C.H. Wilson

# A Compleat Collection of the Resolutions of the Volunteers, Grand Juries, &c

of Ireland, which followed the celebrated resolves of the first Dungannon diet. To which is prefixed a train of historical facts relative to the kingdom.

C.H. Wilson

**A Compleat Collection of the Resolutions of the Volunteers, Grand Juries, &c**
*of Ireland, which followed the celebrated resolves of the first Dungannon diet. To which is prefixed a train of historical facts relative to the kingdom.*

ISBN/EAN: 9783337309619

Printed in Europe, USA, Canada, Australia, Japan

Cover: Foto ©ninafisch / pixelio.de

More available books at **www.hansebooks.com**

A compleat Collection of the

# RESOLUTIONS

OF THE

Volunteers, Grand Juries, &c. of Ireland,

Which followed the celebrated Resolves of the

## FIRST DUNGANNON DIET.

To which is prefixed

A train of HISTORICAL FACTS relative to the Kingdom,
from the Invasion of Henry II. down,

WITH THE

## HISTORY OF VOLUNTEERING, &c.

" We know our Duty to our Sovereign, and are *loyal;* we
know our Duty to *ourselves*, and are resolved to be FREE."

The PEOPLE.

By C. H. WILSON.

VOL. I.

DUBLIN:

PRINTED BY *JOSEPH HILL.*

M DCC LXXXII.

TO THE

# VOLUNTEER BODY

OF

# *IRELAND.*

## SIR,

YOU have promiſed and proved yourſelf to be the warmeſt friend to Liberty and Religious Toleration. I truſt I have ſome claim to your friendſhip; like you, I have endeavoured for the benefit of my country; like you, in the midſt of dangers, I ſpeak bold *truths;* and ſtill farther like you, I glory in the name of an *Iriſh-man:* I, therefore, place this Work under your protection, as a laſting monument of your *public ſpirit.*

C. H. WILSON.

*Dublin,*
*Auguſt* 9, 1782.

# HISTORICAL FACTS

# IRELAND.

THAT the prefent fhining period of Irifh hiftory may not hereafter be clouded from the vague conjecture of literary pride, the affectation of uncommon difcernment, or the prejudice of party, I fhall make no apology for prefenting my countrymen with a full and compleat collection of their firm and liberal refolutions; to which I intend to prefix the Hiftory of Volunteering, and a retrofpect of this kingdom from the invafion of Henry II. &c. merely to exhibit our privileges, the innovation of our rights, the reftriction of our commerce, and the neceffity of our armed affociations; fo that by contrafting the paft time with the glorious profpect of the future, we may be the more truly fenfible of the bleffings we are about to enjoy, the obligations we are under of pioufly tranfmitting them to our children, and the gratitude we owe to Heaven, and thofe virtuous patriots,

a

whofe

whofe firm exertions have reftored us to that liberty, from which happinfs is infeparable.

The Englifh at every period appear to have entertained the higheft contempt for the Irifh *. Nor is there an hiftorian among them who has treated us, or our affairs, with impartiality; nay, even Giraldus Cambrenfis, who attended Henry II. in his expedition here, as Hiftoriographer, has afcribed Mac Murragh's expulfion to an affair of gallantry †, when in fact, it was the tyranny he exercifed over his fubjects, as may more fully appear in Lord Lyttleton's hiftory of Henry II. on authorities furnifhed by that venerable hiftorian, Charles O'Conor, Efq; from whofe lips I have had a further corroboration of this affertion.

King Henry having obtained a bull from Pope Adrian, his countryman, for the inveftiture of this kingdom, I fhall prefent it to my readers, as a proof of the miferable fuperftition, grofs ignorance, and Papal authority of thofe days; and, above all, the religious pretext for the invafion.

" ADRIAN, Bifhop, fervant of the fervants of God, to his deareft fon in Chrift the illuftrious King of England, greeting and apoftolic benediction.

" Full laudably and profitably hath your magnificence conceived the defign of propagating your glorious renown on earth, and completing your reward of eternal happinefs in Heaven; while, as a catholic prince, you are intent on enlarging the borders of the church, teaching the truth of the Chriftian faith to the ignorant and rude, exterminating the roots of vice from the field of the Lord, and for the more

---

* Even the refined Chefterfield, of graceful memory, who dwelt long amongft us, in a letter to the Bifhop of Waterford, reprefents one of our provinces as then in a ftate of the moft profound ignorance and barbarifm.

† The caufe of Dermod's expulfion, fays the legendary monk, was in confequence of his having carried off the wife of Tiergnan O'Rourke King of Breiffne. This lady is reprefented by the Poets and Annalifts of thofe days, as exceedingly beautiful, and of an amorous difpofition; her flight with Mac Murragh it is generally thought carried only the appearance of reluctance; her name was Dervorghal, her father was O'Mallaghlin, King of Meath; fhe lived to the age of 90, and died in a Convent in Drogheda. Mr. Hume calls her Omach, and her hufband Ororic, King of Meath; miftakes which, however trifling, fhould awaken fufpicion to negligence, or ignorance in more important affairs.

convenient execution of this purpofe, requiring the counfel and favour of the apoftolic fee. In which, the maturer your deliberation, and the greater the difcretion of your procedure, by fo much the happier, we truft, will be your progrefs, with the affiftance of the Lord; as all things are ufed to come to a profperous end and iffue, which take their beginning from the ardour of faith and the love of religion.

" There is indeed no doubt but that Ireland, and all the iflands on which Chrift the fun of righteoufnefs hath fhone, and which have received the doctrines of the Chriftian faith, do belong to the jurifdiction of St. Peter and of the holy Roman church, as your excellency alfo doth acknowledge. And therefore we are the more folicitous to propagate the righteous plantation of faith in this land, and the branch acceptable to God, as we have the fecret conviction of confcience that this is more efpecially our bounden duty.

" You then, moft dear fon in Chrift, have fignified to us your defire to enter into the ifland of Ireland, in order to reduce the people to obedience unto laws, and to extirpate the plants of vice; and that you are willing to pay from each houfe a yearly penfion of one penny to St. Peter, and that you will preferve the rights of the churches of this land whole and inviolate. We therefore, with that grace and acceptance fuited to your pious and laudable defign, and favourably affenting to your petition, do hold it good and acceptable, that, for extending the borders of the church, reftraining the progrefs of vice, for the correction of manners, the planting of virtue, and the encreafe of religion, you enter this ifland, and execute therein whatever fhall pertain to the honour of God and welfare of the land; and that the people of this land receive you honourably, and reverence you as their lord: the rights of their churches ftill remaining facred and inviolate; and faving to St. Peter the annual penfion of one penny from every houfe.

" If then you be refolved to carry the defign you have conceived into effectual execution, ftudy to form this nation to virtuous manners; and labour by yourfelf, and others whom you fhall judge meet for this work, in faith, word, and life, that the church may be there adorned, that the religion of the Chriftian faith may be planted and grow up, and that all things pertaining to the honour of God, and the falvation of fouls, be fo ordered, that you may be entitled to the fulnefs of eternal reward from God, and obtain a glorious renown on earth throughout all ages."

As

As the conqueſt of Ireland by Henry the Second, is an ex-preſſion frequent in the mouths of the Engliſh, I ſhall ad-duce Mr. Molyneux's obſervations on this ſubject :

" I come to enquire, whether Ireland might be properly ſaid to be conquered by King Henry II. or by any other Prince in any ſucceeding rebellion. And here we are to un-derſtand by conqueſt, an *acquiſition of a kingdom by force of arms, to which force likewiſe has been oppoſed;* if we are to un-derſtand conqueſt in any other ſenſe, I ſee not of what uſe it can be made againſt Ireland's being a free country. I know *conqueſtus* ſignifies a peaceable acquiſition, as well as an hoſ-tile ſubjugating of an enemy. Vid. Spelman's Gloſ. And in this ſenſe William I. is called the Conqueror, and many of our Kings have uſed the epocha *poſt conqueſtum.* And ſo like-wiſe Henry II. ſtiled himſelf *conqueſtor & dominus Hiberniæ ;* but that his conqueſt was no violent ſubjugation of this king-dom, is manifeſt from what foregoes *: for here we have an intire and voluntary ſubmiſſion of all the eccleſiaſtical and civil ſtates of Ireland, to King Henry II. without the leaſt hoſtile ſtroke on any ſide ; we hear not in any of the chroni-cles of any violence on either part; all was tranſacted with the greateſt quiet, tranquility, and freedom imaginable. I doubt not but the barbarous people of the iſland at that time, were ſtruck with fear and terror of King Henry II's power-ful force which he brought with him ; but ſtill their eaſy and voluntary ſubmiſſions, exempts them from the conſequents of an hoſtile conqueſt, whatever they are ; where there is no op-poſition, ſuch a conqueſt can take no place.

" I have before taken notice of Henry II's uſing the ſtile of *conqueſtor Hiberniæ* †; I preſume no argument can be drawn from hence, for Ireland's being a conquered country ; for we find that many of the Kings of England have uſed the æra of *poſt conqueſtum ;* Edward III. was the firſt that uſed it in England, and we frequently meet with *Henricus poſt con-queſtum quartus,* &c. as taking the Norman invaſion of Wil-liam I. for a conqueſt. But I believe the people of England would take it very ill to be thought a conquered nation, in the ſenſe that ſome impoſe it on Ireland : and yet we find the ſame reaſon in one caſe, as in the other, if the argument from the King's ſtile of *conqueſtor* prevail. Nay, England may be ſaid much more properly to be conquered by Wil-

* See page 11 of this writer.
† Mr. Selden, will not allow that ever Henry II. uſed this ſtile. Tit. Hon. Par. 2. C. 5. Sect. 26.

liam

liam I. than Ireland by Henry II: for we all know with what violence and oppofition from Harold, King Wi liam ob-tained the kingdom, after a bloody battle nigh Haftings. Whereas Henry II. received not the leaft oppofition in Ire-land; all came in peaceably, and had large conceffions made them of the like laws and liberties with the people of Eng-land, which they gladly accepted, as we fhall fee hereafter. But I am fully fatisfied, that neither King William I. in his acquifition of England, or Henry II. in his acqueft of Ire-land, obtained the leaft title to what fome would give to con-querors. Though for my own part, were they conquerors in a fenfe never fo ftrict, I fhould enlarge this prerogative very little or nothing thereby.

" Another argument for Henry II's hoftile conqueft of Ireland, is taken from the oppofition which the natives of Ireland gave to the firft adventurers, Fitz-Stephens, Fitz-Gerald, and Earl Strongbow; and the battles they fought in affifting Mac Murragh, Prince of Leinfter, in the recovery of his principality.

" 'Tis certain there were fome conflicts between them and the Irifh, in which the latter were conftantly beaten; but cer-tainly the conquefts obtained by thofe adventurers, who came over only by the King's licenfe and permiffion, and not at all by his particular command (as is manifeft from the words of the letters patents of licenfe recited by *Giraldus Cambrenfis, Hib. expug.* page 760. *Edit. Francf.* 1603. *Angl. Norm. Hiber. Camd.*) can never be called the conqueft of Henry II. efpe-cially confidering that Henry II. himfelf does not appear to have any defign of coming into Ireland, or obtaining the dominion thereof, when he gave to his fubjects of England this licenfe of affifting Mac Murragh. But I conceive ra-ther the contrary appears, by the ftipulations between Mac Murragh, and the adventurers; and efpecially between him and Strongbow, who was to fucceed him in his principality.

" From what foregoes, I prefume it appears that Ireland cannot properly be faid fo to be conquered by Henry II. as to give the parliament of England any jurifdiction over us; it will much more eafily appear, that the Englifh victo-ries, in any fucceeding rebellions in that kingdom, give no pretence to a conqueft: if every fuppreffion of a rebellion may be called a conqueft, I know not what country will be excepted. The rebellions in England have been frequent; in the contefts between the houfes of York and Lancafter, one fide or other muft needs be rebellious. I am fure the commo-tions

tions in King Charles I's time, are ſtiled ſo by moſt hiſto-
rians. This pretence therefore of conqueſt from rebellions,
has ſo little colour in it, that I ſhall not inſiſt longer on it :
I know conqueſt is an hateful word to Engliſh ears, and we
have lately ſeen a book * undergo a ſevere cenſure, for offering to broach the *doctrine of conqueſt in the free kingdom* of *England.*

    " But, to take off all pretence from this title by conqueſt,
I come in the third place to enquire, *what title conqueſt gives by
the law of nature and reaſon.*

    " And in this particular I conceive, that if the aggreſſor
or inſulter invades a nation unjuſtly, he can never thereby
have a right over the conquered : this I ſuppoſe will be readily granted by all men : if a villain, with a piſtol at my
breaſt, makes me convey my eſtate to him, no one will ſay
that this gives him any right : and yet juſt ſuch a title as this
has an unjuſt conqueror, who with a ſword at my throat
forces me into ſubmiſſion; that is, forces me to part with my
natural eſtate, and birth-right, of being governed only by
laws to which I give my conſent, and not by his will, or the
will of any other.

    " Let us then ſuppoſe a juſt invader, one that has right on
his ſide to attack a nation in an hoſtile manner ; and that thoſe
who oppoſe him are in the wrong : let us then ſee what power
he gets, and over whom.

    " Firſt, 'Tis plain he gets by his conqueſt no power over
thoſe who conquered with him ; they that fought on his ſide,
whether as private ſoldiers or commanders, cannot ſuffer by
the conqueſt, but muſt at leaſt be as much freemen, as they
were before: if any loſt their freedom by the Norman conqueſt, (ſuppoſing King William I. had right to invade England) it was only the Saxons and Britains, and not the Normans that conquered with him. In like manner ſuppoſing
Henry II. had right to invade this iſland, and that he had
been oppoſed therein by the inhabitants, it was only the antient race of the Iriſh, that could ſuffer by this ſubjugation;
the Engliſh and Britains, that came over and conquered with
him, retained all the freedoms and immunities of free-born
ſubjects; they, nor their deſcendants, could not in reaſon
loſe theſe, for being ſucceſsful and victorious ; for ſo, the
ſtate of both conquerors and conquered ſhall be equally ſla-
viſh. Now, it was manifeſt that the great body of the pre-

---

* Biſhop of Salliſbury's Paſtoral Letter.

sent people of Ireland, are the progeny of the English and Britains, that from time to time have come over into this kingdom; and there remains but a meer handful of the antient Irish at this day; I may say, not one in a thousand: so that if I, or any body else, claim the like freedoms with the natural born subjects of England, as being descended from them, it will be impossible to prove the contrary. I conclude therefore, that a just conqueror gets no power, but only over those who have actually assisted in that unjust force that is used against him.

"And as those that joined with the conqueror in a just invasion, hath lost no right by the conquest; so neither have those of the country who opposed him not: this seems so reasonable at first proposal, that it wants little proof. All that gives title in a just conquest, is the opposers using brutal force, and quitting the law of reason, and using the law of violence; whereby the conqueror is entitled to use him as a beast; that is, kill him or enslave him.

"Secondly, Let us consider what power that is, which a rightful conqueror has over the subdued opposers: and this we shall find extends little farther than over the lives of the conquered; I say little farther than over their lives; for how far it extends to their estates, and that it extends not at all to deprive their posterity of the freedoms and immunities to which all mankind have a right, I shall shew presently. That the just conqueror has an absolute power over the lives and liberties of the conquered, appears from hence, because the conquered, by putting themselves in a state of war, by using an unjust force, have thereby forfeited their lives. For quitting reason (which is the rule between man and man) and using force (which is the way of beasts) they become liable to be destroyed by him against whom they use force, as any savage wild beast, that is dangerous to his being.

"And this is the case of rebels in a settled commonwealth, who forfeit their lives on this account. But as for forfeiting their estates, it depends on the municipal laws of the kingdom. But we are now enquiring what the consequents will be between two contesting nations.

"Which brings me to consider how far a just conqueror has power over the posterity and estates of the conquered.

"As to the posterity, they not having joined or assisted in the forcible opposition of the conqueror's just arms, can lose no benefit thereby. It is unreasonable any man should be punished but for his own fault. Man being a free agent, is only

only anfwerable for his own demerits; and as it would be highly unjuſt to hang up the father for the ſon's offence, ſo the converſe is equally unjuſt, that the ſon ſhould ſuffer any inconvenience for the father's crime. A father hath not in himſelf a power over the life or liberty of his child, ſo that no act of his can poſſibly forfeit it. And though we find in the municipal laws of particular kingdoms, that the ſon loſes the father's eſtate for the rebellion or other demerit of the father, yet, this is conſented and agreed to, for the public fafety, and for deterring the ſubjects from certain enormous crimes, that would be highly prejudicial to the common-wealth. And to ſuch conſtitutions the ſubjects are bound to ſubmit, having conſented to them, though it may be unrea-ſonable to put the like in execution between nation and nation, in the ſtate of nature: for in ſettled governments, property in eſtates is regulated, bounded and determined by the laws of the commonwealth, conſented to by the people; ſo that in theſe, 'tis no injuſtice for the ſon to loſe his patrimony for his father's rebellion or other demerit.

" If therefore the poſterity of the conquered, are not to ſuffer for the unjuſt oppoſition given to the victor by their an-ceſtors, we ſhall find little place for any power of the con-querors over the eſtates of the ſubdued. The father, by his miſcarriages and violence, can forfeit but his own life; he involves not his children in his guilt or deſtruction. His goods, which nature (that willeth the preſervation of all man-kind as far as poſſible) hath made to belong to his children to ſuſtain them, do ſtill continue to belong to his children. 'Tis true, indeed, it uſually happens that damage attends unjuſt force; and as far as the repair of this damage requires it, ſo far the rightful conqueror may invade the goods and eſtate of the conquered; but when this damage is made up, his title to the goods ceaſes, and the reſidue belongs to the wife and children of the ſubdued.

" It may ſeem a ſtrange doctrine, that any one ſhould have a power over the life of another man, and not over his eſtate; but this we find every day; for though I may kill a thief that ſets on me in the high-way, yet I may not take away his mo-ney: for it is the brutal force the aggreſſor has uſed, that gives his adverſary a right to take away his life, as a noxious creature: but it is only damage ſuſtained, that gives title to another man's goods.

" It muſt be confeſſed, that the practice of the world is otherwiſe, and we commonly ſee the conqueror (whether juſt or unjuſt) by the force he has over the conquered, compels them with a ſword at their breaſt to ſtoop to his conditions, and ſubmit to ſuch a government as he pleaſes to afford them. But we enquire not now, what is the practice, but what right there is to do ſo. If it be ſaid, the conquered ſubmit by their own conſent: then this allows conſent neceſſary to give the conqueror a title to rule over them. But then we may enquire whether promiſes, extorted by force without right, can be thought conſent, and how far they are obligatory; and I humbly conceive they bind not at all. He that forces my horſe from me, ought preſently to reſtore him, and I have ſtill a right to retake him: So he that has forced a promiſe from me, ought preſently to reſtore it, that is, quit me of the obligation of it; or I may chuſe whether I will perform it or not: for the law of nature obliges us only by the rules ſhe preſcribes, and therefore cannot oblige me by the violation of her rules; ſuch is the extorting any thing from me by force.

" From what has been ſaid, I preſume it pretty clearly appears, that an unjuſt conqueſt gives no title at all; that a juſt conqueſt gives power only over the lives and liberties of the actual oppoſers, but not over their poſterity or eſtates, otherwiſe than as before is mentioned; and not at all over thoſe that did not concur in the oppoſition.

" They that deſire a more full diſquiſition of this matter, may find it at large in an incomparable treatiſe concerning the *true original, extent, and end of civil government*, chap. 16. This diſcourſe is ſaid to be written by my excellent friend, John Locke, Eſq. Whether it be ſo or not, I know not; this I am ſure, whoever is author, the greateſt genius in Chriſtendom need not diſown it.

" But granting that all we have ſaid in this matter is wrong, and granting that a conqueror, whether juſt or unjuſt, obtains an abſolute arbitrary dominion over the perſons, eſtates, lives, liberties, and fortunes of all thoſe whom he finds in the nation, their wives, poſterity, &c. ſo as to make perpetual ſlaves of them and their generations to come; let us next enquire whether conceſſions granted by ſuch a victorious hero, do not bound the exorbitancy of his power, and whether he be not obliged ſtrictly to obſerve theſe grants.

" And here I believe no man of common ſenſe or juſtice, will deny it: none that has ever conſidered the law of nature and nations, can poſſibly heſitate on this matter; the very propoſing it, ſtrikes the ſenſe and common notions of all men ſo forcibly, that it needs no farther proof. I ſhall therefore

b

insist

infift no longer on it, but haften to confider how far this is the cafe of Ireland : and that brings me naturally to the fourth particular propofed, viz. To fhew by precedents, records, and hiftory, what conceeffions and grants have been made from time to time to the people of Ireland, and by what fteps the laws of England came to be introduced into this kingdom.

" We are told by Matth. Paris, hiftoriographer to Henry III. that Henry II. a little before he left Ireland, in a public affembly and council of the Irifh at Lifmore, did caufe the Irifh to receive, and fwear to be governed by the laws of England : ' Rex Henricus (faith he) antequam ex Hibernia redi-
' ret apud Lifmore concilium congregavit ubi leges Angliæ
' funt ab omnibus graranter receptæ, & juratoria cautione
' preftita confirmatæ.' Vid. Matth. Paris, ad An. 1172. Vit. H. 2.

" And not only thus, but if we may give credit to Sir Edward Cook, in the 4th inftit. cap. 1. and 76. and to the infcription to the Irifh *Modus tenendi parliamentum*, it will clearly appear, that Henry II. did not only fettle the laws of England in Ireland, and the jurifdiction ecclefiaftical there, by the voluntary acceptance and allowance of the nobility and clergy, but did likewife allow them the freedom of holding of parliaments in Ireland, as a feparate and diftinct kingdom from England ; and did then fend them a modus to direct them how to hold their parliaments there : the title of which modus runs thus :

' Henricus rex Angliæ conqueftor & dominus Hiberniæ,
  ' &c. mittit hanc formam archiepifcopis, epifcopis, ab-
  ' batibus, prioribus, comitibus, baronibus, jufticiariis,
  ' vicecomitibus, majoribus, præpofitis, miniftris, & om-
  ' nibus fidelibus fuis terræ Hiberniæ tenendi parliamen-
  ' tum.' In primus fummonitio parliamenti præcedere debet quadraginta dies. And fo forth.

" This modus is faid to have been fent into Ireland by Henry II. for a direction to hold their parliaments there. And the fenfe of it agrees for the moft part with the *modus tenendi parl.* in England, faid to have been allowed by William the conqueror, when he obtained that kingdom ; where 'tis alter'd, 'tis only to fit it the better for the kingdom of Ireland.

" I know very well the antiquity of this modus, fo faid to be tranfmitted for Ireland by Henry II. is queftion'd by fome

learned

learned antiquaries, particularly by Mr. Selden * and † Mr. Pryn, who deny alfo the Englifh modus as well as this. But on the other hand, my Lord Chief Juftice Cook, in the 4th inftit. page 12, and 349, does ftrenuoufly affert them both. And the late reverend and learned Dr. Dopping, Bifhop of Meath, has publifh'd the Irifh modus, with a vindication of its antiquity and authority in the preface.

" There feems to me but two objections of any moment raifed by Mr. Pryn againft thefe modi. The one relates both to the Englifh and Irifh modus; the other chiefly ftrikes at the Irifh. He fays the name *parliament*, fo often found in thefe modi, was not a name for the great council of England known fo early as thefe modi pretend to. I confefs I am not prepared to difprove this antiquary in this particular: but to me it feems reafonable enough to imagine that the name *parliament*, came in with William the conqueror: 'tis a word perfectly French, and I fee no reafon to doubt its coming in with the Normans. The other objection affects our Irifh modus, for he tells us, That Sheriffs were not eftablifh'd in Ireland, in Henry II's time, when this modus was pretended to be fent hither; yet we find the word *vicecomes* therein. To this I can only anfwer, that Henry II. intending to eftablifh in Ireland the Englifh form of government, as the firft, and chief ftep thereto, he fent them directions for holding of parliaments, defigning afterwards by degrees, and in due time, to fettle the other conftitutions, agreeable to the model of England. If therefore England had then Sheriffs, we need not wonder to find them named in the Irifh modus, tho' they were not as yet eftablifh'd amongft us, for they were defigned to be appointed foon after, and before the modus could be put regularly in execution; and accordingly we find them eftablifh'd in fome counties of Ireland, in King John's time.

" This Irifh modus is faid to have been in the cuftody of Sir Chriftopher Prefton of Clane in Ireland, An. 6. Hen. 4. and by Sir John Talbot, Lord Lieutenant of Ireland, under King Henry IV. It was exemplify'd by Infpeximus under the great feal of Ireland, and the exemplification was fometimes in the hands of Mr. Hackwel of Lincoln's Inn, and by him was communicated to Mr. Selden. The tenor of which exemplification runs thus:

' Henricus dei gratia rex Angliæ, & Franciæ, & dominus
  ' Hiberniæ, omnibus ad quos prefentes literæ pervene-

---

* Tit hon. par. 2. c. 5. fect. 26. edit. Lond. an. 1672.
† Againft Cook's 4th inftit. c. 76.

' rint

' rint falutem infpeximus tenorem diverforum articulo-
' rum in quodam rotulo pergameneo fcriptorum cum
' Chriftophero Prefton, milite tempore arreftationis fuæ
' apud villam de Clare, per deputatum dilecti & fidelis
' noftri Johannis Talbot de Halomfhire chivaler locum
' noftrum tenentis terræ noftræ Hiberniæ nuper factæ in-
' ventorum ac coram nobis & concilio noftra in eadem
' terræ noftra apud villam de trim, Nono die Januarii
' ultimo præteriti in hæc verba,

" Modus tenendi parliamenta Henricus rex Angliæ con-
" queftor & dominus Hiberniæ, mittit hanc forman ar-
" chiepifcopis, &c." and fo as before, " Et omnibus
" fidelibus fuis terræ Hiberniæ tenendi parliamentum
" imprimis fummonitto, &c." and then follows the modus, agreeable in moft things with that of England, only
fitted to Ireland. Then the exemplification concludes :
' Nos autem tenores articulorum prædictorum de affenfu
' præfati locum tenentis & concilii prædicti tenore prefen-
' tium duximus exemplificandum & has literas noftras
' fieri fecimus patentes. Tefte præfato locum noftrum
' tenente apud Trim. 12 die Januarii anno regni noftri
' fexto.

        ' Per ipfum locum tenentem & concilium.'

" Now we can hardly think it credible (fays the Bifhop of
Meath) that an exemplification could have been made fo folemnly of it by King Henry IV. and that it fhould refer to a
modus tranfmitted into Ireland by King Henry II. and affirm
that it was produced before the Lord Lieutenant and Council
at Trim, if no fuch thing had been done : this were to call
in queftion the truth of all former records and transactions,
and make the exemplification contain an egregious falfhood
in the body of it.

" The Rev. Bifhop of Meath, in his fore-cited preface,
does believe, that he had obtain'd the very original record,
faid by my Lord Cook to have been in the hands of Sir Chriftopher Prefton : it came to that learned Prelate's hands,
amongft other papers and manufcripts of Sir William Domvile, late Attorney General in this kingdom, who, in his life-
time, upon an occafional difcourfe with the Bifhop concerning it, told him, that this record was beftow'd on him (Sir
William Domvile) by Sir James Cuffe, late deputy Vice-trea-
furer of Ireland, that Sir James found it among the papers
of Sir Francis Aungier, mafter of the rolls in this kingdom ;
and the prefent Earl of Longford (grandfon to the faid Sir
                                                    Francis

Francis Aungier) told the Bifhop, that his faid grandfather had it out of the Treafury of Waterford.

"Whilft I write this, I have this very record now before me, from the hands of the faid Bifhop of Meath's fon, my nephew, Samuel Dopping; and I muft confefs it has a venerable ancient appearance; but whether it be the true original record, I leave on the arguments produced for its credit by the faid Bifhop.

"This I am fure of, That whether this be the very record tranfmitted hither by King Henry II. or not; yet 'tis moft certain, from the unanimous conceffions of all the fore-mentioned antiquaries, Cook, Selden, Pryn, &c. that we have had parliaments in Ireland very foon after the invafion of Henry II. For Pryn confeffes that * King Henry II. after his conqueft of Ireland, and the general voluntary fubmiffion, homages, and fealties of moft of the Irifh kings, prelates, nobles, cities, and people, to him, as to their Sovereign Lord and King, anno 1170 (it fhould be 1172) held therein a general council of the clergy at Cafhel, wherein he rectify'd many abufes in the church, and eftablifh'd fundry ecclefiaftical laws, agreeable to thofe in the church of England; ' Ecclefiæ illius ftatum ad Anglicanæ ecclefiæ forman redigere ' modis omnibus elaborando:' To which the Irifh clergy promifed conformity, and to obferve them for time to come, as † Giraldus Cambrenfis, who was then in Ireland, and other ‡ hiftorians, relate: ' Et ut fingulis obfervatio fimilis regnum ' colligaret utrumque' (that is England and Ireland) ' paffim ' omnes unanimi voluntate communi affenfu, pari defiderio ' regis imperio fe fubjiciunt, omnibus igitur hoc modo con-' fummatis, in concilio habito apud Lifmore leges Angliæ ab ' omnibus funt gratantur receptæ, & juratorio cautione præf-' tita confirmatæ §,' fays Matthew Paris.

"Can any conceffion in the world be more plain and free than this? We have heard of late much talk in England of an

* Againft the 4th inftit. c. 76. p. 249.
† Topograph. Hibern. l. 3. c. 18.   Hib. Expug. l. 11. c. 33, 34.
‡ Hoveden an. pars. p. 302.   Brampton chr. col. 1071.   Knighton de Even. Ang. l. c. 10. col. 2394, 2395.   Fol. Virg. hift. Ang. l. 13.   Rad. de Diceto. Walfingham, &c.
§ That each and fingular every obfervation fimilar to one kingdom, fhould be extended to both (England and Ireland) every where with one common confent and one will, with the equal defire of the King they all form themfelves into one empire; this therefore in all things being confummated in a council held at Lifmore, the laws of England are received and confirmed by all, with due caution in law and proper confirmation.

original

original compact between the King and people of England;
I am fure 'tis not poffible to fhew a more fair original compact between a King and people, than this between Henry II.
and the people of Ireland, ' That they fhould enjoy the like
' liberties and immunities, and be govern'd by the fame mild
' laws, both civil and ecclefiaftical, as the people of England."

The Magna Charta of Ireland coming next to hand, I
infert it with the tranflation, that my countrymen may fee
*how far* they have enjoyed thofe privileges, which a fifter
nation in herfelf holds facred.

At the inftance of William Earl Marfhal, this Charter was
granted us, by Henry III. who at the fame time, in the moft
folemn manner, ratified the Britifh one *.

## MAGNA CARTA HIBERNIÆ.

### REGIS HENRICI TERTII.

### XII. DIE NOVEMBRIS, M,CCXVI. ANNO REGNI I.

Ex Libro rubro Scaccharii Dublin.

HENRICUS Dei gratia rex Anglie Dominus Hybernie
dux Normannie et Aquitanie et comes Andegavie archiepifcopis epifcopis abbatibus comitibus baronibus jufticiariis foreftariis vicecomitibus prepofitis miniftris civibus ballivis et fidelibus fuis falutem. Sciatis nos intuitu Dei et pro falute ani-
me noftre et omnium antecefforum et fuccefforum noftrorum
ad honorem Dei et exaltationem fancte ecclefie et emendationem

---

* In the year 1253, there was affembled a very full parliament, to
whom King Henry III. promifed to ratify Magna Charta, and faithfully
to obferve all the articles of it, which King John and he at his coronation, and often fince, had fworn to obferve, and this was done in the
moft folemn and ceremonial manner that could be devifed; for the King,
with all the great nobility of England, all the Bifhops and chief Prelates
in their ornaments, with burning candles in their hands affembled to
hear the terrible fentence of excommunication upon all the infringers of
the fame, and at the lighting of thofe candles, the King bearing one in
his hand, gave it to one of the Prelates, faying, " It becomes not me,
who am no Prieft, to hold this candle, my heart fhall be a greater teftimony;" and withal laid his hand on his breaft the whole time the fentence was reading; which done, the Charter of King John's father was
read. In the end having thrown away their candles they cried out,
" So let them who incur this fentence be extinct, and ftink in hell."

Chron. de Marl. p. 228.

regni

regni noftri per confilium venerabilium patrum noftrorum domini Gaulonis titulo fancti Martini prefbiteri cardinalis apoftolice fedis legati Petri Winton' L. de fancto Afapho J. Bathon' & Glaftom' S. Exon' R. Ciceftr' W. Coventr' W. Roffen' H. London' Menevens' Bangor' et S. Wygorn' epifcoporum et nobilium virorum Willielmi Marifcalli comitis Pembroc' Ranulfi comitis Ceftr' Wiliielmi de Ferrar' comitis de Derbia Willielmi comitis de Aubomarle Huberti de Burgo Jufticiarii noftri Savantii de Malo Leone Willielmi Bruerie patris Willielmi Bruerie filii Roberti de Curtenai Falkefii de Brcante Reginaldi de Vautort Walteri de Laci Hugonis de Mortuo Mari Johannis de Monemute Walteri de Beuchamp Walteri de Clifford Roberti de Mortuo Mari Willielmi de Cantelup' Mathei filii Hereberti Johannis Marifcalli Alani Baffet Philippi de Albiniaco Johannis Extranei et aliorum fidelium noftrorum.

I. Imprimis conceffiffe Deo et hac prefenti carta noftra confirmaffe pro nobis & heredibus noftris imperpetuum quod HYBERNICANA ecclefia libera fit et habeat jura fua integra et libertates fuas illefas. Conceffimus etiam omnibus liberis hominibus de regno noftro pro nobis et heredibus imperpetuum omnes libertates fubfcriptas habendas et tenendas iis et heredibus fuis de nobis et heredibus noftris.

II. Si quis comitum vel baronum noftrorum five aliorum tenentium de nobis in capite per fervicium militare mortuus fuerit et cum decefferit heres fuus plene etatis fuerit et relevium debeatur habeat hereditatem fuam per antiquum relevium fcilicet heres vel heredes comitis de baronia comitis integra per centum libras heres vel heredes baronis de baronia baronis integra per centum folidos ad plus et qui minus debuerit minus det fecundum antiquam confuetudinem feodorum.

III. Si autem heres alicujus talium fuerit infra etatem dominus ejus non habeat cuftodiam ipfius nec terre fue antequam homagium ejus ceperit et poftquam talis heres fuerit in cuftodia ad etatem pervenerit fcilicet viginti et unius annorum habeat hereditatem fuam fine relevio et fine fine ita tamen quod fi ipfe dum infra etatem fuerit miles nichilominus terra remaneat in cuftodia domini fui ufque terminum predictum.

IV. Cuftos terræ hujus et heredis qui infra etatem fuerit non capiat de terra heredis nifi rationabiles exitus et rationabiles confuetudines et rationabilia fervicia et hoc fine deftructione vel vafto hominum vel rerum et fi nos commiferimus cuftodiam alicujus talis terre vicecomiti vel alicui alii qui de exitibus terre illius nobis refpondere debeat et ille deftructionem

de

de cuſtodia fecerit vel vaſtum nos ab eo capiemus emendam
et terre illa committatur duobus legalibus et diſcretis hominibus de feodo illo qui de exitibus nobis reſpondeant vel ei
cui nos aſſignaverimus et ſi dederimus vel vendiderimus alicui cuſtodiam alicujus talis terre et ille deſtructionem inde fecerit vel vaſtum amittat cuſtodiam illam et tradatur duobus
legalibus et diſcretis hominibus de feodo illo qui ſimiliter nobis
inde reſpondeant ſicut predictum eſt.

V. Cuſtos autem quamdiu cuſtodiam terre habuerit ſuſ-
tentet domos parcos vivaria ſtagna molendina et cetera ad
illam terram pertinentia de exitibus terra ejuſdem et reddet
heredi cum ad plenam etatem pervenerit terram ſuam totam
inſtauratam de carucis et omnibus aliis rebus ad minus ſecundum quod illam recepit.   Hec omnia obſerventur de cuſtodia
archiepiſcopatuum epiſcopatuum abbatiarum prioratuum eccle-
ſiarum et dignitatuum vacantium excepto quod cuſtodie hujus
vendi non debent.

VI. Heredes maritentur abſque diſparagatione.

VII. Vidua poſt mortem mariti ſui ſtatim et ſine dilatione
aliqua habeat maritagium ſuum et hereditatem ſuam nec ali-
quid det pro dote ſua vel maritagio vel hereditate ſua quam
hereditatem maritus ſuus et ipſa tenuerunt die obitus ipſius
mariti et maneat vidua in domo mariti ſui per quadraginta
dies poſt mortem ipſius mariti ſui infra quos ei aſſignetur dos
ſua niſi prius ei fuerit aſſignata vel niſi domus illa fuerit caſtrum
et ſi de caſtro receſſerit ſtatim provideatur ei domus competens
in qua poſſit honeſte morari quouſque dos ſua ei aſſignetur
ſecundum quod predictum eſt.

VIII. Nulla vidua diſtingatur ad ſe maritandum duo voluerit vivera ſine marito ita tamen quod ſecuritatem faciat
quod ſe non maritabit ſine aſſenſu noſtro ſi de nobis tenuerit
vel ſine aſſenſu domini ſui ſi de alio tenuerit.

IX. Nos vel ballivi noſtri non ſaiſiemus terram aliquam
nec redditum pro debitum aliquo quamdiu catalla debitoris
preſentia ſufficiunt ad debitum reddendum et ipſe debitor
paratus inde ſatisfacere nec plegium ipſius debitoris diſtringatur
quamdiu ipſe capitalis debitor ſufficit ad ſolutionem debiti et
ſi capitalis debitor defecerit in ſolutione non habens unde reddat aut reddere noluerit cum poſſit plegii reſpondeant de du-
bito et ſi voluerint habeant terras et redditus debitoris quouſque ſit eis ſatisfactum de debito quod ante pro eo ſolverunt
niſi capitalis debitor monſtraverit ſe eſſe quietum verſus eoſdem
plegios.

X. Civitas

X. Civitas Dublin' habeat omnes antiquas libertates et liberas confuetudines fuas preterea volumus et concedimus quod omnes alie civitates ville et burgi et omnes portus habeant omnes libertates et liberas confuetudines fuas.

XI. Nullas diftringatur ad faciendum majus fervicium de feodo militis nec de alio libero tenemento quam inde debetur.

XII. Communia placita non fequantur curiam noftram fed teneantur in aliquo certo loco.

XIII. Recognitiones de nova diffeifina de morte anteceffloris et de ultima prefentatione non capiantur nifi in fuis comitatibus et hoc modo Nos vel fi extra regnum fuerimus capitalis jufticiarius nofter mittemus duos jufticiarios per unumquemque comitatum per quatuor vices in anno qui cum quatuor militibus cujuflibet comitatus electis per comitatum capiant et in comitatu et in die et loco comitatus affifas predictas.

XIV. Et fi in die comitatus affife predicte capi non poffunt tot milites et libere tenentes remaneant de illis qui interfuerunt comitatui die illo per quos poffint fufficienter judicia fieri fecundum quod negotium fuerit majus vel minus.

XV. Liber homo non amercietur pro parvo delicto nifi fecundum modum delicti et pro magno delicto fecundum magnidudinem delicti falvo contenemento fuo et mercator eodem modo falva mercandafia fua et villanus eodem modo amercietur falvo wannagio fuo fi inciderit in mifericordiam noftram et nulla predictarum mifericordiarum ponatur nifi per facramentum proborum et legalium hominum de vifneto.

XVI. Comites et barones non amercientur nifi per pares fuos et non nifi fecundum modum delicti.

XVII. Nullus clericus amercietur nifi fecundum formam predictorum et non fecundum quantitatem beneficii fui ecclefiaftici.

XVIII. Nec villa nec homo diftringetur facere pontes ad riparias nifi qui ab antiquo et de jure facere debent.

XIX. Nullus vicecomes conftabularius coronatores vel alii ballivi noftri teneant placita corone noftre.

XX. Si aliquis tenens de nobis liacum feodum moriatur et vicecomes vel vallivus nofter oftendat literas noftras patentes de fummonitione noftra de debito quod defunctus nobis debuit liceat vicecomiti vel ballivo noftro attachiare et imbreviare catalla defuncti inventa in laico feodo ad valentiam illius debiti per vifum legalium hominum ita tamen quod nichil inde amoveatur donec perfolvatur nobis debitum quod clarum fuerit et refiduum relinquatur executoribus ad faciendum teftamentum

c                                                    defuncti

defuncti et si nichil debeatur abipso omnia catalla cedant de-
functo salvis uxori sue et pueris suis rationabilibus partibus
suis.

XXI. Nullus constabularius vel ejus ballivus capiat blada
vel alia catalla alicujus qui non sit de villa ubi castrum suum est
nisi statim inde reddat denarios vel respectum inde habere possit
de voluntate venditoris si autem de villa fuerit teneatur infra
tres septimanas precium reddere.

XXII. Nullus constabularius distringat aliquem militem ad
dandum denarios pro custodia castri si ipse eam facero voluerit
in propria persona sua vel per alium probum hominem si ipse
eam facere non possit propter rationabilem causam et si nos
duxerimus vel miserimus eum in exercitum erit quietus de
custodia secundum quantitatem temporis quo per nos fuerit in
exercitu.

XXIII. Nullus vicecomes vel ballivus noster vel alius capiat
equos vel carectas alicujus pro cariagio faciendo nisi reddat
liberationem antiquitus statutum scilicet pro carecta ad duos
equos decem denarios per diem et pro carecta ad tres equos
quatuordecim denarios per diem.

XXIV. Nec nos nec ballivi nostri capiemus alienum boscum
ad castra vel alia agenda nostra nisi per voluntatem ipsius cujus
boscus ille fuerit.

XXV. Nos non tenebimus terras illorum qui convicti fuerint
de felonia nisi per unum annum et unum diem et tunc reddan-
tur terre dominis feodorum.

XXVI. Et omnes kydelli deponuntur de cetero per totam
*Avenlich* et per totam *Hyberniam* nisi per costeram maris.

XXVII. Breve quod vocatur precipe de cetero non fiat
alicui de aliquo tenemento unde liber amittere possit curiam
suam.

XXVIII. Una mensura vini sit per totum regnum nostrum
& una mensura cervisie et una mensura bladi scilicet quarterium
DUBLIN' et una latitudo pannorum tinctorum russettorum
haubergettorum scilicet due ulne infra listas de ponderibus autem sit ut de mensuris.

XXIX. Nichil detur de cetero pro brevi inquisitionis de
vita et membris sed gratis concedatur et non negetur.

XXX. Si aliquis teneat de nobis per feodi firmam vel so-
cagium vel por burgagium et de alio terram teneat per ser-
vicium militare nec habebimus custodiam heredis nec terre
sue que est de feodo alterius occasione illius feodi firme vel
soccagii vel burgagii nec habebimus custodiam illius feodi firme vel soccagii vel burgagii nisi ipsa feodi firma debeat servi-
cium

cium militare. Nos non habebimus cuſtodiam heredis vel
terre alicujus quam tenet de alio per ſervicium militare occa-
ſi ne al cujus parve ſerjantie quam tenet de nobis per ſervicium
reddendi nobis cultellos vel ſagittas vel hujuſmodi.

XXXI. Nullus ballivus ponat de cetero aliquem ad legem
ſimplici loquela ſine teſtibus fidelibus ad hoc inductis.

XXXII. Nullus liber homo capiatur vel impriſonetur vel
diſſeiſiatur aut utlegetur aut exulet aut aliquo alio modo de-
ſtruatur nec ſuper eum ibimus nec ſuper eum mittemus niſi
per legale judicium parium ſuorum vel per legem terre.

XXXIII. Nulli vendemus nulli negabimus aut differemus
rectum aut juſticiam.

XXXIV. Omnes mercatores niſi publice antea prohibiti
fueaint habeant ſalvum et ſecurum exire de HYBERNIA et
venire in HYBERNIAM et morari et ire per HYBERNIAM tam
per terras quam per aquas ad emendum et vendendum ſine
omnibus malis toltis per antiquas et rectas conſuetudines pre-
terquam in tempore guerre et ſi ſint de terra contra nos guerrina et ſi tales inveniantur in terra noſtra in principio guerra
attachientur ſine dampno corporum vel rerum donec ſciatur a
nobis vel a capitali juſticiario noſtro quomodo mercatores terre noſtre tractentur que tunc invenientur in terra contra nos
guerrina et ſi noſtri ſalvi ſint ibi alii ſalvi ſint terra noſtra.

XXXV. Si quis tenuerit de aliqua eſcaeta ſicut de honore
Walingeford Notingeham Bolon' Lancaſtr' vel aliis eſcaetis
quæ ſunt in manu noſtra et ſunt baronie et obierit heres ejus
non det aliud relevium nec faciat nobis aliud ſervicium quam
faceret baroni ſi terra illa eſſet in manu baronis et nos eodem
modo eam tenebimus quo baro eam tenuit.

XXXVI. Homines qui maneant extra foreſtam non veniant
de cetero coram juſticiariis noſtris de foreſta per communes
ſummonitiones niſi ſint in placito vel plegii alicujus vel aliquo-
rum qui attachiati ſint pro foreſta.

XXXVII. Omnes homines qui fundaverint abbatias unde
habent cartas regum Anglie vel antiquam tenuram habeant
earum cuſtodiam cum vacaverint ſicut habere debeut et ſicut
ſupra declaratum eſt.

XXXVIII. Omnes foreſte que afforeſtate ſunt tempore
regis Johannis patris noſtri ſtatim deafforeſtentur et ita fiat de
gruariis que per eundem Johannem tempore ſuo poſiti ſunt in
defenſo.

XXXIX. Nullus capiatur vel impriſonetur propter appel-
lum femine de morte alterius quam viri ſui.

XL.

XL. Omnes autem iftas confuetudines prediétas et libertates quas conceffimus in regno noftro tenendas quantum ad
nos pertinet erga noftros omnes de regno noftro tam clirici
quam laici confervent quantum ad fe pertinet erga fuos.

XLI. Quia vero quedam capitula in priori carta contine-
bantur que gravia et dubitabilia videbantur fcilicet de fcuta-
giis et auxiliis affidendis de debitis Judeorum et aliorum et de
libertate exeundi de regno noftro et redeundi in regnum noftrum de foreftis et foreftariis de warrennis et warennariis de
confuetudinibus comitatuum et de ripariis et earum cuftodibus
plaucit fupradiétis prelatis et magnatibus ea effe in refpeétu
quoufque plenius confilium habuerimus et tunc faciemus ple-
niffime tam de his quam de aliis que occurrerint emendanda
id quod ad communem omnium utilitatem pertinuerit et pa-
cem et ftatum noftrum et regni noftri. Quia vero figillum
nondum habuimus prefentem cartam figillis venerabilis patris
noftri domini Gualonis titulo fanéti Martini prefbyteri cardinalis apoftolice fedis legati et Willielmi Marifcalli comitis Pen-
brok' reétoris noftri et regni noftri fecimus figillari. Teftibus
omnibus prenominatis et aliis multis. Dat' per manum pre-
diétorum domini legati et Willielmi Marifcalli apud Briftol-
lum duodecimo die Novembris anno regni noftri primo.

◄◄◄◄►►◄◄◄◄►►◄◄◄◄►

Tranflation of the Magna Charta of Ireland, by Henry III.
    12th day of November, 1216, An. regni 1. From the Red
    Book of the Exchequer.

HENRY by the grace of God, King of England, Duke of
Normandy, &c. To the Archbifhops, Bifhops, Abbots, Earls,
Barons, Juftices, Forefters, Vifcounts, Provofts, Minifters,
and to all his Bailiffs and his Lieges, greeting. Know ye,
that We by the grace of God, and for the faving of our fouls,
and the fouls of all our anceftors, and of our heirs, and for
the honour of God, and the fafety of our holy church, and
for the amendment of our government, by the advice of our
venerable fathers, Saint Martin Lord of Gaul, &c. Peter
Winton, L. of Saint Afaph, J. Bathon, and Glaftom, W.
Coventr, S. Exon, R. Cicefter, W. Roffen, H. London,
Menevens Bangor and S. Hygorn, and of Bifhops and Noble-
men, William Marfhal Earl of Pembroc, Ranulph Earl of
Chefter, William de Ferrar Earl of Derby, William Earl of
Albemarle, Hubert de Burgo, &c.

I. Have

I. Have in the firſt place granted to God, and confirmed by this our preſent Charter, for us and for our heirs for ever, That the churches of Ireland ſhall be free, and ſhall enjoy their rights and franchiſes entirely and fully.

II. We have alſo granted to all the freemen of our kingdom, for us and for our heirs for ever, all the liberties hereafter mentioned, to have and to hold to them and their heirs of us and of our heirs.

III. If any of our Earls, our Barons, or others that hold of us in chief by the knight-ſervice die, and at the time of his death his heirs be of full age, and relief be due, he ſhall have his inheritance by the antient relief; to wit, the heir or heirs of an Earl, for an entire Earldom, C. pounds; the heir or heirs of a Baron, for an entire barony, C. marks; the heir or heirs of a knight, for a knight, for a whole Knight's fee, C. ſhillings at moſt: and where leſs is due, leſs ſhall be paid, according to the antient cuſtoms of the ſeveral tenures.

IV. The guardians of the land of ſuch heirs being within age, ſhall take nothing out of the land of the heirs, but only the reaſonable profits, reaſonable cuſtoms, and reaſonable ſervices, and that without making deſtruction or waſte of men or goods; and if we ſhall have committed the cuſtody of the land of any ſuch heir to a Viſcount, or any other who is to account to us for the profits of the land, and that ſuch committee make deſtruction or waſte, we will take of him amends, and the land ſhall be committed to two lawful and good men of that fee, who ſhall account for the profits to us, or to ſuch as we ſhall appoint. And if we ſhall give or ſell to any perſon, the cuſtody of the lands of any ſuch heir, and ſuch donee or vendee make deſtruction or waſte, he ſhall loſe the cuſtody, and it ſhall be committed to two lawful, ſage, and good men, who ſhall account to us for the ſame, as aforeſaid.

V. And the guardian, whilſt he has cuſtody of the heir's land, ſhall maintain the houſes, parks, ponds, pools, mills, and other appurtenances to the land, out of the profits of the land itſelf; and ſhall reſtore to the heir, when he ſhall be of full age, his land well ſtocked, with ploughs, barns, and the like, as it was when he received it, and as the profits will reaſonably afford.

VI. Heirs ſhall be married without diſparagement.

VII. A widow after the death of her huſband, ſhall preſently and without oppreſſion, have her marriage and her inheritance; nor ſhall give any thing for her marriage, nor for

her

her dower, nor for her inheritance, which she and her huſband were ſeized of the day of her huſband's death: and ſhe
ſhall remain in her huſband's houſe forty days after his death:
within which time her dower ſhall be aſſigned her.

VIII. No widow ſhall be compelled to marry if ſhe be deſirous to live ſingle, provided ſhe give ſecurity not to marry
without our leave, if ſhe hold of us, or without the Lord's
leave of whom ſhe holds, if ſhe hold of any other.

IX. We nor our Bailiffs will not ſeize the lands or rents
of a debtor for any debt ſo long as his goods are ſufficient to
pay the debt: nor ſhall the pledges be diſtrained upon whilſt
the principal debtor have not wherewith to pay the debt, the
pledges ſhall anſwer for it; and if they will, they ſhall have
the lands and rents of the debtor till they have received the
debt which they paid for him, if the principal debtor cannot
ſhew that he is quit againſt his pledges.

X. The city of Dublin ſhall have all her ancient liberties
and freedoms; beſides we will and grant, that every city,
town, and borough have their cuſtoms, and all the ports ſhall
have their liberties, freedoms, and cuſtoms.

XI. None ſhall be diſtrained to do greater ſervice for a
Knight's fee, or for any other frank-tenement than what is
due by his tenure.

XII. Common Pleas ſhall not follow our court, but ſhall
be held in a certain place.

XIII. Recognizance of *novel Diſſeiſin, Mordanceſter,* and
*darrien Preſentment,* ſhall be taken no where but in their proper
counties, and in this manner: we, or our Chief Juſtice (if
ourſelves be out of the realm) will ſend two Juſtices through
every county four times a year; who, with four Knights of
every county, to be choſen by the county, ſhall take the ſaid
aſſizes in the county.

XIV. At a day when the county-court is held, and in a
certain place: and if the ſaid aſſizes cannot be taken upon
that day, ſo many Knights and Free-tenants of them that
were preſent in the county-court that day, ſhall ſtay, as may
give a good judgment, according as the concern may be
greater or leſs.

XV. A freeman ſhall not be amerced for a little offence,
but according to the manner of his offence; and for a great
offence he ſhall be amerced according to the greatneſs of his
offence, ſaving his contentment; and ſo a merchant ſaving
his merchandize; and a villain in like manner ſhall be amerced
ſaving

faving his wainage, if he fall into our mercy: and none of the faid amercements fhall be affeered, but by oath of good and lawful men of the vicinage.

XVI. An Earl and a Baron fhall not be amerced but by their Peers, and according to the manner of their offence.

XVII. No clerk fhall be amerced but according to his lay-fee, and in like manner as others aforefaid, and not according to the quantity of his church-living.

XVIII. No ville nor any man fhall be diftrained to make bridges over rivers, but where they antiently have, and of right ought to make them.

XIX. No Vifcounts, Conftables, Coroners, or other our Bailiffs, fhall hold the pleas of our crown.

XX. If any that holds us a lay-fee die, and our She-riffs, or other our Bailiffs fhew our letters patents of fum-mons for a debt which the deceafed owed to us, our Sheriff or Bailiff may well attach and inventory the goods of the dead, which fhall be found upon his lay-fee, to the value of the debt which the deceafed owed to us, by the view of lawful men, yet fo as nothing be removed till fuch time as the debt, which fhall be found to be due to us, be paid; and the refi-due fhall go to the executors to perform the teftament of the dead: and if nothing be owing to us, all his goods fhall go to the ufe of the dead, faving to his wife and children their reafonable parts.

XXI. None of our Conftables, nor other our Bailiffs, fhall take corn, nor other the goods of any perfon, who may not be of the village where his caftle is, without paying for the fame prefently, unlefs he have time given him by confent of the vendor.

XXII. Our Conftables fhall deftrain no man who ho'ds by knight-fervice, to give money for Caftle-guard, if he has performed it himfelf in proper perfon, or by another good man, if he could not perform it himfelf for fome reafonable caufe: and if we lead him, or fend him into the army, he fhall be difcharged of Caftle-guard for fo long time as he fhall be with us in the army.

XXIII. No Vifcount, Bailiff of our or other, fhall take the horfes or carts of any to make carriage, unlefs he pays according to the antient liberty, to wit, for a cart and two horfes ten pence per day, and for a cart and three horfes four-teen pence per day.

XXIV. Neither ourfelves nor our Bailiffs fhall take an-other man's wood for our caftles, or other occafions, but by his leave whofe wood it is.                          XXV.

XXV. We will hold the lands of such as shall be convict-
ed of felony but a year and a day, and then we will restore
them to the Lords of the fees.

XXVI. All wears shall, for this time forward, be wholly
taken away in the Avenlich * and throughout all Ireland,
except upon the sea-coast.

XXVII. The writ called *precipe* henceforth shall be made
to none out of any tenement, whereby a freeman may lose
his court.

XXVIII. One measure of wine shall be used throughout
our kingdom, and one measure of ale, and one measure of
corn, to wit, the London quart. And there shall be one
breadth of dyed cloths, ruffets, and haubergets, to wit, two
ells within the lifts : and concerning weights, it shall be in
like manner as of measures.

XXIX. Nothing shall be given or taken henceforth for a
writ of inquisition of life or member, but it shall be granted
freely and shall not be denied.

XXX. If any hold of us by fee-farm, or by soccage, and
hold likewise land of others by knight-service, we will not
have the custody of the heir, nor of the land which is of the
fee of another, by reason of such fee-farm, soccage, or bur-
gage, unless such fee-farm owe knight-service.

XXXI. No Bailiff for the time to come shall put any man
to his law upon his bare word, without good witnesses produced.

XXXII. No freeman shall be taken, nor imprisoned, nor
disseized, nor out-lawed, nor exiled, nor destroyed in any
manner ; nor will we pass upon him, nor condemn him, but
by the lawful judgment of his peers, or by the law of the
land.

XXXIII. We will sell none, we will deny nor delay to
none right and justice.

XXXIV. All merchants may, with safety and security, go
out of Ireland, and come into Ireland, and stay, and pass
through Ireland by land and water, to buy and sell without
any evil tolls, paying the ancient and rightful duties, except
in time of war ; and then if they are of the country with
whom we are at war, and are found here at the beginning
of the war, they shall be attached, but without injury to their
bodies or goods, till it be known to us or to our Chief Justice,
how our merchants are entreated which are found in our ene-

* River Liffey.

mies

mies country; and if our's be safe there, they shall be safe in our Land.

XXXV. If any hold of an escheat, as of the honour of Wallingford, Nottingham, Boloin, Lancaster, or of other escheats which are in our hand, and are baronies, and die, his heirs shall owe to us no other relief, nor do us any other service, than was due to the baron of such barony when it was in his Hand; and we will hold the same in like manner as the baron held it.

XXXVI. Men that dwell out of the forest, shall not appear before our justices of the forest by common summons, unless they be in suit themselves, or bail for others who are attached for the forest.

XXXVII. All that have founded Abbies, whereof they have charters from the kings of England, or ancient tenure, shall have the custody thereof whilst they are vacant, as they ought to have.

XXXVIII. All the forests that have been afforested in our time, shall instantly be disafforested; in like manner be it of rivers, that in our time and by us have been put in defence.

XXXIX. None shall be taken nor imprisoned upon the appeal of a woman, for the death of any other than her husband.

XL. Likewise all those customs and liberties, which we grant in our said kingdom, to be held as far as to us belongs towards all our said kingdom, clericks as well as laicks, that they may conserve the same, as far as to them belongs towards theirs.

XLI. But because certain chapters contained in the former charter, may appear heavy and doubtful, to wit, concerning escuages, aids of assessing debts of Jews, and others, liberty of going out of our said kingdom, and returning into our said kingdom, forests and foresters, warrens and warrenners, customs of counties, rivers and their keepers, as they may seem fit to the aforesaid prelates and great men, until we shall have these things examined in a more full council, and then we will make more fully, as well what concerns these things, as others that may hereafter occur to be amended; and whatever shall pertain to the common utility of all, and the peace, and our state, and of our kingdom. And because that we have not yet a seal, we cause this present charter to be sealed, with the seals of our venerable father saint Martin, Lord of Gaul, &c. and William Marischal, Earl of Pembrok our rector, and of our kingdom we cause to be sealed. The

witnesses

witneffes are the perfons above named and many others ; given
by the hand of the aforefaid Lord Legate, and William Mar-
ifcal at Briftol, 12th day of November in the firft year of our
reign.

-‹•◊►•◊►•◊►•◊►•◊►•◊►•◄•◄◄•◄◄•◄‹›-

Soon after the Bill of Rights had paffed in England, the
following heads of a fimilar one, for this kingdom, were prefented for tranfmiffion by our parliament to Lord Capel, then
Lord Deputy of Ireland, on the 14th of October, 1695,
of which no more was heard.

### HEADS of a BILL of RIGHTS.

I. That the pretended power of fufpending of laws, by
regal authority, without confent of parliament, is illegal.

II. That the pretended power of difpenfing with laws,
or the execution of laws by legal authority, as hath been affumed or exercifed, is illegal.

III. That levying money for, or to the ufe of the crown,
by pretence of prerogative, without grant of parliament,
for longer time, or in other manner than the fame is, or fhall
be granted, is illegal.

IV. That it is the right of the fubjects to petition the King,
or the chief governor, or governors of this kingdom, for
the time being, and all commitments or profecutions, or
threats for fuch petition, are illegal.

V. That the fubjects which are proteftants may have arms
for their defence fuitable to their conditions, and as allowed
by law.

VI. That the elections of member of parliament ought to
be free.

VII. That the freedom of fpeech, and debates on proceedings in parliament, ought not to be impeached, or queftioned,
in any place out of parliament.

VIII. That juries ought to be duly impannelled and returned ; and jurors which pafs upon men in trials for high
treafon, ought to be freeholders.

IX. That all grants and promifes, fines and forfeitures of
particular perfons before conviction, are illegal and void.

X. That for redrefs of all grievances in this kingdom,
and for amending, ftrengthening and preferving the laws,
parliaments ought not to be diffolved, as they have been in
the late reigns.

XI. That the free quartering of foldiers on any of this
kingdom, in time of peace, is arbitrary and illegal.

The

The following Extract from a curious Record in the *Calender of Ancient Characters*, will best explain itself.

EDWARDUS Dei gratia rex Angliæ & Franciæ, & dominus Hiberniæ, venerabili in Christo patri M. eadem gratia Archiepiscopo Ardmachono salutem :

Cum alias oneravimus dilectum & fidelem nostrum Nicholaum Dagworth militem, nuncium nostrum versus terram nostram Hiberniæ per nos transmissum, quod ipse in quodam Parliamento in terra nostra prædicta, prætextu literarum nostrarum, dilecto & fideli nostro Willielmi de Wyndesore gubernatori & custodi dictæ terræ nostræ transmissarum, convocando, inter cætera in quadam indentura inter nos & dictum nuncium nostrum confecta, contenta, Prælatis, Magnatibus, & Communibus terræ nostræ prædictæ, ad dictum Parliamentum comparentibus, exponi faceret, quod cum nos, tam excessivas & intolerabiles expensas, circa guerras nostras in terra nostra prædicta, pro salvatione & defensione ejusdem, quales ante hæc tempora apposuimus, propter maximam effusionem expensarum quas circa guerras nostras aliunde necessario nos opponere oportebit, de cætero supportare minime valeamus ; iidem Prælati, Magnates & Communes et eorum quilibet, juxta facultates suas & status sui exigentiam, partem rationabilem hujusmodi expensarum super se capere recusarent, tunc dictus nuncium noster ipsos ex parte nostra oneraret, quod quilibet Episcopus duas personas ecclesiasticas idoneas protestatem sufficientam pro se & clero suæ diocesis, per literas procuratorias ab ipsis episcopo & clero, ac communes cujuslibet comitatus dictæ terræ, duas personas laicas protestatem sufficientam tam pro seipsis, quam Magnatibus ejusdem comitatus, ac Cives & Burgenses cujuslibet Civitatis & Burgi ejusdem terræ, duos Cives & duos Burgenses potestatem sufficientem pro se, & Civibus & Burgensibus civitatum & burgorum prædictorum habentes, versus nos & consilium nostrum in Anglia, ad tractandum, consulendum & concordandum nobiscum, tam super gubernatione dictæ terræ, quam pro auxilio & sustentatione guerræ nostræ ibidem transmitterent. Et licet idem nuncius noster, præmissa omnia & singula Prælatis, Magnatibus & Communibus in Parliamento nostro apud Kilkenn. in octabis Sancti Michaelis proximis præteritis, ex causis præmissis summonito & tento, comparentibus, exposuerit, & ipsos in forma prædicta oneraverit ; ipsi tamen se per eorum insufficientiam excusarunt, quod aliquam partem sumptuum & expensarum, pro guerris nostris ibidem manutenendis, ad

praesens

præfens nequeant fuppo<sup>r</sup>tare : ob quod, hujufmodi perfonas verfus nos in Angliam, ex caufis prædi ftis, in forma fupradicta, tranfmitti volentes, vobis mandamus, quod convocato coram vobis Clero veftræ diocefis, duas perfonas ecclefiafticas hujufmodi poteftatem pro vobis & dicto clero veftro optinentes, de affenfu ejufdem cleri eligi, & coram nobis, & dicto confilio noftro in Anglia ad fumptus veftros, & dicti cleri veftri, citra quindenam purifications beatæ Mariæ proxim' futur', ubicunque tunc fuerimus in Anglia, ad tractandum, confulendum & concordandum, ut prædictum eft, tranfmitti faciatis, nobis in cancellaria noftra Hiberniæ, de nominibus dictarum duarum perfonarum, fic per vos eligendarum, citra feftum Sanctæ Katerniæ virginis prox' futur', ubicunque tunc fuerit fub figillo veftro certificantes, hoc breve nobis tunc ibidem remittentes & hoc fub poena centum librarum de vobis & dicto clero veftro, ad opus noftrum levandarum, nullatenus omittatis.

Tefte Willielmo de Wyndefore gubernatore & cuftode terræ noftræ Hiberniæ, apud Kilkenn. xxv. die Octobris, anno regni noftri Angliæ quadragefimo nono, regni vero noftri Franciæ tricefimo fexto.

✦✦✦✦✦✦✦✦✦✦✦✦✦

## TRANSLATION.

Edward by the grace of God, King of England and France, and Lord of Ireland, to the venerable father in Chrift, M. by the fame grace Archbifhop of Armagh, greeting.

WHEN otherwife we charged our faithful and beloved Nicholas Dagworth, Knight, our Nuncio by us tranfmitted towards our land of Ireland, that he in a certain parliament affembled, in our land aforefaid under the pretext of our tranfmitted letters, to our faithful and beloved William de Wyndesford, governor and keeper of our faid land, among other things exhibited a certain indenture made and contained between us and our faid Nuncio, to the Prelates, Nobles, and Commons of our aforefaid land, at the fame parliament affembled, fhewing the exceffive and intolerable expences of our wars, heretofore in our land aforefaid, for the falvation and defence of the fame, and which on account of the greateft effufion of the expences of our wars elfewhere, we are no longer able to fuftain; that the Prelates, Nobles, Commons, and each of them, as far as in their power, grant a reafonable

part

part of the expences, for the suftenation of our faid war, and for the falvation of our aforefaid land; and if the faid Prelates, Nobles, and Commons, fhould refufe to take on themfelves any reafonable part of the expence for the fuftenation of the war there, and falvation of the aforefaid land, then our faid Nuncio on our part fhall inform them, that every Bifhop fhall have fufficient power for himfelf and the clergy of his diocefe, by letters of procuration from the Bifhop and clergy themfelves, to tranfmit two ecclefiaftical perfons to us and our council in England, to treat, confult, and determine with us, as well for the aid and government of our faid land, as the fuftenation of our war there. And the Commons of every county of the aforefaid land, fhall have fufficient power for themfelves, as the Nobles of faid county, to fend two lay perfons for the fame purpofe, and the citizens and burgeffes of every city and borough, two citizens, and two burgeffes, &c. And although our fame Nuncio, premifed all and figular thefe things to our Prelates, Nobles, and Commons in our parliament at Kilkenny, in the eighth of St. Michael next paft, fummoned and held for the premifed caufes, neverthelefs they excufed themfelves through infufficiency, and at prefent deny to fupport any part of the cofts and the expences of faid war to be maintained in our faid land there, on account of which, and for the caufes abovefaid, we will, that fuch perfons aforefaid, in the form aforefaid, be tranfmitted to us into England. And we command you that you convocate yourfelves before the clergy of your diocefe, chufing for yourfelves and your clergy, two ecclefiaftical perfons, to be elected by the affent of the fame clergy, and before us, and our faid council of England, at your cofts, to appear; and your faid clergy within the fifth of the purification of the bleffed Virgin next coming wherefoever we fhall then be in England, to treat, confult, and agree, as is above faid, that ye caufe to be tranfmitted for us to our Chancellor of Ireland, the names of the aforefaid two perfons, by you thus chofen, within the feaft of the Holy Virgin St. Kathrine, whenfoever it fhall then be, certified under your feal, under the penalty of one hundred pounds from you, and your faid clergy, to be levied for our ufe, on every fuch omiffion, &c.

Witnefs, William de Wyndefore, governor and keeper of our faid land of Ireland, at Kilkenny, the 25th day of October, in the year of our reign of England forty-nine, but in our reign of France, thirty-fix.

We

We have the anfwers of the Archbifhop of Armagh, and of the county of Dublin, to this fummons, diftinctly recorded *. " We are not bound," faid the Prelate, " agreeably to the li- " berties, privileges, rights, laws and cuftoms of the church " and land of Ireland, to elect any of our clergy, and to fend " them to any part of England, for the purpofe of holding " parliaments or councils in England. Yet, on account of " our reverence to our Lord the King of England, and the " now imminent neceffity of the land aforefaid, faving to us " and to the Lords and Commons of the faid land, all rights, " privileges, liberties, laws, and cuftoms before mentioned, we " have elected reprefentatives to repair to the King in Eng- " land, to treat and confult with him and his Council. Ex- " cept, however, that we do by no means grant to our faid " reprefentatives any power of affenting to any burdens or " fubfidies to be impofed on us or our clergy, to which we " cannot yield by reafon of our poverty and daily expence in " defending the land againft the Irifh enemy."

In like manner we find the county of Dublin at firft elect- ing their reprefentatives without power or authority to con- fent to the impofition of any burdens ; the Nobles and Com- mons " unanimoufly with one voice declaring, that accord- " ing to the rights, privileges, liberties, laws and cuftoms of " the land of Ireland, enjoyed from the time of the conqueft " of faid land, they are not bound to fend any perfons from " the land of Ireland to the parliament or council of our " Lord the King in England, to treat, confult, or agree " with our Lord the King in England, as the writ re- " quires. Notwithftanding, on account of their reverence, " and the neceffity and prefent diftrefs of the faid land, they " have elected reprefentatives to repair to the King, and to " treat and confult with him and his Council ; referving to " themfelves the power of yielding or agreeing to any fub- " fidies." At the fame time protefting, " that their prefent " compliance is not hereafter to be taken in prejudice to the " rights, privileges, laws, and cuftoms, which the Lords " and Commons, from the time of the conqueft of the land " of Ireland, have enjoyed, in confideration of the various " burdens which the faid Lords and Commons have borne, " and ftill do bear, and which for the future they cannot fup- " port—*nifi Dominus Rex manum fuam melius apponere voluerit.*"

* MS. Rawlinfon.

In

In 13 year of King Edward I. the statutes of Westminster 1 anno 3 of Gloucester, an. 6 and of merchants, and Westminster 2. an. 13 of his reign, were by his command sent to his chief justice in Ireland, to be there proclaimed and observed, as this one memorandum in the clause roll of that year assures us.

Memorandum, quod die Veneris in festo exaltacionis sanctæ crucis, anno, &c. 13 apud Wynton. liberata fuerunt Rogero Bretun Clerico venerabilis patris W. Waterfordenses episcopi tunc Justic. Hibern. quædam statuta per regem et consilium suum edita et provisa, viz. statuta * Westm. statim post coronationem edita, et statuta Glouc. et statuta pro mercatoribus facta, ac statuta Westm. † in Parliamento regis Pasch. anno prædicto provisa et facta, in Heibern. deferenda, et ibidem proclamanda et observanda.

Cl. 13. Ed. 1. dorso m. 5. De Statutis leboratis.
Writs for free commerce between England and Ireland, as common one to another, 253. Raym. 4 Instit.

Richard II. made a voyage to this kingdom, the particulars of which Howe, the English historian thus relates.

Now somewhat of the former voyage of King Richard into Ireland, as the same was reported to Sir John Froisart, by an Esquire of England, named Henry Christall. Sir John (quoth he) it is not in memory, that ever any King of England made such provision for any journey into Ireland, nor such a number of men of armes nor archers. The King was a nine moneths in the marshes of Ireland to his great cost, and charge to the realme, for they bare all his expences: and the marchant-cities, and good townes of the realm thought it well bestowed, when they saw the King returne home againe with honour. The number that hee had thither, were foure thousand men of armes, and thirty thousand archers, well payed weekly. But to shew the truth, Ireland is one of the euill countries of the world to make warre upon or to bring under subiection, for it is closed strongly and wildly with high forrests, and great waters and marishes. It is hard to enter to doe any of the country any damage: nor yee shall find no towne, nor person to speak withall. For the men draw to the woods, and dwell in caues or small cottages, under trees and among bushes, like wild and sauage beasts: and when they know that any man maketh warre against them, being

* Westm. 1. 3. Ed. 1.          † Westm. 2.

entered

entred into their countries, then they draw together to the
ftraits and paffages to defend them, fo that no man can enter
into them. And when they fee their time they will foone
take their advantage on their enemies, for they know the
country, and are light people. For a man of armes, being
neuer fo well horfed, and runne he neuer fo faft, the Irifhmen will run on foote as faft as hee, and ouertake him, yea,
and leape up upon his horfe behinde him, and throw him
from his horfe; for they are ftrong men in their armes, and
haue fharpe weapons with large blades, two edged, wherewith they will flay their enemie, whom they neuer repute to
be dead till they haue cut his throat, and opened his belly,
and taken out his heart, which they carry away with them,
fome fay they eate it, and haue great delight therein: they
take no man to ranfome. And when they fee that they be
ouer-matched, then they will depart and hide themfelues in
bufhes, woods, and caues, fo that no man fhall finde them:
Sir William Windfore, who had moft vfed the warres in thofe
parts of any other Englifhman, could neuer learne the manner of the countrey. They be hard people, and of rude wit:
and they fet nothing by iollity, nor frefh apparell, nor by
noblefle, for though their country be foueraignly governed
by Kings, whereof they haue many, yet will they abide and
continue in their rudeneffe.

 Truth it is, that 4 of the principall Kings, and moft puif-
fant after the manner of the countrey, are come to the obeyfance of the king of England, by loue and faire meanes, and
not by battell, or conftraint. The Earl of Ormond, who
marcheth upon them, hath taken great paine, and hath fo
intreated them, that they came to Dubline, to the King, and
fubmitted them to him, to be under the obeyfance of the
crowne of England, wherefore the King and all the realme
reputeth this for a great and honourable act. For King Edward did never fo much upon them, as King Richard did in
his voyage. The honour is great, but the profite is but
fmall, &c. The names of the foure Kings were thefe, firft,
the greate Oneale King of Meth, the fecond Otrine of Thomond, King of Thomond, the third Arthur of Mackquemur
King of Leinfter, the fourth Ocomor King of Theuenes
and Drape, they were made Knights by King Richard in the
cathedral church of Dubline: thefe foure Kings watched all
the night before in the church, and the next day at high
maffe time, were made Knights, and with them Sir Thomas
Orphew, Sir Iames Pado, and Sir Iohn Pado, his coufin.

                  Thefe

Thefe Kings fate that day at the table with King Richard, they were regarded of many people, becaufe their behauiour was ftrenge to the manor of England.

When Sir Iohn Froifart defired to know how it came to paffe, that foure Kings of Ireland were fo foone brought to the obeyfance of King Richard, when King Edward the King's grand-father, who was fo valient a Prince, could neuer fubdue them: Sir Henry Chriftall anfwered, he could not tell, but as men faid, the great puiffance that the King had over with him, and remaining there nine moneths, abafhed the Irifhmen. Alfo the fea was clofed from them on all parts, whereby their marchandifes might not enter into their countries, though they that dwell farre within the realme cared little for it, yet fuch as liue on the marches of England and by the fea coaft, vfe feare of merchandife.

King Edward in his time, had to anfwere fo many warres in France, Britaine, Gafcoigne, and Scotland, that his people were divided in divers places, wherefore he could not fend any great number into Ireland. But when the Irifhmen faw the great number of men of warre that King Richard had in this laft iourney, they aduifed themfelues, and came to obeyfance.

⊷⊷⊰⊷⊰⊷⊰⊷⊰⊷⊰✦✦⊷⊷⊷⊷⊷⊷⊷⊷

In thes Articles folowing been comprifed the Kyng's Will, Determination, Commandement, and Plefures, upon the Parliaments holdyn late at the Naafe and Drogheda; and upon the Parliament that fhall be now next holdyn within his lands of Irland. Anno 1418, 19 Ed. IV. Rot. clauf.

WHERE as have been gret variences of late in our faid land of Ireland upon two parliaments ther laft holdyn; the oen at the Naafe, the other at Drogheda, whether of theym fhould be of auctorite; we have thereupon taken fuche directions as folowith:

Furft, We confider that in the faid two parliaments were communed and concludet principaly two acts, the oen touchyng the grauntes of certayn fubfidies for the wele and defence of our faid land, the fecund concerned refumptions afwell of offices as of our revenue.

As touching the fubfidies graunted in our parliament holdyn at Drogheda, for as moche as we underftand, that it was graunted, and alfo in gret part, as we ben enformed,

e                                                    leuced

leveed for the wele and defence abovesaid, We will that the same graunts with all that thereto apperteyneth be gode and effectuell, and also auctorised by the parliament in our said land now next to be holdyn.

As touching the acts of resumptions in eather of the said parliaments passed, which of partialte and malice been, and have been more hurtyng to our subjects ther than to us or the wele of our said land profitable; we will that the same acts be maad void and of none effect in the lawe, except the resumption of offices and Chauncellership and Treforeship, made in the parliament holdyn at Drogheda, the which we will that hit stand in his force and effect. Considering that thereuppon, we have made the Bishop of Meth, our Chanseler, and Sir Rouland Eustace, Knyght, our Treforer there; and we will, that a general act of resumption fro the furst day of Kyng Herry the VIte, be had and made in the next parliament touching our revenue; and that such provision be made upon the same by our Depute Lieutenant there according to our plefure; which our plefure we have shewed to our right trusty and welbeloved cofyn Therle of Kyldare, whom we have ordened to be Depute Lieutenant, and to the reverend father in God the Bishop of Mythe, whom we have ordeyned as is above said to be our Chanseler.

As touching the resumpcion of offices, forafmoche as offices of Chanseler and other in the Deputies commyfion to us oonly reserved, we will that the offices of Chief of the Exchequer and the Maister of our mint there be resumed in this same parliament, and our leters patents be mad there uppon under our gret seall there, to thofe persons to whom we have made our grauntes upon the same.

And as to other offices to us in the said commyffion not reserved, we be contented that such of theym be resumed, and they for the wele of us and our said land, by our said Depute Lieutennant fo difpofed, as shall be thought by him mofte expedient.

We will also, that at thys said parliament be resumed the office of Senefchalfie of the liberte of Methe, with the fees, wages, and rewards therfor by us, or otherwife to any person graunted, and fo to remayn in our hands at our pleafure. We will alfo, that if any act have be made to the prejudice of us, and in derogacion of our Corone in restreyning of tonnage and pondage, it be utterly revoked and adnulled, and in this parliament the old graunt thereof reno-

velled

velled and established, as shall be best for our right, wele and honor.

Item, the Kyng willeth, That such an act as herto before hath be made in the land there restreyning, that noe man within that land shall be called out of the said land by any precept or commandement, made under the Kyng's grete seall, prive seall or signet in England, be utterly revoked and adnulled.

Item, The Kyng willeth, that upon resumption of the Kyng's revenues to be made in this parliament, the townes of Divelyn * and Drogheda be providet fore al suche grauntes as have ben made unto they by the Kyng's auctorite, his progenitours or predocessours, so that they promise to be redy to doo the Kyng service, at suche tymes as by the Kyng's Lieutenant or his depute they shall be designed.

Thes articles folouying conteyne, the Kyng's comanndements and plesere, how his Chanselere of Irland, Clerc of the Rolles, and the Clerk of the Hanaper ther, shall demene them there in executyng of ther offices.

Furst, They and everithe of thems, shall well and trewly serve the Kyng and his liege peple of the same land, in the doyng of their offices.

Item, That they ne none of them shall assent to the hurt, damage, or alienacion of the Kyng's lands, revenues, or rights; but they shall endevoer them selfe for the vauncyng and encresyng therof, and lette all them to the best of theire powere, that wold attempt the contrary therof.

Item, That the sead Chaunseler do serv alweyes in suche place and tymes as the Clerc of the Rolles, the Clerc of the Hanaper, and other ministers of the Chaunsery, may be ther and then present.

Item, That the said Chaunseller do delyvre to the Clerc of the Rolles, all such warrants cummyng to his hands, so as he may kepe them as the Kyng's recordes, according to his office.

Item, That the said Chaunseller sele no pardon under the grete sele, unto any man upon his provisione from the court of Rome, without the King's knowlege and consent.

Item, The Chaunseller in person, shall in true time make his abidyng in the place wher the Kyng's Courts be kept, un leshe ther by a great and urgent cause, by the depute with the advise of the more part of the Kyng's Consele, it be thought his absence to be allowed.

Item,

* Dublin.

Item, That the Clerc of the Rolles do enroll all patents under the Kyng's grete feall, before that they be deliveret to the parties, and kepe fo the Kyng's records, that none of them be rafed, ne befoiled.

Item, That he fee and write at every fele, what profits growith unto the Kyng thereof, and the fpecialtees of the fame ; fo that his boke fo made may be a controllment upon the accompts of the Clerc of the Hanaper, to be made yerly in the Kyng's Efchequer there.

Item, That no lyvere be made to the Kyng's tennant, nor yet reftitution to be made to any Bifhop, Abbot, or Prior, without that the Kyng be furft anfwered of his duete, accordynge to the rate of the tyme that the landes have ben in the Kyng's handes.

Item, That the Clerc of the Hanapier continueley receive the fees of the fele of writts, commiffions and patents ; and alfo, all fuche fynes as fhall be made in the Chauncery, and thereupon pay the Chaunceller his fees, wages, and rewards accuftomed, and deliver the remenant unto the Kyng's Efchequer upon his accompts, which he fhall make yerly therof : and to thentent that noone ignorance may be pretendit, what fines ben to be made them within the Kyng's Chauncery, the fpecialties of them hereafter enfueth.

| | l. | s. | d. |
|---|---|---|---|
| All writs of covenant, every affife and writs in nature, affife and other writts of entry aboye the value of 40s. unto the value of 5 marks, | 0 | 6 | 8 |
| Every fpecial affife, be hit ever fo litell, it maketh a fyne, and *ftreitly*, every 5 marks, | 0 | 6 | 8 |
| Every formedonne above 40s. unto 8 marks, | 0 | 6 | 8 |
| Every pone of Juftices, pone of writts of right, every writt of confpirici, writts of atteynte, and writts of falfe judgment, the fine, | 0 | 6 | 8 |
| Every recordan of dett or trefpaffe, and every dedimus poteftatem upon a writt of covenant, | 0 | 6 | 8 |
| Every writt of dett or trifpaffe, exceeding the fome value or prife of 40l. unto the fome of 60l. | 0 | 6 | 8 |

Alfo an attachments of the privilege of dett or trifpaffe according to the fame, and if hit exceeds more to pay more.

All refpite of homage 6s. 8d. or mark after the quantite of the liveled ; all oyer and determinor at the fuit of the partie, *if gretter* trifpaffe *the grett fyne*. All manner of licence to purchafe temperell livelod to mortmayne the firft yere value of the fame. All manner licence of fpirituell livlihood, as appropriaciery of churches or of benefices, fpirituell

ef

of holy church, four yere value of the fame. All maner
licence of alienacion by the Kyng's tenannt, the third part
of the value thereof. All pardons of alienacions made by
the Kyng's tenaunt, the value of a hole yere. All maneo
licence of marriage of the Kyng's widdows, the third part
of their dower. All manner of confirmacions of offices,
the third part or fourth part of the value thereof, by the yere.
All confirmacions of libertees and franchifees, the third part,
or the fourthe part of the profits or value of the fame franchifees. All patents of devyfing the third part of the value
of his goods. All pardons of the Kyng's widdowes maried
without licence, the value of her dower by the year.

Item, That the Clerc of the Kyng's Hanaper, leave for
him a depute in the court of the Kyng's Bench, another in
the court of the Common Place, which fhall receve for the
Kyng all the profites growing of the Kyng's fele in either of
the faid courts, and thereupon, fhall yeld his accompt in the
Kyng's Efchequer.

Here folouyth the Kyng's comanndements and plefure, to
be fhewed unto Sir Rouland Euftace, Knyght, whom his
Highneffe hath deputed to be Treforer of his land of Irland.

Furft, The faid Sir Rouland, fhall well and trewly behave
hym in the occupieng of his faid office, and juftely and right-
ouifly exercife it, as well betwix the Kyng and his fubjefts,
as betwix the Kyng's fubjefts.

Item, He fhall not affent nore agre to the hurt, dammage,
or difheretyng the Kyng of his lands, revenues, rights, re-
galie or prerogatifs, but in all that hym is, he fhall uphold,
mayntene, encreafe and avaunce them.

Item, That the faid Sir Rouland continually endevour
himfelf, that the Kyng be yerely anfuered of all fuch revenues and rights, as fhall belong unto his highnes within his
land of Irland, and that he do fend unto the Kyng's goode
grace yerly, a trew and pleyn vews thereof, compryfing the
particulers and fpecialtees of the fame.

Item, That the fame Sir Rouland remytte and forgete all
malice and evill will that he hath borne and berith to the Bifhop of Mythe, Bermyngham, the Juftice, and all other the
Kyng's fubjefts within the faid land; for the Kyng's highneffe hath comaundet them in femblable wife to do toward
hym  Alfo the King vol that he delivre his grete fele, beying
in his kepyng, unto the faid Bifhop of Mythe, whom he hath
deputed and made to be his Chaunfeller of his faid land of
Irland.

deputed

Item, That the faid Sir Rouland kepe the appoinment by the Kyng, taken betwix hym and Sir Robert Euſtace in thes articles folouying, beth compriſed the Kyng's comaundments and pleſere, to be executed and accompliſhed by his Juges and Barons of the Eſchequer within his land of Irland.

Furſt, That this and every of them, duely and trewly have them as well towards the Kyng's higheneſſe as towards his ſubjects, in executyng and doyng of their offices, and after their cunyng and difcrecion, juſtely and indeffcrently miniſter juſtice to all the Kyng's ſubjects in theeſe parties.

Item, That nether thei ne eny of them, aſſent nor agree to the hurtyng or damagyng of any ſuche revenues, en his laws, prerogatifs, rights or intereſt to the Kyng in any wiſe belongyng, but that thei and everith of theym endevoir theym to their power to the avauncing and encrecyng thereof.

Item, That they and everith of them, employ them as effectually as they can, that all fines, amerciaments, and all other iſſues and profits, ſhall or ought righturſly to grow within the Kyng's levity, whom they have or ſhall have adminiſtration of juſtice, be truely and duely ceſſed and ordered; and that thereof a due comptes be made yerly in the Kyng's Eſchequer ther, ſo that their fees, wages and rewards, may be paiet and contented of the ſame, as farre as it ſhall ſtretche unto.

Item, In caas that eny variences growe amongſt the Kyng's ſubjects in thes parties, which God defends, whereby the Kyng or the comen wele of his land ther by eny liklyod ſhold be hurted, that thei endevoir themſelf to the beſt of ther power, to appoyſe thoſe variences, and that ſuche direction be taken therupon as ſhall beſt acorde to reſon, and to the wele of the Kyng, and of his ſaid land of Irland.

Item, That the Juges of both the places, aid, aſſiſte, and favoir, ſuch perſons as the Clerke of the Hanaper ſhall depute for hym ther, for the recevyng of profites of the Kyng's ſeles within the ſame places, ſo that the Kyng may be thereby anfwered thereof, as he ought to be.

In the articles folouying ben compriſed the Kyng's pleſure, howe and in what forme Gerard Therle, of Kildare, depute unto his Lieutenant, ſhall be demeaned in the peerceiſing of his office of the ſaid depute, within his land of Irland.

Furſt, The ſeid Erl ſhall wel and trewly ferve the Kyng as depute to his Lieutenant of Irland, in all and every thing compriſed in his commiſſion.

Item,

Item, He fhall to the uttermoft of his power, defend the Kyng's lands and his fubjects within the faid land, againft the Kyng's rebells and Irifh ennemyes.

Item, He fhall not affent to the hurt, damage, or alienacion of the Kyng's lands, revenues, or rights within that land, but to the beft of his power, avance and encres them, and hold all thofe that wold attempt to do the contrary.

Item, He fhall not pardon thentre of any of the Kyng's tennants upon the Kyng's poffeffion, nor yet graunt to deny them licence without a reafonable fyne.

Item, He fhall graunt no pardon to any man upon his provifion purchafed or to be purchafed from the court of Rome, ne therof he fhall addreffe no warrant unto the Chaunfeler, without the Kyng's knowleche and affent.

Item, He fhall favor, aide and affifte all the Kyng's officers within the fame land, in the doing of their offices, and refift all therein that would malicioufly attempt agens them for the doying of the faime.

Item, He fhall effectualy endevour himfelf, that Sir Rouland Euftace deliver unto the Bifhop of Methe, whom the Kyng hath deputed to be his Chaunfeler of the fame land, the Kyng's grete fele.

Item, In neo parliament to be holdyn hereafter ther fhall no fubfidie be axed, ne graunted in the fame upon the commounes ne levied but once in a yere, which fhall not excede the extent of 1200 marks, as hath been accuftumed.

Item, That noo thing that is or fhall be commowned and concluded in Counfele, be taken in ftrenth as an act of Counfele, unlefs the Kyng's Lieutenant or his depute give his affent thereunto, by the advis of the more part of the Kyng's Counfele there, that is to fay, the Chanfelor, the Treforer, the Kyng's Chief Juftys, the Chief Baron of the Kyng's Efchequer, the Clerc of the Rolls, the Kyng's Serjant.

Item, The Kyng will alfo, that the Maifter of the Mint, work his cuniage oonly in the Caftle of Divelin.

Item, That in the fame cuinage touching the fyneffe, it be according to the ftandart of England, and that an unce of fillver of that fyneffe be coyned 4s. 8d. whereof to the merchant 4s. 2d. to the Kyng, the Maifter of the Mynt, for hym, the odyr offieers, and the Coyners 6d.

Item, That all and every of the peces to be coyned, ber a notable difference on eyther fide; on the crofs fide a rofe, and upon the pile fide, a notable difference of the Kyng eafy to be known to every body, accordyng to fuche prints as ben delivered unto the Maifter of the Mynt here.

*  Such parliaments as have been held in Ireland, and such
ts as have been made in them since that year in the reigns
of King Henry VI. Edward IV. Henry VII. VIII. Philip and
Mary, Queen Elizabeth, and King James, and what elſe
concerns the parliament of Ireland, their ſummons, members
privileges, juriſdictions, proceeding, acts and ſettling of the
Engliſh laws, government, ſtatutes in that realm, you may
peruſe at leiſure in the ſtatutes of Ireland, publiſhed by Mr.
Richard Bolton, Dublin, 1621, eſpecially 25 Henry VI.
c. 28, An act that the Lords of parliament in pleas ſhall not
be amerſed, otherwiſe than other perſons ; 3 Edward IV.
c. 5. An act whereby the Lords and Commons of parliament
ſhall have privilege for forty days before and after the parliament ; 15 Edward IV. c. 2. An act concerning the chuſing of
knights and burgeſſes of parliament ; 10 Henry VII. c. 4.
That no parliament be holden in this land, until the acts be
certified into England ; c. 16. An act declaring the effect of
Poyning's act; 33 Henry VIII. c. 1. An act declaring how
Poyning's act ſhall be expounded ; 4 Philip and Mary, An act
authoriſing ſtatutes to be made in this parliament notwithſtanding Poyning's act; 11 Elizabeth, ſeſſi. 2. An act that there
be no bill certified into England, for the repeal or ſuſpenſion
of Poyning's act, before the ſame be firſt argued upon in a
ſeſſion of parliament holden in this realm.

Preſuming that the foregoing references relative to Poyning's act will be peruſed, I ſhall adjoin what Hume ſays on
this ſubject.

The King's (Henry VII.) authority appeared equally pre-
valent and uncontroulable in Ireland ; Sir Edward Poyning
had been ſent over with ſome troops into that country, with
an intention of quelling the partizans of the houſe of York,
and of reducing the natives to ſubjection : he was not ſupported with forces ſufficient for that important enterpriſe.
The Iriſh, by flying into their woods, moraſſes, and mountains, in ſome meaſure eluded his efforts : but Poyning ſummoned a parliament at Dublin, where he was more ſucceſsful. He paſſed that memorable ſtatute, which ſtill bears
his name, and which eſtabliſhes the authority of the Engliſh
government in Ireland. By this ſtatute all the former laws
of England, were made to be of force in Ireland ; and no
bill can be introduced into the Iriſh parliament, unleſs it previouſly receives the ſanction of the council of England. This
latter law ſeems calculated for enſuring the dominion of the
Engliſh over Ireland ; but was really granted at the deſire of
the Iriſh commons, who propoſed, by that means, to ſecure
themſelves from the tyranny of the Lords, particularly of
ſuch Lieutenants as were of Iriſh birth †.

*  Pryn, 4. inſt.      † Sir J. Davies.

I come now to confider our Commercial Reftrictions, which I find already fo happily enumerated, in a work intitled " The Commercial Reftraints of Ireland confidered, in a feries of letters to a noble lord," that I fhall take the freedom with the judicious writer of giving his firft letter entire, and the facts, &c. chiefly of the reft.

## FIRST LETTER.

My Lord,

*Dublin, 20th Aug.* 1779.

YOU defire my thoughts on the affairs of Ireland ; a fubject little confidered, and confequently not underftood in England. The Lords and Commons of Great Britain have addreffed his Majefty to take the diftreffed and impoverifhed ftate of this country into confideration ; have called for information, and refolved to purfue effectual methods for promoting the common ftrength, wealth and commerce of both kingdoms; and his Majefty has been pleafed to exprefs, in his fpeech from the throne, his entire approbation of their attention to the prefent ftate of Ireland.

The occafion calls for the affiftance of every friend to the Britifh empire : thofe who can give material information are bound to communicate it. The attempt however is full of difficulty ; it will require more than ordinary caution to write with fuch moderation as not to offend the prejudices of one country, and with fuch freedom as not to wound the feelings of the other.

The prefent ftate of Ireland teems with every circumftance of national poverty. Whatever the land produces is greatly reduced in its value : wool is fallen one half in its ufual price ; wheat one third ; black cattle of all kinds in the fame proportion, and hides in a much greater : buyers are not had without difficulty at thofe low rates, and from the principal fairs men commonly return with the commodities they brought there : rents are every where reduced, in many places it is impoffible to collect them : the farmers are all diftreffed, and many of them have failed : when leafes expire, tenants are not eafily found : the landlord is often obliged to take his lands into his own hands, for want of bidders at reafonable rents, and finds his eftate fallen one fourth in its

f value.

value. The merchant juſtly complains that all buſineſs is at a ſtand, that he cannot diſcount his bills, and that neither money nor paper circulates. In this and the laſt year, above twenty thouſand manufacturers, in this metropolis were reduced to beggary for want of employment; they were for a conſiderable length of time ſupported by alms; a part of the contribution came from England, and this aſſiſtance was much wanting from the general diſtreſs of all ranks of people in this country. Public and private credit are annihilated: parliament, that always raiſes money in Ireland on eaſy terms, when there is any to be borrowed in the country, in 1778 gave 7½l. per cent. in annuities, which in 1773 and 1775 were earneſtly ſought after at 6l. then thought to be a very high rate. The expences of a country, nearly bankrupt, muſt be inconſiderable; almoſt every branch of the revenue has fallen; and the receipts in the treaſury for the two years, ending lady-day, 1779, were leſs than thoſe for the two years, ending lady-day, 1777, deducting the ſums received on account of loans in each period, in a ſum of 334,900l. 18s. 9½d: there was due on the 25th of March laſt, on the eſtabliſhments, and for extraordinary expences, an arrear amounting to 373,706l. 13s. 6½d.: a ſum of 600,000l. will probably be now wanting, to ſupply the deficiencies on the eſtabliſhments and extraordinary charges of government: and an annual ſum of between 50 and 60,000l. yearly, to pay intereſt and annuities: in the laſt ſeſſion 466,000l. was borrowed; if the ſum wanting could now be raiſed, the debt would be increaſed in a ſum of above 1,000,000l. in leſs than three years, and if the expences and the revenues ſhould continue the ſame as in the laſt two years, there is a probability of an annual deficiency of 300,000l. The nation in the laſt two years has not been able to pay for its own defence; a militia law, paſſed in the laſt ſeſſion, could not be carried into execution for want of money. Inſtead of having forces abroad *, Ireland has not been able in this year to pay the forces kept in the kingdom: it has again relapſed into its ancient ſtate of imbecility, and Great Britain has been lately obliged to ſend over money to pay the army † which defends this impoveriſhed country.

* On account of the inability of Ireland, Great Britain ſince Chriſtmaſs, 1778, relieved her from the burthen of paying forces abroad.

† A ſum of 50,000l. has been lately ſent from England for that purpoſe.

Our

Our diſtreſs and poverty are of the utmoſt notoriety; the proof does not depend ſolely upon calculation or climate, it is palpable in every public and private tranſaction, and is deeply felt among all orders of our people.

This kingdom has been long declining. The annual deficiency of its revenues, for the payment of public expences, has been, for many years, ſupplied by borrowing. The American rebellion, which conſiderably diminiſhed the demand for our linens; an embargo on proviſions continued for three years *, and highly injurious to our victualing trade; the increaſing drain of remittances to England for rents, ſalaries, profits of offices, penſions and intereſt, and for the payment of forces abroad, have made the decline more rapid, but have not occaſioned it.

If we determine to inveſtigate the truth, we muſt aſſign a more radical cauſe: when the human or political body is unſound or infirm, it is in vain to inquire what accidental circumſtances appear to have occaſioned thoſe maladies which ariſe from the conſtitution itſelf.

If in a period of fourſcore years of profound internal peace, any country ſhall appear to have often experienced the extremes of poverty and diſtreſs; if at the times of her greateſt ſuppoſed affluence and proſperity, the ſlighteſt cauſes have been ſufficient to obſtruct her progreſs, to annihilate her credit, and to ſpread dejection and diſmay among all ranks of her people; and if ſuch a country is bleſſed with a temperate climate and fruitful ſoil, abounds with excellent harbours and great rivers, with the neceſſaries of life and materials of manufacture, and is inhabited by a race of men, brave, active, and intelligent, ſome permanent cauſe of ſuch diſaſtrous effects muſt be ſought for.

If your veſſel is frequently in danger of foundering in the midſt of a calm; if by the ſmalleſt addition of ſail ſhe is near overſetting, let the gale be ever ſo ſteady, you would neither reproach the crew, nor accuſe the pilot or the maſter; you would look to the conſtruction of the veſſel, and ſee how ſhe had been originally framed, and whether any new

---

* By a proclamation, dated the 3d of February, 1776, on all ſhips and veſſels, laden in any of the ports in this kingdom, with proviſions of any kind, but not to extend to ſhips carrying ſalted beef, pork, butter and bacon into Great Britain, or proviſions to any part of the Britiſh Empire, except the colonies mentioned in the ſaid proclamation. 4th of January, 1779, taken off as far as it relates to ſhips carrying proviſions to any of the ports of Europe.

works had been added to her, that retard or endanger her
courfe.

But for fuch an examination more time and attention are
neceffary than have been ufually beftowed upon this fubject in
Great Britain; and as I have now the honour to addrefs a
perfon of rank and ftation in that kingdom on the affairs of
Ireland, I fhould be brief in my firft audience, or I may
happen never to obtain the favour of a fecond.

I have the honour to be, my lord, &c.


## SECOND LETTER.


My Lord,

*Dublin, 23d Auguft,* 1779.

FROM the time that king James the firft had eftablifhed a
regular adminiftration of juftice in every part of the kingdom,
until the rebellion of 1641, which takes in a period of between thirty and forty years, the growth of Ireland was confiderable *. In the act recognizing the title of king James,
the Lords and Commons acknowledge " that many bleffings
" and benefits had, within thefe few years paft, been poured
" upon this realm † ;" and at the end of the parliament in
1615, the commons return thanks for the extraordinary pains
taken for the good of this republic, whereby they fay " we
" all of us fit under our own vines, and the whole realm
" reapeth the happy fruits of peace ‡." In his reign the little
that could be given by the people, was given with general
confent § : and received with extraordinary marks of royal
favour ; he defires the lord-deputy to return them thanks for
their fubfidy, and for their granting it with univerfal confent ‖ ; and to affure them that he holds his fubjects of that
kingdom in equal favour with thofe of his other kingdoms;
and that he will be as careful to provide for their profperous
and flourifhing ftate, as for his own perfon.

---

* Its tranquility was fo well eftablifhed in 1611, that king James reduced his army in Ireland to 176 horfe, 1450 foot. Additional judges
were appointed; circuits eftablifhed throughout the kingdom, 2d Cox,
17; and Sir John Davis obferves, that no nation under the fun loves
equal and indifferent juftice better than the Irifh. Davis, p. 184, 196.

† 13 Jac. ch. i.                    ‡ Vol. Com. Journ. p. 92.
§ Ib. 61.                          ‖ Ib. p. 88.

Davis,

Davis mentions the profperous ftate of the country, and that the revenue of the crown, both certain and cafual, had been raifed to a double proportion. He takes notice how this was effected, "by the encouragement given to the maratime " towns and cities, as well to increafe the trade of merchan- " dize, as to cherifh mechanical arts;" and mentions the confequence, " that the ftrings of the Irifh harps were all " in tune."

In the fucceeding reign, Ireland for fourteen or fifteen years appears to have greatly advanced in profperity. The commons granted in the feffion of 1634, fix entire fubfidies, which they agreed fhould amount in the collection to 250,000l. * ; and the free gifts previoufly given to king Charles the firft, at different times, amounted to 310,000l.† ; in the feffion of 1630, they gave four entire fubfidies, and the clergy eight; the cuftoms which had been framed at 500l. yearly, in the beginning of this reign, were in the pro- grefs of it fet for 54,000l

The commodities exported were twice as much in value, as the foreign merchandize imported, and fhipping is faid to have increafed an hundred fold §. Their parliament was en- couraged to frame laws conduciye to the happinefs and prof- perity of themfelves and their pofterities, for the enacting and " confummating" whereof the king paffes his royal word ; and affures his fubjects of Ireland that they were equally of as much refpect and dearnefs to him as any others ‡.

In the fpeaker's fpeech in 1639, enumerating the national bleffings, he mentions as one, "that our in-gates and out-gates do ftand open for trade and traffic**" and as the lord chancel- lor declared his excellency's " high liking of this oration," it may be confidered as a fair account of the condition of Ireland at that time. When the commons had afterwards caught the infection of the times, and were little difpofed to pay compliments, they acknowledge, that this kingdom, when the earl of Stratford obtained the government, " was " in a flourifhing, wealthy and happy eftate ††.

After the reftoration, from the time that the acts of fet- tlement and explanation had been fully carried into execu-

---

* Cox's Hift· of Ireland, 2 Vol. 61.
† Some of thefe fubfidies, from the fubfequent times of confufion, were not raifed.
§ Lord Stafford's Letters, 2d Vol. p. 297.
‡ Leland's Hift, of Ireland, 3d Vol. 41.
** Ir. Com. Jour. 1ft Vol. p. 228, 229.
†† Lord Clarendon. Cox, ib. Ir. Com. Journ. 1 Vol. p. 280, 311.

tion, to the year 1688, Ireland made great advances, and continued, for several years, in a most prosperous condition*. Lands were every where improved; rents were doubled; the kingdom abounded with money; trade flourished to the envy of our neighbours; cities encreased exceedingly; many places of the kingdom equalled the improvements of England; the king's revenue increased proportionably to the advance of the kingdom, which was every day growing, and was *well established in plenty and wealth* † ; manufactures were set on foot in divers parts; the meanest inhabitants were at once enriched and civilized: and this kingdom is then represented to be the most improved and improving spot of ground in Europe. I repeat the words of persons of high rank, great character and superior knowledge, who could not be deceived themselves, and were incapable of deceiving others.

James, the first duke of Ormond, whose memory should be ever revered by every friend of Ireland, to heal the wound that this country had received by the prohibition of the export of her cattle to England, obtained from Charles the Second a letter ‡, dated, the 23d of March, 1667, by which he directed that all restraints upon the exportation of commodities, of the growth or manufacture of Ireland, to foreign parts, should be taken off, but not to interfere with the plantation laws, or the charters to the trading companies, and that this should be notified to his subjects of this kingdom; which was accordingly done by a proclamation from the lord lieutenant and council; and at the same time by his majesty's permission, they prohibited the importation from Scotland of linen, wrollen, and other manufactures and commodities, as drawing large sums of money out of Ireland, and a great hindrance to its manufactures. His grace successfully executed his scheme of national improvement, having by his own constant attention, the exertion of his extensive influence, and the most princely munificence, greatly advanced the woollen, and

---

* Archbishop King, In his state of the protestants of Ireland, p. 52, 53, 445, 446. Lord Chief Justice Keating's address to James the Second, and his letter to Sir John Temple, ib.

The prohibition of the exportation of our cattle to England, though a great, was but a temporary distress; and in its consequences greatly promoted the general welfare of this country.

† Lord Sydney's words in his speech from the throne, in 1692, from his own former knowledge of this country. Ir. Com. Journ. 2d Vol. p. 577.

‡ Carte, 2 Vol. p. 342, 344.

revived

revived * the linen manufactures, which England then encouraged in this kingdom, as a compensation for the loss of
that trade of which she had been deprived; this encouragement, from that time to the revolution, had greatly increased
the wealth, and promoted the improvement of Ireland.

The tyranny and persecuting policy of James the second †
after his arrival in Ireland, ruined its trade and revenue; the
many great oppressions which the people suffered during the
revolution had occasioned almost the *utter desolation* of the
country. § But the nation must have been restored in the
reign of William to a considerable degree of strength and
vigour: their exertions in raising supplies to a great amount,
from the year 1692 to the year 1698, are some proof of it.
They taxed their goods, their lands, their persons, in support
of a prince whom they justly called their deliverer and de-
fender, and of a government on which their own preservation depended.    Those sums were granted ‖, not only without
murmur, but with the utmost chearfulness, and without any
complaint of the inability, or representation of the distressed
state of the country.

The money brought in for the army at the revolution, gave
life to all business, and much sooner than could have been expected retrieved the affairs of Ireland. This money furnished capitals for carrying on the manufactures of this kingdom. Our
exports increased in 96, 97 and 98, and our imports did not
rise in proportion, which occasioned a great balance in our
favour; and this increase was owing principally to the woollen manufacture.    In the last of those years the ballance in favour of Ireland in the accounts of exports and imports was
419,442l. **.

But in the latter end of this reign a law was made in England,
restraining, in fact prohibiting the exportation of all woollen
manufactures from Ireland.    From the time of this prohibition no parliament was held in Ireland until the year 1703.
Five years were suffered to pass before any opportunity was

* Lord Strafford laid the foundation of the linen manufacture in Ireland, but the troubles which soon after broke out had entirely stopped
the progress of it.
† Harris : life of K. W. 116.
§ The Words of Lord Sydney, in his speech from the throne in
1692. Com. Jour. 2 Vol 576.
‖ Ir. Com. Jour. 3 Vol. 45 and 65, that great supplies were given
during this period.
** Dobbs, p. 5, 6, 7, 19.

given to apply a remedy to the many evils which such a prohibition muſt neceſſarily have occaſioned. The linen trade was
then not thoroughlyeſtabliſhed in Ireland ; the woollen manufacture was the ſtaple trade, and wool the principal material
of that kingdom. The conſequences of this prohibition appeared in the ſeſſion of 1703 *.

In an addreſs to the queen †, laid before the duke of Ormond, then lord lieutenant, by the houſe with its ſpeaker,
they mention the diſtreſſed condition of that kingdom, and
more eſpecially of the induſtrious proteſtants, by the almoſt
total loſs of trade and decay of their manufactures, and to
preſerve the country from utter ruin, apply for liberty
to export their linen manufactures to the plantations.

In a ſubſequent part of this ſeſſion ‡, the commons reſolve,
that by reaſon of the great decay of trade and diſcouragement
of the manufactures of this kingdom, many poor tradeſmen
were reduced to extreme want and beggary. This reſolution
was nem. con. and the ſpeaker, Mr. Broderick, then his majeſty's ſolicitor general, and afterwards lord chancellor, in
his ſpeech at the end of the ſeſſion §, informs the lord lieutenant, that the repreſentation of the commons was, as to the
matters contained in it, the unanimous voice and conſent of a
very full houſe, and that the ſoft and gentle terms uſed by the
commons in laying the diſtreſſed condition of the kingdom
before his majeſty, ſhewed that their complaints proceeded
not from querulouſneſs but from a neceſſity of ſeeking redreſs ;
he adds, " it is to be hoped they may be allowed ſuch a por-
" tion of trade, that they may recover from the great poverty
" they now lie under ;" and in preſenting the bill of ſupply
ſays, the commons have granted it " in time of extreme po-
" verty." The impoveriſhed ſtate of Ireland, at that time,
appears in the ſpeech from the throne at the concluſion of the
ſeſſion, in which it is mentioned that the commons could not
then provide for what was owing to the civil and military
liſts **.

The ſupply given for two years, commenced at Michaelmas
1703 ††, was a ſum not exceeding 150,000l. which, conſidering that no parliament was held in Ireland ſince the year
1698, is at the rate of 30,000l. yearly, commencing in 1699,
and ending in the year 1705.

* Com. Jour. 3 Vol. 45.          § Ib. 207, 208.
† Com. Jour. 3 Vol. p. 149.      ** Ib. p. 210.
‡ Ir. Com. Jour. 3 Vol. p. 195.  †† Ib. 79, 94.

The

The great diſtreſs of Ireland, from the year 1699, to the year 1703, and the cauſe of that diſtreſs, cannot be doubted.

Let it now be conſidered, whether the ſame cauſe has operated ſince the year 1703. In the year 1704 * it appears, that the commons were not able, from the circumſtances of the nation at that time, to make proviſion for ‘repairing the neceſſary fortifications; or for arms and amunition for the public ſafety: and the difficulties which the kingdom then laboured under, and the decay of trade, appear by the addreſſes of the commons † to the queen, and to the duke of Ormond, then lord lieutenant, who was well acquainted with the ſtate of this country; by the queen's anſwer ‡, and the addreſs of thanks for it.

In the year 1707 §, the revenue was deficient for payment of the army, and defraying the charges of government; and the commons promiſed to ſupply the deficiency " as far as " the preſent circumſtances of the nation will allow."

In 1709, it appears ** by the unanimous addreſs of the commons to the lord lieutenant, that the kingdom was in an impoveriſhed and exhauſted ſtate: in 1711 ††, in their addreſs to the lord lieutenant, at the cloſe of the ſeſſion, they requeſt, that he ſhould preſent to her majeſty, that they had given all the ſupplies which her majeſty deſired, and which they, in their preſent condition, were able to grant ‡‡: and yet theſe ſupplies amounted, for two years, to a ſum not exceeding 167,023l. 8s. 5d §§; though powder magazines, the council chamber, the treaſury office, and other offices were then to be built.

This laſt period, from the year 1699 to the death of queen Anne, is marked with the ſtrongeſt circumſtances of national diſtreſs and deſpondency.

That the woollen manufactures were the great ſource of induſtry in Ireland, appears from the Iriſh ſtatute of the 17th and 18th of Charles II. ch. 15 ***; from the reſolutions of the commons in 1695 †††, for regulating thoſe manufactures; the reſolutions of the committee of ſupply in that ſeſſion ‡‡‡;

---

* Com. Jour. 3 Vol. p. 298.     † Ib. 225, 266.
‡ Ib. 253, 258.     § Ib, 364, 368, 369.
** Ib. 3 Vol. p. 573.     †† Ib. 827.
‡‡ Ib. 929.     §§ Ib. 876.
*** In the ſame ſeſſion an act was made for the advancement of the linen manufacture, which ſhews that both kingdoms then thought (for theſe laws came to us through England) that each of theſe manufactures was to be encouraged in Ireland.
††† Ir. Com. Jour. 2 Vol. p. 725.     ‡‡‡ Ib. 733.

and

and from the preamble to the Englifh ftatute of the 10th and 11th of William III. ch. 10, in which it is recited, that great quantities of thofe manufactures were made, and were daily increafing in Ireland, and were exported from thence to foreign markets.

Of the exportation of all thofe manufactures the Irifh were at once totally deprived : the linen manufacture, propofed as a fubftitute, muft have required the attention of many years before it could be thoroughly eftablifhed. What muft have been the confequences to Ireland in the mean time, the journals of the commons in queen Anne's reign have informed us. Compare this period with the three former, and you will prove this melancholy truth ; that a country will fooner recover from the miferies and devaftation occafioned by war, invafion, rebellion, maffacre, than from laws reftraining the commerce, difcouraging the manufactures, fettering the induftry, and above all, breaking the fpirits of the people.

## THIRD LETTER.

To an inquirer after truth, hiftory fince the year 1699 furnifhes very imperfect, and often partial views of the affairs of Great Britain and Ireland. The journals of parliament evince the poverty of Ireland for the firft fourteen years of this century. That this poverty continued in the year 1716, appears by the unanimous addrefs of the houfe of commons to George the firft*. A fmall debt of 16,106l. 11s. 0½d. †, due at Michaelmas 1715, was, by their exertions to ftrengthen the hands of government in that year, increafed at midfummer 1717, to a fum of 91,537l. 17s. 1d. ‡, which was confidered as fuch an augmentation of the national debt, that the lord lieutenant, the duke of Bolton, thought it neceffary to take notice in his fpeech from the throne, that the debt was confiderably augmented, and to declare at the fame time that his majefty had ordered reductions in the military, and had thought proper to leffen the civil lift.

In 1721, the fpeech from the throne §, and the addreffes to the king and to the lord lieutenant, ftate, in the ftrongeft

---

* Com. Jour. 4 Vol. p. 249,  † Ib. 296.
† Ib. 335,  § Ib. 694, 700, 701.

terms, the great decay of her trade, and the very low and impoverished state to which she was reduced.

It is a melancholy proof of the desponding state of this kingdom, that no law whatever was then proposed for encouraging trade or manufactures, unless that for amending the laws as to butter and tallow casks deserves to be so called. The remedy proposed by government, and partly executed, by directing a commission under the great seal for receiving voluntary subscriptions *, in order to establish a bank, was a scheme to circulate paper without money; and considering that it came so soon after the south sea bubble had burst, it is more surprising that it should have been at first applauded †, than that it was in the same session disliked, censured and abandoned ‡. The total inefficacy of the remedy proved however the inveteracy of the disease, and furnishes a farther proof of the desperate situation of Ireland, when nothing could be thought of for its relief, but that paper should circulate without money, trade or manufactures.

In the following session of 1727, our manufacturers, and the lowest classes of our people, were greatly distressed; the duke of Grafton, in his speech from the throne, particularly recommends to their consideration the finding out of some method for the better employing of the poor §; and though the debt of the nation was no more than 66,3 8l. 8s. 3½d. ‖ and was less than in the last session; yet the commons thought it necessary to present an address to the king, to give such directions as he, in his great goodness should think proper, to prevent the increase of the debt of the nation. This address was presented ** by the house, with its speaker, and passed nem. con. and was occasioned by the distressed state of the country, and by their apprehensions that it might be further exhausted by the project of Woods' half-pence.

But notwithstanding the success of the linen manufacture, Ireland was in a most miserable condition. The great scarcity of corn had been so universal in this kingdom in the years 1728 and 1729, as to expose thousands of families to the utmost necessities, and even to the danger of famine; many artificers and house-keepers having been obliged to beg for bread in the streets of Dublin. It appeared before the house of commons, that the import of corn for one year and six months, ending the 29th day of September, 1729, amounted

* Ir. Com. Jour. 4 Vol. p. 694.   † Ib. 720.
‡ Ib. 832.   § Ib. 5 vol. p. 12.
** Ib. 108.   ‖ Ib. 102.

in value to the fum of 274,ccol. an amazing fum compared with the circumftances of the kingdom at that time! and the commons refolve that public granaries would greatly contribute to the increafing of tillage, and providing againft fuch wants as have frequently befallen the people of this kingdom, and hereafter may befal them, unlefs proper precautions fhall be taken againft fo great a calamity.

The great fcarcity which happened in the years 28 and 29, and frequently before and fince, is a decifive proof that the diftreffes of this kingdom have been occafioned by the difcouragement of manufactures.

In the year 1731 there was a great deficiency in the public revenue, and the national debt had confiderably increafed. The exhaufted kingdom lay under great difficulties by the decay of trade, the fcarcity of money, and the univerfal poverty of the country, which the fpeaker reprefents * in very affecting terms, in offering the money-bills for the royal affent, and adds, " that the commons hope from his majefty's " goodnefs, and his grace's free and impartial reprefentation " of the ftate and condition of this kingdom, that they may " enjoy a fhare of the bleffings of public tranquillity, by " the increafe of their trade, and the encouragement of their " manufactures."

But in the next feffion, of 1733, they are told in the fpeech from the throne what this fhare was to be. The lord lieutenant informs them, that the peace cannot fail of contributing to their welfare, by enabling them to improve thofe branches of trade and manufactures † which are properly their own, meaning the trade and manufacture of linen. Whether this idea of property has been preferved inviolate, will hereafter appear.

The years 40 and 41 were feafons of great fcarcity, and in confequence of the want of wholefome provifions, great numbers of our people perifhed miferably ; and the fpeech from the throne recommends it to both houfes, to confider of proper meafures to prevent the like calamity for the future. The employment of the poor and the encouragement of tillage, are the remedies propofed by the lord lieutenant, and approved of by the commons ; but no laws for thofe purpofes were introduced.

* Ir. Com. Jour. 6 Vol. p. 143.    † Ib. 189.

For

For above forty years after making thofe reftrictive laws *
Ireland was always poor, and often in great want, diftrefs
and mifery †, tho' the linen manufacture had made great progrefs during that time. In the war before the laft, fhe was
not able to give any affiftance. The duke of Devonfhire, in
the year 1741, takes notice from the throne, that during a
war for the protection of the trade of all his majefty's dominions, there had been no increafe of the charge of the eftablifhment; and in the year 1745 the country was fo little able
to bear expence, that lord Chefterfield difcouraged and prevented any augmentation of the army, tho' much defired by
many gentlemen of the houfe of commons, from a fenfe of
the great danger that then impended. An influx of money
after the peace, and the further fuccefs of the linen trade, encreafed our wealth, and enabled us to reduce by degrees,
and afterwards to difcharge the national debt. This was not
effected until the firft of March 1754. This debt was occafioned principally by the expences incurred by the rebellion
in Great Britain in the year 1715; an unlimited vote of credit was then given ‡. From the lownefs of the revenue, and
the want of refources, not from any further exertions on the
part of the kingdom in point of expence, the debt of 16,106l.
11s. 0½d. due in 1715, was encreafed at Lady Day, 1733,
to 37 ,3 2l. : 2s. 2½d.

After the payment of this debt, the wealth and ability of
Ireland were greatly over-rated, both here and in Great Britain.

A large redundency of money in the treafury, gave a de-
lufive appearance of national wealth. At Lady Day, 1755,
the fum in credit to the nation was 471,404l. 5s. 6½d§, and the
money remaining in the treafury of the ordinary unappro-
priated revenue on the 29th day of September, 1755,
457,959l. 12s. 7½d. But this great increafe of revenue arofe
from an increafe of imports, particularly in the year 1754,
by which the kingdom was greatly overftocked, and which
raifed the revenue in that year 208,309l. 19s. 2d. higher
than it was in the year 1748, when the revenue firft began
to rife confiderably ‖; and though what a nation fpends is
one method of eftimating its wealth; yet, a nation, like an

* The act intitled an act for better regulation of partnerfhips, and to
encourage the trade and manufactures of this kingdom, has not a word
relative to the latter part of the title.
† Com. Jour. 6 Vol. 694; 7 Vol. 742.   ‡ Ib. 4 Vol. p. 195.
§ 9 Vol. p. 35.                          ‖ Ib. 10 Vol. p. 751.

individual, may live beyond its means, and spend on credit which may far exceed its income. This was the fact as to Ireland in the year 1754, for some years before and for many years after; it appeared in an enquiry before the house of commons in the session of 1755, that many persons had circulated paper to a very great amount, far exceeding not only their own capitals*, but that just proportion which the quantity of paper ought to bear to the national specie. This gave credit to many individuals, who without property became merchant importers, and at the same time increased the receipts of the treasury and lessened the wealth of the kingdom. At the very time that so great a balance was in the treasury, public credit was in a very low way, and the house of commons was employed in preparing a law to restore it. In 54 and 55 three principal banks † had failed, and the legislature took up much time in enquiring into their affairs, and in framing laws for the relief of their creditors.

## LETTER IV.

THE revenue, for the reasons already given, decreased in 1755, fell lower in 1756, and still lower in 57. In the last year the vaunted prosperity of Ireland was changed into misery and distress; the lower classes of our people wanted food ‡; the money arising from the extravagance of the rich was freely applied to alleviate the sufferings of the poor. One of the first steps of the late duke of Bedford's administration, and which reflects honour on his memory, was obtaining a king's letter, dated 31st March, 1757, for 20,000l. to be laid out as his grace should think the most likely to afford the most speedy and effectual relief to his majesty's poor subjects of this kingdom. His grace, in his speech from the throne, humanely expresses his wish, that some method might be found out to prevent the calamities that are the consequences of a want of corn, which had been in part felt the last year, and to which this country had been too often exposed; the commons acknowledge that those calamities had

---

* Com. Jour. 9 Vol. p. 818.

† March 6, 1754, Thomas Dillon, and Richard Ferral, failed. 3d March, 1755, William Lennox and George French. Same day John Wilcocks and John Dawson.

‡ Com. Jour. 10 Vol. p. 16. Speech from the throne, and ib. 25, address from the house of commons to the king.

been

been frequently, and were too fenfibly and fatally experienced in the courfe of the laft year; thank his grace for his early and charitable attention to the neceffities of the poor of this country in their late diftreffes, and make ufe of thofe remarkable expreffions, " that they will moft chearfully embrace * every *practicable* method to promote tillage †." They knew that the encouragement of manufactures were the effectual means, and that thefe means were not in their power.

The ability of the nation was eftimated by the money in the treafury, and the penfions on the civil eftablifhment, exclufive of French, which at Lady-day, 1755, were 38,003l. 15s. od. amounted at Lady-day, 57, to 49,293l. 15s. od ‡.

The fame ideas were entertained of the refources of this country in the feffion of 1759. Great Britain had made extraordinary efforts, and engaged in enormous expences for the protection of the whole empire. This country was in immediate danger of an invafion. Every Irifhman was agreed that fhe fhould affift Great Britain to the utmoft of her ability, but this ability was too highly eftimated. The nation abounded rather in loyalty than in wealth §. Our brethren in Great Britain had, however, formed a different opinion, and furveying their own ftrength, were imcompleat judges of our weaknefs. A lord lieutenant of too much virtue and magnanimity to fpeak what he did not think, takes notice from the throne, " of the profperous ftate of this country, " improving daily in its manufactures and commerce ‖." His grace had done much to bring it to that ftate, by obtaining for us fome of the beft laws ** in our books of ftatutes. But this part of the fpeech was not taken notice of, either in the addrefs to his majefty, or to his grace, from a houfe of commons well-difpofed to give every mark of duty and refpect, and to pay every compliment confifting with truth. The event proved the wifdom of their referve. The public expences were greatly increafed, the penfions on the civil eftablifhment, exclufive of French, at Lady-day, 1759, amounted

---

* Com. Jour. 10 Vol. 25.

† They brought in a law for the encouragement of tillage, which was ineffectual (fee poft 42) but the preamble of that act is a legiflative proof of the unhappy condition of the poor of this country before that time. The preamble recites, " the extreme neceffity to which the poor of this " kingdom had been too frequently reduced for want of provifions. "

‡ Com. Jour. 10 Vol. 285.

§ 11 Vol. 472, Speaker's fpeech.    ‖ Ib. 16.

** The acts paffed in 58, giving bounties on the land-carriage of corn, and on coals brought to Dublin.

to 55,497l. 5s. od. * there was at the same time a great augmentation of military expence †. Six new regiments and a
troop were raised in a very short space of time. An unanimous and unlimited address of confidence to his grace ‡, a
specific vote of credit for 150,000l. ||, which was afterwards
provided for in the loan-bill § of that session; a second vote of
credit in the same session for 300,000l. **, the raising the rate
of interest paid by government, one per cent. and the payment out of the treasury †† in little more than one year, of
703,957l. 3s. 1½d. ‡‡ were the consequences of those encreased
expences. The effects of these exertions were immediately and
severely felt by the kingdom. These loans could not be supplied by a poor country, without draining the bankers of their
cash; three of the principal houses §§ among them stopped
payment; the three remaining banks in Dublin discounted no
paper, and in fact, did no business. Public and private credit,
that had been drooping since the year 1754, had now fallen
prostrate. At a general meeting of the merchants of Dublin,
in April 1760, with several members of the house of commons, the inability of the former to carry on business was uni-
versally acknowledged, not from the want of capital, but from
the stoppage of all paper circulation, and the refusal of the remaining bankers to discount the bills even of the first houses.
The merchants and traders of Dublin, in their petition |||| to
the house of commons, represent " the low state to which
" public and private credit had been of late reduced in this
" kingdom, and particularly in this city, of which the suc-
" cessive failures of so many banks, and of private traders in
" different parts of this kingdom, in so short a time as since
" October last, were incontestable proofs. The petitioners,
" sensible that the necessary consequences of these misfortunes
" must be the loss of foreign trade, the diminution of his ma-
" jesty's revenue, and what is still more fatal, the decay of
" the manufactures of this kingdom, have in vain repeatedly
" attempted to support the sinking credit of the nation by as-
" sociations and otherwise; and are satisfied that no resource
" is now left but what may be expected from the wisdom of
" parliament, to avert the calamities with which this king-
" dom is at present threatened."

The

The committee, to whom it was referred, refolve * that they had proved the feveral matters alledged in their petition ; that the quantity of paper circulating was not near fufficient. for fupporting the trade and manufactures of this kingdom ; and that the houfe fhould engage, to the firft of May 62, for each of the then fubfifting banks in Dublin, to the amount of 50,000l. for each bank ; and that an addrefs fhould be prefented to the lord lieutenant, to thank his grace for having given directions, that bankers notes fhould be received as cafh from the feveral fubfcribers to the loan ; and that he would be pleafed to give directions, that their notes fhould be taken as cafh in all payments at the treafury, and by the feveral collectors for the city and county of Dublin.   The houfe agreed to thofe refolutions, and to that for giving credit to the banks, nem. con.

The fpeech from the throne takes notice of the care the houfe of commons had taken for eftablifhing public credit, which the lord lieutenant fays, he flatters himfelf will anfwer the end propofed, and effect that circulation fo neceffary for carrying on the commerce of the country †.

The great law which we owe to his interpofition (I fpeak of that which gives a bounty on the land carriage of corn and flour to Dublin ‡) has faved this country from utter deftruction ; this law, which reflects the higheft honour on the author and promoter, is ftill a proof of the poverty of that country where fuch a law is neceffary.   Its true principle is to bring the market of Dublin to the door of the farmer, and that was done in the year, ending the 25th of March, 1777, at the expence of 61,789l. 18s. 6d. to the public ; a large, but a moft ufeful and neceffary expenditure §.

In the beginning of the next parliament, the rupture with Spain occafioned a new augmentation of military expence. The ever loyal commons return an addrefs of thanks to the meffage mentioning the addition of five new battalions ‖, and unanimoufly promife to provide for them ; and with the fame unanimity pafs a vote of credit for 200,000l **.   The amount of penfions on the civil eftablifhment, exclufive of French, had for one year, ending the 25th of March, 1761, amounted to 64,127l. 5s. †† and our manufacturers were then

---

* Com. Jour. 11 Vol. p. 993, 994.    † Ib. 1049.
‡ Brought in by Mr. Pery, the prefent Speaker.
§ In the year ending lady-day, 1778, it amounted to 71,533l. 1s. and in that ending lady-day, 1779, to 67,864l. 8s. 10d.
‖ Com. Jour. 12 Vol. p. 700.    ** Ib. 728.    †† Ib. 443.

diftreffed

diftreffed by the expence and havock of a burthenfome war *.

The ftate of penfions remained nearly the fame †; by the peace the military expences were confiderably reduced; of the military eftablifhment to be provided for in the feffion 1763, compared with the military eftablifhment as it ftood on the 31ft of March, 1763, the net decreafe was 119,037l. 0s. 10d. per annum; but as a peace eftablifhment it was high, and compared with that of the 31ft of March, 1756 ‡ being the year preceding the laft war, the annual increafe was 110,422l. 9s. 5d. the debt of the nation at Lady-day 1763, and which was entirely incurred in the laft war, was 521,161l. 16s 6d §. and would have been much greater, if the feveral lord lieutenants had not ufed with great œconomy the power of borrowing, which the houfe of commons had from feffion to feffion given them.

The fame miftaken eftimate of the ability of Ireland, that occafioned our being called upon to bear part of the Britifh burthen during the war, produced fimilar effects at the time of the peace, and after it. The heavy peace eftablifhment was increafed by an augmentation of our army in 1769, which induced an additional charge, taking in the expences of exchange and remittance, of 54,118l. 12s. 6d. yearly, for the firft year; but this charge was afterwards confiderably increafed, and amounted from the year 1769, to Chriftmas 1778, when it was difcontinued, to the fum of 620,824l. 0s. 9d. and this increafed expence was more felt, becaufe it was for the purpofe of paying forces out of this kingdom.

As our expences increafed our income diminifhed; the revenue for the two years, ending the 25th of March, 1771 ‖, was far fhort of former years, and not nearly fufficient to pay the charges of government, and the fums payable for bounties and public works **. The debt of the nation at lady-day, 1771, was increafed to 782,320l. 0s. 0d ††. The want of income was endeavouring to be fupplied by a loan. In the money-bill of the October feffion, 1771, there was a claufe impowering government to borrow 200,000l. Immediately

---

* Com. Jour. 929, Speech of Lord Hallifax from the throne, 30th of April, 1762.

† For a year ending 25th March, 1763, they were 66,477l. 5s.; they afterwards rofe to 89,095l. 17s. 6d. in September 1777 at the higheft; and in this year, ending the 25th of March laft, amounted to 85,971l. 2s. 6d.

‡ Com. Jour. 13 Vol. p. 576.    § Ib. 574. 621.

‖ Ib. 14 Vol. 715.    ** Ib. 15 Vol. 710.    †† Ib. 153.

after the linen trade declined rapidly; in 1772, 1773, and 1774, the decay in that trade was general in every part of the kingdom where it was established; the quantity manufactured was not above two-thirds of what used formerly to be made, and the quality did not fell for above three-fourths of it's former price; the linen and linen yarn exported for one year, ending the 25th of March, 1773 *, fell short of the exports of one year, ending the 25th of March 1771, to the amount in value of 788,821l. 1s. 3d. At lady-day, 1773 †, the debt increased to 994,890l. 10s. 10d. 1-8th. The attempt in the session of 1773 ‡, to equalize the annual income and expences failed, and borrowing on tontine in the sessions of 1773, 1775 and 1777, added greatly to the annual expence, and to the sums of money remitted out of the kingdom. The debt now bearing interest amounts to the sum of 1,017,600l. besides a sum of 740,000l. raised on annuities, which amount to 48,900l. yearly, with some incidental expences. The great increase of those national burdens, likely to take place in the approaching session, has been already mentioned.

The debt of Ireland has arisen from the following causes: the expences of the late war, the heavy peace establishment in the year 1763, the increase of that establishment in the year 1769, the sums paid from 1759 to forces out of the kingdom, the great increase of pensions and other additional charges on the civil establishment, which however considerable, bears but a small proportion to the increased military expences, the falling of the revenue, and the sums paid for bounties and public works; these are mentioned last, because it is apprehended that they have not operated to increase this debt in so great a degree as some persons have imagined; for though the amount is large, yet no part of the money was sent out of the kingdom, and several of the grants were for useful purposes, some of which made returns to the public and to the treasury exceeding the amount of those grants.

When those facts are considered, no doubt can be entertained but that the supposed wealth of Ireland has led to real poverty; and when it is known, that from the year 1751 to Christmas 1778, the sums remitted by Ireland to pay troops serving abroad, amounted to the sum of 1,401,925l. 19s. 4d. it will be equally clear from whence this poverty has principally arisen.

---

* Com. Jour. 16 Vol. p. 372.    † Ib. p. 190. 191, 193.    ‡ Ib. 256.

In 1762, lord Hallifax, in his speech from the throne*, acknowledges that our manufactures were distressed by the war. In 763, the corporation of weavers, by a petition to the house of commons, complain that, notwithstanding the great increase both in number and wealth of the inhabitants of the metropolis, they found a very great decay of several very valuable branches of trade and manufactures † of this city, particularly in the silken and woollen.

In 1765, there was so great a scarcity of potatoes, spring corn, &c. that it was thought necessary to appoint a committee‡ to inquire what may be the best method to reduce it; and to prevent a great dearth, two acts passed early in that session, to stop the distillery, and to prevent the exportation of corn, for a limited time.

In 1778 and 1779 there was great plenty of corn, but the manufacturers were not able to buy, and many thousands of them were supported by charity; the consequence was that corn fell to so low a price that the farmers in many places were unable to pay their rents, and every where were under great difficulties.

## FIFTH LETTER.

FOR several years the exportation of live cattle to England § was the principal trade of Ireland. This was thought most erroneously ‖, as has since been acknowledged**, to lower the rents of lands in England. From this, and perhaps from some less worthy motive †† a law passed in England ‡‡, to restrain and afterwards to prohibit the exportation of cattle from Ireland. The Irish, deprived of their principal trade, and reduced to the utmost distress by this prohibition, had no

* Com. Jour. 12 Vol. p. 928.        † Ib. 13 Vol. p. 987.
‡ Ib. 14. Vol. p. 69, 114, 151.
§ Carte, 2 Vol. 318, 319.
‖ Sir W. Petty's Political Survey, 69, 70. Sir W. Temple, 3 Vol. 22, 23.
** By several British acts (32 G. 2, ch. 11. 5 G. 3, ch. 10, 12. G. 3, ch. 56.) allowing from time to time the free importation of all sorts of cattle from Ireland.
†† Personal prejudice against the duke of Ormond. (2 Carte, 332, 337.
‡‡ 15 Ch. 2, ch. 7. 18 Ch. 2, ch. 2.

resource but to work up their own commodities, to which they applied themselves with great ardor *. After this prohibition they increased their number of sheep, and at the revolution were possessed of very numerous flocks. They had good reasons to think that this object of industry was not only left open, but recommended to them. The ineffectual attempt by lord Strafford in 1639, to prevent the making of broad cloaths in Ireland †, the relinquishment of that scheme by never aferwards receiving it, the encouragement given to their woollen manufactures by many English acts of parliament from the reign of Edward the 3d, ‡ to the 12th of Ch. 2d, and several of them for the express purpose of exportation: the letter of Charles the 2d, in 1667, with the advice of his privy council in England, and the proclamation in pursuance of that letter, encouraging the exportation of their manufactures to foreign countries; by the Irish statutes of the 13th Hen. 8, ch. 2, 28th Hen 8, ch. 17, of the 11th Elizabeth, Ch. 10, and 17 and 18 Ch. 2, ch. 15, (all of which, the act of 28 Henry 8th excepted, received the approbation of the privy council of England, having been returned under the great seal of that kingdom) afforded as strong grounds of assurance as any country could possess for the continuance of any trade or manufacture.

An act, in its title, professes the encouraging the importation of wool from Ireland.

By a report from the commissioners of trade in that kingdom, dated on the 23d December 97, and laid before the house of commons, in 1698, they find that the woollen manufacture in Ireland had increased since the year 1665, as follows:

| Years. | New draperies. Pieces. | Old draperies. Pieces. | Frize. Yards. |
|--------|------------------------|------------------------|---------------|
| 1665 | 224 | 32 | 444,381 |
| 1687 | 11,360 | 103 | 1,129,716 |
| 1696 | 4,413 | 34½ | 104,167 |

The bill for restraining the exportation of woollen manufactures from Ireland, was brought into the English house of commons on the 23d of Feb. 97, but the law did not pass until the year 1699, in the first session of the new parliament. I have not been able to obtain an account of the exportation

---

* 2 Carte, 332.
† Com. Jour. 1 Vol. p. 208, by a clause to be inserted in an Irish act.
‡ See post, those acts stated.

of woollen manufactures for the year 1697 *, but from the 25th of December 1697, to the 25th of December 1698, being the first year in which the exports in books extant, are registered in the custom-house at Dublin, the amount appears to be of

| New drapery. | Old drapery. | Frize. |
|---|---|---|
| Pieces. | Pieces. | Yds. |
| 23,285½ | 281h | 666,901 |

Though this encrease of export shews that the trade was advancing in Ireland, yet the total amount, or the comparative increase since 1687 could scarcely "sink the value of lands, " and tend to the ruin of the trade and woollen manufactures " of England †.

King William in his answer, says, " his majesty will take " care to do what their lordships have desired ;" and the lords direct, that the lord chancellor should order that the address and answer be forthwith printed and published ‡.

Of what Ireland gains it is computed that one-third centers in Great Britain §. Of our woollen manufacture the greatest part of the profit would go directly there. But the manufacturers of Ireland would be employed.

Mr. Dobbs, who wrote in 1729 ‖, affirms, that by this law of 1699, our woollen manufacturers were forced away into France, Germany and Spain ; that they had in many branches so much improved the woollen manufacture of France, as not only to supply themselves, but to vie with the English in foreign markets, and that by their correspondence, they had laid the foundation of the running of wool thither both from England and Ireland. He says that those nations were then so improved, as in a great measure to supply themselves with

---

* In a pamphlet cited by Dr. Smith, (v. 2, p. 244) in his memoirs of wool, it is said that the total value of those manufactures exported in 1697, was 23,614l. 9s. 6d. namely, in frizes and stockings 14,625l. 12s; in old and new draperies 8,988l. 17s. 6d. and that though the Irish had been every year increasing, yet they had not recovered above one-third of the woollen trade which they had before the war (ib. 243). The value in 1687, according to the same authority, was 70,521l. 14s. of which the frizes were 56,481l. 16s. Stockings 2,520l. 18s. and old and new drapery (which it is there said could alone interfere with the English trade) 11,514l. 10s.

† Preamble of English act of 1699.

‡ Lords Jour. page 315.

§ Sir M. Decker's decline of foreign trade, p. 155, and Anderson on commerce, 2 vol. p. 149.

‖ Essay on the trade of Ireland. p. 6, 7.

many

many forts they formerly had from England, and fince that time have deprived Britain of millions, inftead of the thoufands that Ireland might have made.

It is now acknowledged that the French underfel the Englifh; and as far as they are fupplied with Irifh wool, the lofs to the Britifh empire is double what it would be, if the Irifh exported their goods manufactured. This is mentioned by Sir Matthew Decker*, as the caufe of the decline of the Englifh, and the increafe of the French woollen manufactures; and he afferts that the Irifh can recover that trade out of their hands. England, fince the pafling this law, has got much lefs of our wool than before†. In 1698, the export of our wool to England amounted to 377,520 ftone; at a medium of eight years, to lady-day 1728, it was only 227,049 ftone. which is 148,000 ftone lefs than in 1698, and was a lofs of more than half a million yearly to England. In the laft ten years the quantity exported has been fo greatly reduced, that in one of thefe years ‡ it amounted only to 1007ft. 11lb. and in the laft year did not exceed 1665ft. 12lb.§. The price of wool, under an abfolute prohibition, is 50l. or 60l. per cent. under the market price of Europe, which will always defeat the prohibition ‖.

The impracticability of preventing the pernicious practice of running wool is now well underftood. Of the thirty-two counties in Ireland, nineteen are maritime, and the reft are wafhed by a number of fine rivers that empty themfelves into the fea. Can fuch an extent of ocean, fuch a range of coafts, fuch a multitude of harbours, bays and creeks be effectually guarded?

The prohibition of the export of live cattle forced the Irifh into the re-eftablifhment of their woollen manufacture; and the reftraint of the woollen manufacture was a ftrong temptation to the running of wool. The fevereft penalties were enacted, the Britifh legiflature, the government and houfe of commons of Ireland, exerted all poffible efforts to remove this growing evil, but in vain, until the law was made in Great Britain** in 1739, to take off the duties from

---

* Decline of foreign trade, p. 55, 56, 155.   † Dobbs, p. 76.
‡ In 1774.
§ Nor was this deficiency made up by the exportation of yarn. The quantities of thefe feveral articles exported from 1764 to 1778, are mentioned in the appendix, Numb.
‖ Smith's Memoirs of Wool, 2 Vol. p. 554. The only way to prevent it, is to enable us to work it up at home. Ib. 293.
** This was done for the benefit of the woollen manufacture in England. Eng. Com. Jour. 22 Vol. p. 442.

woollen or bay yarn exported from Ireland, excepting worfted yarn of two or more threads, which has certainly given a confiderable check to the running of wool, and has fhewn that the policy of opening is far more efficacious than that of reftraining. The world is become a great commercial fociety, exclude trade from one channel, and it feldom fails to find another.

To fhew the abfolute 'neceffity of Great Britain's opening to Ireland fome new means of acquiring, let the annual balance of exports and imports, returned from the entries in the different cuftom-houfes, in favour of Ireland, on all her trade with the whole world, in every year from 1768 to 1778, be compared with the remittances made from Ireland to England in each of thofe years, it will evidently appear that thofe remittances could not be made out of that balance. The entries of exports made at cuftom-houfes are well known to exceed the real amount of thofe exports in all countries, and this excefs is greater in times of diffidence, when merchants wifh to acquire credit by giving themfelves the appearance of being great traders.

This balance in favour of Ireland on her general trade, appears by thofe returns to have been in 1776, 606,190l. 11s. 0d. in 1777, 24,203l. 3s. 10d. in 1778, 386,384l. 5s. 7d. and taken at a medium of eleven years, from 1768 to 1778, both inclufive, it amounts to the fum of 605,083l. 7s. 5d. The fums remitted from Ireland to Great-Britain for rents, interefts of money, penfions, falaries, and profits of offices, amounted, at the loweft computation, from 1768 to 1773, to 100,000l. yearly* ; and from 1773, when the tontines were introduced, from which period large fums were borrowed from England, thofe remittances were confiderably increafed, and are now not lefs than between 12 and 13,000l. yearly. Ireland then pays to Great-Britain double the fum that fhe collects from the whole world in all the trade which Great Britain allows her. It will be difficult to find a fimilar inftance in the hiftory of mankind.

What was the information given by the trading towns in 1697 and 1698, on the fubject of the woollen manufacture of Ireland? feveral of their† petitions ftate that the woollen manufacture was *fet up* in Ireland, as if it had been lately intro-

---

* This is ftated confiderably under the computation made in the lift of abfentees, publifhed in Dublin in 1769, which makes the amount at that time 1,208,982l, 14s, 6d.

† Eng. Com. Jour. 12 Vol. 64, 68.

duced

duced there; and one of them goes so far as to represent the
time and manner of introducing it. " Many of the poor of
" that kingdom (says this extraordinary petition) during the
" late rebellion there, fled into the West of England, where
" they were put to work in the woollen manufacture to learn
" that trade, and since the reduction of Ireland, endeavours
" were used to set up those manufacturers there."

Would any man suppose that this could relate to a manufacture, in which this kingdom excelled before the time of
Edward the 3d, which had been the subject of so many laws
in both kingdoms, and which was always cultivated here, and
before this rebellion with more success than after it? the trading towns gave accounts totally inconsistent of the state of this
manufacture at that time in England : from Exeter it is represented as greatly decayed and discouraged * in those parts,
and diminished in England.   But a petition from Leeds represents this manufacture as having very much increased †,
since the revolution in all its several branches, to the general
interest of England ; and yet, in two days after the clothiers
from three towns in Gloucestershire assert, that the trade
has decayed, and that the poor are almost starved ‡.   The
commissioners of trade differ in opinion from them, and by
their report, it appears that the woollen manufacture was then
very much increased and improved §.   The traders have sometimes mistaken their own interests on those subjects ; in 1698,
a petition for prohibiting the importation from Ireland of all
worsted and woollen yarn, represents that the poor of England
are ready to perish by this importation ‖ ; and in 1739, several petitions were preferred against taking off the duties **
from worsted and bay yarn exported from Ireland to England.
But this has been done in the manner before-mentioned, and
is now acknowledged to be highly useful to England.   Trading people have ever aimed at exclusive privileges ; of this
there are two extraordinary instances ; in the year 1698, two
petitions were preferred, from Folkestone and Aldborough,
stating a singular grievance that they suffered from Ireland,
" by the Irish catching herrings at Waterford and Wexford ††,
" and sending them to the Streights, and thereby forestalling
" and ruining petitioners markets ;" but these petitioners had
the hard lot of having motions in their favour rejected.

* English Com. Jour. Vol. 12, p. 7.     † Ib. 527.     ‡ Ib. 530.
§ Ib. 434.                               ‖ Ib. 387.
** Ib, vol. 22.          †† Ib. 178.

It

It is hoped, many of the excellent obfervations contained in the remainder of thefe letters, will not appear improperly applied to the fupport of a few remarks fuggefted from a review of the foregoing pages.

In the mean time I fhall lay the following letter before my readers, as no unpleafing picture to an Irifhman of the confequence of his country.

LETTER II. of the juftly efteemed OWEN ROE O'NIAL To the Men of Ireland.

*SUÆ quifque faber fortunæ eft*, is one of thofe truths which the experience of ages has handed down as a proverb.

What is true of every individual muft be fo of nations— " Their fortune muft depend upon *themfelves*."

It is a truth well worthy the deep confideration of Ireland —I have, in my former letter, endeavoured to convince her by reafoning, and an appeal to hiftorical facts, of what fhe fhould long ere this have learned from experience ; that whatever juftice or generofity exifts among individuals, it is vain to look for it in the mutual intercourfe of nations. Their principle is policy.

It is time for Ireland to take thought for herfelf.

That Ireland hath been, and is, fubordinate to, and dependent on the imperial crown of Great Britain, and that the King's Majefty, with the confent of the Lords and Commons of Great Britain in Parliament, hath power to make laws to bind the people of Ireland *, is a truth too melancholy to admit contradiction. That it of right " ought" to be fo, was referved for the modefty and good fenfe of an Englifh parliament to affert, and would therefore be a *blunder* in Irifhmen to deny.

That no nation can by conqueft, or by any other means, acquire a right of perpetual dominion over another ; that no confent or contract, however exprefs or folemn, can bind pofterity to their injury ; that no prefcription or length of time can fanctify oppreffion ; that little deference is due to names impofed by the oppreffors upon the act of affuming rights unalienable in their nature, and only overborne by force, or overlooked by folly ; thefe are propofitions which I fhall not attempt to enlarge upon. Time, with moft minds, gives a facrednefs to error : enquiry then bears the name of impiety : but the idols of one age are trampled under foot in another, and the prejudices which once required a Locke to remove, are in thefe days but themes to the fchools.

* 6 Geo. I. c. 5.

I shall not then war with the dead; nor shall I offend the delicacy of an English Judge, by doubting the propriety, or disputing the omnipotence of an English act of parliament. That would be " to oppose my private Irish judgment to public English authority *." And, in so plain a case, the opposition " must be virulent and factious †." Authority must be ever in the right! The demand of Magna Charta was but a successful rebellion; the reformation was an impious defection from the church; and the author of Christianity was an heretic and a traitor! Ireland then, by right, ought to be, nay more, for ever must be, subordinate to the sovereign legislative parliament of Great Britain. I acknowledge it! my reason is a strong one; she thinks so herself; and who dare deny the competency of her judgment? She thinks herself formed by nature an humble attendant upon England. She crouches under what she calls necessity. Her loyalty dares not form a wish for the preservation of her crown in the house of Hanover, united with the separate independency of her own legislature: because she looks upon that wish as hopeless. The very thought to her seems madness! the attempt, she apprehends, would be ruin!

I owe a deference to the general opinion, and shall submit to it; yet, as all found judgment on this question can only be built upon experience, it seems not unreasonable to enquire, were it but as matter of speculation, into the fate of other countries, which having been nearly in the same situation with Ireland, endeavoured to mend their condition. One advantage will certainly result from the enquiry, which cannot fail of proving acceptable to a people, who have hitherto appeared more delighted with their fears, than with any other feelings of the human heart. It will lead us, by the consideration of our superior resources, to estimate infallibly the quantum of national punishment, likely to be superadded to our present burdens, by our masters, the parliament of Great Britain, for the efforts of this day, when their leisure and security shall permit them to turn their thoughts to us. In proportion to our superior power of resisting, will the means be of preventing, in future, the possibility of the operation of such a resistance.

A late respectable writer (Guatimozin) has already enumerated the natural advantages of Ireland. It appears that

* 6 George I. ch. 5.
† See Blackstone's Comment. book 4, p. 50, Irish edition.

she

she possesses within herself, or immediately within her reach, almost every advantage that nature or situation can give, or that is necessary to make a nation rich, great, and happy.

A climate of the finest temperature ; a soil of most extraordinary fertility ; mines that encouragement might convert into sources of national industry and national superiority ; seas that teem with fish ; harbours numerous, safe, commodious, and well situated for commerce ; and, to conclude, a people with capacity for every thing, and who want but leave to acquire habits of industry, as persevering as spirited.

These are the natural advantages of Ireland. How few nations can boast so many and so great ? Compare her rank and consequence in the world, with what these advantages might entitle her to. Enquire then, whence arises the difference, and thank England, if you can, for the generosity of her protection !

Are either the United Provinces, or Switzerland, to be compared to Ireland in natural advantages ? I cannot think they are. The former is but one-third, the latter only one-half her size. Ireland is an island, and such an one as I have described ; rich in climate, soil, mines, and harbours. Switzerland is in the heart of the Continent, and is poor in all these,—the latter she cannot possess at all. The Duch States are joined to the Continent ; their shore is dangerous from its flats ; does not afford them a single good harbour ; and the frost binds up their commerce during a considerable part of the winter. I need not mention the fish which the lakes of Switzerland afford. The fisheries of Holland lie upon our coast. They enjoy more from their unchecked industry, than we from nature and the protection of England. The Dutch have no mines. The Swiss don't work theirs, except for their necessary instruments of war and agriculture. Neither Holland nor Switzerland produces corn for half their inhabitants. In the latter half the harvest produced by a stubborn soil is often destroyed by storms, and but part of the remainder is allowed by the climate to ripen.

The Swiss may be said to have neither commerce nor navigation, since the latter they have only on their lakes, the former is concerned wholly in necessaries.

Of the timber of the Swiss I need not speak. They can have no navy, nor do they require one. As to Holland, the spongy produce of marshes is useless in trade or navigation. Her navy must be purchased by industry. Ireland may be as industrious as Holland, but she requires it less. She may

raise

raise a navy at home, if she cannot with more advantage bring marerials from abroad. The climate of Switzerland may make an hardy race of foldiers or husbandmen, but to a nation that would aim at more than a penurious exifence, it cannot be a subject of envy. The climate of Holland, marshy in its foil, and interfected by fo many ftagnated canals, is not wholefome. Some of their towns are formed on the foil left by the ftagnation of rivers. In others the folid foundations of the earth feemed to have forfaken them, and they laid new ones. The fea threatens to overwhelm them. They oppofe it with mounds, which require a continual repair, and dream not of danger, though the failure of a bank would give them a fecond deluge.

Labour and induftry are in Holland neceffary. They cannot otherwife exift. This, it is true, will keep them laborious and induftrious. But what they are from neceffity, other nations may be from nobler motives ; and Ireland fets out from a point which, in Holland, it required the labour and induftry of years to gain.

Holland muft be a drudge, as fhe fubfifts on the wants of other nations, and thefe, we know, are moftly artificial. She is their factor and carrier. She may fuffer from their caprice. She muft languifh in their ill-humour. Their induftry, or even frugality, would ftarve her. Ireland is more independent. She can fubfift by her internal refources, though the world fhould refufe her either commerce or employment. She is rich in herfelf. Nature, that made her an ifland, and gave her fertility, qualified her equally for abfolute independence, and unlimited intercourfe with other nations. She can fubfift without other nations. She can trade with them to mutual advantage.

Such are the natural advantages of Holland and Switzerland, and fuch are they compared with Ireland. America I fhall briefly confider hereafter. Each of the former is furrounded by powerful empires. Each of them was once oppreffed by all the rigours of flavery. Each of them burft her fhackles, and baffled the moft inveterate attacks of enemies, whofe power feemed to approach them with the irrefiftability of fate.

Holland, inferior to Ireland in every natural advantage, and equal to but a third of her in fize, threw off the yoke of the moft powerful monarch then in Europe. The firmnefs and courage which fhe difplayed, will appear incredible to thofe who are unacquainted with the power of enthufiafm.

The

The feven provinces we are fpeaking of furmounted every difficulty—they thought they could defend themfelves. The ten other provinces, fays Voltaire, would have a foreign Prince to protect them, and are in flavery to this day.

One Prince [Henry the IVth of France] to whom they applied for affiftance, was himfelf engaged in civil wars, and yet tottered on his throne. The extreme caution of another, [Queen Elizabeth] in foreign enterprize, correfponded but ill with her magnanimity and refolution in domeftic affairs; and from the reprimands fhe was daily giving to the Houfe of Commons, for prefuming to judge of the duty they were called to, fhe feemed little likely to tempt the wrath of a powerful tyrant or turn abettor of rebellion. The fuccours received by the States were accordingly for a long time feeble and clandeftine. To obtain open affiftance from Elizabeth required a longer ftruggle: and even the offer of their fovereignty. But before any affiftance had been received by the States, they had gotten poffeffion of what Doctor Johnfon calls " the choice of evil:" Their darling object *liberty*. The very women had formed regiments for the defence of their cities; and, rather than again fall under the hated tyranny of Spain, the dykes and fluices had been opened, and the very Peafants, fays Hume, had been active in ruining their own fields by an inundation; they preferred the mercy of the waters to that of tyrants.

Thefe fame people have fince withftood the moft formidable attacks of a Monarch, who thought his power equal to univerfal empire. They have fupported themfelves with more than equal honour againft the combined fleets of France and England. They have fwept the channel of England, and their infults in the Thames have carried confternation to the capital.

In little more than half a century from the time, at which, unprepared as they muft have been, they firft ventured to take up arms againft Spain in defence of their liberty, they beat one of her formidable Armadas *. They obliged it to take fhelter in the Downs under the Englifh flag. They retire for a reinforcement;—they refolve—that the fleet of England fhall no longer protect their enemy; they return to the charge; and the Spanifh navy, in its flight, received from them a blow which at this day, after near a century and an half, it has

* The Duke of Alva left the Low Countries in the year 1574. They beat the Spanifh Armada in 1639.

not

not fully recovered. A few years more, affifted by a few more defeats, foftened the obftinacy of Spain. She acknowledged the independence of the States *, and in twenty years after they protected her provinces againft France †.

The Swifs, now that they are free, are more fecure from attacks, than when they were dependent. They are defended by their mountains and the barrennefs of their country; by their poverty, by their valour, and by the mutual jealoufies of the neighbouring empires. A partition is not eafily agreed upon, and none will confent to their becoming an acceffion to the power of another, if fuch an acceffion were practicable. But it muft be confeffed that of all the advantages I have mentioned, their valour alone, at the time they threw off the yoke, feemed moft in their favour. The enemy had poffeffion of their country. The balance of power was then lefs underftood, or lefs attended to, and their poverty and commercial infignificance muft have been feeble inducements to the protection of their neighbours. Accordingly they had to work out their own liberty, and above three centuries elapfed before the Houfe of Auftria acknowledged their independence ‡.

I believe there are few will deny that America has already eftablifhed her independence. She would not come over and proftrate herfelf at the feet of England; fo England, with the magnanimity of a conqueror, appointed ambaffadors to her by act of Parliament. Upon England's condefcending " to treat with armed rebels," they refufed to treat with England. They had procured friends, and they preferred them to mafters. For the fituation of America in the beginning of the conteft, hear her own unexaggerated defcription: " Without arms, ammunition, difcipline, revenue, government, or ally, almoft totally ftript of commerce, and in the weaknefs of youth, as it were, " with a ftaff and a fling only," fhe dared, " in the name of the Lord of Hofts," to engage a gigantic adverfary, prepared at all points, boafting of his ftrength, and of whom even mighty warriors were greatly afraid."

When to this enumeration of difficulties, which, one is tempted to think, requires little addition, we fubjoin the fol-

---

* Treaty of Munfter, 1648.　† Triple alliance in 1658.

‡ They took up arms in the year 1308. Their independence was acknowledged in 1648, by the treaty of Munfter, the fame by which Spain acknowledged the independence of the United Provinces.

It would be fingular enough if the fame period which eftablifhes American independence, fhall be found to have deftroyed the ufurpation of the Britifh Parliament over the legiflative rights of Ireland.

lowing;

lowing; that thefe Colonies were not more difunited by diftance of place, than by difference of opinion, manners, fpirit,
religion and government; that they were fo difunited in all
thefe, that it feemed the dream of a dotard to think of connecting them in one intereft, or of bringing them to co-operate, if they could be convinced that their intereft was the
fame; that they were expofed to the navy and arms of England on their fea-coafts, to the incurfions of Indians (perhaps
too juftly enraged) on their rear; and, in fome provinces,
to the more dangerous infurrections of their domeftic flaves,
whofe difpofitions to revenge muft have been expected to burft
on their more immediate oppreffors; when all thefe particulars, I fay, are confidered, befides thofe which America herfelf has enumerated, I think fcarce any nation on the earth
fhould abfolutely defpair.

Let us confider the prefent fituation of Ireland. I need
fcarce fay, that there is not a maritime power in Europe to
which her alliance would not, in itfelf, be an object of emulation. What then would it appear to the enemies of England? If Ireland fhould afk their protection, would they
require to be founded at a diftance, or to be affailed by pre-
paratory arguments and leading propofitions? Would they
think it prudent to act as they did by America, to ftand by,
cool fpectators of our ftruggle, till they judged how far we
fhould be able to perfevere or be likely to fucceed? or, if they
determined to affift Ireland, would they be obliged to have
recourfe to art in order to deceive a credulous minifter, and
to mafk their intentions until they could declare them with
fafety? No, my countrymen: diftant propofitions, prepara-
tory arguments, negociation, art,—all thefe are to us unneceffary! Conviction has long been confirmed. Their refolution is already taken. Their arms are already in their hands.
They have croffed the Atlantic for their own intereft and for
the humiliation of England. Will a few leagues terrify them
when their fcheme is fo near arriving at almoft unhoped-for
perfection? They were then at peace, yet, they engaged in
war. They are now at war, will they not carry it on? The
fole queftion with them at prefent muft be this: will they
chufe to vifit us as enemies, or as friends? For vifit us they
probably will. Will they attempt a conqueft to which they
are probably unequal; or will they chufe the eafier road, and
offer an alliance, which will have every real advantage to be
expected from dominion, without the danger of an unfuccefsful attempt, or the inconveniencies and hazards of the moft

fuccefsful

fucce'sful execution? Will they not offer an alliance fuch as their good fenfe has been content with from America, and which they have thought worthy of fupporting by a war with England? fuch an alliance as, from its liberality, it will be the intereft of the other European powers, at leaft, by a tacit acquiefcence, to fupport? An alliance that will not contribute more to the weakening of an haughty adverfary, and the dif-appointment of an infatiable monopolift, than to their own re-gal power, aggrandifement and glory.

And here, my countrymen, occurs an awful paufe! What inducements hath Britifh policy fuffered, to take root in the hearts of Irifhmen, to enable them to refift fuch neceffary and proffered protection. None, my friends! Loyalty, the faireft flower that can ornament the bofom of a Prince, finds in Ireland its happieft foil. Perfona lattachment to the King of Ireland, and his illuftrious houfe, is the cord which binds us to our burden, and furnifhes to a Britifh people the occafion of load-ing us without bounds or mercy. Had we as little attach-ment to the Houfe of Hanover as Scotland, or Manchefter, we had long fince in defpair implored the protection of other powers, for fo long as the " Parliament of Great Britain can bind us in all cafes whatfoever," the worft that could happen to us would be to change our mafters*. The word is not my own. It is by an Englifh Judge and commentator di-rectly applied to the fituation of this kingdom, and its fu-bordination to England by right of conqueft.

But has England learned nothing from her late experience in America? Will fhe for ever truft to our loyalty alone, and will our King for ever leave us at the mercy of a Britifh Par-liament? As to the Englifh people, the power of God has been

* It may be feen by Blackftone, b. I. p. 100, what an Englifh lawyer' thinks the *neceffary* confequence of *all* dependence upon *England!* We are bound by *every law* fhe, in her wifdom or wantonnefs, *thinks proper* to prefcribe. We fhall foon, I fuppofe, be on a footing with thofe flaves of the Romans who were *bound to the glebe*, or foil. England will *think proper* that we fhould not *depart* from the foil, but be transferred with it by *deed*, *roll*, or *indenture*. This will fave us a multitude of difputes about *our pro-perty*, for we fhall then, like the Roman flaves, become perfect THINGS, and ceafe to be PERSONS. The Englifh prints will then afford entertain-ment to thofe who can relifh it. If any of us are miffing from our *ftalls* or *lumber-rooms*, we fhall be *advertifed* for, and defcribed, as " LOST, STRAYED, STOLEN, or MISLAID."—We fhall be taken *damage feafant* (perhaps *rider* and all!) and if we happen to die of cold and hunger, in an *open pound*, it will be at the fuit of *the owner!*—O Ireland! Ireland! Doft thou retain one fpark of feeling, to make the oppreffion of thee *a* crime?

k　　　　　　　displayed

difplayed to them in vain. They feem to have revived the age of miracles, and to have left the Egyptians at a diftance. All that fhould have infpired them with awe, humility, and wifdom, feems but to have darkened their underftandings and hardened their hearts! But let it be our duty, my countrymen, to confider the crifis, and profit of it! Let us adore that wonder-working God, who in the intoxication of our oppreffors has laid the foundation of our relief, and who in the mifcarriages of Britifh tyranny beyond the Atlantic, has taught Irifhmen the practicability of their own emancipation from the authority of an ufurping Englifh Parliament.

But we are nearer to England. I hear my countrymen lament it, and often have lamented it myfelf! Yet, (indulge me, my countrymen, while I explain my paradox!) *on that very proximity does the weal of Ireland depend.*

We are near to England; but we are near to affiftance alfo. The Atlantic rolls not between us and England; but neither does it roll between us and her enemies. Thefe enemies are on the way. Before the wind changes they are here. Our proximity to England is to us, in the prefent pofture of affairs, what the diftance of America was in the beginning of the conteft, to her. The latter was a barrier againft Britain; the former is a bridge for her foes. In this refpect then we are equal to America. We have however an advantage from our proximity, which fhe never can derive from her diftance. It is a *perpetual guarantee* againft the oppreffion of any felf-created protector. It is perpetual, becaufe it depends not on the policy or caprice of kings or of nations. It is fixed in the nature of things.

America might have been ruined by the treachery of France, or fhe may yet fall by Congrefs, as England has done by a parliament.

Let Ireland be fubject to her own legiflation only, and one might venture to fay fhe is free for ever. Her fituation and fize fit her for that moderate degree of ftrength and power which is moft likely to be permanent.

Let thefe things be weighed, and perhaps that man could not be acquitted of prefumption, who would venture to point out another fpot upon the globe, to which Ireland fhould now wifh to be removed.

From this proximity of Eugland, I would deduce *this truth,* which I wifh to be engraven on the heart of every Irifhman: *England is the only power that can enflave us further, or keep us as we are.* And this is the important moment

ment when our own firm conftitutional refiftance will derive additional fupport from the dread of her enemies, towards fhaking of the fhackles off an ufurping Englifh people.

But, unlefs we entertain for each other a mutual and general confidence, unlefs we lay afide all rancour of prejudice on account of diftinctions either political or religious, to attempt fuch a relief from thofe fhackles would be only to folicit confufion.

There are, however, many inftances of ftates differing very much in religion, and yet united in ftrict civil confederacy and union. Scarce fix of the Cantons of Switzerland are Proteftants, the feven remaining are Roman Catholics; and, what feems a little extraordinary, the greater number of the Roman Catholic Cantons are democratical, that of the Proteftant Cantons ariftocratical in their government. In the United Provinces the majority of the people are either Prefbyterians or Roman Catholics, and though Prefbyterianifm is the eftablifhed religion, yet, the toleration or connivance which all fects meet with from the government, has produced a general moderation and peace, and, in its natural confequences, has added power, grandeur, and ftability to the ftate. The ftate of Pennfylvania is equally various in its religion. The laws of this province are more liberal than the fpirit of any other province. They give no preference to any fect. They tolerate all fects. All fects are therefore not only peaceable, but content. Moft of the other ftates of America, fo firm in their union againft England, are fcarcely more oppofite than they are inveterate in the feveral prejudices and opinions which they carried with them from Europe. In fhort, from all the facts we can collect, our uniform conclufion muft be, that that nation is moft likely to be great, powerful, and happy, which finds political and civil moderation neceffary to its very being. Where there are no fects or parties, I may venture to fay there cannot be fenfe, fcience, liberty, or commerce. Where, from circumftances internal or external, different fects are nearly ballanced in power, the laws muft be moderate, and the fpirit of the laws will become the fpirit of the people. The nation will be in harmony within itfelf, and that moderation and good fenfe which will diftinguifh it in its internal government and policy, muft characterife it in its conduct towards other nations.

It is very fenfibly obferved by a Roman Catholic Prieft *, in a late addrefs to thofe of his own perfuafion in Ireland,

* Rev. Arthur O'Leary.

that

that " conquerors, (and, let me add, traders and politicians)
are of no religion." The English established popery in
Canada. The French entered into alliance with Presbyterians
in North America; and, I dare say, would have done the
same, if their Deity had been the sun or a serpent, an onion or
a monkey. The Dutch, it is said, tread upon the cross at
Japan, and the English make alliances with Moors and with
Indians.

The French are, perhaps, even in religion, as liberal a
nation as any in Europe. I judge not of them by their creeds,
confessions, or articles of belief: God forbid that I should
judge by these alone of the hearts or understandings of any
people upon earth, who have public creeds, confessions, or
articles! These are not always formed by the wisest or most
religious people of a nation. The wisest and most religious
are generally better employed. I judge of the French nation
by the general conduct of the people; and I believe it will
be owned that they are more liberal to Englishmen, than
Englishmen are to them. The absurdity of supposing that
even conquerors would make violent alterations in private
property, and involve themselves in the perplexed disputes
and antiquated claims of families, that have suffered by forfeiture, has been well exposed by the Reverend Divine just
mentioned. Were the question indeed between two pretenders
to the crown, the case might be different. He who succeeded
must reinstate some of his adherents, and gratify others.
This must be done at the expence of the opposite party. But
a conqueror, who is not able to crush the subdued nation at a
single effort, will think himself happy in prevailing upon the
people to remain quiet as he found them. He will make no
alteration which he can avoid; he will avoid every alteration
which can disgust or displease. What then is to be expected
from even a powerful protector, that offers independence to a
nation so divided into parties that no one of them has power
to crush the others, supported as they would be, by the nation
that formerly enslaved them? I say that, in this case, we
might expect such a moderation as would over-rule every petty
distinction or jealousy, and would unite the nation by community of interest. To make an alteration in the established
religion, or to deny to all denominations of Protestant Dis-
senters that toleration which they at present enjoy, would be
the madness of folly. Those we speak of are neither fools
nor madmen.

The

The Roman Catholics might, with juſtice indeed, expect a more compleat toleration. But it would require peculiar delicacy to grant this without offending thoſe Proteſtants who at preſent enjoy but a toleration themſelves. The interference of Roman Catholic protectors, confcious of the prudence their ſituation required, muſt be of the moſt temperate kind. The alterations made would be gentle, gradual, and rather the effect of an infenſible alteration of opinion and removal of prejudice, than an act of force or power in the ſtate. And, from the co-operation of all theſe cauſes, I am inclined to think there would naturally ariſe a mildneſs of government, and a benevolence of toleration which is unknown to the laws of any other country in Europe, and which enthuſiaſm itſelf has ſcarce dared to think conſiſtent with the littleneſs of human nature.

But whatever may be the natural dignity and ſtrength of Ireland, or whatever advantages ſhe might derive from the preſent poſture of affairs, there are ſome who cannot readily give up their attachment to the people of England, or think themſelves juſtified in refiſting them in their preſent ſtate of misfortune, while there are others who yet dread her power, and tremble at her name. To the former I ſhall ſpeak more particularly hereafter, and hope to ſhew that we are not bound by any ties of duty, gratitude, or honour, to remain in ſubjection to the parliament of England.

At preſent I would addreſs myſelf to the latter. That the power of England is not yet an imagination I readily will own. Great even yet is the power of England, and great is the memory of her glory! but her glory lives but in memory, and the finews of her power are withered. Exhauſted and foiled by America, whom, in the hour of her inſolence, ſhe treated with a contempt that would have robbed victory of its honour, but has covered defeat with aggravated diſgrace, returning reaſon can ſuggeſt but one conſolation for her folly; that ſomething yet remains for madneſs to ſquander, that there is yet a remnant which penury may ſave. The arbitreſs · of empires may yet exiſt among nations! the patroneſs of nations may yet be an houſe-wife!

There was a time when the world and the Roman Em[r] were ſynonimous terms.

There was a time too when the very name of Rom[e]; and the Provinces in awe, though ſhe could ſcarce have fears ago, her walls; England has fallen by her own weight ·

ſhews

wanted wifdom to balance. Thofe days are paft in which her hiftory went hand in hand with romance. France has ftruck terror into *her conquerors*, and has fhaken the throne of *her* King! The Englifh channel has become a term of mockery. It has feen the navy of England in its *flight!* The navy of England has left her coafts to be infulted! That the navy of England was able to fecure the protection of a port has, to a fovereign of England, become a theme of congratulation!

While England thus protects herfelf, need I afk what protection fhe is likely to afford to Ireland? If we remain by her bad policy in our prefent impoverifhed ftate, can fhe protect us from the arms or infults of her enemies?

Have we not men in arms already? Men whom England, and the flaves of England, would long ere this have difarmed, had they dared to do fo! Men whofe fpirit they now affect to approve, becaufe they find their approbation is indifferent to them! Men whofe fpirit muft obtain a momentary protection, and to whom a very little time will render protection unneceffary! Men who may yet teach England that the foil of their own country benumbs not their courage; that it is not on the plains of Flanders or America alone that *Irifhmen* can *conquer!*

The fubject, my countrymen, has rifen upon me. I have (I hope you will think unavoidably) been led into fome details. My indignation, upon other occafions, I have found it difficult to reprefs. You will confider the defign, and pardon any involuntary failure in the execution. But, before I take my leave for the prefent, allow me to afk one fhort queftion:

Shall we truft to other nations for a temporary protection, which (judging from human nature, and their particular line of conduct) I aver it to be equally their intereft and their inclination to give, and the bounds of which, as I have endeavoured to prove, they cannot exceed; or, fhall we depend to eternity on the generofity of a nation, who has fhewn herfelf as incapable of generofity as of juftice, and whofe folly has difabled her from performing the duties of either? She thunders forth the mandates of her *omnipotence;* but, is her di ovidence fo particular, fo watchful, fo active, and fo benemu nt, that we fhould leave to her more than the God of relig re demands for himfelf, that we fhould leave agency to fenter. nd addrefs her but in prayer? Is the night of religious the ma ion paffed away, and muft that of political idolatry nor madh rightful viciffitude of day? Our night of both has iently long? But the fun of England, in whofe

meridian

meridian beams our feebler light was loft, is now fet, perhaps, for ever : and the Hefperian ftar of America, which
fet with England, for a time, is now rifen, a Lucifer to light
us into day. It has moved, 'till it is vertical in glory, and
points to *our political falvation!*

OWEN ROE O'NIAL.

As the author of the foregoing excellent letter, in enumerating the natural advantages of Ireland, juft mentions her
mines, it may not be thought unneceffary to add· what Mr.
O'Halloran fays on this fubject :

Thus Gerard Boate * tells us, " All the mines which are at
" this day found out in Ireland, have been difcovered by the
" new Englifh, that is, fuch of them as came here in, and
" fince the days of Queen Elizabeth, and thefe, he tells us, are
" Iron, Lead and Silver. As to the Irifh themfelves (he
" fays) *being one of the moft barbarous nations of the whole earth,*
" they have been, *at all times,* fo far from feeking out any,
" that even in thefe laft years, and fince the Englifh have be-
" gun to difcover fome, none of them all, great or fmall,
" have applied themfelves to, or furthered that bufinefs." In
the next fection, he thinks mines of Gold are in Ireland ; and
he mentions a drachm of pure gold being got in a rivulet in
the county of Tyrone, from which he prefumes that the adjacent mountains are replete with this metal. In cap. 18, he
mentions a filver mine, in the county of Antrim, fo very rich
that every 30 pounds of ore yielded one of pure filver. This
candid writer was ftate phyfician to the common-wealth juftices of Ireland ; and was too well acquainted with the fentiments of his mafters, to lofe any opportunity of infulting a
nation, fo remarkably attached to Monarchy.

Let us now fee, how far doctor Boate's cenfure is fupported by truth and hiftory. Stanihurft, who wrote a century
earlier, and no very warm Irifhman, tells us, that Ireland
was then known to be rich in mines of different metals ; and
Adrianus the Dutchman, ftill earlier, thus celebrates them,

> . . . . . . *Stannique fodinas*
> *Et puri argenti venas.*——

Cambrenfis himfelf bears teftimony to our mines † ; and
Donatus, bifhop of Fefcoli, who wrote about 1100 years ago,

* Natural Hiftory of Ireland, cap. 16. fect. 11.
† Topograph, Hibern. Dift. 3. cap. 10.

fhews

shews that Ireland was even then highly renowned on the same account,

*Insula dives opum, gemmarum, vestis & auri.*

From these foreign evidences, let us now recur to the accurate pages of the Irish History. In the reign of Tighernmas, who flourished about 1000 years before Christ, we are told that the first gold mine found in Ireland, was discovered near the banks of the Liffy: and our annalists have been minute enough to tell us, that Juachadhan of Cualane, in the county of Wicklow, was the principal conductor of these works *, whose knowledge in metals and colours, they have not neglected to mention. In more than a century after we find that targets of pure silver were fabricated, and distributed to the bravest of the soldiery; and in the reign of Muincamhuin, who founded the order of the Golden Collar (so called from each knight wearing a collar of gold hung round his neck by a chain of the same metal) helmets were made with the neck and fore-pieces of pure gold. The handles of the swords of our antient knight, were made of pure gold, and the blades of a mixt brass, numbers of which have been and are daily discovered in bogs and other recesses. It appears among the hostages delivered to the Emperors of Ireland by the provinces, as well foreign as domestic, that those of Orgial were particularly distinguished from the rest, by having their shackles of pure gold, and the very word signifies the Golden Hostage. Part of the *Boirimhe-Laighen*, or tax on the kingdom of Leinster, and regularly paid into the monarch's treasury, for near 400 years, was 6000 ounces of pure silver. These facts it should seem are sufficient proofs of the great riches of antient Ireland, and her superior knowledge and industry to the modern. But if her own history will not be allowed as evidence in her favour, without modern collateral proofs, we are even abundantly furnished with these.

Mr. ô Flaherty †, from Nenius, an author of the 9th century, and from old manuscripts, gives an account of the antiently supposed wonders of Ireland, some of which have been found true, others false. Among others we find the following account of mines about Louch-Lene, or Killarney in the county of Kerry.

*Mamoniæ stagnum* Lochlenius *undique Zonis*
*Quatuor ambitur : prior est ex ære ; secunda*
*Plumbea ; de rigido conflatur tertia ferro :*
*Quarto residenti pallescet linea Stanno.*

* Keating p. 1. ô Flaherty, p. 195. Grat. Lucius, &c.
† Ogygia, p. 220.

We also find, that in said lake, large quantities of pearls have been found.

It is not above thirty years since a very rich copper mine was discovered on the border of this lake, and worked with very great profit to the proprietors for many years; but what is greatly to our purpose, is, that on pushing on their works, they found shafts had been regularly sunk, and implements of mining were found. These works were ignorantly imputed to the Danes, who, it appears, had very inconsiderable settlements here, and who, it must be confessed, seem to have been little qualified for such undertakings. As to the lead mine it is an uncontroverted fact, that about fifty years ago, an English company worked one at Castle Lyons, on the side of the Lake; and many years after, the same works were resumed under the inspection of one Longstaff, from which they extracted large quantities of silver. Though the tin mine has not been yet found, nor, I suppose, searched for, yet Smith * confesses to have found near the lake an ore which contained tin; and as for the iron mines, the proofs that they were largely carried on here are many, and at this day one is worked near Mucrofs. A. C. 1094, we read of an elegant present of Kerry pearls, from Gilbert Bishop of Limerick, to Anselm Archbishop of Canterbury †. At this day pearls are frequently found in the lake; nor can it be denied but the finest amethysts, emeralds, and other precious stones, and the hardest, are found in this country; and the common Kerry stone nearly approaches the diamond in lustre and hardness. Yet it is not above fifty years since such have been discovered; though we read, that our early princes and nobles wore them in their ears and on their cloaths; and that the Bishop of Fesicoli has mentioned these among the other productions of Ireland! In opening of many other mines, old shafts have been discovered, and implements of mining found, particularly in a rich lead one, on the estate of Thomas Westrop, Esq; in this county, and bordering on the Shannon. In working the lead mines of Knocaderry, since called Silver Mines, in the county of Tipperary, in the beginning of the last century, shafts were seen, and every other proof of its being worked centuries earlier. The rich copper mines in the county of Wicklow, and these latter ones in the county of Tipperary, are still further proofs of the great plenty of this metal formerly; and will explain why

* Nat. History county of Kerry, p. 125.
† Epist. Hibern, Syl. p. 81, &c.

l

the

the fharp edges of the blades of our antient fwords, &c. were of a mixt brafs; and how the people of Leinfter were ena-bled to give fix thonfand copper cauldrons to the Monarch's tax-gatherers, every fecond year, being a part of their famous tribute, the caufe of fo much bloodfhed in Ireland.

When the Spaniards, in Queen Elizabeth's days, landed at Smerwic bay, in the county of Kerry, on erecting a fort near it, from the many pieces of gold they found here they called it Fort de l'or; and fome years ago fome country peo-ple, in trenching potatoes near it, found feveral corfelets of pure gold. Mr. Smith * fuppofes this to be part of the trea-fures fent from Spain, in thefe days; but is it probable that gold corfelets were fent to relieve a diftreffed people, who only wanted powder and ball, and which they fought for at an immenfe expence? Befides, Sir George Carew, then pre-fident of Munfter, and an indifputable authority, tells us †, that thefe treafures were in money, fafely landed by Mac Eagan, Apoftolic Vicar, and by him diftributed to the Irifh chiefs; nay, he is even minute enough to tell us each per-fon's fhare. But numbers of thefe, as well as handles of fwords, and gold of a particular colour and hardnefs, made for the purpofe of lodging the poll-axes of our antient *Marc-Sloigh*, or cavalry, have been frequently found. Of thefe corfelets alone, I have feen above twenty, and purchafed one, the gold of which was fo ductile as to roll up, like paper. Thefe likewife prove the reality of our Niagha-Nafc, or Knights of the Golden Collar, as well as the fuperior know-ledge of our anceftors in the natural hiftory of their country. They fhew the care taken to advance nothing but what was ftrictly true, in our antient hiftory; and at the fame time, point out to the public, the great lofs the learned world, as well as this kingdom, has fuftained by the deftruction of fo many of our antient annals, and the neceffity of attending more diligently to what remain. Even our old odes and bal-lads, fhould not be too flightly regarded. The Bifhop of London, in his edition of Cambden, p. 1411, tells us, " That " The Bifhop of Derry being one day at dinner, an Irifh harp- " er came in, and fung an old ode to the harp, the fubftance " of which was, that in fuch a place, pointing to the very " fpot, near Ballyfhannon, a man of gigantic figure lay bu- " ried; and that over his breaft and back were plates of pure " gold, and on his fingers rings of the fame; the place was

* Hiftory of Kerry, p. 186.    † Parai. Hibern. p. 306.

" fo

" fo minutely defcribed, that two of the company were
" tempted to examine into it, and did accordingly find two
" thin pieces of pure gold," a figure of one of which, Mr.
Harris gives. The great plenty of gold in antient Ireland
cannot be contefted. We have feen that part of the furniture
of Tara was of pure gold, as was moft of the church plate
through the kingdom: even the bells for the altars were of
gold, or of filver inlaid with gold, and ornamented with precious ftones, many of which exifted in the laft century, as
the learned Colgan witneffes *; and we yet call them Muil-
lean-oir. Nay this luxury extended to private life; thus,
the ó Cowhig's, a family in the county of Cork, are, in a very
antient poem, diftinguifhed from their neighbours, the ó Dif-
coll's, and ó Flain's, by the epithet of ó Colhtaice, na N'ard-
Ceorn oir, or ó Cowhig of the lofty gold drinking cup. Should
any doubt yet remain of the wealth of antient Ireland, the
Airigid-Sron, or Nofe-money, being an ounce of gold paid
annually by the head of every family, under the Danifh
power to thefe tyrants, may, furely, remove it.

→>·>·<<·→>·→>·→>·<<·<>·→>

When I firft propofed to myfelf the compilation of the following work, I did not intend the prefent fubject fhould extend beyond a general reference to a pamphlet which ought
to be dear to every Irifhman, I mean, Mr. Molyneaux's Cafe
of Ireland, &c. and a copy of the Irifh Magna Charta, which
laft, even to every difpaffionate reader, ought to be fufficient,
as ratified in the fame folemn manner, and containing the
fame facred privileges and immunities of the Englifh one, to
which they very juftly hold no law fuperior †. I fhall, however, claim the reader's indulgence, and proceed further:

All the charters and grants of liberties from Edward ‡ the
Confeffor's time down to the 9th of Henry the III. were but
confirmations one of another, and all of them declarations
and confirmations of the common law of England. And by
the feveral eftablifhments, which we have formerly mentioned,
of the laws of England to be of force in Ireland: Firft, in
the 13th of Henry II. Secondly, in the 12th of king John.

---

* Act. Sanctor. Hibern. p. 149

† Magna Charta is only an abridgment of our ancient laws and cuftoms; the King that fwears to it, fwears to them all, and is not admitted
to be interpreter of it, or to determine what is good or evil, fit to be obferved or annulled in it, and he can have no more power over the reft.
Lord Somers on the Rights of the people.

‡ Molyneux.

Thirdly,

Thirdly, in the 12th of Henry III. All thofe laws and cuftoms of England, which by thofe feveral charters were declared and confirmed to be the laws of England, were eftablifhed to be of force in Ireland. And thus Ireland came
to be governed by one and the fame common law with England; and thofe laws continue as part of the municipal and
fundamental laws of both kingdoms to this day.

It now remains that we enquire, how the ftatute laws and
acts of parliament made in England, fince the 9th of Henry
III. came to be of force in Ireland; and whether all or any
of them, and which, are in force here, and when and how
they came to be fo,

And the firft precedent that occurs in our books, of acts
of parliament made in Ireland, particularly mentioning and
confirming fpecial acts of parliament in England, is found in
a marginal note of Sir Richard Bolton's, formerly lord chief
baron of the Exchequer in Ireland, affixed in his edition of
the Irifh ftatutes, to ftat. 10 Hen. 7, cap. 22. to this purport,
That in 13 Ed. II. ' by parliament in this realm of Ireland
' the ftatutes of Merton, made the 20th of Henry II. and
' the ftatutes of Marlbridge, made the 25th of Henry III.
' the ftatute of Weftminfter the firft, made the 3d of Edward
' I. the ftatute of Gloucefter, made the 6th of Edward I.
' and the ftatute of Weftminfter the fecond, made the 13th
' of Edward I. were all confirmed in this kingdom, and all
' other ftatutes which were of force in England, were re-
' ferred to be examined in the next parliament; and fo many
' as were then * allowed and publifhed, to ftand likewife for
' laws in this kingdom. And in the 10th of Henry the
' IV. it was enacted in this kingdom of Ireland, " That
" the ftatutes made in England fhould not be of force in
" this kingdom, unlefs they were allowed and. publifhed
" in this kingdom by parliament." ' And the like ftatute
' was made again in the 29th of Henry VI. Thefe fta-
' tutes are not to be found in the rools, nor any parliament
' roll of that time; but he (Sir Richard Bolton) had feen the
' fame exemplifyed under the great feal, and the exempli-
' fication remaineth in the treafury of the city of Waterford.'
Thus far the note. If we confider the frequent troubles and
diftractions in Ireland, we fhall not wonder that thefe, and
many other rolls and records, have been loft in this kingdom:
For from the 3d year of Edward the II. which was anno

* Vid. lib. rubr fcaccar. Dubl.

13 o, through the whole reigns of Edward the III. Richard II. Henry IV. and Henry V. and so to the 7th year of Henry VI. anno 1428, which is about 118 years, there are not any parliament rolls to be found * ; yet certain it is, that divers parliaments were held in Ireland in those times †. The same may be said from Henry II's coming into Ireland, anno 1172, to the 3d year of Edward II anno 1310, about 138 years.

Perhaps it may be said, that if there were such statutes of Ireland as the said acts of the 10th of Henry IV. and the 29th of Henry VI. as they shew, that the parliaments of Ireland did think that English acts of parliament could not bind Ireland ; yet they shew likewise, that, even in those days, the parliaments of England did claim this superiority; or else to what purpose were the said acts made, unless in denial of that claim.

All which I hope may be readily granted without any pre-judice to the right of the Irish parliaments : there is nothing so common, as to have one man claim another man's right: and if bare pretence will give a title, no man is secure : and it will be yet worse, if when another so pretends, and I insist on my right, my just claim shall be turned to my prejudice, and to the disparagement of my title.

We know very well, that many of the judges of our four-courts have been from time to time sent out of England; and some of them may easily be supposed to come over hither prepossessed with an opinion of our parliament's being subordinate to that of England. Or, at least, some of them may be scrupulous, and desirous of full security in this point ; and on their account, and for their satisfaction, such acts as afore-said, may be devised, and enacted in Ireland. But then, God forbid that these acts should afterwards be laid hold of to a clear other intent than what they were framed for ; and instead of declaring and securing our rights, should give an handle of contest, by shewing that our rights have been ques-tioned of ancient time.

In conclusion of all, if this superiority of the parliament of England have been doubted a great while ago, so it has been as great a while ago strenuously opposed, and absolutely denied by the parliaments of Ireland : and by the way, I shall take notice, that from whencesoever this ancient pre-tence of Ireland's subordination proceeded in those days, it did

---

* Annals of Ireland, at the end of Camden's Britain. Edit. 1634. page 195, 197, &c.

† Ibid. page 160. Pryn against the 4th Instit. chap. 76.

not·

not arife from the parliament of England itfelf: for we have, not one fingle inftance of an Englifh act of parliament exprefsly claiming this right of binding us: but we have feveral inftances of Irifh acts of parliament exprefsly denying this fubordination, as appears by what foregoes.

Afterwards, by a ftatute made in Ireland the 18th of Henry VI. cap. 1. All the ftatutes made in England againft the extortions and opprefsions of purveyors, are enacted to be ' holden and kept in all points, and put in execution in this ' land of Ireland.'

And in the 32d year of Henry VI. cap. 1. by a parliament in Ireland 'tis enacted, ' That all the ftatutes made againft ' provifors to the court of Rome, as well in England as in ' Ireland, be had and kept in force.'

After this, in a parliament at Drogheda the 8th of Edward IV. cap. 1. it was ratifyed, that the Englifh ftatute againft rape, made the 6th of Richard II. fhould be of force in Ireland, from the 6th day of March laft paft: ' And that ' from henceforth the faid act, and all other ftatutes and acts ' made by authority of parliament within the realm of Eng- ' land, be ratifyed, and confirmed, and adjudged, by the ' authority of this parliament in their force and ftrength, ' from the faid fixth day of March.' We fhall hereafter have occafion of taking farther notice of this ftatute upon another account.

Laftly, in a parliament held at Drogheda the 10th of Henry VII. cap. 22. it is enacted, ' that all ftatutes late' (that is as the * learned in the laws expound it, before that time) ' made ' in England, concerning the common and public weal of the ' fame, from henceforth be deemed effectual in law, and be ' accepted, ufed and executed within this land of Ireland in ' all points, &c.'

† And in the 14th year of the fame king's reign, in a parliament held at Triftle-Dermot, it was enacted, That all acts of parliament made in England for punifhing cuftomers, controulers, and fearchers, for their mifdemeanors; or for punifhment of merchants or factors, be of force here in Ireland, provided they be firft proclaimed at Dublin, Drogheda, and other market-towns.

Thus we fee by what fteps and degrees all the ftatutes which were made in England, from the time of Magna Charta, to the 10th of Henry VII. which did concern the public commonweal,

---

* Cook's 4th inftit. cap. 76, p. 351.    † Vid. Irifh Stat.

were

were received, confirmed, and authorized to be of force in Ireland; all which was done by affent of the lords fpiritual and temporal, and the commons in the parliament of Ireland affembled, and no otherwife.

We fhall not enquire, whether there are not other acts of the Englifh parliament, both before and fince the 10th of Henry VII. which were and are of force in Ireland, though not allowed of by parliament in this kingdom. And we fhall find, that by the opinion of our beft lawyers, there are divers fuch; but then they are only fuch as are declaratory of the ancient common law of England, and not introductive of any new law: for thefe become of force by the firft general eftablifhment of the common laws of England in this kingdom, under Henry II. king John, and Henry III. and need no particular act of Ireland for their fanction.

As to thofe Englifh ftatutes fince the 10th of Henry VIIth, that are introductive of a new law, it was never made a queftion whether they fhould bind Ireland, without being allowed in parliament here; till of very late years this doubt began to be moved; and how it has been carried on and promoted, fhall appear more fully hereafter.

I fay, till of very late years; for the ancient precedents which we have to the contrary, are very numerous. Amongft many, we fhall mention the following particulars.

In the 21ft of Henry VIIIth, an act was made in England, making it felony in a fervant that runeth away with his mafter's or miftrefs's goods. This act was not received in Ireland till it was enacted by a parliament held here in the 33d of Henry VIIIth, c. 5. Sef. 1.

In the 21ft of Henry VIII. c. 19. there was a law made in England, that all lords might diftrain on the lands of them holden, and make their avowry not naming the tenant, but the land. But this was not of force in Ireland till enacted here in the 33d of Henry VIII. c. 1. Sef. 1.

An act was made in England, anno 31 Henry VIII. that joint-tenants and tenants in common fhould be compelled to make partition, as co-parceners were compellable at common law. But this act was not received in Ireland till enacted here, anno 33 Henry VIII. c. 10.

Anno 27 Henry VIII. c. 10. the ftatute for transferring ufes into poffeffion was made in England; but not admitted in Ireland till 10 Car. 2, Sef. 2.

In

In like manner, the Englifh ftatute 33 Henry VIII. c. 1. directing how lands and tenements may be difpofed by will, &c. was not of force in Ireland till 10 Car. 2. Sef. 2.

The act of uniformity of common prayer and adminiftration of the facraments was made in England the uft of Eliz. c. 2. but was not eftablifhed in Ireland till the 2d of Eliz. c. 2. And fo that of England 14 Car. 2. c. 14. was not received in Ireland till 17 & 18 Car. 2. c. 6.

The ftatute againft wilful perjury made in England 5 Eliz. c. 9. was not enacted in Ireland till 28 Eliz. c. 1.

So the Englifh act againft witchcraft and forcery made 5 Eliz. c. 16. And another act againft forgery 5 Eliz. c. 14. were neither of them in force in Ireland till the 28th of her reign, cap. 3, and 4.

The Englifh ftatute againft piracies was made the 28th of Henry VIII. c. 15. but not in Ireland till the 12th of King James, c. 2.

In England an act was made the 27th of Eliz. c. 4. againft fraudulent conveyances ; but it was not in force in Ireland till enacted here the 10th of Charles, c. 3. Sef. 2.

In the 15th year of king Charles I. in a parliament held at Dublin, there were fix Englifh ftatutes made laws of this kingdom, with fuch alterations as beft fitted them to the ftate thereof, viz.

21 Jac. c. 14. For pleading the general iffue in intrufions brought by the king, by chap. 1 of the Irifh ftatutes.

31 Eliz. c. 2. For abridging of proclamations on fines, by chap. 2.

2 and 3 Edw. VI. c. 8. concerning offices before the efcheator, by chap. 4.

31 Eliz. c. 1. Difcontinuance of writs of error in the Exchequer chamber, by chap. 5.

8 Eliz. c. 4. and 18 Eliz. c. 7. concerning clergy, by chap. 7.

24 Hen. VIII. c. 5. concerning killing a robber, by chap. 9.

There are fix Englifh ftatutes likewife paffed in the time of king Charles II. upon and foon after the reftoration, fome of which were not paffed into laws in Ireland till a year, two or three, afterwards : as will appear by confulting the ftatute books *

* Irifh ftat. 13 C. 2, c. 2. 13 C. 2, c. 3. 14 & 15 C. 2, c. 1. 14 & 15 C. 2, c. 19, 17 & 18 C. 2, c. 3. 17 & 18 C. 2, c. 11. Englifh ftat. 12 C. 2, c. 12. 12 C. 2, c. 3. 12 C. 2, c. 14. 12 C. 2, c. 24. 12 C. 2, c. 33. 16 & 17 C. 2, c. 5.

And

And in the firſt year of William and Mary, Seſ. 2. c. 9. an act paſſed in England, declaring all attainders and other acts made in the late pretended parliament under king James at Dublin, void : but was not enacted here in Ireland till the 7th year of king William, c. 3. And this was thought requiſite to be done upon mature conſideration thereon before the king and council of England *, notwithſtanding that the Engliſh act does particularly name Ireland, and was wholly deſigned for, and relates thereto.

The like may we find in ſeveral other ſtatutes of England paſſed ſince his preſent majeſty's acceſſion to the throne, which have afterwards been paſſed here in Ireland, with ſuch alterations as make them practicable and agreeable to this kingdom, ſuch as are amongſt others, the act for diſarming papiſts. The act of recognition. The act for taking away clergy from ſome offenders. The act for taking ſpecial bail in the country, &c. The act againſt clandeſtine mortgages. The act againſt curſing and ſwearing.

Theſe, with many more, are to be found in our ſtatute books in the ſeveral reigns of Henry VIII. Edward VI. queen Elizabeth, king James, king Charles I. and II. and king William. But it is not to be found in any records in Ireland, that ever any act of parliament, introductive of a new law made in England ſince the time of king John, was by the judgment of any court, received for law, or put in execution in the realm of Ireland, before the ſame was confirmed and aſſented to by the parliament in Ireland.

And thus I preſume we have pretty clearly made out, and plainly ſhewn the ſeveral ſteps by which the Engliſh form of government, and the Engliſh ſtatute laws were received in this kingdom ; and that this was wholly by the people's conſent in parliament, to which we have had a very ancient right, and as full a right as our next neighbours can pretend to, or challenge.

It were endleſs to mention all the records and precedents that might be quoted for the eſtabliſhment of the laws of England; I ſhall therefore enter no farther into that matter but therein refer to lord chief juſtice Cook, † Pryn ‡, Reyly §, &c.

---

* For we have had two ſeveral acts tranſmitted to us at different times, to this very purpoſe. One we rejected in the lord Sidney's government, t'other paſſed under the lord Capell.

† Fourth inſt.  ‡ Againſt the fourth inſt.   § Placita parliamentaria.

The

The hand of Englifh power may be faid then to have grafped at Irifh freedom only, under the deteftable reign of Charles II\*.

In the year 1663 the diftinctions † between the trade of England and Ireland ‡, and the reftraints on that of the latter commenced. By an Englifh act paffed in that year, intitled an act " for the encouragement of trade," a title not very applicable to the parts of it that related to Ireland, befides laying a duty nearly equal to a prohibition on cattle imported into England from that kingdom, the exportation of all commodities, except victuals, fervants, horfes, and falt for the fifheries of New England and Newfoundland, from thence to the Englifh plantations, was prohibited from the 25th of March, 1764. The exports allowed were ufeful to them, but prejudicial to Ireland, as they confifted of our people, our provifions, and a material for manufacture which we might have ufed more profitably on our own coafts.

In 1670 another act ‖ paffed in England, to prohibit from the 24th of March 1671, the exportation from the Englifh plantations to Ireland of feveral materials for manufactures §, without firft unloading in England or Wales. We are informed by this act that the reftraint of the exportation from the Englifh plantations to Ireland was intended by the act of 1663; but the intention is not effectuated, though the importation of thofe commodities into Ireland *from England*, without firft unloading there, is, in effect, prohibited by that act.

The prohibition of importing into Ireland any plantation goods, unlefs the fame had been firft landed in England, and had paid the duties, is made general, without any exception, by the Englifh act of the 7th and 8th W. 3d, ch. 22.

---

\* This I am fure of, that before thefe acts (cattle, tobacco, and navigation acts) in King Charles II. time, (the eldeft of which is not over thirty-feven years) there is not one pofitive full precedent to be met with in all the ftatute-book, of an Englifh act binding the kingdon of Ireland. And on this account we may venture to affert, that thefe are at leaft innovations on us, as not being warranted by any former precedents.

And fhall proceedings only of thirty-feven years ftanding, be urged againft a nation, to deprive them of the rights and liberties which they enjoyed for five hundred years before, and which were invaded without and againft their confent, and from that day to this have been conftantly complained of? Let any Englifh heart that ftands fo juftly in vindication of his own rights and liberties, anfwer this queftion, and I have done.
　　　　　　　　　　　　　　　　　　　　Molyneux, p. 40.

† Commer. Reftr.
‡ 15 Ch. 2, ch. 7.　　　　‖ 22d and 23d Ch. 2d, ch. 26.
§ Sugar, tobacco, cotton, wool, indigo, fteel or Jamaica wood, fuftick, or other dying wood, the growth of the faid plantations.

By

By comparing the reſtrictive law of 1699, with the ſtatutes which had been previouſly enacted in England from the 15th year of the reign of Charles the Second, relative to the Colonies, it appears that this reſtrictive law originated in a ſyſtem of colonization. The principle of that ſyſtem was, that the Colonies ſhould ſend their materials to England, and take from thence her manufactures, and that the making thoſe manufactures in the Colonies ſhould be prohibited or diſcouraged. But was it reaſonable to extend this principle to Ireland? The climate, growth and productions of the Colonies were different from thoſe of their parent country. England had no ſugar-canes, coffee, dying-ſtuff, and little tobacco. She took all thoſe from her Colonies only, and it was thought reaſonable that they ſhould take from her only the manufactures which ſhe made. But in Ireland, the climate, ſoil, growth and productions are the ſame as in England, who could give no ſuch equivalent to Ireland as ſhe gave to America, and was ſo far from conſidering her, when this ſyſtem firſt prevailed, as a proper ſubject for ſuch regulations, that ſhe was allowed the benefits ariſing from thoſe Colonies equally with England, until the 15th year of the reign of King Charles * the Second. By an act paſſed in that year, Ireland had no longer the privilege of ſending any of her exports, except ſervants, horſes, victuals and ſalt, to any of the Colonies; the reaſons are aſſigned in the preamble, "To make "this kingdom a ſtaple, not only of the commodities of thoſe "plantations, but alſo of the commodities of other countries "and places for the ſupplying of them, and it being the "uſage of other nations to keep their plantation trade to "themſelves †." At the time of paſſing this law, though leſs liberal ideas in reſpect of Ireland were then entertained, it went no further than not to extend to her the benefit of thoſe Colony regulations; but it was not then thought that this kingdom was a proper ſubject for any ſuch regulations. The ſcheme of ſubſtituting there, inſtead of the woollen, the linen trade, was not at that time thought of. The Engliſh were deſirous to eſtabliſh it among themſelves, and by an act of parliament ‡ made in that year for encouraging the manufacture of linen, granted to all foreigners who ſhall ſet it up in England, the privileges of natural born ſubjects.

---

* 15 Ch. II. ch. 7.

† As other nations did the ſame, Ireland was ſhut out from the new world, and a conſiderable part of the old in Aſia and Africa.

‡ 15 Ch. II. ch. 15.

But it appears by the Englifh ftatute of the 7th and 8th Will. III *. that this fcheme had not fucceeded in England ; and from this act it is manifeft that England confidered itfelf, as well as Ireland, interefted to encourage the linen manufacture there; and it does not then appear to have been thought juft, that Ireland fhould purchafe this benefit for both, by giving up the exportation of any other manufacture. But in 1698 a different principle prevailed ; in effect the fame, fo far as relates to the woollen manufacture, with that which had prevailed as to the commerce of the Colonies. This is evident from the preamble of the Englifh law † made in 1699, " For as much as wool and woollen manufactures of cloth, " ferge, bays, kerfies and other ftuffs, made or mixed with " wool, are the greateft, and moft profitable commodities of " this kingdom, on which the value of lands and the trade " of the nation do chiefly depend; and whereas great quan- " tities of like manufactures have of late been made and are " daily encreafing in the kingdom of Ireland, and *in the* " *Englifh plantations* in America, and are exported from thence " to foreign markets, heretofore fupplied from England, " which will inevitably fink the value of lands, and tend to " the ruin of the trade and woollen manufactures of this " realm; for the prevention whereof, and for the encourage- " ment of the woollen manufactures in this kingdom, &c."

The ruinous confequences of the woollen manufactures of Ireland to the value of lands, trade and manufactures of England, ftated in this act, are apprehenfions that were entertained, and not events that had happened; and before thofe facts are taken for granted, I requeft the mifchiefs recited in in the acts ‡ made in England to prevent the importation of cattle dead or alive from Ireland, may be confidered.

Connecting this preamble of the act of 1699, with the fpeech made from the throne to the parliament of Ireland in the year 1698, with the addreffes of both houfes in England, and with the prohibition, by this and by other acts formerly made in England, of exporting wool from Ireland except to that kingdom, the object of this new commercial regulation is obvious. It was to difcourage the woollen manufacture in Ireland, and in effect, to prohibit the exportation from thence, becaufe it was the principal branch of

* Ch. 39.
† 10th and 11th W. III. ch. 10.
‡ 15 Ch. II. ch. 7.  18 Ch. II. ch. 2.  20 Ch. II. ch. 7.  22d and 23d Ch. II. ch. 6.  3 Ch. II. ch. 2.

manufacture,

manufacture, and trade in England, to induce us to send to them our materials for that manufacture, and that we should be supplied with it by them ; and to encourage, as a compensation to Ireland, the linen manufacture, which was not at that time a commercial object of any importance to England.

The supposed compensation was no more than what Ireland had before ; no further encouragement was given by England to our linen manufacture until six years after this prohibition, when at the request of the Irish house of commons, and after a representation of the ruinous state of this country, liberty was given by an English act of parliament * to export our white and brown linens into the colonies, which was allowing us to do as to one manufacture, what, before the 15th of king Charles the second, was permitted in every instance.

For several centuries before this period Ireland was in possession of the English common law +, and of magna charta. The former secures the subject in the enjoyment of property of every kind; and by the latter, *the liberties of all the ports of the kingdom are established.*

The statutes made in England for the common and public weal, are ‡ by an Irish act of the 10th of Henry the 7th, made laws in Ireland ; and the English commercial statutes, in which Ireland is expresly mentioned, will place the former state of commerce in this country in a light very different from that in which it has been generally considered in Great-Britain.

By the 17th of Edward the 3d, ch. 1. all sorts of merchandizes may be exported from Ireland, except to the king's enemies.

By the 27th of Edward the 3d, ch. 18. merchants of Ireland and Wales may bring their merchandize to the staple of England ; and by the 34th of the same king, ch. 17. all kinds of merchandizes may be exported from and imported into Ireland, as well by aliens as denizens. In the same year there is another statute, ch. 18. that all persons who have lands or possessions in Ireland, may freely import thither,

---

* 3 and 4 Ann. ch, 8.

† 4 Inst. 349. Matth. Paris, anno 1172. p. 121, 220. Vit H. '. Pryn, against the 4th Inst. 76, p. 250, 251. Sir. John Davis's Hist. 71. Lord Lyttleton's Hist. of H. 2. 3 Vol. 89, 90. 7 Co. 22. 23. 4th Black. 429.

‡ Cooke's 4th Inst. 351.

and

and export from that kingdom *their own commodities*; and by the 5th of Edward the 3d, ch. 8. no alnage is to be paid, if frize ware, which are made in Ireland.

The reign of Edward the 4th furnishes still stronger instances of the *regard* shewn by England to the trade and manufactures of this country.

In the third year of that monarch's reign, the artificers of England complained to parliament that they were greatly impoverished and *could not live* by bringing in divers commodities and wares ready wrought *. An act passed reciting those complaints, and ordaining that no merchant born a subject of the king, denizen or stranger, or other person should bring into England or Wales any woollen cloths, &c. and enumerates many other manufactures, on pain of forfeiture; provided that all wares and " chaffers" made and wrought in Ireland or Wales, may be brought in and sold in the realm of England, as they were wont before the making of that act. †

In the next year another act ‡ passed in that kingdom, that all woollen cloth brought into England and set to sale, should be forfeited, except cloths made in Wales or Ireland.

In those reigns England was as careful of the commerce and manufactures of her ancient sister kingdom, particularly in her great staple trade, as she was of her own.

Of this attention there were further instances in the years 1468 and 1478. In two treaties concluded in those years between England and the duke of Bretagne, the merchandize to be traded in between England, Ireland and Calais on the one part, and Bretagne on the other, is specified, and woollen cloths are particularly mentioned §.

And in a treaty between Henry the 7th and the Netherlands, Ireland is included, both as to exports and imports ‖.

From this time until the 15th of king Charles the 2d, which takes in a period of 167 years, the commercial constitution of Ireland was as much favoured and protected as that of England; " the free enlargement of common traf-
" fic which his majesty's subjects of Ireland enjoyed," is

* 3d Edw. 4. ch. 4.
† The part of this law which mentions that it shall be determinable at the king's pleasure, has the prohibition for its object, and does not lessen the force of the argument in favour of Ireland.
‡ 4th Edw. IV. ch. 1.        § Anderson on Commerce, 1 Vol. 285.
‖ Ib. 319

taken

taken notice of incidentally, in an English statute, in the reign of king James the 1st* ; and in 1627 king Charles the 1st made a strong declaration in favour of the trade and manufactures of this country. By several English statutes in the reign of king Charles the 2d, an equal attention was shewn to the woollen manufactures in both kingdoms; in the 12th year of his reign † the exportation of wool, wool-felts, fuller's earth, or any kind of scowering-earth, was prohibited from both. But let the reasons, mentioned in the " preamble, for passing this law be adverted to: " For pre-" venting inconveniencies and losses that happened, and that. " daily do and may happen to the kingdom of England, " dominion of Wales, and kingdom of Ireland, through the " secret exportation of wool out of and from the said king-" doms and dominions; and for the *better setting on work the* " *poor people* and inhabitants of the kingdoms and dominions " aforesaid, and to the intent that the full use and benefit of " *the principal native commodities* of the same kingdom and " dominion may come, redound, and be unto the subjects and " inhabitants of the same.

The shipping and navigation of England and Ireland were at this time equally favoured and protected. By another act of the same year, no goods or commodities ‡ of the growth, production or manufacture of Asia, Africa or America, shall be imported into England, *Ireland* or Wales, but in ships which belong to the people of England or *Ireland*, the dominion of Wales, or the town of Berwick upon Tweed, or which are of the built of the said lands, and of which the master and three-fourths of the mariners are English ; and a subsequent statute § makes the encouragement to navigation in both countries equal, by ordaining that the subjects of Ireland and of the Plantations shall be accounted English within the meaning of that clause. Another law ‖ of the same reign shews that the navigation, commerce and woollen manufactures of both kingdoms were equally protected by the English legislature. This act lays on the same restraint as the above-mentioned act of the 12th of Charles II. and makes the transgression still more penal. It recites that wool, wool-felts, &c. are secretly exported from England and Ireland to foreign parts, to the great decay of the woollen manufactures and

---

* 2d James, ch. 6.      † 12th Ch. 2, ch. 3.
‡ 12 Ch. 2, ch. 18.      § 13th and 14th Ch. 2, ch. 11.
‖ 13th and 14th Ch. 2, ch. 18.

the deſtruction of the navigation and commerce of *theſe kingdoms*.

From thoſe laws it appears that the commerce, navigation and manufactures of this country were not only favoured and protected by the Engliſh legiſlature, but that we had in thoſe times the full benefit of their Plantation trade ; whilſt the woollen manufactures were protected and encouraged in England and Ireland, the planting of tobacco in both was prohibited, becauſe " it was one of the main products of ſeveral " of the plantations, and upon which their welfare and ſub- " ſiſtence do depend\*." This policy was liberal, juſt and equal ; it opened the reſources, and cultivated the ſtrength of every part of the empire.

This commercial ſyſtem of Ireland was enforced by ſeveral acts of her own legiſlature ; two ſtatutes paſſed in the reign of Henry VIII. to prevent the exportation of wool, becauſe, ſays the firſt of thoſe laws, " it hath been the cauſe of dearth " of cloth, and idleneſs of many folks †," and " tends to the " deſolation and ruin of this poor land." The ſecond of thoſe laws inforces the prohibition ‡ by additional penalties ; it recites, " that the ſaid beneficial law had taken little effect, but " that ſince the making thereof, great plenty of wool had been " conveyed out of this land, to the great and ineſtimable hurt, " decay and impoveriſhment of the King's poor ſubjects within " the ſaid land ; for redreſs whereof, and in conſideration that " conveying of the wool of the growth of this land out of the " ſame is one of the greateſt occaſions of the idleneſs of the " people, waſte, ruin and deſolation of the King's cities and " borough towns, and other places of his dominion within " this land." The 11th of Elizabeth § lays duties on the exportation equal to a prohibition ; and the reaſon given in the preamble ought to be mentioned ; " That the ſaid commodities " may be more abundantly wrought in this realm ere they ſhall " be ſo tranſported, than preſently they are, which ſhall ſet " many now living idle on work, to the great relief and com- " modity of this realm ‖."

By the preamble of one of thoſe acts, made in the reign of Charles II. it appears that the ſale of Iriſh woollen goods

---

\* 12 Ch. 2, ch. 27.      † Ir. act, 13 H. 8, ch. 2.
‡ 28 H. 8, ch. 17.        § Ch. 10.
‖ The neceſſity of encouraging the people of Ireland to manufacture their own wool, appears, by divers ſtatutes, to have been the ſenſe of the legiſlature of both kingdoms for ſome centuries.

in

in foreign markets was encouraged by England; "whereas
" there is a general complaint in *England*, France, and other
" parts beyond the feas, (whither the woollen cloths and other
" commodities made of wool in this his Majesty's kingdom of
" Ireland are transported) of the false, deceitful, uneven, and
" uncertain making thereof, which cometh to pass by reason
" that the clothiers and makers thereof do not observe any cer-
" tain affize for length, breadth and weight for making their
" cloths and other commodities aforesaid in this kingdom, as
" they do in the realm of England, and as they ought also to
" do here; by which means the merchants, buyers and users of
" the said cloth and other commodities are much abused and
" deceived, and the credit, esteem and sale of the said cloth and
" commodities is thereby much impaired and undervalued, to
" the great and general hurt and hindrance of the trade of
" clothing in this whole realm."

After the ports of England were shut against our cattle,
and our trade to the English Colonies was restrained, still
this commercial system was adhered to by encouraging the
manufactures of this country, and the exportation of them to
foreign countries. In 1667, when the power of the crown
was not so well understood as at present, the proclamation before mentioned was published by the Lord Lieutenant and
Privy Council of Ireland *, in pursuance of a letter from
Charles II. by the advice of his council in England, notify-
ing to all his subjects of this kingdom, the allowance of a
free trade to all foreign countries, either at war or at peace
with his Majesty.

※ ※ ※ ※ ※ ※ ※ ※ ※ ※ ※

In 1698 a most unjustifiable attack was made on the judicial privilege of the Irish House of Lords, by the English,
which gave birth to the following

## ORDER of the HOUSE of LORDS in ENGLAND,

### Die Martis, 24th Maij, 1698.

WHEREAS a petition and appeal was offered to the house
on the 7th of January last, of the society of the governor
and affiftants of London, of the new plantation in Ulster,
in the kingdom of Ireland, against a judgment given by the
Lords Spiritual and Temporal of Ireland in parliament there
affembled, on the 24th day of September last, upon the petition and appeal of William, Lord Bishop of Derry, against

* Carte, 2 Vol. p. 344.

the

the decree or order made in the faid caufe in the court of
Chancery there : whereupon a committee was appointed, to
confider of the proper method of appealing from the decrees
made in the court of Chancery in Ireland, and that purfuant to the order of the faid committee, and a letter fent to
the Lords Juftices of Ireland, by order of this houfe, feveral precedents have been tranfmitted by the Lords Juftices to
this houfe, copies whereof were ordered to be delivered to
either fide: after hearing counfel upon the petition of the
focie'v of London, prefented to this houfe the 20th of April
laft, praying that they might be heard, as to the jurifdiction
of the houfe of lords in Ireland, in receiving and judging
appeals from the Chancery there, as alfo counfel for the bifhop
of Derry : after due confideration of the precedents, and of
what was offered by counfel thereupon ; it is this day ordered, adjudged and declared, by the lords fpiritual and
temporal in parliament affembled, that the faid appeal by the
bifhop of Derry, to the houfe of lords in Ireland, from the
decree or order of the court of Chancery there made, in the
caufe wherein the faid bifhop of Derry was plaintiff, and the
faid fociety of the governors and affiftants of London, of the
New plantation in Ulfter, in Ireland, were defendants, was
*coram non judice*, and that all the proceedings thereupon are
null and void ; and, that the court of Chancery in Ireland
ought to proceed in the faid caufe, as if no fuch appeal had
been made to the houfe of lords there ; and if either of the
faid parties do find themfelves aggrieved by the faid decree or
order of Chancery, they are at liberty to purfue their proper
remedy by way of appeal to this houfe.

Ordered, That the Lord Chancellor do write to the lords
Juftices of Ireland, and fend them this order.

                              MAL. JOHNSON, *Cler. Parli.*

## REASONS againft the foregoing ORDER,
### By WILLIAM MOLYNEUX, Efq.*

1ft. Becaufe upon the conqueft † of Ireland by Henry
the IId. he introduced the laws of England in that kingdom,
and fent over the *Modus Tenendi Parliamentum in Terminis*, the

---

* Found in the hand writing of the author in blank leaves of one of
his cafes, &c. fent to the then bifhop of Meath, and now in the poffeffion
of John Evans, Efq; St. Stephen's-green, Dublin.

† Mr. Molyneux here ufes the word *conqueft*, in compliance with the
Englifh idea of Henry's invafion, in order, we may fuppofe, to render
his arguments more fubfervient to their object.

                                                        fame

fame with that of England, in which record it is faid that fuch things may be examined and corrected, *in Pleno parliamento et non alibi.*

2dly. Becaufe in the 20th year of king Henry the third, it was provided, that all laws and cuftoms which are enjoyed in England, fhall be alfo in Ireland, and that the land fhall be fubject thereunto and governed thereby, *ficut Dominus Johannes Ker cum ultimo effet in Hibernia ftatuit et fieri mandavit et quod brevia de communi jure quæ currunt in Anglia fimiliter currant in Hibernia.*

3dly. Becaufe king Edward III. in the 29th year of his reign, ordained for the quiet and good government of the people in Ireland, that in all cafes whatfoever, errors in judgment, in records, and proceedings in the courts of Ireland, fhall be corrected and amended in parliament in Ireland.

4thly. Becaufe it appears by other ancient records *quod terra Hiberniæ intra fe omnes et omnimodas habet curias prout in Anglia.*

5thly. Becaufe a conqueror by the laws of England and of nations, having power to introduce what laws he will in the conquered country, and king Henry II. purfuant to that power, having introduced the laws of England, and particularly that of holding parliaments in Ireland the houfe of lords in parliament in Ireland, may proceed to hear and determine judicially fuch matters as fhall be brought before them, in the fame manner as the lords in parliament in England.

6thly. Becaufe purfuant to the many conceffions made by king Henry II. king John, king Henry III. and other kings of England, the Lords in parliament in Ireland, have proceeded to correct and amend errors in judgment and decrees in the courts of Ireland, (as appears by the feveral precedents certified over to your lordfhips) and their judgments never before this called in queftion, many of them being very irregular. It is therefore prefumed to have been by a good and lawful jurifdiction, otherwife they would have been by our anceftors (who were zealous affertors of their rights) long before this called in queftion.

7thly. The order declaring the appeal was *coram non judice*, and null and void, will call all other judgments and decrees in queftion, under which many eftates have been purchafed, fettled, and enjoyed, which will be of fatal confequence to many families, and create great difcontent and diffatisfaction in that kingdom.

8thly. Becaufe the declaring the faid appeal to be *coram non judice*, and null and void, ftrikes at and tends to the de

tion of the jurifdiction of this houfe, for Ireland having *omnes et omnimodus curias prout in Anglia*, muft include the high court of parliament, and if their high court of parliament, being an exact picture of the high court of parliament in England, cannot judicially hear and determine appeals, writs of error, and impeachments, it may from thence be alleged that this here cannot.

9thly. Becaufe this refolution ftrikes at and tends to abridge the king's prerogative in Ireland; all appeals and writs of error in parliament being *coram rege in parliamento*, and therefore thefe words *coram non judice* takes from the king the judicial power which is given to him there.

10thly. Becaufe the peers of Ireland have little elfe left them befide their judicature, which if taken away, they will be of little efteem there, and many of the peers of England have fome of their titles of honour from that kingdom.

11thly. Becaufe it is the glory of the Englifh laws, and the blefling attending Englifhmen, that they have juftice adminiftered at their doors, and not to be drawn as formerly to Rome, by appeals which greatly impoverifhed the nation; and by this order the people of Ireland muft be drawn from Ireland hither, whenfoever they receive any injuftice from the Chancery there, by which means poor men muft be trampled upon, not being able to come over to feek for juftice.

12thly. The danger of altering, changing, or leffening a conftitution, for above five hundred years unfhaken, or fo much as called in queftion in any one thing, (the cuftom and ufage of courts being the law of courts) may occafion the deftruction of the whole, for the judicial power of the houfe of peers in Ireland, in criminal caufes by way of impeachment or otherwife, may by the fame reafon be called in queftion, as their judicature in civil caufes, which will encourage evil difpofed men, efpecially thofe in employment in that kingdom (who are generally very arbitrary) to act wickedly; and the better we preferve the conftitution of Ireland, and of thofe plantations dependant on England, the better we fhall preferve our own; and they will be barriers to ours, to prevent any invafion of theirs; and fince the Kings of England have in all times in matters relating to their revenue, their grants by letters patent, and their minifters not only empowered the parliament of Ireland to hear, correct, reform and amend them, but alfo acquiefced in their judgment, it ought not now to be queftioned.

13thly.

13thly. Becaufe this taking away the jurifdiction of the lords houfe in Ireland, may be a means to difquiet the lords there, and difappoint the king's affairs.

14thly. Becaufe the judicial power of the houfe of peers in Ireland is in no refpect altered by an act of parliament, the ftatute of the 10th of Henry 7, c. 4, called Poyning's law, only directs a new form of paffing bills into laws, but alters nothing of the judicial power, and their argument of their having the interpretation of all laws by a judicial power being allowed them, will enable them to make the laws what they pleafe, will as well hold againft the jurifdiction of this houfe, which ought not to be fuffered.

*Proteſt of the Iriſh Lords on the preceding Order.*

Die Veneris 11° Februarii, 1703°

PRESENT.

Lord Chancellor, Speaker.

Lords Spiritual

| | |
|---|---|
| Lord Archbp. of Armagh, | Lord Bifhop of Killalla, |
| Lord Archbp. of Dublin, | Lord Bifhop of Offory, |
| Lord Archbp. of Cafhel, | Lord Bifhop of Lromore, |
| Lord Archbp. of Tuam, | Lord Bifhop of Clogher, |
| Lord Bifhop of Meath, | Lord Bifhop of Limerick, |
| Lord Bifhop of Kildare, | Lord Bifhop of Killalo, |
| Lord Bifhop of Kilmore, | Lord Bifhop of Raphoe, |
| Lord Bifhop of Ferns, | Lord Bifhop of Downe, |
| Lord Bifhop of Clonfert, | Lord Bifhop of Cork. |

Lords Temporal.

| | |
|---|---|
| Earl of Rofcommon, | Lord Vifc. Dungannon, |
| Earl of Londonderry, | Lord Vifc. Charlemont, |
| Earl of Meath, | Lord Vifc. Powerfcourt, |
| Earl of Cavan, | Lord Vifc. Lanefborough, |
| Earl of Inchiquin, | P. Pr. Ld. Vifc. Mountjoy, |
| Earl of Mount Alexander, | Lord Vifc. Strabane, |
| Earl of Longford, | Lord Vifc. Doneraile, |
| Lord Vifc. Ely, | Lord Baron of Kerry, |
| Lord Vifc. Skerrin, | Lord Baron of Santry, |
| Lord Vifc. Maffareene, | Lord Baron of Shelburne. |

Ordered on motion, That the petition of Edward earl of Meath, and Cecilia Countefs of Meath, his wife, be read.

Read accordingly.

Ordered on motion, That the clerk of the rolls, do bring into this houfe, the roll of the acts of parliament of the 38th of Henry VI.

Refolved

Refolved on the queftion *nem con.* That by the ancient and known laws and ftatutes of this kingdom, her majefty hath an undoubted jurifdiction and prerogative in this her high court of parliament, in all appeals and caufes within this her majefty's realm of Ireland.

Refolved on the queftion *nem con.* That the determinations and judgments of this high court of parliament are final and conclufive, and cannot be reverfed or fet afide by any other court whatfoever.

Refolved on the queftion *nem con.* That if any fubject or refident within this kingdom, fhall hereafter prefume to remove any caufe determined in this high court of parliament, to any other court, fuch perfon or perfons, fhall be deemed betrayers of her majefty's prerogative and jurifdiction, and the undoubted ancient rights and privileges of this houfe, and of the rights and liberties of the fubjects of this kingdom.

Refolved on the queftion *nem con.* That if any fubject or refident within this kingdom, fhall prefume to put in execution any order from any other court, contrary to the final judgment and determination of this high court of parliament, fuch perfon or perfons, fhall be deemed betrayers of her majefty's prerogative and jurifdiction, and the undoubted ancient rights and privileges of this houfe, and of the rights and liberties of the fubjects of this kingdom, &c.

In the Irifh Houfe of Lords, in the year 1703, upon the petition of Edward, then earl of Meath, and Cecilia, countefs of Meath, his wife, againft the lord Ward, complaining of their having been difpoffeffed of certain lands in the county of Tipperary, under a pretended order of the houfe of lords of Great Britain ; we find the lords of Ireland*, unanimoufly adopt the refolutions on the foregoing appeal, in 1698.

On the 12th day of February, 1703, their lordfhips made the following order:

Whereas, upon hearing the complaint of the right hon. Edward, earl of Meath, and Cecilia, countefs of Meath, his wife, exhibited to this houfe on the 9th of October laft, it has appeared upon full proof, that they have been illegally difpoffeffed of the lands of part of Rocheftown, Corruta, Loughloughery, Keating, Milfield, Richardfon alias Richeftown, Cloughnecody, Ardfinane and Faren-Englifh, Rathcordane and Grumgill, Gortneerannah, Drumtrafney, Kilnemaun, Gurtinebamagh, and Garriglifh, all lying and being

---

* Jour. Houfe of Lords, fol. 52.

in

in the county of Tipperary, the actual poſſeſſion whereof was given them, purſuant to an order of this houſe, dated the 29th of October 1695: We the lords ſpiritual and temporal in parliament aſſembled, this 2th day of Feb. 703, do order, require, and command the Sheriff of the ſaid county of Tipperary, for the time being, forthwith to put the ſaid earl and counteſs of Meath into the actual, quiet and peaceable poſſeſſion of all the aforeſaid lands and premiſes, as he will anſwer the contrary at his peril.

From this period until the year 1717, we find the houſe of Lords of Great Britain did not attempt to interfere with the rights and privileges of the lords and people of this kingdom.

But about the year 717, that houſe thought proper once more to endeavour the eſtabliſhment of their uſurped authority, and accordingly entertained an appeal from Maurice Anneſly, Eſq; againſt a deciſion of the lords of Ireland, reverſed their decree, and ordered the ſheriff of the county of Kildare to reſtore to Mr. Anneſley the poſſeſſion of certain lands, of which he had been diſpoſſeſſed by the order of the Iriſh Lords.

And to enforce this order, the Britiſh lords had recourſe to the authority of the Barons of the court of Exchequer here, who ordered the Sheriff of Kildare to reſtore Mr. Anneſley to the poſſeſſion of his lands, according to the order of the Lords of Great Britain.

The ſheriff (Alexander Burrowes, Eſq;) Hampden-like, refuſed obedience to this illegal order: the barons endeavoured to enforce it by the impoſition of heavy fines; whereupon he petitioned the Iriſh Lords for relief, which having been referred to a committee of the houſe, they, on the 28th July, 1719, made the following report, and entered into the following reſolutions and proceedings *.

On the 17th of October, 17 9, the houſe proceeded on the order of the day, for reading the repreſentation to his majeſty of the proceedings of the houſe upon the petition of Alex. Burrowes, Eſq; in the cauſe of Sherlock and Anneſley †.

And the ſaid repreſentation was read, and agreed to by the houſe, and is as follows, viz.

To the King's moſt excellent Majeſty.
The humble repreſentation of the Lords ſpiritual and temporal in Parliament aſſembled.

---

* Lords Journals, Vol. Ii, fol. 621 to 625.
† Ib. 654.

Moſt

Moſt gracious Sovereign,

IT is with the greateſt concern that we, your Majeſty's moſt dutiful and loyal ſubjects, the lords ſpiritual and temporal in parliament aſſembled, do find ourſelves under a neceſſity of making this our humble repreſentation to your Majeſty.

It evidently appears, by many antient records, and ſundry acts of parliament paſſed in this kingdom, and particularly by one in the 11th of Queen Eliz. intitled, " An act for attainder of Shane O'Neil, &c." that the kings, with all the princes and men of value of the land, did, of their own good wills, and without any war or chivalry, ſubmit themſelves to your Majeſty's royal anceſtor, King Henry II. took oaths of fidelity to him, and became his liege ſubjects, who (as it is aſſerted by the Lord Chief Juſtice Coke and others *) did ordain and command, at the inſtance of the Iriſh, that " ſuch laws as he had in England, ſhould be of force and obſerved in Ireland." By this agreement the people of Ireland obtained the benefit of the Engliſh laws, and many privileges, particularly that of having a diſtinct parliament here, as in England†, and of having weighty and momentous matters, relating to this kingdom, treated of, diſcuſſed and determined in the ſaid parliament.

This conceſſion and compact thus made, and afterwards, by ſucceeding kings, confirmed to the people of this land, in proceſs of time, proved a great encouragement to many of the Engliſh to come over and ſettle themſelves in Ireland, where they were to enjoy the ſame laws and liberties, and live under the like conſtitution as they had formerly done in the kingdom of England ‡; which, thro' God's good providence, has proved a means of ſecuring this kingdom to the crown of England, and we truſt will do ſo to all futurity. By this happy conſtitution, and theſe privileges by us for ſo

---

* Coke, 4th Inſt. p. 349. Matt. Paris, anno 1172, p. 105.　　† Ib. 350.
‡ Pryn, on 4th Inſt. p. 287 . Anno 31 Ed. III.
" Rex Juſtic. &c. Cancellar. ſuis Hibern. ſalutem, &c.—Item volumus " & precipimus quod noſtra & ipſius terræ negotia præſertim majora " & ardua in conſiliis perperitos conſiliarios noſtros ac prælatos, & mag- " nates, & quoſdam de diſcretioribus et probrioribus hominibus de par- " tibus vicinis, ubi ipſa conſilia teneri contigerit propter hoc evocandos. " In parliamentis vero, per ipſos conſiliarios noſtros ac prælatos, & pro- " ceres alioſque de terra prædicta prout nos exigit ſecundum juſtitiam, " legem, conſuetu & dinem rationem tractentur, deducantur, & fide· " liter, timore, favore, odio aut pretio, poſt poſitis diſcutiantur & etiam " terminentur."

many

many years enjoyed, the Englifh fubjects of this kingdom have been enabled faithfully to difcharge their duty to the crown of England, and vigoroufly fet themfelves, upon all occafions, to affert the rights thereof, againft all the rebellions which have been raifed by the Irifh enemies. And therefore, we, your Majefty's loyal fubjects, do, with all fubmiffion to your Majefty, *infift* upon them, and hope, through your Majefty's goodnefs, to have them preferved inviolable.

And we beg leave to reprefent to your Majefty, that though the imperial crown of this realm was formerly infeparably annexed to the imperial crown of England, and is now to that of Great-Britain *, yet this kingdom being of itfelf a diftinct dominion, and no part of the kingdom of England, none can determine concerning the affairs thereof, unlefs authorized thereto, by the known laws and cuftoms of this kingdom, or by the exprefs confent of the king †

And as your royal anceftors have always enjoyed the right and power of determining all matters that related only to this kingdom, by their royal authority, in their parliaments held here, fo we humbly hope your Majefty will always look on this right as a moft valuable jewel of your crown, which none fhould prefume to touch without your Majefty's confent ; and that your Majefty will gracioufly allow us to reprefent it, as an invafion of your prerogative, and a grievance to your loyal fubjects in this kingdom, that any court of judicature fhould take upon them to declare, that your Majefty cannot determine all controverfies between your fubjects of this kingdom, and about matters relating wholly to the fame, by your royal authority, in your parliament fummoned to meet here ; or that your fubjects of Ireland appealing to your Majefty in your parliament in Ireland, in matters wholly relating to this kingdom, do bring their caufe before an incompetent judicature.

We have (may it pleafe your facred Majefty) endeavoured with our utmoft care, to enquire into the grounds of all fuch appeals or removals of caufes from this kingdom, as have at any time been made into England, and are perfuaded that fuch ufages have been introduced by flow degrees, at firft the judges here being to determine the caufes that came before them by the common laws of England, and fometimes not knowing well the ufages there, applied to Henry III ‡,

* Anno 2 Eliz. p. 214, c. 5. c. 7. p. 218.
† Coke, 4th Inft. p. 350.
‡ 14th Henry III. ftat. Hibern. made at Weftminfter.

their

their then king, for information, who gave them an account
what the common law and custom of England in like cases
was, and this undoubtedly by the advice of the Justices of
the King's Bench, who then were obliged to attend the
King wherever he should be *; and in process of time, when
his successors had settled the court of King's Bench after
another manner, and had forborne to sit there themselves in
person, the application which formerly used to be made to
the King who presided in that court, came of course to be
brought before the Justices of the court, although the King
was not there personally present. And this, as we conceive,
gave rise to that custom of removing causes, by writs of
error, from the King's Bench in Ireland to the King's Bench
in England; but from hence to infer, that therefore appeals
from the Parliament of Ireland may be brought before the
House of Peers in England or Great-Britain, is a consequence
for which there appears to be no manner of ground.

As for the practice of appealing from the High Court of
Chancery in Ireland to the Lords of Great Britain, we can
find but two precedents of such appeals before the late happy
Revolution, one in 1670, and the other in 1679; and we
can account for them no otherwise than by observing, that
they happened at a juncture when no opposition could be
given them from this kingdom, because through the preva-
lency of a Popish interest, no parliament had been held here
for some years before, nor were we then in any likelihood of
having any called here for many years to come; nor can we
find, that any like subsequent appeals from that court have
any other foundation than those two precedents.

And such appeals (though they had been of longer standing, and better founded) yet were never supposed to preclude
the King's Majesty from his right of giving redress to his subjects of Ireland in his parliament, when assembled here, any
more than writs of error to the King's Bench in England
had hindered the like writs from being returnable in the parliament here.

And accordingly when, by God's blessing on the late happy
Revolution, this kingdom came to have a parliament, after
twenty-six years intermission, complaints were heard, writs of
error and appeals were received, and proper orders were made
thereon as formerly; nor were they, as far as we can find,
ever questioned, or their validity doubted, till the year 1699,
when two appeals from the parliament here were carried be-

* 28th Edward I ch. 5.

fore the Lords in England, though no pleadings to the jurisdiction of the parliament of Ireland had been offered or mentioned by either party, on hearing the said causes here.

And though the parliament of Ireland could not then interpose, or any way assert their jurisdiction, because it was not sitting, yet the Lords of England declared the said causes to be *Coram non Judice*, and without hearing the merits of the causes, reversed the decrees that had been made here.

Upon which occasion, we cannot but observe, that the parliament of Ireland (as the constitution thereof has been for some hundreds of years) being convened by the same authority and writs of summons, and consisting of like members and distinct Houses of Peers and Commons, and the former having the same assistance and attendance from the Judges of the several courts and Masters of Chancery as in England or Great Britain, either some record, act of parliament, or antient usage must be shewn, whereby to make a difference (which has never yet been attempted) or else, from our very constitution it must, as we conceive, appear, that whatever power of judicature is lodged in the English or British parliament, with respect to that kingdom and its inferior courts, the same must also be allowed to be in the parliament of Ireland, with like respect to the kingdom and courts thereof. And if it be looked upon as illegal for any inferior court in Great Britain to act in direct opposition to, or contempt of the orders and decrees of the House of Lords in parliament there assembled, the same must also be concluded upon the like opposition given, or contempt shewn, to such parliamentary orders and decrees, as are or shall be made within this kingdom.

And therefore, in the year 1703, when a parliament of Ireland met on a complaint of Edward, Earl of Meath, and Cecilia, Countess of Meath, his wife, setting forth, that during the interval of parliament they had, by order of the Lords in England, been dispossessed of the lands that had been here decreed them, the said parliament *unanimously* restored the said Earl and Countess to the lands they had been so dispossessed of so effectually, that neither they nor their heirs have been disturbed in the possession of them.

And we may very justly conclude, from the strong resolutions in which the parliament here did on that occasion assert their jurisdiction, that they would have proceeded as effectually in vindicating the decree on the other appeal, if the removal of the Lord Bishop of Derry, the appellant here, and a composition

position made by his succeffor with the Irish fociety of Londonderry, the appellants in England, had not prevented it.

After the time of thofe two appeals, feveral writs of error and appeals were brought into your parliament in this kingdom, and among them an appeal wherein Maurice Annefley, Efq; was refpondent, which were determined, and the judgment given on them took effect accordingly. But the fame Maurice Annefley being refpondent in an appeal brought lately from the Chancery of the Exchequer, before the parliament of Ireland, by Hefter Sherlock, appellant, after having appeared to the jurifdiction here, appealed to the Lords of Great Britain, from a decree made here in juftice to the appellant Hefter Sherlock, and found fuch countenance there, as has given your loyal fubjects juft reafon to complain of much injury done both to your Majefty's prerogative and their privileges.

For it having (after a full and fair hearing) been decreed in your Majefty's parliament of Ireland, and accordingly ordered, that the appellant, Hefter Sherlock, fhould be put into poffeffion of certain lands in the faid order named, until fhe fhould receive thereout a certain fum of money to her decreed, to be due and chargeable on the faid lands. And the faid decree and order having accordingly been obeyed, and put in execution by the then High Sheriff of the county of Kildare, to whom the faid order was directed; and the faid Hefter Sherlock being accordingly in the actual poffeffion of the faid lands, the Lord Chief Baron, together with the other Barons of your Majefty's court of Exchequer in this kingdom, have taken upon them, in an illegal and unprecedented manner, to caufe the faid Hefter Sherlock to be difpoffeffed of the faid lands, and to lay feveral great fines upon the late High Sheriff of the faid county of Kildare, for refufing to give obedience unto the orders of them, the faid Barons, in that cafe iffued, although their faid orders were manifeftly contrary to the laws, cuftoms, and antient ufages, of this your Majefty's kingdom, as well as to the above-mentioned refolutions formerly made in the cafe of the late Earl of Meath, and continuing upon record in the journals of parliament, of which refolutions, as well as of the feveral refolutions and decrees in like manner made upon the appeal of the faid Hefter Sherlock, the faid Barons had fufficient and timely notice before the iffuing of any of their above-mentioned illegal orders, as in a report of this whole proceeding, now alfo entered in the Journals of parliament (a copy whereof of we herewith humbly lay before your Majesty) may more fully and at large appear.

Hereupon we humbly crave leave to represent unto your Majesty, that although appeals from the courts of equity in this kingdom to the Lords of England or Great Britain, are but a very late practice, (as we have already set forth); yet in all such cases, it has been the constant and received practice here, that no copy of any order of the said Lords was ever allowed, or demanded to be allowed, as authentic in any such court, except the same were expresly directed unto the court which was to put the same in execution, and proved by a witness *viva voce*, upon oath, to be a true copy of the original order. Nor does it appear, that any such court ever claimed, or pretended to any authority, to supply any defects supposed at any time to be in any such order, or by virtue of such order in the least to go beyond what expresly and in words was in such order contained. And yet so it is, that although the only pretence of the said Barons for these their illegal proceedings, is grounded upon certain copies of orders, or pretended orders, from the Lords of Great Britain, yet neither were the said orders, or any of them, directed to the Court of Equity or Chancery-side of the Exchequer, (where the cause originally lay, and from whence the appeal was) but only to the Lord Chief Baron and other Barons, which is the stile of the common law-side thereof; nor were the said copies, or any of them, in manner aforesaid proved. to agree with the original orders; neither were the names of any lands, or so much as of any county, inserted in the said copies, or any of them. And yet notwithstanding all these notorious defects and nullities of the said pretended orders, the said Barons have proceeded not only in their own names, to whom the said pretended orders were directed, but also in the names of the Chancellor and Treasurer of the court of Exchequer, (to whom the said orders were no way directed) to issue forth several injunctions and orders, and therein, without any warrant for so doing, to insert the names of lands, and of the county wherein they are supposed to lie, in order to dispossess the said Hester Sherlock of lands whereof she had been put into possession, as is herein above-mentioned.

And that your Majesty may be yet more fully apprised of the arbitrariness as well as the illegality of the proceedings of the said Barons, We further, in all humble manner, lay before your Majesty, that whereas, amongst other rules of practice in all your Majesty's courts throughout this your kingdom, by ancient law and cuſtom eſtabliſhed, it is univerſally received, that every order or other rule of court ought to be made upon the motion of ſome Counſel or Attorney, or other perſon by law or cuſtom allowed to make ſuch motion ; that no injunction or writ, ought to iſſue out of any of your Majeſty's courts, (except in the crown's cauſe) without the name of a Six Clerk or Attorney, thereunto ſubſcribed, who is to be accountable unto every perſon, who through any undue practice of his, ſhall be aggrieved by ſuch writ or injunction), and that no proceedings ſhall be grounded upon any written affidavit, which is known to be either falſe, or defective in any material part thereof, (except ſuch defect be firſt ſupplied or falſity expunged), the ſaid Barons in theſe their proceedings, have acted in open violation of theſe, as well as other rules, which by the law they ought to have obſerved and ſtrictly kept to.    The Barons having ordered an injuction to iſſue for the diſpoſſeſſing of the ſaid Heſter Sherlock, without any motion for the ſame made either by Counſel or Attorney, or by any other perſon, except what was offered in court by the ſaid Lord Chief Baron himſelf; the ſaid injunction, alſo, having no name of any Attorney thereunto affixed or ſubſcribed ; and the affidavit of John Anneſley (upon which the ſaid Barons afterwards proceeded to fine the ſaid late High Sheriff) having ſeveral notorious falſities in it, of which, though the ſaid Barons were publicly advertiſed at the time when the ſaid affidavit was read in open court, yet, they took on them to act thereupon, without cauſing the ſame to be rectified, or the ſaid falſities to be expunged or altered.

And, although the ſaid orders from the Lords in Great Britain expreſsly required no more, but that Maurice Anneſley ſhould be reſtored to the poſſeſſion of thoſe lands, of which the ſaid Maurice was diſpoſſeſſed, pending the appeal before the ſaid houſe ; yet, the ſaid Barons in their ſaid injunction, not only ordered poſſeſſion of certain lands by name, to be given to the ſaid Anneſley, as is already mentioned, but alſo, grounded this their injunction upon an affidavit, wherein it is not ſo much as alledged that the ſaid Maurice was at all poſſeſſed or diſpoſſeſſed of any lands whatſoever pending the ſaid appeal.

And whereas it is the duty of the Barons of your Majeſty's Court of Exchequer in this kingdom, and a part of the oath by each of them taken at their entrance upon their ſaid office, " That where they may know any wrong or prejudice to be " done to the King, they ſhall put and do all their diligence

" that

" that to redress.  And if they may not do it, they shall
" tell it to the king, or them of his council, or to the King's
" Majesty's Lieutenant, or other Chief Governor or Gover-
" nors of this Realm for the time being."  So far have the
said Barons in the present case been from doing all their diligence to redress the wrong or prejudice done to your Majesty's prerogative, of finally determining in your parliament
here, matters relating wholly to this your kingdom, that
they seem to have acted with great diligence and zeal in direct
opposition thereto, and to have taken such measures as will,
in effect, establish a jurisdiction superior to that which your
Majesty undoubtedly has in your High Court of Parliament
in this kingdom ; nor does it in the least appear, or is it at all
pretended, that the said Barons, or any of them, during all
the abovementioned proceedings, did ever tell, or make known
the same, either to your Majesty's Lieutenant, or other Chief
Governor or Governors, or to your Majesty's Privy Council,
who, if they had been timely acquainted therewith, might
(according to their duty) have made the same known to your
Majesty, or otherwise have done what was fit and proper for
the supporting your Majesty's royal prerogative, and defending the just rights and privileges of this your Parliament and
People.

And here we beg leave to lay before your Majesty some of
the many evil consequences which we apprehend must necel-
farily follow from such exorbitant practices as these, if a timely,
and effectual stop be not put to them.

It is the right and happiness of the subjects of this kingdom, as well as of those of Great Britain, that by their refpective constitutions, the administration of justice is near at
hand, and within the kingdom whereunto they belong.  So
that if any of your Majesty's liege people are at any time
wronged or oppressed in any of the courts of law or equity,
they may, without any great trouble or expence, have recourse
to your Majesty, in your high Court of Parliament, where
they may assure themselves of speedy redress.  But if this
your Majesty's Highest Court within this kingdom is deprived
of the power of finally determining the causes which come
before them, all such of your subjects as do not abound in
wealth, and thereby are not able to follow their causes, or
bear the expence of them in Great Britain, will be under a
perpetual necessity of sitting down with the greatest wrong or
oppression which at any time, under the colour of justice, or
by the management of rich and potent adversaries may be
said upon them, which (considering the poverty that every

where prevails throughout this kingdom) muſt, if not prevented in a ſhort time, become a moſt grievous and intolerable evil. And your Majeſty's royal predeceſſor, Edward the
III. was ſo ſenſible of the hardſhips that his loyal ſubjeĉts of
this kingdom ſuffered for want of having a means of rever-
ſing erroneous judgments within this kingdom, that by his
Charter, dated Auguſt 30th, in the 29th year of his reign,
on the complaint of his ſubjeĉts of Ireland, " he command-
" ed all his Judges and Miniſters before whom any proceſſes
" ſhould be held at the proſecution of the parties aggrieved,
" to return the Rolls of the Records, and proceſſes into the
" Parliaments to be held in the kingdom of Ireland, and
" that the Records and Proceſſes ſhould be recited and
" examined, and the errors (if any ſhould be found in them)
" duly correĉted. *

It is, under God, the great ſecurity of this your Majeſty's
kingdom of Ireland, that by the laws and ſtatutes thereof,
the ſame is annexed and united to the Imperial Crown of
England, and declared to be depending upon, and for ever

---

* Pryn, on 4th Inſt. pag. 286. Anno 29 Edw. III. " Edwardus Dei
" gratia, &c. Ex parte non nullorum fidelium noſtrorum communitatis
" terræ noſtræ Hiberniæ: nobis eſt graviter conquerendo monſtratum
" ut cum ipſi damna & gravamina quam plurima a magno tempore ſuſ-
" tinuerint ex hoc; et etiam ex hoc, quod errores qui in Recordis &
" Proceſſibus placitorum nec in Parliamentis in eadem terra corrigi
" nequeunt, nec alias juſtitia inde fieri ſine remedia in Anglia quærendo
" propter quod quidem propter labores & expenſas circa præmiſſa appoſi-
" tas ad maximum miſeriam & inopiam deducuntur; & quidam omnino
" ex hæredati exiſtunt, per quod pro quiete & indemnitate populi noſtri
" in terra prediĉta, ſub noſtro regimine exiſtentis cui in exhibitione
" juſtitiæ ſumus debitores: Ordinamus quod, &c. et quod ad proſecutio-
" nem omnium & ſingulorum qui conqueri voluerint errores in Recordis
" & Proceſſibus coram aliquibus juſtic. ſeu aliis miniſtris prædiĉtis habiti
" interveniſſe Rotuli eorundem Recordorum & Proceſſuum in Parliamen-
" tis noſtris in eadem terra tenend. per juſtic. ſeu miniſtros coram quibus
" Rocorda & Proceſſus illa fuerint deferantur & ibidem eadem Recorda
" & Proceſſus diligentur recitenter & examinentur; & errores, ſi quos
" in eiſdem inveniri contigerit debite corrigantur; & ideo vobis manda-
" mus quod ordinationem prædiĉtam in terra noſtra prædiĉta teneri &
" partibus conquerentibus plenam & celerem juſtitiam fieri fac. in forma
" prædiĉta quibuſcunque mandatis vobis aut aliis in terra prædiĉta ante
" hæc tempora in contrarium direĉtis non obſtantibus ita quod aliquis
" materiam non habeat nobis pro defeĉtu juſtitiæ ſuper caſibus prædiĉtis
" de cætero conquerendi. Teſte apud Weſtminſter, 30 die Auguſti."

It appears from the latter end of this Record, that the original power
of Parliaments in Ireland, ſettled by King Henry the Second, (as is
above ſet forth) had afterwards been reſtrained, as to writs of error, by
ſome ſubſequent Mandates of the Kings of England, which Mandates
are hereby recalled and made void.

belonging

belonging to the fame : but if all judgments, decrees, and determinations made in this your Majefty's High Court, within this your kingdom, are fubject to be nulled and reverfed by the Lords in Great Britain, the liberties and properties of all your fubjects of Ireland muft thereby become finally dependant on the Britifh Peers, to the great diminution of that dependence, which by law we always ought to have immediately upon the Crown itfelf.

That your Majefty has, by the conflitution of this your realm of Ireland, the full power of judging and determining all caufes that belong to it alone in Pleno Parliamento, is what no man hitherto has ventured openly to deny or doubt of.

But if in all cafes that relate to this kingdom, the *dernier refort*, (as fome of late have affected to fpeak) ought to be to the Houfe of Lords in Great Britain, however this your Majefty's power may ftill in words be acknowledged, the force and effect of it is in reality taken away and wholly vefted in the Britifh Peers.

And we cannot but obferve, with the utmoft concern, that by this practice of the Peers of Great Britain, juft and unjuft caufes will meet with equal encouragement. For however rightly fuch caufes may be determined in Parliament here, the decrees will be annulled and reverfed by the Peers of Great Britain, without hearing or entering into the merits of the caufe, upon pretence that the proceedings were *Coram non Judice*.

The writs for fummoning the Lords fpiritual and temporal, and electing the Commons to affemble in parliament here, being the very fame with thofe in England or Great-Britain, as has been before obferved, either the refpective powers in each kingdom muft ftill be the fame, or elfe the Peerage of this your Majefty's kingdom muft remain little more than an empty title, and the Commons thereof ftand for ever deprived of that moft valuable privilege of impeaching in parliament, which cannot poffibly be maintained if there be no fuch thing as a parliamentary judicature within this realm ; *and if the power of the judicature may, by a vote of the Britifh Lords, be taken away from the Parliament of Ireland, no reafon can be given why the fame may not, in like manner, deprive us of the benefit of our whole conflitution.*

It is notorious, that the Lords of Great Britain have not, in themfelves, either by law or cuftom, any way of putting their decrees in execution within this kingdom, of which they

P                                                    have

have given moſt undoubted evidence by their late application
to your Majeſty, to cauſe ſuch their decrees to be executed by
an extraordinary interpoſition of your royal power.   And
ſhould your Majeſty think fit to yield to this their deſire, we
humbly preſume to think it would highly affect the liberty of
your Majeſty's loyal ſubjects of this kingdom.

In order to prevent the appellant, Heſter Sherlock, above-
mentioned, from making any further application to your Parliament here, your Majeſty's Deputy-receiver, John Pratt,
Eſq; thought fit to pay above £1800 to the ſaid Heſter Sherlock, which, on examination, he alleged to be his own money ; and that he made an agreement with the ſaid Heſter,
of himſelf, without any order from any perſon whatſoever ;
but that from ſome converſation which he had with perſons
of judgment, he thought he had reaſon to hope and expect,
that ſince what he had done was for the public good, the government would not permit him to be a ſufferer.   What particular grounds the ſaid John Pratt had thus to hope and
expect, has not as yet been made known to us.   But if ſuch
hopes and expectations as theſe are from time to time to be
ſatisfied, we leave your Majeſty, in your royal wiſdom, to
judge what the evil conſequences thereof may be.

And we farther humbly repreſent to your Majeſty, that
theſe proceedings of the Lords of England have greatly em-
baraſſed your Parliament, and diſquieted the generality of
your moſt loyal Proteſtant ſubjects of this your kingdom, and
muſt, of neceſſity, bring all ſheriffs and officers of juſtice
under great hardſhips, by reaſon of the claſhing of different
juriſdictions.   Nor can we but with grief obſerve, that whilſt
many of the Peers and commons who ſat in Parliament were
Papiſts, their judicature was never queſtioned ; but of late,
ſince only Proteſtants are qualified to have a ſhare in the ligiſ-
lature, their power, and the right of hearing cauſes in Parliament, hath been denied, to the great diſcouragement and
weakening of the Proteſtant intereſt in Ireland.

And having thus, with all humility, laid before your Majeſty your undoubted power and prerogative within this your
kingdom of Ireland, the immediate dependence of the ſame
upon your Majeſty's crown, the right your Majeſty has to
hold Parliaments here, as in Great-Britain, and of finally determining therein all matters that wholly relate to this realm,
together with the great incroachments that of late have been
made upon your Majeſty's prerogative, and the rights of this
your Parliament, and the illegal unprecedented proceedings
                                                         of

of the Lord Chief Baron, and the other Barons of your Majefty's Court of Exchequer, whereby they have endeavoured to fupport thofe encroachments with the evil confequences of fuch proceedings, in cafe that a fpeedy and effectual ftop be not thereunto put. We moft humbly hope, that all thefe things being duly confidered and weighed with your Majefty's ufual wifdom, will abundantly juftify us in the methods we have taken, as well for the fupporting of your Majefty's royal prerogative, as the prefervation of the juft rights and liberties of ourfelves and our fellow fubjects, as the fame are fet forth in the feveral refolutions we have come to, (a copy whereof we have hereunto annexed,) with all humility affuring your Majefty, that no difficulties which we may be laid under, fhall hinder us from giving the utmoft difpatch to all your Majefty's affairs, or from moft chearfully demonftrating that loyalty and affection to your Majefty's perfon, and attachment to your intereft, which becomes your Majefty's dutiful and obedient fubjects, whereof we again, from our hearts, make an humble tender to your moft facred Majefty.

Refolved, That a committee be appointed to draw up an humble Addrefs to his Grace the Lord Lieutenant, to defire his Grace to lay the faid Reprefentation before his Majefty, in the beft and moft effectual manner.

The Declaratory Act of the 6th of George I. was formed in confequence of thefe appeals, which ftatute exprefsly declares, "That the kingdom of Ireland hath been, is, and of right ought to be, fubordinate unto and dependent upon the imperial crown of Great Britain, as being infeparately united and annexed thereunto, and that the King, with the confent of the Lords and Commons of Great Britain in parliament affembled, hath power to make laws of fufficient force to bind the kingdom and people of Ireland.

" And that the Houfe of Lords of Ireland have not, nor ought of right to have, any jurifdiction to judge of, affirm, or reverfe any judgment or decree made in any court within the faid kingdom; and that all proceedings before the faid Houfe of Lords upon any fuch judgment or decree, are void."

It is prefumed that no political cafuift, after a view of the foregoing pages, will affect to talk of England's title to Ireland by *conqueft.*

The titles of the Kings of England to this kingdom appear to have been very precarious, even to Henry VIII. as the very act which conftitutes him King of Ireland, exprefsly

prefsly fays " That the Irifhmen and inhabitants of this realm of Ireland, have not bene fo obedient to the Kings highneffe and his moft noble progenitors, and to their lawes, as they of right and according to their allegeance and bounden duties ought to have been*. Wherefore at the humble purfuit, &c." Befides, what are all the papers in Bermingham and London Tower, but attempts to footh, foften, bribe and tame, by indulgence and art, the fpirit of Irifh independence? What parties, divifions, hatred, and animofities among the clergy! fometimes acknowledging the power of the King, fometimes the Pope's, and at others difavowing both! one time fomenting infurrections, and at others attempting to quell them. Pryn has preferved us a number of thefe tranfactions †, horrid picture of ecclefiaftical tyranny, from which we are now, thank heaven, happily delivered! horrid picture of the minifters of that gofpel, *which preaches peace on earth, and good will to all men!* pious minifters, indeed! whofe feet, inftead of being fhod with the preparation of the gofpel of peace, were rather fwift to fhed blood!

Richard II. in perfon invaded this kingdom, for the purpofe of fubjugating it: Howes gives us the number of his forces, and the lines following their fate.

Richard was at length prevailed on to march againft the enemy commanded by Art Mac-Murchad, who, notwithftanding the penfions he had received, and the fubmiffions he had lately made, was ftill the inveterate enemy of the Englifh; and in the violence of national pride, enflamed by the

---

* The following anecdote fhews the high ideas entertained by the Irifh dynafts, of their own independence and dignity.

' Mac-Gillipatrick, the Irifh chieftain of Offory, had received fome injury from the earl of Ormond, or at leaft found fome pretence of complaint againft the prefent deputy, better known among the Irifh by the name of *Piers the Red*. In all the dignity of offended grandeur, he determined to apply to the king of England for redrefs; but not with the humility of a fupplicant or a fubject. His ambaffador was fent to the court of England to obtain juftice, or elfe to denounce the vengeance of an injured potentate. He appeared at the chapel door, when the king was going to his devotions, and advancing with a compofed undifmayed gravity of deportment, delivered his commiffion in thefe words—" Sta " pedibus! Domine Rex! Dominus meus Gillapatricius me mifit ad te " juffit dicere, quod fi non vis caftigare Petrum Rufum, ipfe faciet bel- " lum contra te." Stand on your feet! lord King! my lord Gillipatrick has fent me to tell you, that if you do not chaftife Peter Rufus, he himfelf will make war againft you.

† II Vol. Eccl. Jur. p. 372, 373, 378, 382, 393, 397, 422, 423, 458, 474, 475, 480, 481, 482, 559, 603, 616, 632, 633, 634, 635, 690, 719, 735, 756, 768, 784, 807, 808, 810, 827, 828, 857, 858, 859, 957, 939, 956, 990, &c. &c.

prospect of success, vowed the most desperate vengeance against his invaders.  To secure himself from the superiour numbers of the enemy he retired to his woods; and at their approach, appeared at the head of three thousand men so well armed and appointed, and with such an appearance of determined valour, as were perfectly astonishing to the English, who had been taught to despise their rude and undisciplined violence.  The royal army was drawn out in order of battle, expecting a vigorous attack ; but the Irish forces, who thought of nothing less than a regular engagement in the field, suddenly disappeared ; and Richard, elevated by this retreat, ordered the adjacent villages and houses to be set on fire, and the royal standard to be advanced, under which he created several knights, and among these the young Lord Henry the fifth, who on this occasion gave the first proofs of his distinguished valour.

To facilitate the pursuit of an enemy who appeared to fly, a large body of peasants was employed to open a passage through the woods, which the Irish had by every means endeavoured to render impassable.  As the king's army marched through all the difficulties of an encumbred road, perpetually impeded, and sometimes plunged into deep and dangerous morasses, the enemy frequently assailed them with loud and barbarous ululations; cast their darts with such force as no armour could withstand, slaughtered their detached parties, retired, and advanced with astonishing agility, so as continually to annoy and harrass the English forces, though they could not be brought to a general engagement.  Some of the Irish lords, less penetrating than their subtile chieftain, and among those his uncle, were indeed terrified by the numbers of the king's forces, and with all the marks of humiliation submitted to Richard.  They appeared before him with halters round their necks, fell at his feet, imploring peace and forgiveness, and were graciously received.  Art Mac-Murchad was summoned to make the like submissions ; and, to prevail upon him to accept of grace, and return to his allegiance, Richard was weak enough to promise large rewards, territories, and castles in Leinster.  The Irishman, who well knew the difficulties to which the King's army was reduced, and the impossibility of their subsisting for any time in their present situation, returned a haughty answer of defiance, and declared his resolution of opposing the King of England to the utmost.  Richard had the mortification to find, that the distress of his soldiery, which had encouraged the adversary to this insolence,

could

could no longer be concealed, and every day grew more intolerable. Numbers of his men perished by famine; their horses, from want and severity, grew incapable of service; a general gloom spread through his camp, and his braveſt Knights murmured at their fate, who were to perish in a service attended with so little honour, and such severe diſtress. A few ships laden with proviſions from Dublin having landed on the neighbouring coaſt, the famiſhed soldiers plunged into the sea, seized and rifled them, ſhedding each others blood in a furious conteſt for relief. The neceſſity of decamping was too apparent, and too urgent to admit of the leaſt delay. Richard, with his numerous forces, was compelled to retire before an inconſiderable band of enemies whom he had deſpiſed, who purſued, and inceſſantly harraſſed him in his retreat *.

It is univerſally acknowledged, that no prince ever brought into this kingdom such an army as Richard, II. for reducing it, and we ſee he did not ſucceed therein †.

After reading this account, I know not how it can be said that the Iriſh chieftains ſubmitted to Henry II. ‡ through fear, an affection they appear not to be much influenced by; the moſt probable cauſes for this tranſaction was pride, malice, and, above all, the hopes of revenging public and private inſults, or ſuppoſed inſults, to the impreſſions of which they were exceedingly ſuſceptible; to this aſſertion the following letter and anſwer, which paſſed in the 14th century, authenticated by Cox, will bear no inconſiderable teſtimony.

O'Nial to O'Donnell.

" Pay me your tribute, or if you don't"——

O'NIAL.

O'Donnell to O'Nial.

" I owe you no tribute, and if I did"——

O'DONNELL.

The ſtrength of the kingdom thus divided at firſt, became an eaſy prey to every invader.

---

* Story of Richard II. his laſt being in Ireland. By the Earl of Tothneſs.

† It is not in memory, that ever any king of England made ſuch proviſion for any journey into Ireland, nor ſuch a number of men of arms nor archers.     Howes.

‡ Henry II. brought with him into this kingdom a train of 500 Knights, the Kings of the land, &c. of *their own good wills*, without any war or chivalry, ſubmitted and took oaths of fidelity to him.

Parliam. debates, vol. 7, p. 274, &c.

To

To this cause was owing the first invasion of Greece by Darius with a numerous and mighty army, the destruction of which, by the few intrepid troops of the Athenians, will ever be remembered.

The following are the three principal charges brought against the earl of Strafford by Mr. St. John, which plainly shew that he did not consider Ireland as a *conquered nation.*

1. There at Dublyn, the principal city of that kingdome whither the subjects of that country came for justice, in an assembly of Peeres and others of greatest ranke, upon occasion of a speech of the Recorder of that city thouching their Franchises and legal rights, he tels them, that *Ireland was a conquered nation, and that the king might do with them what he pleased.*

2. Not long after, in the *parliament* 10 *Car.* in the chaire of state, in full parliament againe, That *they were a conquered nation, and that they were to expect laws as from a conqueror ; before the King might do with them what he would ; now, they were to expect it, that he would put this power of a conqueror in execution.*

3. Upon like occasion of pressing the lawes and statutes, that he would make *an act of counsell board in that kingdom binding as an act of parliament.*

My Lords, continued he, I have done with the three treasons within the stat. of 25 Ed. III.

◆▶◆▶◆◀◆▶◆▶◆◀◆◀◆◀◆◀◆▶◆◀

From a perusal of the collections of Pryn *, Rymer, &c. it will plainly appear that the Monarchs of England paid every attention to the welfare of their subjects in this kingdom till Char. time. Henry II. we see gave them a *Modus tenendi Parliamenta,* in the same terms with that of England, and considering it as a *distinct kingdom,* settled it on his son John for an appenage, who confirmed to the Irish, by charter, his father's grant of the *Common Law* of England, and a free parliament with immunities to the city of Dublin †, and Waterford ‡, even beyond those of London, which Henry VI farther confirmed. Henry III. granted us a Magna Charta.

In the fifth of Edward I. the English laws were confirmed to the Irish §.

* Animad. p. 7, 11, 50, 59, 60, 111, 120, 12`, 123, 127, 143, 415, 146, 160, 229, 248 250, 254 to 327, 408 to 414. See also index to 4 Inst. under Ireland.

† Charta Johanni regis Angl. et dom. Hibern. civib. Dub. facta 30 die Julii reg. 17. Ex lib nig. eccl. S. Trin. Dub. A. D. 1214.

‡ Pat. 9, Hen. VI. No. 7.

§ De legibus Anglicanis Hibernis concedendis ex bundella literarum in Turr. Lond. Pryn, tom. 3, p. 1218.

The ſtatutes of force in England, which, in the time of Edward II. were referred to be examined in the next parlia-, ment, ſo many as were then allowed and publiſhed to ſtand likewiſe for laws in this kingdom *.

Edward III. ordained that the affairs of the land (Ireland) eſpecially the weightieſt, ſhould be handled, diſcuſſed, and determined by the Prelates, Nobles, and other diſcreet men of the King's Council there; and by his Council, Prelates, and others in parliaments according to juſtice, law, cuſtom, reaſon, &c †.

Richard III. on uſurping the Engliſh crown, expreſſed theſe words : " From this moment, I take upon me the govern-" ment of the two kingdoms of *England* and *France;* the " former to be governed and defended; and the latter, by " God's help, and my peoples' aſſiſtance, to be ſubdued." That he in no wiſe conſidered Ireland as annexed to that crown, which certainly at this time was a ſeparate and diſtinct nation, wherein the ſtate of *England* had not leiſure or abilities to bring about a reformation, till their own civil diſſentions were appeaſed.

The Declaratory Act in the reign of Henry IV. expreſsly ſays, " That Engliſh ſtatutes bind not, unleſs retracted here ‡," and the ſimilar one of Henry VI. ſpeaks its attention to this great object; in the 18 of Henry VI. ceſſing of horſe or foot upon the King's ſubjects here is made treaſon; even the act of Poyning in the time was intended as ſalutary to the ſubject, as may appear from the following copy of it.

An act that no Parliament be holden in this land, until the acts be certified into England.

Item, At the requeſt of the Commons of the land of Ire-land, be it ordained, enacted and eſtabliſhed, That at the next parliament that there ſhall be holden by the king's command-ment and licence, wherein amongſt other the king's grace en-tendeth to have a general reſumption of his whole revenues ſith the laſt day of the reign of King Edward II. no parlia-ment hereafter be holden in the ſaid land but at ſuch ſeaſon as the king's lieutenant and counſaile there firſt do certifie the king under the great ſeale of that lande the cauſes and con-ſiderations, and all ſuch acts as to them ſeemeth ſhould paſs in the ſame parliament, and ſuch cauſes, conſiderations and acts

* See marginal note of Sir Richard Bolton, in his edit. of the Iriſh ſtatutes. See alſo, Pryn 264, 265, 266. An. 20, Edw. 2.

† Pat. ſtat. 31 Edw. III. m. 11, 12, exemplified likewiſe in Pat. 17, R. 2, m. 34. See likewiſe Rylye's appendix, p. 582, &c. Pryn 287.

‡ See p. lxxxvii of theſe Facts.

affirmed

affirmed by the king and his counfaile to be good *and expedient for that land*, and his licenfe thereupon, as well in affirmation of the faid caufes and acts, as to fummon the faid parliament under his great feal of England had and obtained, that done, a parliament to be had and holden after the form and effect afore rehearfed, and if any parliament be holden in that land hereafter, contrary to the form and provifion aforefaid, it be deemed void and of none effect in Law.

Ir. Stat. 28 H. 8. cap. 4 & 20. 11 El. cap. 1 and 8.

In the Irifh act paffed 28 Henry VIII. it is fully afferted, and enacted, " That the faid *Englifh* act, and every thing and
" things therein contained, fhall be eftablifhed, affirmed, taken,
" obeyed, and accepted within this land of *Ireland*, as good
" and perfect law, and fhall be within the faid land of the
" fame force, effect, quality, condition, ftrength and virtue
" to all purpofes and intents, as it is within the realm of
" *England*, and that all fubjects and refidents within this faid
" land of *Ireland*, fhall obferve, keep, obey, accomplifh and
" execute the effects and contents fpecified in the faid *Englifh*
" act, and fhall have and enjoy the profit and commodity of
" the fame; as the *Englifh* fubjects are thereby bound, or in-
" tituled, &c."

Notwithftanding that it is allowed, that there were a few Englifh ftatutes reftraining our commerce before 1663 *, yet they appear to have been fo little felt, that our commercial reftriction may properly be faid to have commenced at the foregoing period, when an Englifh act was formed to prevent exportation from Ireland to the Englifh Colonies, and in 1670, another act was made to prevent importation from thence.

Let the hiftories of both kingdoms †, and the ftatute-books of both parliaments be examined, and no precedent will be found for the act of 1699 ‡, or for the fyftem which it intro-duced.

The whole tenor of the Englifh ftatutes relative to the trade of this country, and which by our act of the 10th of Henry VII. became a part of our commercial conftitution, breath a fpirit totally repugnant to the principle of that law, and it

---

* Stat. Hib. 14 Hen. III. Ordin. Irifh ftat. Hib. 17 Edw. I. 2 Hen. VI, &c.
† Commer. Reftr.
‡ When the act paffed in England reftraining the exportation of all woollen manufactures from Ireland, which was then the fource of in-duftry in that kingdom, and the difcouragement of them, the principal caufe of her diftrefs, the encouragement of the linen manufacture was not an equivalent at this time, and if it was, has long fince ceafed to be fo.

is

is therefore with the utmoſt deference ſubmitted to thoſe who have the power to decide, whether this law was agreeable to the commercial conſtitution of Ireland, which for 500 years has never produced a ſimilar inſtance.

It might be naturally ſuppoſed, by a perſon not verſed in our ſtory, that in the ſeventeenth century * there had been ſome offence given, or ſome demerit on our part. He would be ſurprized to hear, that during this period our loyalty had been exemplary, and our ſufferings on that account great. In 1641, great numbers of the proteſtants of Ireland were deſtroyed, and many of them were deprived of their property, and driven out of their country from their attachment

* 6 Geo. I. cap. 21. ſect. 49. If any tobacco entered out for foreign parts and exported, ſhall afterwards be landed in *Ireland*, the ſame and double the drawback ſhall be forfeited, and every debenture for the drawback ſhall become void, as if the tobacco were relanded in *Great Britain ;* which forfeitures may be recovered in any of the courts of record of *Weſtminſter* or *Dublin*, or in the Exchequer of *Scotland*.

Brit. ſtat. 5 Geo. I. No wrought ſilks, Bengals, ſtuffs mixed with ſilk and herba, or muſlins or other callicoes, of the manufacture of *Perſia*, *China*, or *Eaſt India*, ſhall be imported into *Ireland*, from any place other than *Great Britain*, on forfeiture of the goods or value thereof, as alſo of the ſhip, with all her guns and tackle, &c. &c.

Brit. ſtat. 6 Geo. I. cap. 21. § 52. Where any ſhip or veſſel of the burthen of fifty tons or under, laden with cuſtomable or prohibited goods, ſhall be found at anchor, or hovering on the coaſts of Ireland, within two leagues of the ſhore, and not proceeding on her voyage (wind and weather permitting), it ſhall be lawful for any Officer of his Majeſty's cuſtoms of that kingdom, to go on board every ſuch ſhip, &c.——The *Britiſh* parliament regulating his Majeſty's cuſtoms in *Ireland !* It is but a ſtep, one ſmall ſtep, from the regulation of revenue to the impoſition of taxes.——See the remainder of that ſection, and alſo the following one. The ſtat. 11 & 12 W. III. cap. 7 ; 4 Geo. I. cap. 11. § 7 ; and 8 Geo. I. cap. 24. for the puniſhment of piracies.——And 2 Geo. II. cap. 28. 19 Geo. II. cap. 12. ſect. 23. no perſon ſhall import into *Ireland* any crown glaſs, flint, or white glaſs ; or any common bottles, or other green glaſs ; or glaſs of any kind or denomination, other than the manufacture of *Great Britain*. And if any kind of glaſs, other than the manufacture of *Great Britain*, ſhall be landed out of any veſſel in *Ireland*, it ſhall be forfeited and deſtroyed within ten days after condemnation thereof ; and the veſſel alſo, with her tackle and furniture, &c. ſhall be forfeited ; and the maſter of the veſſel, and every other perſon concerned in importing or landing the ſame, ſhall forfeit ten ſhillings for every pound weight thereof, and ſo in proportion for any quantity.

7 Geo. II. cap. 19. If any foreign hops, other than of *Britiſh* growth, ſhall be landed in *Ireland*, all ſuch hops ſhall be forfeited and burnt within ten days after the ſame ſhall be lawfully condemned ; and the perſons concerned in importing of the ſame, or that ſhall have aſſiſted in landing the ſame, ſhall forfeit five ſhillings for every pound weight thereof.

to

to the English government in this kingdom, and to that religion and constitution which they happily enjoyed under it. At the Revolution they were constant in the same principles, and successfully staked their lives and properties against domestic and foreign enemies, in support of the rights of the English crown, and of the religious and civil liberties of Britain and of Ireland. They bravely shared with her in all her dangers, and liberally partook of all her adversities. Whatever were their rights, they had forfeited none of them. Whatever favours they enjoyed, they had new claims, from their merit and their sufferings, to a continuance of them. They now wanted more than ever the care of that fostering hand, which by rescuing them twice from oppression (obligations never to be forgotten by the protestants of Ireland) established the liberties, confirmed the strength, and raised the glory of the British Empire.

Besides our exclusion from foreign markets, England had two objects in the discouragement of our woollen trade.

It was intended that Ireland should send her wool to England, and take from that country her woollen manufactures *. It has been already shewn that the first object has not been attained; the second has been carried so far as, for the future, to defeat its own purpose. Whilst our own manufacturers were starving for want of employment, and our wool sold for less than one half of its usual price, we have imported from England in the years 1777 and 1778 woollen goods to the enormous amount of 715,740l. 13s. od. as valued at our custom-house, and of the manufactures of linen, cotton and silk mixed, to the amount of 98,086l. 1s. 11d. making in the whole in those two years of distress 813,826l. 14s. 11d. Between 20 and 30,000 of our manufacturers in those branches were, in those two years, supported by public charity. From this fact it is hoped, that every reasonable man will allow the necessity of using our own manufactures. Agreements

---

* The commissioners of trade, in their representation, dated the 11th of November, 1697, relating to the trade between England and Ireland, advise a duty to be laid upon the importation of oil, upon teasles, whether imported or *growing* there, and upon *all the utensils* employed in the making any woollen manufactures; on the utensils of worsted-combers, and particularly a duty by the yard upon all cloth and woollen stuffs, except frizes, before they are taken off the loom. Eng. Com. Journ. 12 v. 428.

among

among our people for this purpofe are not, as it has been fuppofed, a new idea in this country.   It was never fo univerfal
as at prefent; but has been frequently reforted to in times of
diftrefs. . In the feſſions of 1703, 1705 and 1707 \*, the
Houſe of Commons refolved unanimoufly, That it would
greatly conduce to the relief of the poor and the good of
the kingdom ; that the inhabitants thereof fhould ufe none
other but the manufactures of this kingdom in their apparel
and the furniture of their houfes; and in the laft of thofe
feſſions the members engaged their honours to each other,
that they would conform to the faid refolution.   The not importing goods from England, is one of the remedies recommended by the council of trade in 1676, for alleviating fome
diftrefs that was felt at that time † ; and Sir William Temple,
a zealous friend to the trade and manufactures of England,
recommends to Lord Effex, then Lord Lieutenant, " to in-
" troduce, as far as can be, a vein of parfimony throughout
" the country, in all things that are not perfectly the native
" growths and manufactures ‡."

The Englifh law ‖ of 1663, reftraining the exportation
from Ireland to America, was at that time, and for fome
years after, fcarcely felt in this kingdom, which had then
little to export, except live cattle; not proper for fo diftant a
market.

The act of fettlement paffed in Ireland the year before this
reftrictive law, and the explanatory ftatute for the fettlement
of this kingdom, was not enacted until two years after.   The
country continued for a confiderable time in a ftate of litiga-
tion, which is never favourable to induftry.   In 1661 the people muft have been poor ; the number of them of all degrees,
who paid poll money in that year was about 360,000 §.   In
1672, when the country had greatly improved, the manufacture beftowed upon a year's exportation from Ireland, did not
exceed eight thoufand pounds \*\*, and the clothing trade had
not then arrived to what it had been before the laft rebellion.
But ftill the kingdom had much increafed in wealth, tho' not
in manufactured exports.   The cuftoms which fet in 1656
for 12,000l. yearly, were in 1672 worth 80,000l. †† yearly,
and the improvement in domeftic wealth, that is to fay, in

---

\* Com. Journ. 3 vol. 348, 548.
† Sir W. Petty's Political Survey, 312.
‡ Sir W. Temple, 3 v. 11.
‖ Ib. 9. and 110.        § Sir W. Petty, p. 9.
\*\* 15 Ch. II.              †† Ib. 89.

building, planting, furniture, coaches, &c. is said to have advanced from 1652 to 1673 in a proportion of from one to four, Sir William Petty in the year 1672 complains not of the reſtraints on the exportation from Ireland to America *, but of the prohibition of exporting our cattle to England, and of our being obliged to unlade in that kingdom † the ſhips bound from America to Ireland ; the latter regulation he conſiders as highly prejudicial to this country.

The immediate object of Ireland at this time, ſeems to have been to get materials to employ her people at home without thinking of foreign exportations. When we advanced in the export of our woollen goods, the law of 1663 ‡, which excluded them from the American markets, muſt have been a great loſs to this kingdom; and after we were allowed to export our linens to the Britiſh colonies in America, the reſtraints impoſed by the law of 1670 upon our importations from thence became more prejudicial, and will be much more ſo if ever the late extenſion of our exports to America ſhould, under thoſe reſtraints, have any effect ; for it is certainly a great diſcouragement to the carrying on trade with any country, where we are allowed only to ſell our manufactures and produce, but are not permitted to carry from them directly to our own country their principal manufactures or produce. The people to whom we are thus permitted to ſell, want the principal inducement for dealing with us, and the great ſpring of commerce, which is mutual exchange, is wanting between us.

As the Britiſh legiſlature has thought it reaſonable to extend, in a very conſiderable degree, our exportation to their colonies, and has doubtleſs intended that this favour ſhould be uſeful to Ireland, it is hoped that thoſe reſtraints on the importation from thence, which muſt render that favour of little effect, will be no longer continued.

From thoſe conſiderations it is evident, that many ſtrong reaſons reſpecting Ireland are now to be found againſt the continuance of thoſe reſtrictive laws of 1663 and 1670, that did not exiſt at the time of making them.

' Ireland was by thoſe laws excluded from almoſt all the trade of three quarters of the globe, and from all direct beneficial intercourſe with her fellow-ſubjects in thoſe countries, which were partly ſtocked from her own loins. But ſtill, though deprived at that time of the benefit of thoſe colonies,

---

* Sir W. Petty, p. 9 and 10.  † Ib. 34, 71, 125.  ‡ 15 Ch. II. ch. 7,

the

fhe was not then confidered as a colony herfelf; her manufacturers were not in any other manner difcouraged, her ports
were left open, and fhe was at liberty to look for a market
among ftrangers, though not among her fellow-fubjects in
Afia, Africa or America*.

By the proceedings in the Englifh parliament in the year
1698, and the fpeech of the Lords Juftices to the Irifh parliament in that year it appears, that the linen was intended to
be given to this country as an equivalent for the woollen manufacture. The opinion that this fuppofed equivalent was
accepted of as fuch by Ireland is miftaken. The tempera-
ment, which the commons of Ireland in their addrefs faid
they hoped to find, was no more than a partial and a temporary duty on the exportation, as an experiment only, and not
as an eftablifhed fyftem, referving the exportation of frize,
then much the moft valuable part to Ireland †. The Englifh
intended the linen manufacture as a compenfation, and declared they thought it would be much more advantageous to
Ireland ‡ than the woollen trade.

This idea of an equivalent has led feveral perfons, and
among the reft two very able writers §, into miftakes, from
the want of information in fome facts which are neceffary to
be known, that this tranfaction may be fully underftood, and
therefore ought to be particularly ftated.

The Irifh had before this period applied themfelves to the
linen trade. This appears by two of their ftatutes, in the
reign of Elizabeth, one laying a duty on the export of flax
and linen yarn ‖, and the other, making it felony to fhip

---

* Sir William Petty mentions that " the Englifh who have lands in
" Ireland were forced to trade only with ftrangers, and became unac-
" quainted with their own country, and that England gained more than
" it loft by a free commerce (with Ireland), as exporting hither three
" times as much as it received from hence;" and mentions his furprize
" at their being debarred from bringing commodities from America di-
" rectly home, and being obliged to bring them round from England
" with extreme hazard and lofs.—Political Survey of Ireland, p. 123.

† The Lords commiffioners of trade in England, by their report of
the 31ft of Auguft 1697, (Eng. Com. Jour. 12 vol. p. 428) relating to
the trade between England and Ireland, though they recommend the
reftraining of the exportation of all forts of woollen manufactures out of
Ireland, make the following exception, " except only, that of their frize,
" as is wont, to England."

‡ See before fpeech of Lords Juftices.

§ Mr. Dobbs, and after him Dr. Smith.    ‖ 11 Eliz. feff. 3, ch. 10.

them

them without paying such duty *. In the reign of Charles I. great pains were taken by Lord Strafford to encourage this manufacture; and in the succeeding reign † the great and munificent efforts of the first Duke of Ormond were crowned with merited success. The blasts of civil dissentions nipped those opening buds of industry, and when the season was more favourable, it is probable that, like England, they found the woollen manufacture a more useful object of national pursuit; which may be collected from the address of the English house of commons, "that they so unwillingly promote "the linen trade ‡;" and it was natural for a poor and exhausted country to work up the materials of which it was possessed.

In 1696 the English had given encouragement to the manufactures of hemp and flax in Ireland, but without stipulating any restraint of the export of woollen goods.

In 1699, there was no equivalent whatever given for the prohibition of the export of our woollen manufactures.

But perhaps it may be necessary to inform the reader, that the foregoing privileges at first extended only to the English adventurers in the pale ‖ and five Irish families, the O'Briens, the O'Cavanaghs, the O'Neals, the O'Conors, and O'Mea Loughlins of Meath, the rest were deprived of their lives, lands, and liberties by the English with impunity; and, to compleat their misfortunes, the celebrated statute of Kilkenny, which here follows, was passed in 1365, which proved a more respectable and numerous assembly than had hitherto been convened in Ireland. The prelates of Dublin, Cashel, Tuam, Lismore, Waterford, Killaloe, Ossory, Leighlin, Cloyne, obeyed the summons of the king's son. The temporal peers and commons chearfully attended. Both estates sat together: and the result of their deliberations was, that the English of the realm § of Ireland, before the arrival of the duke

---

* 13 Eliz. sess. 5, ch. 4.

† 17 and 18 Ch. 2, ch. 9, for the advancement of the linen manufacture.     Carte.     ‡ See before.

‖ Which included Dublin, Meath, Uriel, now Louth, the cities of Kildare, Waterford, Cork, and Limerick.

" Tho' a Prince assume the title of Sovereign of an entire country, (as our Kings did of Ireland,) yet if there be *two-thirds* of that country, wherein he cannot punish treason, or murder, or theft, if the jurisdiction of his ordinary courts of justice doth not extend to these parts; if he have no certain revenues, no escheats or forfeitures, I cannot say, that such a country is conquered. Davis's Hist. of Ire. p. 9.

§ MSS. Lamb. G. No 608. fol. 1.

of

of Clarence, were become mere Irish in their language, names, apparel, and manner of living; had rejected the English laws, and submitted to those of the Irish, with whom they had united by marriage-alliance, to the ruin of the general weal. It was therefore enacted, that marriage, nurture of infants, and gossipred with the Irish, should be considered and punished as high-treason.   Again, if any man of English race shall use an Irish name, the Irish language, or the Irish apparel, or any mode or custom of the Irish, the act provides that he shall forfeit lands and tenements, until he hath given security in the court of Chancery, to conform in every particular to the English manners; or, if he have no lands, that he shall be imprisoned until the like security be given.   The Brehon law was pronounced, to be a pernicious custom and innovation lately introduced among the English subjects *.   It was therefore ordained that in all their controversies they shall be governed by the common law of England; and that whoever should submit to the Irish jurisdiction, was to be adjudged guilty of high-treason.   As the English had been accustomed to make war and peace with the bordering enemy at their pleasure, they were now expressly prohibited from levying war upon the Irish, without special warrant from the state.   It was also made highly penal to the English, to permit their Irish neighbours to graze their lands, to present them to ecclesiastical benefices, or to receive them into their monasteries or religious houses; to entertain their bards, who perverted their imaginations by romantic tales; or their news tellers, who seduced them by false reports.   It was made felony to impose or cess any forces upon the English subject against his will.   And as the royal liberties and franchises were become sanctuaries for malefactors, express power was given to the king's sheriffs to enter into all franchises, and there to apprehend felons or trai-

* *Finglas*, chief Baron of the Exchequer in King H. VIII. time says, "That the English statutes passed in Ireland, are not observed above eight days after passing them; whereas those laws and statutes made by the Irish on their hills, they keep firm and stable, *without breaking them for any favour or reward.*" Baron Finglas's Breviate of Ireland.

"There is no nation under the Sun, that love equal and indifferent justice, better than the Irish, or will rest better satisfied with the execution thereof, although it *be against themselves.*" Sir J. Davice's Hist. Ire.

"I have been informed by many of them that have had judicial places there (in Ireland) and partly of mine own knowledge, that there is no nation of the Christian world, that are greater lovers of justice than they are; which virtue must of necessity be accompanied by many others. Cooke's Inst. chap. 76.

tors.

tors. Laftly, becaufe the great lords, when they levied forces for the public fervice, acted with partiality, and laid unequal burdens upon the fubjects, it was ordained, that four wardens of the peace in every county fhould adjudge what men and armour every lord or tenant fhould provide. The ftatute was promulgated with particular folemnity; and the fpiritual lords, the better to enforce obedience, denounced excommunication on thofe who fhould prefume to violate it in any inftance.

Voltaire, whofe acquaintance with Irifh hiftory appears to be very flight, afferts, " That the Irifh always behaved fhamefully at home." I am confident, with all his ingenuity, he would not be able to fupport this on any principle of philofophy or common fenfe: he fhould, however, firft have recollected the celebrated battle of Clontarf, which was the 99th in which Boroimhe was victorious over the Danes; he fhould alfo have recollected the battle of Aughrim, * where 15000 Irifh, ill-paid, and worfe cloathed, fought with 25000 men, highly appointed, and the flower of all Europe, compofed of *Englifh, Dutch, Flemings* and *Danes*, vying with each other. That after a moft bloody fight of fome hours, thefe began to fhrink on every fide; and would have received a moft complete overthrow, but for the treachery of the commander of the Irifh horfe, and the death of their general, killed by a random fhot.

At the firft fiege of Limerick, a fmall party of Irifh, headed by the gallant *Sarsfield*, cut off a confiderable body of thefe aliens near Cullen, and deftroyed all the cannon and amunition, intended for the expediting this work; and in this enterprife it is difficult to determine which to admire more, the wifdom of the plan, or the intrepidity with which it was executed. Soon after this, when a breach was made in the walls 40 feet wide, which the Englifh, with their accuftomed bravery, mounted, and poured into the city, the Irifh rallied in the centre of the Irifh-town; in their turn attacked the enemy, beat them back to the difmantled walls, and from thence to the Foffe. They did not ftop here: they purfued them to their camp with great flaughter; and though they did not fet fire to the Englifh hofpital, where the wounded, unable to fly, were perifhing in the flames, yet, it is a known fact, that they partly prevented the effects of this unnatural order, by quenching the fire, and faving numbers of thefe half-expiring wretches. The cenfure which King William paffed on his troops, after this defeat, is too glorious for the Irifh to be here omitted: " *Had I* (faid he) *but the handful of*

---

* O'Halloran, page 270.

" *men*

" *men who defended this city, and that you were all shut up in it,*
" *I would take it in spite of you.*" M. de Voltaire makes but a
poor atonement to this injured nation, when he rapidly
tells us, " that they behaved well abroad." He knew that
their valour abroad was such, that in many capital defeats
of the French armies they alone remained conquerors. Witness the battle of the *Woods*, where Clare's regiment alone cut
to pieces one of two battalions, so that none but the colonel
(Gore) and a very few survived the action. While the whole
army were complimenting the *great Marlborough*, on this signal
victory, he alone appeared melancholy and dejected. *I wish,*
(said a young colonel) *that my regiment had been on that service.*
*I wish they had* (answered this officer, cooly) *for then I should be*
*at the head of* 1500 *brave fellows, and you not have ten.* The
affair of Cremona, were there no other instance, one should
think would secure them immortality in France, were gratitude the characteristic of the French nation ; and the remark
of a senator, in the British house of commons the winter following, shews how sensibly the high allies felt the check :
" Two Irish regiments (said he) have done at Cremona
" more real injury to the high allies, than the fee-simple of
" all their forfeited estates is worth !"

If time and the limits of this work permitted, numerous
examples of Irish prowess and disinterested generosity could
be adduced, but every invidious remark to the contrary may
be overthrown, from the bare transactions of the great *Hugh*
*O'Nial,* and his intrepid followers :

> O sacred LIBERTY ! shall faction's train
> Pervert the reverend archives of thy reign ?
> Shall slaves traduce the blood thy votaries spilt,
> Blaspheming glory with the name of guilt ?
> And shall no son of thine, their wiles o'erwhelm,
> And clear the story of *our* injur'd realm ?
> To this bright task some *Irish* spirit raise,
> With power surpassing even a Livy's praise ;
> Thro' this long wilderness his march inspire,
> And make thy temperate flame his leading fire !
> Teach his keen eye, and comprehensive soul,
> To pierce each dark recess, and grasp the whole !
> Let truth's undoubted signet seal his page,
> And glory guard the work from age to age ;
> That *Irish* minds from this pure source may draw
> Sense of thy *rights*, and passion for thy *law* ;
> Wisdom to prize, and honour that inspires,
> To reach that virtue which adorns our sires.    HAYLEY.

Approaching to a clofe, I prefume, my endeavours may at leaft lay fome claim to the laudable verfes of old Ennius:

Anteiqua fepolta vetufta,
Quai faciunt mores veterefq. novofque tenentem,
Moltarum veterum legum divomque hominumque.

And though accuracy may be difappointed in arrangement, judgment in felection, and indulgence wearied with length; to balance thefe, difcernment may difcover a defire to paufe, where candour feemed fatisfied, till hurried on by frefh information to eftablifh truth, or difpel prejudice, repetition confequently following: however, fhould the former prevail, youth, hafte, and avocation to neceffary bufinefs, could be produced in my favour, if the pleafing reflection of having endeavoured to ferve my country, did not at leaft, though at the fame time with every poffible refpect to public opinion, prepare my feelings againft every ill-natured attack; in confidence of which, I fhall add a few remarks, unwilling to quit a fubject which has left fuch pleafing impreffions on a heart, which only laments the inability of a head to gratify its warmeft wifhes.

Videmus quid deceat non affequimur.  *Cicero.*

It is plain, *then*, that Ireland *never was* conquered by the Englifh; it is not probable to fuppofe, that Strongbow with 400, and Henry II. with 500 Knights, fhould prevail where 60,000 and upwards, ignominioufly failed. In addition to what has been faid on this fubject, the following may not be deemed inappofite.

The very beft view of the political ftate of this kingdom (from the reign of Henry the fecond to that of James the firft) is given by Sir John Davies, Attorney-General, who was fent hither in that character, foon after his royal mafter's acceffion to the throne of Great Britain. His book bears the title of ' Hiftorical collections: or, a difcovery of the ' true caufes why Ireland was never entirely fubdued, nor ' brought under obedience to the crown of England, until ' the beginning of the reign of king James.' The caufes are affigned under two general heads: 1ft. The faint profecution of the war. Both Henry the fecond and his fon (King John) contented themfelves with gaining a fuperficial homage from the kings of three provinces; and Sir John Courcy, earl of Ulfter, made little more impreffion on the fourth. No force fufficient to fupport the Englifh intereft, appeared before the thirty-fixth of Edward the third; and this was reckoned an intolerable burden upon the treafury of England. So was Richard the fecond's expedition in the latter end of his reign;

from

from which time, to the 39th of queen Elizabeth, there never was a competent ſtrength ſent over. The author, in this part of his diſcourſe, ſhews at large what hindrances every preceding reign was cloged with, running through the moſt material occurrences in each.  2. The other chief cauſe of this ſlow progreſs he attributes to the defects and looſneſs in the civil adminiſtration.  There was from the beginning, he obſerves, a ſhew of giving Engliſh laws and franchiſes to the natives in general ; but, in fact, theſe privileges were only allowed, by the courts of judicature, to five Iriſh ſepts, the reſt being always treated as aliens and enemies.  In proof of this, he entertains his reader with ſeveral curious caſes and pleadings in ſaid courts.  A like fault in policy was the paſſing of exhorbitant grants, whole countries and provinces, to the firſt adventurers, who, inſtead of winning over the natives to the obedience of their Sovereign, fell into endleſs quarrels among themſelves.  Theſe ſtruggles put them under a neceſſity of living under the old Iriſh faſhion, for, to increaſe the numbers and powers of their reſpective families and clans, they obſerved the laws of Tainiſtry and Gavelkind ; and, as their forces grew numerous, they were ſubſiſted by the wicked extortion of Buanachd, Coigna and Livery.  The ſtatutes of Kilkenny made ſome proviſion for the cure of this epidemic diſtemper : and theſe enacted by Sir Edward Poyning, under king Henry the ſeventh, ſeemed to ſecure an univerſal obſervance of the Engliſh laws.  Yet, in the very next reign, there was room enough for a farther reformation both in church and ſtate : when the Lord Grey, having (among other wholeſome acts of parliament) procured an eſtabliſhment of the king's ſupremacy, firſt diſcovered that the Iriſh made no ſcruple in renouncing the Pope, when they had once reſolved to obey the king.  However, the advances that were afterwards made by the Earl of Suſſex under Queen Mary, ſeconded by thoſe of Sir H. Sidney, and Sir Charles Blount (Lord Mountjoy) under Queen Elizabeth, finiſhed the martial part of a plenary reduction of the whole kingdom; leaving only the peaceful diſtribution of juſtice, and the ſettlement of trade and commerce, to the miniſtry of King James.  This is the ſum and ſubſtance of that excellent treatiſe, which abounds with ſuch a maſterly knowledge in the hiſtory and ſtate of Ireland, as is truly incomparable.

It is plain then that we enjoyed all the commercial liberties of England, until the 15th of Charles II. * In 1663, our

* Additionl proofs to thoſe I have already advanced in favour of this aſſertion, ſee 3d James I. ch. 6, 12 Ch. II. ch. 32.  Matth. Paris,

exportation to the Colonies was prohibited. In 1670, our im-portation thence. In 1699, King William III. declared he would reftrict our wool trade as *far as in him lay,* which he accordingly did.

As nine-tenths of the prefent inhabitants of this king-dom are allowed to be defcended from thofe Englifh fettlers, and the natives, who from time to time were permitted the ufe of the Englifh laws * ; it is clear, beyond contradiction, that *we* were as FREE as the Englifh during 500 years. Our liberties were firft infringed by the deteftable Strafford, *but the cries of this oppreffed country purfued, and overtook him* †. Since that period, you have borne " the whips and fcorns of " time ‡, the oppreffor's wrongs, the proud man's contumely,

anno. 1172, p. 121, 220. Vit. H. 2. Pryn 4 Inft. 349. Againft the 4 Inft. c. 76, p. 250, 252. Lord Lyttelton's hift. H. II. 3d vol. 89, 90. 7 Co. 22,23. Sir J. Davis's hift. 71. 4th Black 419. Cooke's 4th Inft. 351. Lucas's works. Irifh Hift. Lib. p. 136, &c.

* De legibus ab Anglicanis in Hibernia ufitatis meri Hibernicis con-cedendis. A. D. 1280, Pryn, an. 257, Pat. 8, Ed. I. m. 12.

† See Mr. Flood's fpeech, December 18, 1781.

‡ Lucæ De Linda, Defcriptio Orbis. Amfterdam 1665. p. 385. Mores Hibernorum noftri temporis. Baptizatis infantibus nomina impo-nunt profana matrimonia contrahunt, non de præfenti, fed de futuro, ideo facile divortium admittunt, ubi fine negotio maritus aliam quærit uxorem et mulier alterum maritum filveftres Irlandi in genua procum-bunt, cum novilunium fpectant frumentum pro equis, quorum ingentem gerunt curam, fervant, urgente nimium fame etiam crudas carnes comedunt, vaccæ fanguinem coagulatum butyro fuperfundunt, et ita comedunt. Adhæc Anglo-Hiberni adeo ab antiquis illis Hibernis funt feperati ut colonorum omnium ultimus qui in Anglica provincia habitat, filiam fuam, vel nobiliffimo Hibernorum principi in matrimonium non daret, Tales vero lites æftimare folent certi homines quos *Brehonios* appellant, qui tam juris civilis, quam Britannici ignorantes funt, judicantque folum ex do-mefticis confuetudinibus, quæ ufu et frequentia actuum receptæ funt. In fuam et montanis velut feræ oberrant locis quod illorum fpectat eruditio-fuam, illa valde exigua eft. Medicos ibi hæreditas, non doctrina facit fatifque fe doctos putant, fi illud Hippocratis, *ars longa vita brevis* recitare queant.                                                                Grafton.

Manners of the Irifh of our days. Their baptifmal names are prophane; they wed for the future, not the prefent, whereby divorces are eafily ob-tained, and the hufband at liberty to chufe another wife, and the wife ano-ther hufband; the favage Irifh fall on their knees at fight of the new moon; they pay great attention to their horfes, feeding them with corn; preffed by great hunger, they eat raw flefh, they likewife eat cow's blood, covered with butter. The Englifh Irifh as yet are feparated from the old natives, and the Englifh who inhabit the Pale, being the laft of all the colo-nies, would not give one of their daughters in marriage to the nobleft Prince of the Irifh. Their difputes are determined by certain men, called *Brehons,* who are as ignorant of the civil law as of the Britifh; they judge wholly from domeftic cuftoms, which, confirmed by frequency of

acts

"and the laws delay ;" your history confidered as fable, your courage fool-hardinefs, and your hofpitality intemperance.

And now, my countrymen and fellow-fubjects, fince ye have fet fo bright an example to pofterity in the redemption of your liberties, continue to preferve them inviolate; watch them with the eye of circumfpection and caution; truft not to the fpecious profeffions of national friendfhip and generofity, they are the words only of fpeculation and fophiftry. The dreams of Puffendorf and Montefquieu may amufe in the clofet, but they vanifh in the field. Power only is the law of nations : when affured of the confidence of Britain, yield her every confiftent aid; one of her fons had the prefumption already to ring the fhackles ye have nobly broken in your ears, and to brand ye with difcontent; the voice of your unanimity has already reached the throne; ye have given the higheft marks of gratitude for a *fimple act of juftice*. What would Britain require?

acts, are received; they live in mountains and woods like wild beafts; they fcarcely poffefs any learning; their phyficians are hereditary, and illiterate; they conceive themfelves learned enough, if they are able to repeat the fentence of Hippocrates, *Ars longa, vita brevis,* art is long, life fhort.

Lucæ de Linda Amfteldam. 1665.

In Irelande there be two kinde of men, one foft, gentle, ciuile, and curteous: And to thefe people, as to the moft richeft, and beft nurtured perfons, doth many merchantmen of the Countryes adjoynyng, dayly refort. But becaufe the moft refort thether is of the Englifhe nation, the Irifhe men folow and counterfeyt their ciuile manners, and honeft conditions. And by reafon of the the common trade and entercourfe betwene them, they have learned the Englifh tongue, and can both fpeake and underftand it. And all this kind of people is under the fubjection and dominion of the king of England. The other kinde is cleane contrary from this, for they be wylde, rufticall, foolifhe, fierce, and for their unmanerly behauier, and rude fafhions are called wilde and fauage Irifhemen. And thefe men have many gouernours and feuerall rulers, which kepe continuall battaile, and dayly warre amongeft themfelues, for the which caufe they be more fierce, more bolde and hardie then the other Irifh men, and they be uery defyrous of newe thinges, and ftraunge fights and gafyngs, and after robery, theft, and rapine, and in nothing fo much delightyng as with tumulteous fedition and continuall ftrife. And to thefe wilde Coltes, Perkyn fhewed himfelfe firft, eafily perfwadyng them to beleue that he was the fame very perfon whom he falfly fained and counterfeited.                                    Grafton.

"Some nations feem formed for fubjection to others. The Englifh always had a fuperiority over the Irifh, in genius, as well as arms and riches, nor has Ireland ever been able to fhake off the yoke, *fince fhe was firft fubdued by an Englifh baron.*"                          Voltaire.

"The Irifh, from the beginning of time, had been buried in the moft profound barbarifm and ignorance."                          Hume.

See more on this fubject, particularly in the introduction to Dr. Carry's hift. of the Civil Wars of Ireland.

" Let the favour received be what it will, liberty is too
" dear a price for it. A state that has been *obliged*, is not
" therefore to be *enslaved*. It ought, if possible, make an
" adequate return for the services done to it ; but to suppose
" that it ought to give up the power of governing itself, and
" the disposal of its property, would be to suppose, that in
" order to shew its gratitude, it ought to part with the power
" of ever afterwards exercising gratitude." Dr. *Price*.

Arouse! be awakened and guard the freedom that is justly
your due! guard the precious fruit of your own exertions
with *breathing fire*. Place your confidence, therefore, in Heaven and *yourselves* alone.

Wisdom and moderation have already marked your councils ; ye have proceeded, and may ye continue so to do, with
the firmness of men resolved to be FREE.

It is not my wish to awaken discontents or jealousies. Englishmen cannot blame ye for adoring what themselves admire :
they are generous, so are ye ; they are brave, so are ye. May
Britain—but a favourite Poet conveys my wish, &c.

May Britain soon her better interest know,
Nor spurn the good Ierne can bestow ;
Her paltry pride, her mean suspicions chace,
And win, by bounteous acts, a grateful race.
In many a maze, while commerce flows around,
New force and value shall to her redound ;
Wide, and more wide, the genial currents born,
With rising herbage shall their banks adorn ;
And scatter plenty, as their path they sweep,
Then sink in her, as in their parent deep :
Or like the blood, with heat informing roll,
Strength to the limbs, and spirit to the soul.

# VOLUNTEERING, &c.

BEFORE we enter on the unexampled period that must ever raife the page of Irish hiftory fuperior to all others, let us take a fhort view of this ifland immediately preceding it; happily fituated, placed beneath one of the fineft climates, behold the richeft foil no longer entrufted with the hopes of harveft, but configned to the fuftenance of cattle as the only marketable commodity; a fpiritlefs peafantry, ill-lodged, worfe cloathed, and coarfely fed; a ruined tenantry; every heretofore crowded hamlet and village experiencing the real miferies of Doctor Goldfmith's *Deferted One;* the fpirit of freedom broken by oppreffion into defpondence; the languid eye only lifted to take in frefh images for forrow; life meafured by length; and death or emigration, the living death of population, prefented as the only refource from mifery; every fpecies of induftry blafted in the bud; public credit failed, merchants became bankrupts, our artificers begged in our ftreets, the numbers of our poor grew greater as the means of relieving them grew lefs; our charity only was not chilled, but our hands could not obey the warm dictates of our hearts; wool reduced one half in its ufual price; wheat one third; black cattle of all kinds in the fame proportion, and hides in a much greater; buyers not had without difficulty at thofe low rates, and from the principal fairs men commonly returned with the commodities they brought there. Many faithful pictures of our mifery * were given,

* Were I, fays the ingenious Dr. Campbell, to devife an emblematic figure of Ireland, in her prefent ftate, it fhould not be a Manerva-like figure with her fpear and harp, nor fhould it be a Diana with her wolf dogs, coupled, and the moofe deer in the back ground; but my picture of Ireland fhould be *Mulier formofa fuperne,* a woman exquifitely beautifully,

even the voice of verse arose to aid *slighted truth*, a piece of cloth of Irish manufacture, presented to the Queen by Lord Clare, was accompanied by the following lines, so truly descriptive of our situation, that an apology for their insertion must be needless.

> And O! might poor Ierne hope,
> In sober freedom's liberal scope,
> To ply the loom, to plough the main,
> Nor see Heaven's bounties pour'd in vain ;
> Where starving hinds, from fens and rocks,
> View pastures rich with herds and flocks ;
> And only view, forbid to taste—
> Sad tenants of a dreary waste ;
> For other hinds our oxen bleed,
> Our flocks for happier regions feed ;
> Their fleece to Gallia's looms resign,
> More rich than the Peruvian mine ;
> Her fields with barren lillies strown,
> Now white with treasures not her own :
> In vain Ierne's piercing cries
> Plaintive pursue the golden prize ;
> While all aghast the Weaver stands,
> And drops the shuttle from his hands:
> Barter accurst ! but mad distress
> To ruin flies from wretchedness.
> Theirs be the blame, who bar the course,
> Of commerce from her genuine source,
> And drive the wretch his thirst to slake
> With poison, in a stagnant lake.
>
> Hence ports secure from ev'ry wind,
> For trade, for wealth, for pow'r design'd ;
> Where faithful coasts and friendly gales
> Invite the helm and court the sails ;
> A wide deserted space expand,
> Surrounded with uncultur'd land.
> Thence Poverty, with haggard eye,
> Beholds the British streamers fly ;
> Beholds the Merchant doom'd to brave
> The treacherous shoal, and adverse wave ;

fully, with her head and neck richly attired, her bosom full, but meanly drest, her lower parts lean and emaciated, half covered with tattered weeds, her legs and feet bare with burned shins, and all the squalor of indigent sloth.          Philosop. Survey

Conftrain'd to rifk his precious ftore,
And fhun our interdicted fhore.
Thus Britain works a Sifter's woe;
Thus ftarves a friend, and gluts a foe.

So fhackled were we in our trade, by the interefted policy
of England, and by the power fhe had affumed of making
laws to bind us, that we even ftooped to follicit the liberty
of fome trifling manufactures, and they were refufed, though,
the requeft was founded in juftice, and begged as a favour;
in fo low an eftimation were we held in the fcale of the empire,
that the trivial intereft of every infignificant town was preferred to the juft rights of an extenfive nation, and every
attempt to eftablifh any manufacture their jealous avarice
deemed injurious, met with immediate oppofition, and the
attempt itfelf was treated as an infolent violation of the rights
of Britain; nay, to complete our mifery, the landed property of the kingdom was fhaken, the principal export trade
ruined by a repeated embargo *, to ferve the low corrupt in-
trigues of an Englifh minifter, to bribe a vote, and fill the
pockets of a contractor. To add, if poffible, a further dif-
grace, we were made the inftruments of our humiliation;
we were upbraided with a langour, and inattention, of which
England alone was the caufe; and while every exertion and
every art were ufed to forge and rivet our chains, we were
charged with the vices that refult from a ftate of defpondent
fervitude, and they were made the infolent plea for refufing
our juft demands. It muft however, be acknowledged, that
in the midft of tyranny, they thought on mercy; and, when
they had loft America, they were pleafed, with all the
kindnefs of infulting condefcenfion, to indulge us in the unfollicited favour of cultivating tobacco; and, to give the laft
gloomy finifhing to the picture of our diftrefs, the property
of the kingdom, feverely injured and threatened with total
and immediate deftruction, by a combination of fecret vil-
lains, hardened in iniquity, and made defperate by want.

It is a juft obfervation that there are moments big with the
fate of nations, as well as of perfons: 1779 appears to be
peculiarly fo with refpect to Ireland; the combination of

---

* By a proclamation, dated the 3d of February, 1776, on all fhips and
veffels, laden in the ports in this kingdom, with provifions of any kind,
but not to extend to fhips carrying falted beef, pork, butter and bacon
into Great-Britain, or provifions to any part of the Britifh empire, except the Colonies mentioned in the faid proclamation. 4th of January,
1779, taken off as far as it relates to fhips carrying provifions to any of the
ports of Europe.

feveral happy circumftances, happily attended, produced the defired effect; feveral literary luminaries arofe on our hitherto almoft darkened hemifphere; the re-illumined mind recognized her long loft liberties, and determined to reclaim them; the thunder of Britain died at a diftance, and the fea only trembled beneath the flight of her fleet; informed in the language of confidence that we were unjuftly oppreffed by a fifter kingdom, whofe extent of territory exceeded ours only in one-third, and her inhabitants one-half, and if a narrow fea divided us, a ftill narrower divided her and France, which muft ever be her enemy, let her be the ally of whom fhe will; we fmiled at our ftrength and the juftnefs of our caufe; the fparks of liberty were ftill alive, and only required to be fanned; the flame caught even the pulpit, the hallowed lip touched with fire, the manly exertions for our liberty, as a grand principle of the focial and moral duties, was warmly ufhered on the wings of religion.

    And hark! *Ierne* calls her fons to arms,
From plain to plain we hear the glad alarms!
On ev'ry breeze the facred banners ftream;
From hill to hill the marfhall'd fquadrons beam!
Not fhepherd's carrol, now, nor hunter's horn,
But piercing fifes awake the ling'ring morn!
Not rural fports the village throng delight,
But warlike leffons, and the mimic fight!
See, gayly dread, the virtuous bands appear,
Dear to their country, and to freedom dear!
No venal flaves, by fome poor ftipend led,
To fell their worthlefs blood for daily bread;
No ready engines, at a tyrant's word,
'Gainft human rights to draw the guilty fword:
Awake, alive, poffeft with glory's charms,
'Tis virtue, virtue calls the hoft to arms.
They blend the citizen's and foldier's name,
And reafon fanctifies the martial flame.
Each facred pledge that human life endears,
Each awful call that founds to virtuous ears:
The rifing energies of free-born mind,
The glorious ties that honour loves to bind;
And laft, the promife of a deathlefs meed,
See prompts, nor vainly prompts th' heroic deed.
What honeft flames from ev'ry eye-ball dart!
What god-like tranfports heave the burfting heart!
Now virtue reigns, fublime, fupreme, confeft;
A nation feels her like a fingle breaft!

Lord Nugent, whose name Irish gratitude should remember, on the 19th of January, 1779, called the attention of the British senate to the situation of our affairs, by moving for " an account of the imports from Ireland, and the exports to that kingdom, from the year 1768." His motion, he said, would, if carried, enable gentlemen to see at once the rapid decay of trade in Ireland ; and to judge whether the bills passed last session in favour of Ireland, had been productive of that good which the house, at the time of passing them, intended to do. He assured gentlemen, that the situation of the Irish was truly deplorable ; want and poverty were visible every where throughout the kingdom ; manufactures were at a stand ; and famine had so overspread the country, that nothing but the miseries of our people at Calcutta, during the dreadful scarcity of provisions there, could equal the present situation of the Irish, The whole revenue of the kingdom was scarcely adequate to the support of the military establishment, and the payment of interest for the debts contracted in the *cause* of Britain. The value of estates : had sunk to 17 and 14 years purchase ; and even at that low rate no purchasers were to be found, and for want of trade there was no money in circulation. The loyalty of the Irish in such a distracted condition was eminently conspicuous ; no sooner was France leagued with America, than the parliament of Ireland voted 300,000l. for the service of his Majesty ; and actually pays the enormous interest of seven and a half per cent. because the poverty of the nation prevented it from settling a loan filled upon easier terms.

He offered to produce a letter from Sir George Saville to confirm what he advanced, and still farther appealed to Lords North, and Germaine, as *they knew what he had said was too true.*

The narrow policy of confining the trade of an empire to one part, and excluding all the others from a participation in it, was no less absurd than prejudicial to the whole. It was singular and unparalleled in Europe. There was no Prince on the continent, whose dominions were composed of different states, who absurdly cherished the interest of one to the ruin of the rest. The house of Austria possesses Austria, the Netherlands, the Milanese, Hungary and Bohemia, and finds it her interest in granting the benefit of a free and equal trade to all France, makes no distinctions between the ancient possessions of the crown and its newly acquired dominions, Alsace, Franche Comte, Lorraine, and what are called Les Pays

Reconque

Reconques, all participate in trade equally with the other provinces of the kingdom. Spain acted formerly as we do now; but our misfortunes had made them wise. Cadiz was the only port in Spain allotted for American commerce: but that foolish system had been lately exploded; and now that all the Spanish ports are opened, the Spaniards find their manufactures revived; but above all, they see their navy raised to a degree of strength unknown to Spain at any other period. We in our turn ought to learn from them. Ireland had always been our best customer; she had taken our manufactures off our hands, and gave bread to our workmen. To disable her from continuing to do so, is to rob our manufacturers of the means of subsisting. Our tanning-bark, which was formerly sold in Ireland at four guineas a ton, brought at present only half that sum: The other commodities of this kingdom had sunk in proportion. Was that policy? Was that justice either to English or Irish? The prosperity of one country he always understood to be beneficial to the other; and as their interests were inseparable, so their advantage should be mutual. Ireland, situated as it is, would be still more advantageous to Great Britain, than if it was placed in the very centre of England; because from the situation it must always be of service to our navigation.

Mr. T. Townshend, lord Newenham, lord Beauchamp, and latterly Mr. Burke, appeared equally warm in the cause of Ireland. Sir George Yonge, our *worthy* vice-treasurer, indeed appeared wholly averse to the inquiry, and insisted; that our distress arose from indolence, and not from the restraints we lay under.

His Excellency John Earl of Buckinghamshire, Lord Lieutenant General, and General Governor of Ireland, his Speech to both Houses of Parliament, at Dublin, on Tuesday the 12th Day of October, 1779.

"*My Lords and Gentlemen,*

"AT a time when the trade and commerce of this kingdom are, in a more particular manner, the objects of public attention, it were to be wished, that the general tranquility, ever desireable, had been restored, so as to have left you entirely at liberty to deliberate on those great and important subjects. But I am persuaded, you will not permit any interests, however dear to you, to impede your efforts or disturb your unanimity at this most important period: and I have it expressly in command from his majesty, to assure you, that the cares and solicitudes, inseparable from a state of hostility,

have

have not prevented him from turning his royal mind to the
interests and distresses of this kingdom with the most affectionate concern; of which the money remitted to this country
for its defence, when England had every reason to apprehend a most formidable and immediate attack, affords a convincing proof. Anxious for the happiness of his people, his
majesty will most chearfully co-operate with his parliaments,
in such measures, as may promote the common interest of all
his subjects.

" I have the pleasure to inform you of an accession to
his majesty's family, since the last session of parliament, by
the birth of another prince. May the same Providence, that
continues to increase his domestic felicity, protect the honour
of his crown, and the happiness of his people.

" *Gentlemen of the House of Commons,*

" It is with great concern, I am to inform you, that on
account of the extraordinary decline of the revenues, the very
liberal supplies of the last session have proved inadequate to
the exigencies of government; so that, contrary to my most
sanguine expectations, and most earnest endeavours, there is
a considerable arrear now to be provided for.

" His majesty, from his paternal attention to the interests
of his people, and his solicitude to obviate, to the utmost,
the necessity of increasing their burdens, has graciously commanded me to declare to you, that the greatest œconomy shall,
in every instance, be exerted, as far as may be consistent
with the honour of his crown, and the real interests of the
nation.

" I have ordered the public accounts, and other necessary papers to be laid before you: and I have no doubt that
your known loyalty to your king, and attachment to your
country, will induce you to go as far, as the national abilities
will admit, in making a provision suitable to the exigency of
the times, and the honourable support of his majesty's government.

" *My Lords and Gentlemen,*

" The united efforts and great military preparations of the
house of Bourbon, seem only to have rouzed the courage
and called forth the exertions of his majesty's brave and loyal
subjects of this kingdom. I have only to lament, that the
exhausted state of the treasury, has hitherto put it out of my
power to give those exertions the most extensive and constitutional operation, by carrying the militia-law into execution.

" I am persuaded, you will not suffer any dangers, that
may be threatened from abroad, to draw off your attention

from wife and neceffary domeftic regulations; and that, among the many fubjects worthy of your confideration, the Proteftant charter fchools and linen manufacture, will continue to be objects of your ferious attention.

"In promoting thefe, and in all other meafures, that may tend to increafe the profperity and improve the true interefts of this kingdom, I am bound to co-operate with you by a double tie, of inclination and of duty. Nothing can ever effect me with more real fatisfaction, than the exerting my beft endeavours for the welfare of Ireland; nor can I ever render a more acceptable fervice to my fovereign, than in promoting the happinefs of his people."

Houfe of Lords, Wednefday, October 13. Committees fat upon the addreffes to his majefty and the lord lieutenant, which were reported and agreed to unanimoufly, and ordered to be prefented. That to his majefty contained a paragraph fimilar to the one introduced into the commons one, relative to a free trade.

Houfe of Commons, Tuefday October 12. As foon as the Speaker had, according to cuftom, read the lord lieutenant's fpeech,

Sir Robert Deane arofe, and after an exordium, lavifh in its encomiums on the lord lieutenant's adminiftration, and the good difpofitions of his majefty and the Britifh miniftry toward this kingdom, moved for an addrefs to the throne, expreffing in the warmeft terms the greatful fenfe the houfe entertained of the above difpofitions, and, in the ufual language of thefe addreffes, ecchoing the fpeech. He was feconded by

Mr. R. H. Hutchinfon, who faid this was a great, critical, and important period, in which the declarations of the king, the beft of princes, and the Britifh legiflature, left us no room to doubt but every good was defigned for Ireland; that his majefty's fpeech in the Britifh houfe, at the clofe of the laft feffion, was the harbinger of good tidings and great events, which was this day confirmed in the lord lieutenant's fpeech, who fays he has it in command to declare his wifh to co-operate in fuch meafures as may beft promote our interefts, interefts which, in the hands of the prefent adminiftration, muft be well managed, as their defigns are pure; that under fuch an adminiftration the general benefit of the empire would be attended to, above all partial and felfifh confiderations; and the veil of calumny, which fo long traduced them, would difappear, and the factious calumniators, touched with truth, as with the

fpeak

spear of Ithuriel, would start into shape. What thanks were
due to our chief governor, who so respectfully mentions the
societies of armed patriots throughout the kingdom? What
must our opinion be of a chief governor who speaks so honourably of that great bulwark of constitutional liberty, a
national militia? though our distresses are great, from them
prosperous days may spring, like that fair flower the fabling
poets tell of, which sprung from a hero's blood.

Mr. Grattan said, the speech contained nothing explicit;
nothing satisfactory; it meant to quiet the minds of the people without any declaration whatever. After his majesty had
been addressed by his Irish subjects for a free export trade,
did such addresses require no answer? Were the people of Ireland undeserving the notice of the British ministers? Was there
no respect for the interests of these kingdoms among the servants of the crown on this side of the water? Were not these
servants of the crown also representatives of the people?
Why not then speak out? Are our distresses of so private a
nature that they must not be mentioned? [Here he gave an
eloquent and pathetic picture of the miserable condition of
this kingdom.] It is plain we have nothing to expect, since
applications from the people, backed with the same from the
officers of the crown, are not attended to. Ireland, then, has
nothing to depend upon but her spirit; no redress of grievances, no extension of trade, but from the efforts of her
people! and will it be politic, will it be safe, here or elsewhere,
to oppose these efforts? Why does not our address also speak
out? Why have we less spirit than the people? Shall the commons of Ireland shew less spirit than the most insignificant
corporation? Are we so fallen, so despicable, as to be more
afraid of England's censure, than of the cries of our starving
manufacturers.

The distresses of this kingdom are two fold, the beggary of
the people, and the bankrupcy of the state. The first he
would ask the commissioners of the revenue to prove, but he
would ask them upon oath, whether the restrictions on our
trade was not the cause? whether the prohibitions laid on by
England against the exports of woollen clothes did not
occasion it? Whether there were not too many inhabitants in
this kingdom, though not half peopled; whether to those inhabitants was the American continent still open, would
they not have migrated thither rather than pine in their native land, the victims of English tyranny, rather than starve
in it by an English act of parliament? And lastly, was there
one

one rich merchant in the kingdom? This kingdom, (he continued) ruined by a balance of trade against her for so many years, and the drain of absentees, owes its present existence to associations; it is but a temporary expedient, and something more effectual must be done.

As to the bankruptcies of the state, they are the consequence of a system of boundless prodigality, profligacy, and violence; a boundless prodigality, while our means were limited; a profligacy and violence uniformly maintained. One instance will suffice, where the late attorny general obliged the merchants of Cork to sign an illegal bond, as a collateral security to an illegal oath. The peace establishment of this poor country amounts to one-sixth of that of England; what proportion is there in our means? What is this establishment? infamous pensions to infamous men! [here he launched into some personalities] and will those men, whom we pay, vote against an extension of our trade? vote against the means of supporting them! To what pass have these profligate administrations reduced this kingdom! to be insulted with our poverty in the speech from the throne; to be told of our beggary; that the officers of the crown here have begged 50,000l. from England, or the troops could not have marched into camp; when it is known, that it is this profligacy that has unnerved the arm of government, and made the sword of defence fall in its hand.

He then moved an amendment to the address, to be inserted in the following words:

"That we beseech your majesty to believe, that it is with the utmost reluctance we are constrained to approach you on the present occasion; but the constant drain to supply absentees, and the unfortunate prohibition of our trade, have caused such calamity; that the natural support of our country has decayed, and our manufacturers are dying for want. Famine stalks hand in hand with hopeless wretchedness, and the only means left to support the expiring trade of this miserable part of your majesty's dominions, is to open a free export trade, and let your Irish subjects enjoy their natural birthright." Lord Westport seconded Mr. Grattan's motion for the amendment. Mr. Flood considered the address as inexplicit.

Sir Henry Cavendish declared he would vote against the amendment, apprehending (with a view we may suppose to inefficacy and procrastination) that this business would be better effected by opening a committee on purpose, or rather following

t

lowing a precedent in the year 1661, when the Lords and
Commons of Ireland appointed commiffioners to attend the
King, to *fupplicate* the redrefs of grievances.

Mr. Ogle, in a ftrain of honeft indignation, reprobated the
idea of entering into a committee on the fubject of our
grievances; he was fick, he faid, of that mode of trifling with
the nation in order to gain time; that the ghoft of the committee on the embargo haunted him every time he heard a
committee mentioned; and laftly, if we did not mention
fomething in the addrefs, the miniftry might again fhelter
themfelves under the old excufe, "That truly they did not
" know what the Irifh wanted, as their parliament was filent
" on the head," and fo go on with the old fyftem of duplicity.

Sir Edward Newenham, in a fpirited and warmly decided
ftrain, conjured the houfe, by all they held dear, to re-affume
their wonted dignity and power, the early claims to which
he happily and unanfwerably traced; charged the Britifh miniftry with contempt and neglect to the nation, and called on
their warmeft advocate to deny the affertion; faid he perfectly
agreed with Mr. Flood, that the addrefs did not go far
enough, and that he thought the original addrefs a fervile
echo to the fpeech.

The Provoft drew a moft pathetic picture of the melancholy
fituation of his native country, declaring, on this queftion,
that no adminiftration fhould bias him from the welfare of
his country.

The Attorney General, without arguments to fupport, or
art to deceive, delivered a ftudied eulogium on the fenfibility
of the King, and the humanity of his minifter.

The debate now took a new turn; feveral of the minifterial
party declared, that though they thought this bufinefs might
have come more properly otherwife, yet, that there might be
an unanimity, they would not oppofe the amendment.

Hon. Henry Flood declared for the amendment, and entered largely into a juftification of his political conduct,
which, he faid, had unfortunately been much mifreprefented;
that the office he held was the unfollicited gift of his Sovereign, which he had received with gratitude, and held with
honour; that when a time came that he could no longer do
it, he would gladly throw the bracelet into the common
cauldron.

Mr. Prime Serjeant, after expaciating on the neceffity of
immediately laying, in an unequivocal manner, the ftate of our
diftreffes at the foot of the throne, moved in lieu of the
amendment propofed, "that it is not by temporary expedi-
" ents,

" ents, but by a Free Trade alone, that this nation is now to
" be faved from impending ruin."

The amendment was carried *nem. con.* as was alfo the addrefs to the Lord Lieutenant.

We fhall here give a flight review of this feffion: every
object now wore the appearance of beauty, contrafted with
the deformity we have defcribed; our liberties reftored!
our commerce emancipated! a people, no longer divided
by religious prejudice and factious animofity, but, endeared
to each other by the firmeft ties of gratitude and affection;
united to her fifter kingdom, in the ftrongeft bonds of intereft and amity; content and fatisfaction diffufed on every
countenance; the loweft individual taught, by experience, to
know his own importance, and actuated by a fpirit of emulation, to attain a higher rank amongft his fellow-citizens.
The acts of commerce encouraged by the rich, and purfued
with induftry by the poor; convinced that their activity will
now be followed by fuccefs; the nation itfelf, roufed from
indolence, governed folely by a fpirit of freedom, and elevated to the moft exalted fituation in the opinions of mankind,
which, while it gratifies their pride, infures its ftability; her
natural rank in the political fcale of Europe afcertained; no
longer confidered a meer appendage to Great Britain; fupported wholly by that confequence, to which the fertility of
her foil, the peculiar happinefs of her fituation, and the fpirit of her people incitle her.

Immediately previous to this, the patriotic town of Galway entered into a non-importation agreement, which was
inftantly followed over all the kingdom, now clothed in her
native manufacture :                     ——with ruftic air,
    Blooming fhe ftands, and innocently fair.
    Let polifh'd arts the bafhful nymph refine,
    In filken raiment let her beauties fhine;
    Th' admiring world fhall own her peerlefs charms,
    And diftant bofoms pant with foft alarms.

Military affociations arofe unnumbred over the land. England,
indeed forgetful, or pretending to be fo, of the liberal plan
on which the majefty of the people ftept forth, affected to de-
fpife them; and even Lord Shelburn, who draws a very confiderable part of his fources from our ifle, had the prefumption
in the Britifh houfe to call us an *enraged mob*,* but an opportunity foon offered, which convinced our enemies of the eftimation in which we were to be held.

* See his fpeech in the Houfe of Lords, May the 11th, 1779.

. Late

Late in the fummer of the year 1779, while the combined fleet of our enemies rode triumphant in the channel, and menaced the kingdom with immediate invafion, the affrighted maratime towns made application to government for protection, the eftablifhed forces of the nation having been called away to fupport the war in America; the chief governor was forced to confefs himfelf unable to afford any effectual affiftance in this alarming ftate of urgent necefiity; the people of Ireland refolved to defend themfelves; government, forgetting their jealoufy in their fears for the fafety of the empire, yielded to the impulfe of the nation, and, with reluctant confidence, placed arms in the hands of men, that fhewed themfelves worthy of the important truft. The fleets of the enemy, alarmed at our military preparations, beheld the banners of defiance, and fled precipitate from our coafts.

For this never to be forgotten fervice, the Duke of Leinfter, and Mr. T. Conolly moved, " That the thanks of the " houfe be given to the feveral Volunteer Corps, for their " fpirited exertion at this time fo necefsary in defence of this " country," (which paffed *nem. con.*)

This the Lord Chancellor and Lord Annally feemed defirous to oppofe, by wifhing to know under what authority the Volunteers arofe; forgetful, it feems, that power only originates from the people, which, once for all, that they may perfectly know, I have fubjoined the plain, but truly fenfible remarks of Mr. Locke hereon, &c.

The reafon why men enter into fociety, is the prefervation of their property; and the end why they chufe and authorize a legiflative, is, that there may be laws made, and rules fet, as guards and fences to the properties of all the members of the fociety; to limit the powers, and moderate the dominion of every part and member of the fociety; for fince it can never be fuppofed to be the will of the fociety, that the legiflative fhould have a power to deftroy that which every one defigns to fecure by entering into fociety, and for which the people fubmitted themfelves to legiflators of their own making, whenever the legiflators endeavour to take away, or to deftroy the property of the people, or to reduce them to flavery under arbitrary power, they put themfelves into a ftate of war with the people [*i e.* Rebellant, they bring back the ftate of war] who are thereupon abfolved from any farther obedience, and are left to the common refuge which God hath provided for all men againft force and violence.

Whenfoever,

Whensoever, therefore, the legiflative shall tranfgrefs this fundamental rule of fociety, and either by ambition, fear, folly, or corruption, endeavour to grafp themfelves, or put into the hands of any other, an abfolute power over the lives, liberties and eftates of the people; by this breach of truft they forfeit the power the people had put into their hands for quite contrary ends, and it devolves to the people again, who have a right to refume their original liberty; and by the eftablifhment of a new legiflative (fuch as they fhall think fit) to provide for their own fafety and fecurity, which is the end for which they are in fociety.   What I have faid here concerning the legiflative in general, holds true alfo concerning the fupreme executor, who having a double truft put in him, both to have a part in the legiflative and the fupreme execution of the law, acts againft both when he goes about to fet up his own arbitrary will as the laws of the fociety.   He acts alfo contrary to his truft when he either employs the force, treafure, and office of the fociety, to corrupt the reprefentatives, and gain them to his purpofes, or openly pre-engages the electors, and prefcribes to their choice fuch whom he has, by folicitations, threats, promifes or otherwife, won to his defigns, and employs them to bring in fuch who have promifed beforehand what to vote and what to enact.   Thus to regulate the candidates and electors, and new model the ways of election, what is it but to cut up the government by the roots, and to poifon the very fountain of public fecurity? for the people, having referved to themfelves the choice of their reprefentatives, as the fence to their properties, could do it for no other end but that they might always be freely chofen, and fo chofen, freely act and advife, as the neceffity of the common wealth and the public good fhould, upon examination and mature debate, be judged to require.   This thofe who give their votes before they have heard the debate, and have not weighed the reafons on all fides, are not capable of doing.   To prepare fuch an affembly as this, and to endeavour to fet up the declared abettors of his own will for the true reprefentatives of the people, and the law-makers of the fociety, is certainly as great a breach of truft, as perfect a declaration of a defign to fubvert the government, as is poffible to be met with; to which if one fhall add, rewards and punifhments vifibly employed to the fame end, and all the arts of perverted law made ufe of, to take off and deftroy all that ftand in the way of fuch a defign, and will not comply and confent to betray the liberties of

their

their country, it will be paſt doubt what is doing. What power they ought to have in the ſociety, who thus employ it contrary to the truſt that went along with it in its firſt inſtitution, is eaſy to determine; and one cannot but ſee, that he who has once attempted any ſuch thing as this cannot any longer be truſted.  Locke on Gov. chap. 19, § 222.

The fears of an invaſion ſubſided; but the people, now accuſtomed to aſſociate in arms, and ſenſible of their importance, conferred, began to ſpeak and think with more freedom of that ſtate of ſubjection, in which they had too long been held, and which was aggravated by the diſtreſs felt at this time, in a peculiar degree, convinced of their rights, and conſcious they were now in a ſituation to demand a reſtitution of them, they looked forward to redreſs, and they thought it juſt, that whilſt they protected Ireland from the enemies of Britain, it ſhould be made of ſome value to themſelves. The fire of Liberty ſpread through their different aſſociations; their union ſerved to ſtrengthen and diffuſe the flame; they talked amongſt themſelves of their preſent degenerate ſtate; wondered at their puſillanimous conduct, and reſolved to redeem themſelves in the eyes of mankind; at this critical period, the ſeſſion of 79 opened :—The Secretary entered on the buſineſs of government with the uſual confidence of ſucceſs; a confidence authorized by the experience of the former ſeſſion, in which, aſſiſted by a numerous and *corrupt* majority in parliament, he had triumphed over the efforts of the virtuous part of the people, and by continuing an odious embargo, had brought the nation to the verge of bankruptcy; how great then muſt have been the ſurprize of the miniſter to meet with unaccuſtomed oppoſition! to feel himſelf obliged to give way to an unanimous reſolution of the Houſe of Commons, inſerted even in the addreſs to the throne; " That, it was not by temporary expedients, but by a Free Trade alone, this country could be ſaved from impending ruin." This great reſolution, in the opinions of the repreſentative, can be attributed only to that ſpirit of liberty, which the armed aſſociations had diffuſed through the whole nation; they ſeemed ſenſible of this, and gave a ſanction to their aſſemblies, by voting them *unanimouſly*, an addreſs of thanks; the words, " *Free Trade*" echoed through the kingdom, and the people pledged themſelves to ſupport the requiſition of the commons; the nation however had not yet learned to ſpeak out, nor had the gallant

lant affociations yet infpired or affumed that confidence, their
refpectability of character eminently ent.:led them to.  A remarkable inftance of this occurs in the printed debates of the
houfe in the early part of this feffion ; on a motion for retrenchment, it being fagacioufly infinuated by Sir Benjamin
Chapman, that, it would be prudent in government to comply cheartully with the reafonable demands of the people, now
with arms in their hands, determined to defend their rights.
He was anfwered by Luke G—r, and John D—n, Efqrs.
that, the Volunteers had taken up arms, *only*, for the purpofe of defending the country from external violence, and
internal infurrection, and not, by any means, with the
view fuggefted. So little was the true fpirit of the Volunteer
combinations at that time underftood or afferted in parliament. A Free Trade, with the acquiefcence of England, was
the confequence of thofe fpirited meafures ; the people were
not to be refufed, but England, while fhe was forced to yield
to the ftrong remonftrances of the nation, endeavoured (and
in a great meafure effected her plan) to make the acquifition
of little value, by forcing, through the weight of parliamentary influence, fuch regulations as were inapplicable and
injurious to the purpofes of commerce.  Thefe attempts to
evade our requifitions awakened the attention, and confirmed the fpirit of Ireland ; fhe began to fee, that it was idle
and in vain to expect, that the freedom of trade would be
inviolate, while the freedom of the conftitution remained
ftill unafferted; thefe wife and generous fentiments fo worthy
of a great people, fhe was taught to feel and maintain in a
manner becoming her dignity, by one of the firmeft and moft
diftinguifhed patriots a grateful nation was ever bleffed with :
Mr. Grattan directed the efforts of the Volunteers to the attainment of an object that merited all their exertions ; a total
emancipation from the intruded power of England, and a
perfect reftoration of that freedom to which they were entitled by Magna Charta.  While he infpired the armed forces
of the nation with an idea of their own confequence, he at
the fame time fupported their claims in parliament with fuch
purfuafive eloquence, fuch power of argument, that each
individual of the commons abjured for himfelf, the fupremacy
of Great Britain ; and, it cannot be faid he was defeated,
though he did not, at that time, prevail in carrying his motion for a parliamentary declaration of rights.  He fucceeded
however in eftablifhing the idea in the minds of every individual in the kingdom.  He was looked up to as their leader

in

in the glorious work of liberty; he deferved the honourable
ftation, and was regarded by all parties, as the glory, ornament, and faviour of his country. The people having now
difclaimed all obedience to the acts of the Englifh legiflature,
as we had no law of our own, to regulate the conduct of the
army, it was neceffary that a mutiny bill fhould be immediately enacted; it paffed here, and was fent to England for
the royal affent: here fhe again fhewed, how tenacious fhe
was ftill of the power fhe had affumed; the bill was altered,
and the law made *perpetual* though it had been limited by
our parliament to two years only. Still the arts of venality,
which had triumphed with fuch avowed fuccefs in the former
feffions, again prevailed, and the bill was paffed in its prefent
difgraceful form: arguments were not wanting to fupport or
palliate corruption; it was attempted to be proved, that a
perpetual law was of equal fervice to the nation, and that the
alteration of the Englifh council ought not to alarm the jealoufy of this kingdom, as their admitting at all, the neceffity of a new law was a fufficient relinquifhment of their
right to bind Ireland. This flimfy reafoning however did
not fatisfy the people; they faw with aftonifhment and contempt the interefted venality of their reprefentatives: the
Volunteers entered inftantly into the moft fpirited and decided refolutions expreffive of their difcontent, and difappro-
bation; and the parliament was prorogued while the nation
remained thus unfatisfied. The general diffatisfaction had
fpread itfelf into the remoteft corners of the kingdom; every
man was called upon to lend his affiftance, and enlift under
the banner of freedom. If any before remained inatten-
tive, they were now convinced of the neceffity of uniting in
the general caufe: fcarcely was one individual found indo-
lent or bafe enough to look on an idle fpectator. Reviews
were appointed; new corps were added; provincial mufters
were directed; encampments were formed; inftructions came
from the conftituents to their reprefentatives, and the people
waited in military array, until the hour came, when they
could with firmnefs and dignity demand from parliament a
legal fanction to their claims.

April 20, 1780, Mr. Grattan, uninfluenced by power,
ftrengthening from defeats, and brightening from minifterial
collifion, moved, " that the King's moft excellent Majefty, and
" the Lords and Commons of Ireland, are the only power
" competent to make laws to bind Ireland: " yet fuch, at
this time, was the corruption of the fenate, that this moft

falutary

falutary motion was negatived, though urged with the cleareft arguments, and delivered with the warmeft pathos.

It was originally intended that this work fhould clofe with the laft feffion, (in 1782,) but finding on a clofer view, the tranfactions from this to that period numerous, deeply interefting, and worthier of higher difcuffion than time has hitherto permitted, they are referved for the continuation of a fecond volume; and as the principle defign of this work is to diffufe information, and convey, to the lateft moment, thofe important determinations which the unanimous voice of a whole nation has uttered, and their tranfactions conformed, a few obfervations and extracts are added, as a mirror in which the fubject may view his own importance, &c. as a member of the empire; the duty he owes to, and in return expects from his fovereign; the futility of kings reigning by *divine right*, fo frequently urged by fleepy church dignitaries, court fycophants, and the gilded pen of minifterial hirelings.

The King is chofen as head of the community, to prefide in their councils, and to execute their laws in times of peace; not to controle the one, or make the other; and. to conduct and command their armies, in times of war. This *fupreme Magiftrate*, and *chief General* they dignified with the *honours* and *title* of KING. All the rights, powers and privileges neceffary to fupport the regal rank, and fovereign dignity of this great officer, confiftent with the great end of the inftitution, now called prerogatives of the crown, were annexed; with an abfolute freedom and exemption to his perfon, from all coercive or offenfive acts of violence whatfoever; except on his committing a breach of the *implied* or *written* CONTRACT between KING and PEOPLE; in which cafe, they have referved to themfelves, and conftantly exercifed, the power of dethroning their King, and that of appointing and limiting the fucceffion to the throne.

The legiflative power of the Lords extends to the framing, and paffing bills, for all purpofes of good government; excepting the granting *taxes*, or *fubfidies*; fuch bills muft take rife in the Commons only, their affent and confent, being of *original right*, firft to be obtained.     LUCAS.

The *election* of commoners, to be immediate truftees and apt reprefentatives of the people in parliament, is the hereditary and indefeafible privilege of the people. It is the privilege which they accepted, and which they retain, in exchange of their origionally inherent and hereditary right of fitting with the King and Peers, *in perfon*, for the guardianfhip of their own liberties, and the inftitution of their own laws.

Such

Such reprefentatives, therefore, can never have it in their power to give, delegate, or extinguifh the whole, or any part of the peoples infparable and undiftinguifhable fhare in the legif-lative power; neither to impart the fame to any one of the other eftates, or to any perfons or perfon whatever, either in or out of parliament. Where plenepotentaries take upon them to abolifh the authority of their principals; or where any fecundary agents attempt to defeat the power of their primaries; fuch agents and plenepotentaries defeat their own commiffion, and all the powers of the truft neceffarily revert to the conftituents.

The perfons of thefe temporary truftees of the people, du-ring their feffion, and for fourteen days before and after every meeting, adjournment, prorogation, and diffolution of parliament, are equally exempted, with the perfons of peers, from arreft and durefs of every fort.

They are alfo, during their feffion, to have ready accefs to the King or Houfe of Lords, and to addrefs or confer with them on all occafions.

No member of the Houfe of Commons, no more than of the Houfe of Peers, fhall fuffer, or be queftioned, or com-pelled to witnefs or anfwer, in any court or place whatfoever, touching any thing faid or done by himfelf, or others, in parliament; in order that perfect freedom of fpeech, and action, may leave nothing undone for the public weal.

They have alfo (during feffion) an equal power with the Houfe of Lords, to punifh any who fhall prefume to traduce their dignity, or detract from the rights or privileges of any Member of their Houfe.

They commons form a court of judicature, diftinct from the judicature of the Houfe of Lords. Theirs is the peculiar privilege to try and adjudge the legality of the election of their own members. They may fine and confine their own members, as well as others, for delinquency or offence againft the honour of their houfe. But, in all other matters of ju-dicature, they are merely a court of *inquifition* and *prefentment*, and not a tribunal of *definitive judgment*.

In this refpect, however, they are extremely formidable. They conftitute the *grand inqueft* of the nation; for which great and good purpofe, they are fuppofed to be perfectly qualified, by a perfonal knowledge of what hath been tranf-acted throughout the feveral fhires, cities, and boroughs, from whence the affemble, and which they reprefent.

Over and above their inquiry into all public grievances, *wicked Minifters, tranfgreffing Magiftrates, corrupt Judges and*

*Justiciaries*, who sell, deny, or delay justice; *evil Counsellors* of the crown, who attempt or devise the subversion or alteration of any part of the constitution; with all such overgrown malefactors as are deemed above the reach of inferior courts, come under the particular cognizance of the Commons, to be by them impeached, and presented for trial at the bar of the House of Lords. And these inquisitory and judicial powers of the two Houses, from which no man under the crown can be exempted, are deemed a sufficient allay and counterpoise to the whole executive power of the King by his Ministers.

The legislative department of the power of the Commons is, in all respects, co-equal with that of the peers. They frame any bills at pleasure for the purposes of good government. They exercise a right, as the Lords also do, to propose and bring in bills, for the amendment or repeal of old laws, as well as for the ordaining or institution of new ones. And each house alike hath a negative on all bills that are framed and passed by the other.

But the capital, the incommunicable privilege of the House of Commons, arises from that holy trust which their constituents repose in them; whereby they are impowered to borrow from the people a small portion of their property, in order to restore it threefold, in the advantages of peace, equal government, and the encouragement of trade, industry, and manufactures.

To impart any of this trust would be a breach of the constitution: and even to abuse it, would be a felonious breach of common honesty.

By this fundamental trust, and incommunicable privilege, the Commons have the sole power over the money of the people; to grant or deny aids, according as they shall judge them either reqisite, or unnecessary to the public service. Theirs is the province, and theirs alone, to enquire and judge of the several occasions for which such aids may be required, and to measure and appropriate the sums to their respective uses. Theirs also is the sole province of framing all bills or laws for the imposing of any taxes, and of appointing the means for levying the same upon the people. Neither may the first or second estate, either King or Peerage, propound or do any thing relating to these matters, that may any way interfere with the proceedings of the Commons, save in their negative or assent to such bills, when presented to them, without addition, deduction, or alteration of any kind.

After

After such aids and taxes have been levied and difpofed of,
the Commons have the further right of enquiring and ex-
amining into the application of the faid aids; of ordering all
accounts relative thereto, to be laid before them; and of
cenfuring the abufe or mifapplication thereof.

The royal affent to all other bills is expreffed by the terms,
*Le Roy le veut, the King wills it.* But, when the Commons
prefent their bills of aid to his Majefty, it is anfwered, *Le Roy
remercier fes loyal fubjeɑs et ainfi le veut, The King thanks his loyal
fubjeɑs and fo willeth.* An exprefs acknowledgment that the
right of granting or levying monies for public purpofes, lies
folely, inherently, and incommunicably, in the people and
their reprefentatives.

This capital privilege of the Commons, conftitutes the
grand counterpoife to the King's principal prerogative of
making peace or war; for how impotent muft a warlike
enterprize prove, without money, which makes the finews
thereof; and thus the people and their reprefentatives ftill
retain in their hands the *grand momentum* of the conftitution,
and of all human affairs.

Diftinguifhed reprefentatives! Happy People! Immutably
happy, while *worthily reprefented.*

As the fathers of the feveral families throughout the kingdom, nearly and tenderly comprize and reprefent the perfons,
cares, and concerns of their refpeɑive houfhoulds; fo thefe
adopted fathers immediately reprefent, and intimately con-
centrate, the perfons and concerns of their refpeɑive conftituents, and in them the colleɑive body, or fum of the nation.
And while thefe fathers continue true to their adopting children, a fingle ftone cannot lapfe from the *great fabric of the
conftitution.*

### The Three Eſtates in Parliament.

With the King, Lords, and Commons, in parliament affembled, the people have depofited their *legiflative* or *abfolute
power, in truft* for their whole body; the faid King, Lords,
and Commons, when fo affembled, being the *great* reprefentative of the whole nation, as if all the people were then convened in one general affembly.

As the inftitution, repeal, and amendment of laws, together with the redrefs of public grievances and offences, are
not within the capicity of any of the three eftates, diftinɑ
from the others, the *frequent holding of Parliaments* is the vital
food, without which the conftitution cannot fubfift.

The three eftates originally, when affembled in parliament
fat together confulting in the open field. Accordingly, a

Running-Mead, five hundred years ago. King John paſſed the great charter, (as therein is expreſſed) by the advice of the Lords Spiritual and Temporal, by the advice of ſeveral Commoners (by name recited) *et aliorum fidelium*, and of others his faithful people. And in the twenty-firſt clauſe of the ſaid charter, he covenants, that, " For having " the Common Council of the kingdom to aſſeſs aids, he will cauſe " the Lords ſpiritual and temporal to be ſummoned by his writs ; " and, moreover, he will cauſe the principal Commoners, or " thoſe who held from him in chief, to be generally ſummoned " to ſaid parliaments by his Sheriffs and Bailiffs."

In the ſaid aſſemblies, however, the concourſe became ſo great and diſorderly, and the conteſt frequently ſo high between the ſeveral eſtates, in aſſertion of their reſpective prerogatives and priviliges, that they judged it more expedient to ſit apart, and ſeparately to exerciſe the offices of their reſpective departments.

As there is no man, or ſet of men, no claſs or corporation, no village or city, throughout the kingdom, that is not virtually repreſented by the delegates in parliament, this *great body politic*, or *repreſentative of the nation*, conſiſts, like the body natural, of a head and ſeveral members, which, being endowed with different powers for the exerciſe of different offices, are yet connected by one main and common intereſt, and actuated by *one life or ſpirit of public reaſon*, called the *laws*.

In all ſteps of national import, the King is to be conducted by the direction of the parliament, his great national council ; a council on whom it is equally encumbent to conſult for the King with whom they are connected, and for the people by whom they are delegated, and whom they repreſent. Thus the King is conſtitutionally to be guided by the ſenſe of his parliament ; and the parliament alike is conſtitutionally to be guided by the general ſenſe of the people. The two eſtates in parliament are the conſtituents of the King ; and the people, mediately or immediately, are the conſtituents of the two eſtates in parliament.

Now, while the three eſtates act diſtinctly, within their reſpective departments, they effect and are reciprocally affected by each other. This *action and re-action* produces that general and *ſyſtematic controul* which, like *conſcience*, pervades and ſuperintends the whole, checking and prohibiting evil from every part of the conſtitution. And from this confinement of every part of the rule of *right reaſon*, the great *law of liberty to all* ariſeth.

For inſtance, the King has the ſole prerogative of making war, &c. But then the means are in the hands of the people and their repreſentatives.

Again, to the King is committed the whole executive power. But then the minifters of that power are accountable to a tribunal, from which a criminal has no appeal or deliverance to look for.

Again, to the King is committed the cognizance of all caufes. But fhould his Judges or Jufticiaries pervert the rule of righteoufnefs, an inquifition, impeachment, and trial impends, from whofe judgment the Judges cannot be exempted.

Again, the King hath a negative upon all bills, whereby his own prerogatives are guarded from invafion. But fhould he refufe the royal affent to bills tending to the good of the fubject, the Commons can alfo with-hold their bills of affeffment, or annex the rejected bills to their bill of aids: and they never failed to pafs in fuch agreeable company.

Laftly, to the King is committed the right of calling the two eftates to parliament. But, fhould he refufe fo to call them, fuch a refufal would be deemed *an abdication of the conftitution;* and no one need be told, at this day, *that an abdication of the conftitution* is an *obdication of the throne.*

Thus, while the King acts in confent with the parliament and his people, he is limitlefs, irrefiftable, omnipotent upon earth; he is the free wielder of all the powers of a free and noble people; a King throned over all the Kings of the children of men. But fhould he attempt to break bounds, fhould he caft for independence, he finds himfelf hedged in and ftraightened on every fide; he finds himfelf abandoned by all his powers, and juftly left to a ftate of utter impotence and inaction.

Hence is imputed to the fovereign head, in the conftitution of Great Britain, the high and divine attribute, *the King can do no wrong;* for he is fo circumfcribed from the poffibility of tranfgreffion, that *no wrong can be permitted to any King in the conftitution.*

While the King is thus controuled by the Lords and Commons; while the Lords are thus controuled by theCommons and the King, and while the Commons are thus controuled by the other two eftates, from attempting any thing to the prejudice of the general welfare, the three eftates may be aptly compared to three pillars divided below at equidiftant angles, but united and fupported at top, merely by the bearing of each pillar againft the others. Take but any of thefe pillars away, and the other two muft inevitably tumble. But while all act on each other, all are equally counteracted, and thereby affirm and eftablifh the general frame.

How

How deplorable then would it be, should this elaborate structure of our happy constitution, within the short period of a thousand years hence, possibly in half the time, fall a prey to effeminacy, pusilanimity, venality, and seduction; like some ancient oak, the lord of the forest, to a pack of vile worms that lay gnawing at the root; or, like Egypt, be contemptibly destroyed by *lice and locusts*.

Should the morals of our constituents ever come to be debauched, *consent*, which is *the salt of liberty*, would then be corrupted, and no salt might be found wherewith it could be seasoned. Those who are inwardly the servants of *sin*, must be outwardly the servants of *influence*. Each man would then be as the Trojan *horse* of old, and carry the enemies of his country within his bosom. Our own appetites would then induce us to betray our own interests; and state policy would seize us a *willing sacrifice to our own perdition*.

Should it ever come to pass, that corruption, like a dark and low-hung mist, should spread from man to man, and cover these lands. Should a general dissolution of manners prevail. Should vice be countenanced and communicated by the leaders of fashion. Should it come to be propagated by ministers among legislators, and by the legislators among their constituents. Should guilt lift up its head without fear of reproach, and avow itself in the face of the sun, and laugh virtue out of countenance by force of numbers. Should public duty turn public strumpet, Should shops come to be advertised, where men may dispose of their honour and honesty at so much per ell. Should public markets be opened for the puachase of consciences with an *oyez!* We bid most to those who set themselves, their trusts, and their country to sale! If such a day, I say, should ever arrive, it will be doom's-day, indeed, to the virtue, the liberty, and constitution of these kingdoms. It would be the same to Great Britain, as it would happen to the universe; should the laws of of cohesion cease to operate, and all the parts be dissipated, whose orderly connection now forms the beauty and *commonwealth of nature*. Want of sanity in the material, can never be supplied by any part in the building. A constitution of *public freemen* can never consist of *private prostitutes*.

BROOKE.

We here see the harmoney of the whole arises from the mutual connection, and the mutual opposition of the several constituent parts. The three different orders which compose the system, including every part of the community, and possessing felling the unlimited authority of the whole, are connected together by a power of ordaining belonging jointly to them all ; they are oppofed to one another by a power of hindering, belonging feparately to each ; by the former, they are enabled to provide for the good of the community in general ; by the latter, they are difabled from encroaching on each others rights, or oppreffing any part. The legiflative power, which requires much council and mature deliberation, is very properly placed in the hands of the many ; the executive power, which requires immediate action, is, with equal propriety, committed to the one. How hath the wifdom of nature been ftretched! how have the veins of the valiant been exhaufted, to form, fupport, reform, and bring to maturity this unexampled conftitution, this coalefcence and grand effort of every human virtue, *Britifh Liberty!*

If it was poffible for any man who hath the leaft knowledge of our conftitution, to doubt in good earneft, whether the prefervation of public freedom depends on the prefervation of parliamentary freedom, his doubts might be removed, and his opinion decided, one would imagine, by this fingle obvious remark, that all the defigns of our Princes againft liberty, fince parliaments began to be eftablifhed on the model ftill fubfifting, have been directed conftantly to one of thefe two points ; either to obtain fuch parliaments as they could govern, or elfe to ftand all the difficulties, and run all the hazards of governing without parliaments. The means principally employed to the firft of thefe purpofes have been, undue influences on the elections of members of the Houfe of Commons, and on thefe members when chofen. When fuch influences could be employed fuccefsfully, they have anfwered all the ends of arbitrary will ; and when they could not be fo employed, arbitrary will has been forced to fubmit to the conftitution.

Bolingbroke's Differtat. Letter XI page 15.

The King at his coronation folemnly fwears to the following effect : " That he will govern the people of the realm according to the ftatutes in parliament made, that is by the reprefentatives of the people ; and agreeable to the laws, and cuftoms by them eftablifhed ; that he will caufe law and juftice in mercy and equity to be difpenfed and executed ; that he will protect and maintain, to the utmoft of his power, the laws of God, the true religion and profeffion of the gofpel, and the general rights and liberties of all the people, whether clergy or laity, without diftinction."

It

Man, without *religious* and *civil liberty*, is a poor and abject animal, without a conscience, bending his neck to the yoke, and crouching to the will of every silly creature who has the insolence to pretend to authority over him.

All *taxes* are free-gifts for public services. All *laws* are particular provisions or regulations established by *common consent* for gaining protection and safety.

PRICE.

In governing of the people, the King has above him the *law*, by which he is constituted King, and his parliament.

*Bracton, l. 2. c. 16.*

Glanville, who was a learned Lawyer, and Chief Justice in Henry the second's time (now above 500 Years ago) writ a book of the common laws of England, touching the subject; and he informs us, that there was, in his time, such a thing as high treason against the kingdom. His words are these: " *Crimen quod in legibus dicitur crimen læfa Majestatis, ut de nece* " *vel seditione personæ Domini Regis, vel regni,*"

*Glanv. l. 1. c. 2. p. 1.*

But why detain ye with the writings of others? Your own resolutions teem with the very soul of liberty; they abound in the bold *relief* of expression; they do honour to the head, but immortalize the heart. Therein ye have openly vowed, in the eye of Heaven, to be *governed only by laws that ye form yourselves;* to fill the senate only with honest men, worthy of the immortal honour of representing a free people, and the holy trust of their lives and properties. Ye confess that ye hold the *right of private judgment in matters of religion to be equally sacred in others as well as in yourselves*; ye have given the highest proofs of your brotherly affection, in rejoicing *at the relaxation of the Penal Laws against* your Roman Catholic brethren, as conscious that the God in humanity diffused the precepts of his Gospel in the mildness of his power, and that his *service is perfect freedom.* Ye have rightly resolved, That a seat in parliament was never intended by our constitution as an instrument of emolument to individuals; and that the representative who perverts it to such a purpose, is guilty of betraying the trust reposed in him by the people, for *their*, not *his*, benefit; and, that the people who could tamely behold their suffrages made the tool of private avarice or ambition, are still more criminal than the venal representative, as they become the pandors, without even the wages of prostitution. Ye have rightly observed, that a freeholder · is answerable only to God for his vote, and that whosoever shall

x

attempt

attempt to influence him by any other means than that of argument, is an enemy to the freedom of election, and consequently to the real intereft of his country. Ye have folemnly declared, that ye will pay obedience to thofe laws only, which are made by our own legiflature, the King, Lords, and Commons of Ireland, as the very terms of our original compact with Great Britain are, that we fhall poffefs and exercife the full enjoyment of the Britifh conftitution. As external greatnefs and conftitutional extention were the objects of Great Britain in that compact; as external fecurity and conftitutional liberty were the objects of Ireland, whatever leads to feparation on the part of the latter, or infringments on the part of the former, is a violation of both. With becoming dignity, ye have reprobated the expreffion of *that* man, who, fhielded only by his infignificance, had the audacity to declare, " *That power makes right.*" Ye have been too long the dupe of venal fenators; but the meafure of their iniquity is full, and the page of time fhall witnefs their vice, whether fenced with power, characterifed by rage, or lulled in the down of dedication: *tremble thou wretch, that haft within thee crimes unwhipt of juftice!* The fruits of your land has been devoted to ftalled Divinity, and pampered wealth; oppreffion ftalked at large, and fcience, fhorn of her beams, fhed a feeble ray; but the profpect brightens.

That you have been for the laft century under the dominion of England, has been owing not to your want of native fpirit, but to the unhappy divifions which, from the many fovereigns that exifted early on your ifland, and the difference of religion which has fubfifted fince, have prevented you from making one united and entire refiftance. Every nation of Europe is witnefs of your gallantry abroad, and to know that a man is brave, it is fufficient to fay 'That he is an Irifhman.' You have too long fhone the fatellite of a larger planet; guard againft future contingencies; Britain, recovering courage with the abfence of danger, may yet repent of her approach to equity, and ftep back to defpotifm once more. It is unfafe to live incautioufly connected with a neighbouring people of the fame manners, the fame language, and fuperior ftrength; the propinquity of fituation will give frequent opportunities, and the influence arifing from the feamnefs of language, and fimilarity of manners, will infenfibly prevail, and eftablifh an intereft in the fmaller kingdom *

* Montefquieu.

The.

The plains are yet warm with the blood of Irishmen in defence of Britain, which, if yet faithful to us, our veins are ready to bleed afresh in the same cause ; if not, we shine the centre of our own interest, and danger is a cloud that mocks at a distance.  The King of England is also King of Ireland ; the liberty of England, is the liberty of Ireland.  But why deduce from her the Heavenly gift ?  It is the privilege of individuals, breathed with our breath, and wrote on the heart by the finger of God !  Let no little party-spirit disunite you ; twigs gather strength from combination ; the dignity of your prince, the aggrandisement of your kingdom, and the welfare of Britain is your object ;   discuss your affairs with spirit and moderation !

Persevere ; your cause is good ; your sufferings have been great ; your complaints just ; your spirit is roused, and you *cannot* be enslaved.

It is a maxim that the *King can do no wrong ;* let it be now, that he *shall* do no wrong.

Watch over the sacred freedom of the press * that great medium of information, through which we think aloud ; friends will not be wanting on all occasions to wield the pen:

> O sacred weapon, left for Truth's defence,
> Sole dread of folly, vice, and insolence.

Quid de reliquis republicæ malis ?  Licet-ne dicere ?  Mihi vero licet et semper licebit dignitatem tueri, mortem contemnere.  Protestas modo veniendi in hunc locum sit, dicendi periculum non recuso.                                CIC. ORAT.

I contemplate with joy, and wait with impatience, the happy moment that is to crown your glorious exertions with something more than human felicity, when the unwearied

---

* Private individuals, unknown to each other, are forced to bear in silence those injuries in which they do not see other people take a concern. Left to their own individual strength, they tremble before the formidable and ever ready power of those who govern ; and, as the latter well know, nay, are apt to over-rate the advantages of their own situation, they think they may venture upon any thing.  But when they see that all their actions are exposed to public view, that in consequence of the celerity with which all things are communicated, the whole nation seems as it were one continued *irritable* body, no part of which can be touched without exciting an universal *tremor ;* they become sensible that the cause of *each* individual is really the cause of *all ;* and that to attack the *lowest among the people,* is really to attack the *whole people.*

DELOLME, a Foreigner.

Newenham is to exert himlelf for the more due reprefentation of the people; when the difcerning and comprehenfive Flood, with irrefiftable eloquence, fhall help to fix our liberties on the moft durable bafis; when an *Irifh Bill of Rights* fhall fhine as the rainbow of our political fky; when the placemen and penfioners fink beneath public execration, and the voice of virtue refound in the fenate; when the tranfactions of the bifhops, thofe expletives of fociety, and other lumber of the church, fhall be more duly examined: to doubt of thefe would be to doubt of our exiftence! to miftruft that Providence, which has fmiled on our endeavours, and the difinterefted flame, that pervades the moft inanimate bofom. Your progreffion to perfection is quick, and I fee you will not ceafe till you attain it; the wide, the unbounded profpect lies before you,

Nor " fhadows, clouds, nor darknefs reft upon it."
Then fhall the fun of freedom rufh forth as a bridegroom out of his chamber, and rejoice as a giant to run his courfe. May it go forth from the uttermoft part of the Heaven, and run about to the end of it again, and nothing be hid from the heat thereof.

Before I part the reader, I muft make another obfervation or two, which is, that whoever attempts to fupprefs Volunteering, or but whifpers, that it ought to be done, let his rank or fituation be what it may; let him do it with a tongue dipt in oil, and with a countenance dreffed by the graces; or with lightening in his eye, and thunder leaping from his brow; whether he does it in the fenate or out of the fenate; whether tyrannically to a fet of trembling dependents, or fervilely cringing to fome lordly fuperior, he is qually the detefted enemy of Ireland, and fhould be looked upon with abhorrence: and if we are anxious to have our conftitution and liberty fully afcertained, and the extention of our commerce indifputably eftablifhed on a lafting foundation, there is no other means under Heaven of doing fo, but by perfevering in the prefent fpirit, and keeping up, unimpaired, our Volunteer army. For, O my country! fhould your *chofen fons* put off their warlike attire, you may drefs in fable, and mourn indeed!

Ulfter

# Ulster Volunteers.

◄·◄·◄·◄·◄·◄·◄ ◄·◄·◈·✦·✦·✿·◑·►·►·►·►·►·►·►·►

*At a Meeting of the Representatives of* ONE HUNDRED *and*
FORTY THREE CORPS *of* VOLUNTEERS *of the*
*Province of* ULSTER, *held at* DUNGANNON *on Friday*
*the* 15th *Day of February*, 1782.

CoLoNeL WILLIAM IRVINE in the Chair.

**W**HEREAS it has been afferted, " That Volunteers, as
fuch, cannot with propriety, debate or publifh their opinions
on political fubjects, or on the conduct of parliament, or public men."

Refolved unanimoufly, That a citizen, by learning the ufe
of arms, does not abandon any of his civil rights.

Refolved unanimoufly, That a claim of any body of men.
other than the King, Lords, and Commons of Ireland, to
make laws to bind this kingdom, is unconftitutional, illegal,
and a *grievance*.

Refolved (with one diffenting voice only) that the powers
exercifed by the Privy Council of both kingdoms, under, or
under colour or pretence of the Law of Poyning's, are unconftitutional, and a *grievance*.

Refolved unanimoufly, That the ports of this country are,
by right, open to all foreign countries, not at war with the
king, and that any burthen thereupon, or obftruction thereto,
fave only by the parliament of Ireland, are unconftitutional,
illegal, and a *grievance*.

Refolved (with one diffenting voice only) That a Mutiny
Bill, not limited in point of duration, from feffion to feffion,
is unconftitutional, and a *grievance*.

A                                          Refolved

Refolved unanimoufly, That the independence of judges
is equally effential to the impartial adminiftration of juftice in
Ireland, as in England, and that the refufal or delay of this
right to Ireland, makes a diftinction where there fhould be no
diftinction, may excite jealoufy where perfect union fhould
prevail, and is, in itfelf, unconftitutional, and a *grievance*.

Refolved (with eleven diffenting voices only) that it is our
decided and unalterable determination, to feek a redrefs of
thofe grievances; and we pledge ourfelves to each other, and
to our country, as freeholders, fellow-citizens, and men of
honour, that we will, at every enfuing election, fupport
thofe only, who have fupported, and will fupport us therein,
and that we will ufe all conftitutional means to make fuch
purfuit of redrefs fpeedy and effectual.

Refolved (with one diffenting voice only) That the right
honourable and honourable the minority in parliament, who
have fupported thefe our conftitutional rights, are entitled to
our moft grateful thanks, and that the annexed addrefs be
figned by the chairman, and publifhed with thefe refolutions.

Refolved unanimoufly, That four members from each
county of the province of Ulfter, eleven to be a quorum, be,
and are hereby appointed a committee till next general meeting, to act for the Volunteer Corps here reprefented, and as
occafion fhall require, to call general meetings of the province, viz.

| | |
|---|---|
| Ld. Vifc. Ennifkillen | Major Charles Duffin |
| Col. Mervyn Archdall | Capt. John Harvey |
| Col. William Irvine | Capt. Robert Campbell |
| Col. Rob. M'Clintock | Capt. Jofeph Pollock |
| Col. John Fergufon | Capt. Wad. Cunningham |
| Col. John Montgomery | Capt. Francis Evans |
| Col. Charles Leflie | Capt. John Cope |
| Col. Francis Lucas | Capt. James Dawfon |
| Col. Tho. M. Jones | Capt. James Atchefon |
| Col. James Hamilton | Capt. Dan. Eccles |
| Col. And. Thompfon | Capt. Tho. Dickfon |
| Lieut. Col. C. Nefbitt | Capt. David Bell |
| Lieut. Col. A. Stewart | Capt. John Coulfton |
| Major James Patterfon | Capt. Rob. Black |
| Major Francis Dobbs | Rev. Wm. Crawford |
| Major James M'Clintock | Mr. Rob. Thompfon. |

Refolved unanimoufly, That faid committee do appoint
nine of their members to be a committee in Dublin, in order
to communicate with fuch other Volunteer affociations in the
other

other provinces, as may think proper to come to fimilar refolutions, and to deliberate with them on the moft conftitutional
means of carrying them into effect. In confequence of the
above refolution, the committee have appointed the following
gentlemen for faid committee, three to be a quorum, viz.

Col. Merv. Archdall          Capt. Francis Evans
Col. Wm. Irvine              Capt. James Dawfon
Col. John Montgomery         Capt. Jofeph Pollock
Col. T. M. Jones             Mr. Robert Thompfon.
Major Francis Dobbs

Refolved unanimoufly, That the Committee be, and are
hereby inftructed to call a general meeting of the province,
within twelve months from this day, or in fourteen days after the diffolution of the prefent Parliament, fhould fuch an
event fooner take place.

Refolved unanimoufly, That the Court of Portugal have
acted towards this kingdom (being a part of the Britifh empire) in fuch a manner as to call upon us to declare and pledge
ourfelves to each other, that we will not confume any wine
of the growth of Portugal, and that we will, to the extent of
our influence, prevent the ufe of faid wine, fave and except
the wine at prefent in this kingdom, until fuch time as our
exports fhall be received in the kingdom of Portugal, as the
manufactures of part of the Britifh Empire.

Refolved (with two diffenting voices only, to this and the
following refolution) That we hold the right of private judgment, in matters of religion, to be equally facred in others
as in ourfelves.

Refolved therefore, That as Men and as Irifhmen, as
Chriftians and as proteftants, we rejoice in the relaxation of
the *Penal Laws* againft our *Roman Catholic fellow-fubjects*,
and that we conceive the meafure to be fraught with the happieft confequences to the union and profperity of the inhabitants of Ireland.

Refolved unanimoufly, That the Dundalk Independent
Troop of Light Dragoons, commanded by Captain Thomas
Read, having joined a regiment of this province (the firft
Newry regiment or Newry Legion) and petitioning to be re-
ceived as part of this body, and under its protection, is ac-
cordingly hereby received.

Whereas a letter has been received by the chairman of this
meeting from the united corps of the county of Cavan, Colonel Ennery in the chair, declaring their readinefs to co-
operate

operate with their brother Volunteers in every conftitutional fupport of their rights ;

Refolved unanimoufly, That the thanks of this meeting be prefented to the faid united corps of the faid county of Cavan for their fpirited refolution, and that a copy of the proceedings of this meeting be inclofed by the chairman to Colonel Ennery, to be by him communicated to the faid united corps, and that they fhall have a right, if they choofe, to affociate with the corps reprefented at this meeting, to nominate four members to act with thofe already appointed as a committee by the delegates at this meeting.

Refolved unanimoufly, That the thanks of this meeting be prefented to Captain Richardfon and the Dungannon Light Company, for their politenefs in mounting guard this day.

Refolved unanimoufly, That the thanks of this meeting be prefented to the Southern Battalion of the Firft Ulfter Regiment, commanded by the Earl of Charlemont, for that patriotic zeal which we are convinced induced them to call this meeting.

Refolved uanimoufly, That the thanks of this meeting be prefented to Colonel William Irvine, for his particular propriety and politenefs of conduct in the chair.

Refolved unanimoufly, That the thanks of this meeting be prefented to Captain James Dawfon, for his readinefs in undertaking the office of Secretary to this meeting, and for his particular attention and ability in the laborious duty thereof.

Refolved unanimoufly, That thefe refolutions be publifhed.

*To the Right Honourable and Honourable the Minority in both Houfes of Parliament.*

*My Lords and Gentlemen,*

We thank you for your noble and fpirited, though hitherto ineffectual efforts in defence of the great conftitutional and commercial rights of your country. Go on—the almoft unanimous voice of the people is with you ; and, in a free country, the voice of the people *muft* prevail. We know our duty to our Sovereign, and are loyal.—We know our duty to ourfelves, and are refolved to be free. We feek for our rights, and no more than our rights, and, in fo juft a purfuit, we fhould doubt the being of a Providence, if we doubted of fuccefs.        Signed by order,

WM. IRVINE.

I:

*In Committee.*

Refolved unanimoufly, That the corps of this province, not reprefented at the meeting held this day, be, and they are hereby invited to join in the refolutions of faid meeting, and to become members of the faid affociation on the moft equal footing.

Refolved unanimoufly, That fuch corps as may choofe to join the faid affociation be, and they are hereby requefted to communicate their intentions to our Secretary, Capt. Dawfon, Union-lodge, Loughbrickland, who will lay the fame before the Chairman and Committee.

WM. IRVINE, Chairman.

ROYAL EXCHANGE, Feb. 17, 1782.

*At a numerous Meeting of the Corps of* Independent Dublin Volunteers.

WM. M'CLEARY, Efq. Capt. Grenadiers, in the Chair.

The following refolutions were unanimoufly agreed on.

NATURAL juftice and equity having eftablifhed the univerfal rights of mankind upon an equal footing, the inhabitants of Ireland have a claim to a *free trade* with all nations in amity with Great Britain ; yet, their ports have been kept fhut, their trade has been monopolized, and their induftry has but ferved to aggrandize the proud traders of a neighbouring kingdom.

Neceffity, which compels to ingenuity, has lately held up that trade, dignified with the fpecious name of *Free ;* yet, trade which enriches induftrious nations, ferves but to impoverifh the natives of this kingdom; becaufe they have purchafed, at an high price, an illufion. Defrauded thus of their birth-right, there is nothing left but œcenomy as a counterpoife. This unfubftantial freedom of commerce having originated from the united fpirit of the people againft the ufe of *foreign manufactures*, the fame fpirit which procured the fallacious grant, may yet, by a perfevering unanimity, eftablifh a *real*, permanent, and fubftantial trade.

Therefore refolved, That thefe our thoughts and opinions be laid before our countrymen, reminding them, at the fame time,

time, that not only they, but their posterity, are interested in the event; that, to do away effectually the yoke of monopoly, a non-confumption and non-importation agreement should be entered into without delay.

Resolved, That for the more effectually furthering this great national point, the several Corps (as private citizens) of this city, be requested to send each a Delegate to the Royal Exchange, on Monday the 25th inst. at seven o'clock in the evening.

Resolved, That the foregoing resolutions be published three times in Saunders's News-Letter, and Dublin Evening Post.

WILLIAM M'CLEARY, Chairman.

*∻∻∻∻∻∻∻∻∻∻∻∻∻∻∻∻∻∻∻∻∻∻∻∻∻∻*

*At a full Meeting of the Lawyers Corps (assembled by public Notice) on the 24th Day of February, 1782, they came to the following Resolutions.*

### Col. EDWARD WESTBY, in the Chair.

R ESOLVED (with two differing voices only) That we do highly approve of the resolutions and address of the Ulster Volunteers, represented at Dungannon on the 15th day of February inst.

Resolved unanimously, That as citizens and Volunteers, we will co-operate with the several corps, whose Delegates met at Dungannon, in every constitutional mode of obtaining a redress of the grievances mentioned in their resolutions.

Resolved, That the above resolutions be published in Saunders's News-Letter, the Hibernian Journal, and the two Evening Posts.

Signed by order,

SAMUEL ADAMS, Secretary.

C L A N.

# CLANRICARDE INFANTRY.

*At a general Meeting of the* Clanricarde Infantry *at Head Quarters,* Loughrea, *on Sunday the 24th of February,* 1782.

### Captain DAVID POWER in the Chair.

RESOLVED, That the late refolutions of the Delegates from the Ulster Affociations, entered into at Dungannon on Friday the 15th inst. appear to us to be truly fpirited and patriotic, and if adopted by the different other Volunteer Corps of this kingdom, cannot fail of being productive of the happieft confequences.

Refolved therefore, That a meeting of Delegates from all the Volunteer Corps of the province of Connaught is hereby requefted, on Friday the 15th of March next, at Ballinafloe, being deemed the moft central town, in order to fpeak the fentiments of their conftituents in fuch refolutions as their wifhes, and the exigency of public affairs, demand.

Refolved, That thefe refolutions be inferted in the Dublin Evening Poft and Connaught Journal.

Signed by order,
MYLES-BURKE TULLY, Secretary.

---

# MARYBOROUGH VOLUNTEERS.

*At a full Meeting of the* Maryborough Volunteers, *the 25th of February,* 1782.

### Major CASSAN in the chair.

RESOLVED, That the refolutions entered into by the Delegates of the Ulster Affociations at Dungannon, are truly fpirited and patriotic, and highly neceffary at this time, and we are determined to fupport them, and all other fuch laudable undertakings, and think that a general meeting of Delegates from all the Queen's county corps is, at this time, much wanting, in order to fpeak the fentiments of their conftituents, and enter into fuch other refolutions as the exigency of the times may require.

Signed by order,
JOHN BALDWIN.

*At a Meeting of the Deputies of the First Independent County of Down Regiment, assembled at Newtown-Ards, the 26th of February, 1782, to take into Confideration the Refolutions entered into by the Volunteers met at Dungannon.*

### Lieut. Col. STEWART in the Chair.

The following refolutions were unanimoufly agreed to.

RESOLVED, That it is our unalterable opinion, and that we think it a duty incumbent on us, and every individual, or body of individuals, to ufe their utmoft exertions at all times to promote the profperity and welfare of the community; and that it appears to us to be, now more efpecially, neceffary to ftep forward, when the decay of public virtue is fo apparent, and the dereliction of the public intereft become fo common.

Refolved, That we are fully fatisfied and convinced, that a general union and correfpondence among the Volunteer Corps throughout this kingdom, may be of moft effential fervice to this country in the prefent fituation of its affairs; and, that we do not fee how it can be fo effectually accomplifhed, as by concurring with the refolutions of the Dungannon meeting.

Refolved, That the Dungannon refolutions are entitled to, and do meet our warmeft approbation; which, while they are dictated with moderation, are animated with a fpirit fuitable to men who have the intereft of their country at heart, and who, though they wifh to affert their rights with temper, yet, fhew their determination to perfevere in the purfuit of them with fteadinefs.

Refolved therefore, That we do moft willingly accede to the Dungannon affociation; and we do hereby declare our firm determination to co-operate with our brethren Volunteers in every legal meafure, and conftitutional mode of reftoring and afferting the rights of this country, and of eftablifhing them on fo fure a bafis, as may fecure them to lateft pofterity.

Refolved, That the Chairman be requefted to tranfmit the foregoing refolutions to the Secretary of the Dungannon meeting, and to publifh the fame in the Belfaft News-Letter, and Dublin Evening Poft.

A. STEWART, Chairman.

Major

Major CRAWFORD having taken the Chair,

Refolved, That the warmeft thanks of this meeting be given to our worthy Lieutenant-colonel, for his conftant attention to the regiment, for convening us together, and for his very proper and polite conduct this day in the chair.

JOHN CRAWFORD.

*At a Meeting of the* Drumbridge Volunteers, *held at* Ballydrain, *the* 26th *of* February, 1782.

Major A. G. STEWART in the Chair.

The Refolutions entered into and publifhed by the Volunteers of Ulfter, affembled at Dungannon on the 15th inftant, having being read and deliberated, paragraph by paragraph;

RESOLVED unanimoufly, That this Corps highly approve of, and moft cordially accede to, the faid refolutions, in the whole and in every part, as calculated to promote the juft rights, and no more than the juft rights, of Ireland; and we do pledge ourfelves to each other and to our country, as freeholders, fellow-citizens and men of honour, that we will ufe our utmoft efforts, by every conftitutional means, to carry the fame into effectual execution.

Refolved unanimoufly, That our Chairman do communicate our approbation of, and acceffion to, faid refolutions, to Captain James Dawfon, Secretary to the Committee of Ulfter Volunteers, and inform him, that we cordially accept of the invitation to become members of that Affociation.

Refolved, That thofe refolutions be publifhed in the Dublin Evening Poft, and in all the news-papers of this province.

A. G. STEWART, Chairman.

B        LAWYERS

# LAWYERS CORPS.

*At a full Meeting of the* Lawyers Corps, *the 28th of February,* 1781, *purfuant to notice.*

### Colonel EDWARD WETSBY in the Chair.

The following Refolutions were unanimoufly agreed to:

RESOLVED, That the members of the Houfe of Commons are the reprefentatives of, and derive their power folely from the people, and that a denial of this propofition by them, would be to abdicate the reprefentation.

Refolved unanimoufly, That we conceive that the people of this country are now called upon to declare, that the King, Lords, and Commons of Ireland are the only power competent to make laws to bind this kingdom.

Refolved unanimoufly, That we do expect fuch Declaration of Rights from our reprefentatives in parliament, and that we will fupport them with our lives and fortunes in whatever meafures may be neceffary to render fuch declaration an effectual fecurity.

Refolved, That the above refolutions be publifhed.
Signed by order,
SAMUEL ADAMS, Secretary.

*At a full Meeting of the*
## LIBERTY VOLUNTEERS,
*Purfuant to general Summons, on Thurfday the 28th of February,* 1782.

### Lieut. Col. ALEXANDER GRAYDON in the Chair.

RESOLVED unanimoufly, That the Delegates of this Corps are hereby empowered, and defired to confent to the propofition, that all the Corps of the county and city of Dublin do form themfelves into a legion, to confift of a Squadron of Horfe, a Train of Artillery, and one Regiment of Infantry ; the latter to adopt one uniform, with only fome diftinctive mark on the button.

The

The feveral refolutions, and addrefs of the Ulfter Volunteers, reprefented in Dungannon, on the 15th day of February inft. having been read, paragraph by paragraph,

Refolved unanimoufly, That we do highly approve of the faid refolutions and addrefs.

Refolved unanimoufly, That we hereby pledge ourfelves to co-operate with the feveral Corps, whofe Delegates met at Dungannon, in every conftitutional mode of obtaining redrefs of the grievances mentioned in their refolutions.

Refolved unanimoufly, That the above refolutions be figned by the Secretary, and publifhed in the Hibernian Journal, and Dublin Evening Poft.

Signed by order,

ROBERT WALKER, Sec.

✦◆✦◆✦◆✦◆✦◆✦◆✦◆✦✦◆✦◆✦◆✦◆✦◆✦◆✦◆✦◆✦

*At a Meeting of the Principal Freeholders of the* Manors *of* Teemore *and* Johnftown, *at* Hamilton's Bawn, *on Thurfday the* 28*th of February*, 1782, *they agreed to the following Refolutions.*

BENJAMIN BELL, Efq; in the Chair.

R ESOLVED unanimoufly, That this meeting do highly approve of the refolutions entered into at the Dungannon meeting, and in particular, that in favour of our fellow-fubjects, the Roman Catholics of this kingdom.

That we highly approve of the addrefs of faid meeting to the minority of both houfes of parliament.

That we will not ufe any of the produce of Portugal (not even its falt) until that country fhall receive our manufactures on the fame terms as thofe of Great Britain.

The following vote of thanks to our reprefentatives was unanimoufly agreed to :

To the Right Honourable WILLIAM BROWNLOW, and THOMAS DAWSON, Efqs.

Receive our warmeft thanks for fupporting Mr. Grattan's motion for an addrefs to our Sovereign; we have heard with furprife, that under the Britifh conftitution, *power makes right;* yet, we are bold to fay, no power on earth can now

(and

(and we hope never will be able to) effect with force in this kingdom, what is not pretended to be established by its laws.

After the meeting, most of the members, being volunteers, assembled on their parade, and passed the evening in military manœuvre and exercise.

●◆●◆●◆●◆●◆●◆●◆●◆◆◆●◆●◆●◆●◆●◆●◆●◆◆●

ROYAL EXCHANGE, Dublin, 1st March, 1782.

*At a meeting of the Delegates from the following thirteen associated Corps of the City and County of* Dublin, *this Day, pursuant to public Notice, to wit,* Union Light Dragoons, Hibernian Light Dragoons, Dublin. Volunteers, Goldsmiths, Lawyers, Merchants, Liberty, Independent Dublin Volunteers, Upper Cross *and* Coolock, Newcastle *and* Donore Union, Finglas, Builders *and* Attornies, *in order to take into Consideration the Resolutions and Address of the* Ulster Volunteers, *represented at* Dungannon, *on the 15th of February last.*

Colonel TALBOT in the Chair.

The said Resolutions and Address of the *Ulster Volunteers* being first separately read, and the question put on each,

RESOLVED unanimously, That we do highly approve of the said resolutions and address.

Resolved . unanimously, that as citizens and . Volunteers, we will co-operate with the several corps, whose Delegates met at Dungannon, in every constitutional mode of obtaining a redress of the grievances mentioned in their resolutions ; and, the more effectually to carry those resolutions into execution, we do request the several corps in the province of Leinster to send Delegates, to meet at the Royal Exchange, Dublin, on Wednesday the 17th of April next, at ten o'clock in the morning.

Resolved unanimously, That the thanks of this meeting be returned to the Delegates who met at Dungannon the 15th of February last, for appointing nine of their members to be a committee in Dublin, in order to communicate with other Volunteer Associations in the other provinces, and that we shall be happy to confer and deliberate with them upon the

most

moſt conſtitutional means of carrying their reſolutions into
Execution.

Reſolved unanimouſly, That a copy of the laſt reſolution,
ſigned by the chairman, be ſent to the nine gentlemen of the
ſaid committee.

Reſolved unanimouſly, That the thanks of this meeting
be turned to our ſecretary, for his great trouble and attention to the buſineſs of this aſſociation.

R. TALBOT, Chairman.

Col. Talbot having left the chair, it was afterwards reſolved
unanimouſly, That the thanks of this meeting be returned
to him for his very upright and impartial conduct therein.

By order,<br>
J. T. ASHENHURST, Sec.

---

## LOYAL LIMERICK VOLUNTEERS.

*At a general Meeting of the* Loyal Limerick Volunteers, *commanded by Brigadier General* Thomas Smyth, *at the Council-
Chamber,* Limerick, *March the 1ſt,* 1782.

Captain GEORGE PITT in the chair.

The following Addreſs was unanimouſly agreed to.

To Colonel Mervyn Archdall, and the other members of the
Committee, appointed to communicate with ſuch Volunteer
Corps as approve of the Reſolutions entered into at *Dun-
gannon,* on the 15th of February, 1782.

GENTLEMEN,

WE, the Loyal Limerick Volunteers, impreſſed with
the ſtrongeſt conviction of the neceſſity of your late ſpirited
and patriotic reſolutions, take this early and public opportunity of declaring our fulleſt approbation of them, and our
determined reſolution to co-operate in ſuch conſtitutional
meaſures as ſhall appear moſt expedient for rendering them
effectual.

As citizens of a free ſtate, we hold ourſelves indiſpenſably
obliged at all times to aſſert our rights and privileges, and
ſhould the complexion of the times render a peculiar attention

to

to this great object neceſſary, we truſt that our conduct will fully evince the ſincerity of this declaration.

Convinced of the rectitude of your intentions, and of the great ſhare which you have always had in the emancipation of your country, we read with particular pleaſure the reſolves of your body, and ſhall ever feel the greateſt ſatisfaction in a communication of ſentiments with men who have thus honourably diſtinguiſhed themſelves as ſupporters of their country's rights.

Signed by order,

MITCHELL BENNIS, Sec. L. L. V.

<hr />

## RAFORD BRIGADE.

*At a meeting of the* Raford Brigade, *held at the* New Inn, *in the County of* Galway, *the firſt of March,* 1782.

The following Reſolutions were unanimouſly entered into.

Captain HYA. CUNIFF in the chair.

RESOLVED, That true praiſe, and heart-felt thanks are moſt juſtly due to the honeſt ſpirit, the ſterling loyalty, and liberality of ſentiment, that in a peculiar manner, ſtamp the reſolutions of the Ulſter Delegates at Dungannon.

Reſolved, That we will uſe every right, and exert every efficatious and conſtitutional means, as Iriſhmen, freemen, and freeholders, to ſhew that they are ours alſo.

Reſolved, That with true gladneſs of heart, we behold bigotry and religious prejudices giving way in every ſect to true chriſtian liberty and brotherly love; but that notwithſtanding indulgence in point of religious opinions muſt be conſidered a bounteous, a charitable, and manly act, characteriſtic of Proteſtant benevolence, it is ſtill but a partial reſtoration of our brethrens natural rights; defective to the grand end, it muſt unite with all our rights, conſtitutional and commercial, to beget the juſtly ſtiled confidential ſtrength and glory of a nation.

Reſolved, That to neglect ſupporting and cultivating our natural rights, the gift of heaven, and which no civil inſtitution can legally prevent, but ought to ſecure to the ſtate,

and

and use every kind and parental endeavour to render inviting and improvable, would be ingratitude to God, disaffection to our country, and injustice to our posterity.

Resolved, That as laws ought to guide the liberty of the people to their strength and happiness, and of consequence beget the dignity, security, and internal satisfaction of the sovereign, and not cramp or pervert it, we do hereby promise and engage, that we will most cordially unite and cooperate with our virtuous countrymen and brethren, as shall be deemed most expedient and effectual (becoming good and faithful subjects) to remove the many illegal, unconstitutional, and intolerable restraints and checks that now, or may hereafter, tend to destroy the final end of every connection between the sovereign and people, and restore and preserve to our country, her legal and rightful constitution—*Her birth-right.*

Resolved, That the warmest thanks and acknowledgments of this corps be given to our colonel, Denis Daly, Esq; for his unremitted and unwearied exertions and aid, to give us a title to the name of fellow-citizens, in seventeen hundred and eighty two; for his supporting the police and quiet of this country, and for his wonted and honestly animated alacrity, in convening us at this crisis; and that we do pledge ourselves, as *Irishmen* and *Volunteers,* to him and our country, that we will endeavour to be at least not unworthy part of the virtuous *whole.*

Resolved, That the above resolutions be published in the Dublin Evening Post.

Signed by order,

EDMOND O'DONNEL, Sec.

*At a meeting of the corps of* Dublin Volunteers, *at the Eagle,* Eustace-street, *on Friday the 1st of March,* 1782.

His Grace the DUKE of LEINSTER in the chair.

RESOLVED, That the resolutions of this corps, of the 9th of June 1780, be re-published three times, in the Dublin Journal, and which are as follow.

Resolved, That Great Britain and Ireland, are, and ought to be, inseparably connected, by being under the dominion
of

of the fame king, and enjoying equal liberty and fimilar conftitutions.

That it is the duty of every good citizen to maintain the connection of the two countries, and the freedom and independence of this kingdom.

That the King, Lords, and commons, of Ireland only, are competent to make laws binding the fubjects of this realm, and that we will not obey, or give operation to any laws, fave only thofe enacted by the King, Lords, and Commons of Ireland, whofe rights and privileges, jointly and feverally, we are determined to fupport with our lives and fortunes.

Signed by order,

JOHN WILLIAMS, Sec.

## DROGHEDA ASSOCIATION.

*At a full meeting of the* Drogheda Affociation *(convened by public notice) at the Tholfel of* Drogheda, *the 1ft of March,* 1782.

Colonel HUGH MONTGOMERY LYONS in the chair.

RESOLVED unanimoufly, That we do approve of, and highly applaud the fpirited refolutions and addrefs of the Delegates from the feveral corps of Volunteers, affembled at Dungannon, the 15th day of February laft.

Refolved unanimoufly, That we will co-operate with our fellow-volunteers in every conftitutional mode of obtaining a redrefs of the grievances juftly complained of infaid refolutions.

Refolved unanimoufly, That colonel Ogle, colonel Lyons, major Chefhire, captain Fairtlough, and lieutenant Holmes, or any three of them, be appointed a committee, on behalf of this corps, to communicate with the committee of nine, appointed on behalf of the Ulfter corps to meet in Dublin.

Refolved unanimoufly, That the thanks of this meeting be given to colonel Lyons, for his polite conduct in the chair.

Refolved, That thefe refolutions be figned by captain Fairtlough, fecretary to this meeting, and publifhed in the Dublin and General Evening Pofts, and Drogheda Journal.

OLIVER FAIRTLOUGH, Sec.

MER

MERCHANTS, &c. of BELFAST.

Belfaft, March 1, 1782.

*To* Travers Hartley, *Efq; one of the Reprefentatives in Parlia-*
*ment for the City of* Dublin.

SIR,

WE the merchants and other principal inhabitants of the
town of Belfaft, take this earlieft opportunity to offer you our
fincere congratulations on the happy event of your being
elected a reprefentative of the city of Dublin. We confider
it as a proof of the freedom and independence of the Electors of that city. We rejoice in it, as an addition to the
wifdom and virtue of the Senate: from the choice of fuch
men we forefee the confirmation of all our national rights; and
we behold it as a pledge, that the principles of trade, and
facts regarding our commerce, fhall be more clearly explained,
and more fully ftated to the Commons of Ireland, than they
ever can be, without the aid of men poffeffed of real commercial knowledge.

We moft fincerely wifh, that on every future occafion the
reft of the kingdom may follow the illuftrious example of the
City of Dublin, both in the uninfluenced wifdom of their choice,
and the incorruptible freedom and independency of their proceedings,

We have the honour to be,

SIR,

Your moft obedient humble fervants.

| | | |
|---|---|---|
| Val. Jones, Chair-man. | James Hamill, | Samuel M'Tier, |
| Tho. Sinclaire, | Hu. M'Ilwain, | John Mathers, |
| James Weir, | William Seed, | T. Batefon and Co. |
| Thomas Hyde, | Robert Linn, | T. Hardin and Co. |
| Richard Batefon, | Herc. M'Comb, | Stewarts, Thomfon |
| W. and J. Brown, | James Stevenfon, | and Co. |
| Thomas Lyons, | Alex. Armftrong, | R. Hu. & A. Hynd- |
| J. and J. Holmes, | Hugh Crawford, | ham, |
| W. Cunningham, | James Pinkenton, | Samuel Brown, |
| Thomas Gregg, | James Fergufon, | Brown, Cunning- |
| J. Campbell & Co. | James Colt Smite, | ham and Co. |
| Wm. Ramfey, | Daniel Blow, | Annefly and Lilly, |
| Will. Irvin, | David Tomb, | Robert Gotty, |
| | Henry Joy, | Ifaac Miller, |

C

Tho.

Tho. Stewart,
Robert Wallace,
John Ewing,
And. Hyndman,
Alex. Arthur,
Cunning. Greg,
Sam. Afhmore,
Robert Carfon,
John Neilfon,
J. Henderfon,
Arch. Scott,
Ja. Graham,
Francis Taggart,
Patrick Gaw,
Jof. Stevenfon,
Cavan and Seed,
Tho. Hardin,
Wm. Bryfon,
James Park, jun.
Alex. Blackwell,

James Park,
John Bafhford,
Tho. Andrews,
Thomas Lyle,
John Smith,
Alexander Orr,
Robert Gordon,
William Magee,
James Magee,
John Hay,
John Luke,
John Craig,
Michael Linn,
David M‘Tier,
M‘Kedy & Steven-
fon,
Crawford and Cun-
ningham,
Tho. Milliken,
John Campbell,

Rob. Thomfon,
Lukes, Murphy,
Hazlett & Co.
Wm. Boyle,
D. Berweck & Co.
Robert Knox,
Robert Lylburn,
Walter Crawford,
Wilfon, Joyce and
Kennedy,
James Fergufon,
Rob. Stevenfon,
Wm. Harrifon,
John Brown,
Nath. Wilfon,
Robert Joy,
John Carfon,
John Clarke,
James Beggs.

---

*To the* Merchants *and other principal* Inhabitants *of the Town of*
Belfaft.

*Gentlemen,*

THE very honourable teftimonial your moft obliging addrefs has conveyed to me, is not conferred on a man infenfi-
ble of the value of it. The efteem and confidence of fo
refpectable a body of men, as the Merchants and other principal inhabitant of the town of Belfaft, affect me with the moft
pleafing and grateful fenfations.

You have been long diftinguifhed by your zeal for the commercial interefts and conftitutional rights of your country; a
zeal always directed by knowledge and found judgment. The
fenfe you exprefs of the virtuous, independent fpirit of the
electors of this city, is a tribute moft juftly due to them, and
which I greatly prefer to any thing perfonally relating to myfelf. The diftinguifhed honour which I enjoy, is that of their
confidence; and in a faithful difcharge of my truft to them,
I fhall be always fecure, Gentlemen, of your approbation.

I have the honour to be,
Gentlemen,
Your obliged and obedient fervant,

TRAVERS HARTLEY.

*Dublin,*
*March* 6, 1782.

# BELFAST BATTALION.

*At a Meeting of the* Belfaſt Battalion, *March* 1, 1782.

### Reverend JAMES BRYSON in the Chair.

RESOLVED unanimouſly, That the following addreſs be tranſmitted by our Chairman, Major Brown, Captains Cunningham and Bateſon, to *Travers Hartley*, Eſq; one of the repreſentatives in parliament for the city of Dublin.

S I R,

WHEN you were called forth by your fellow-citizens to ſtand as a Candidate at the late election of a repreſentative for the metropolis of the kingdom, we felt the greateſt ſatisfaction; the invitation did honour to their diſcernment and wiſdom; and no more than juſtice to your excellent and acknowledged character. When the attempt to ſend a member to the Houſe of Commons was crowned with ſucceſs, through your perſeverance, and the firmneſs, integrity, public virtue, and unconquerable independence of the electors, our ſatisfaction was raiſed into emotions of a more excellent nature—ſuch emotions as the triumphs of ſtruggling virtue muſt ever inſpire.

As the patriotic conduct of your fellow-citizens has done honour to the metropolis, we hope that the illuſtrious example will convey inſtruction to the whole kingdom, and univerſally excite that ſpirit of freedom and independence in the choice of the repreſentative body, which alone can reſtore to us our injured rights, and preſerve us from the deſtructive influence of ſenatorial venality and court dependence.

Permit us, therefore, to congratulate you, Sir, to congratulate the city of Dublin, to congratulate the whole kingdom on this happy event: an event which has done you the greateſt honour, added one man more of unſuſpected virtue to the ſenate, and taught the nation how to ſtruggle with ſucceſs for liberty.

May your parliamentary conduct reflect back on your conſtituents as much honour as they have already conferred on you.

We have the honour to be, Sir, your very humble ſervants.
Signed by order of the Belfaſt battalion,

JAMES BRYSON, Chairman and Chapl. of 1ſt company,
JOHN BROWN, Major of the Belfaſt battalion,
WADDELL CUNNINGHAM, Capt. firſt company,
RICHARD BATESON, Capt. Whitehouſe Volunteers.

*To*

*To the Gentlemen compofing the* Belfaft Battalion.

*Gentlemen,*

   I DO not wonder that a body of men, formed not only for the protection of their country againft foreign enemies, but for the conftant affertion of its conftitutional rights, fhould highly enjoy the triumph of the free and independent electors of the metropolis over the exertions of power and undue influence ; there is a fympathy between virtuous minds. The favourable idea which you have conceived of me, correfponding with that of my worthy fellow-citizens, does me great honour. In acting a part agreeably to the fenfe of my conftituents, which I fhall ever invariably do, I fhall be fecure of your approbation, and that of every friend to his country throughout the whole kingdom. With the heart-felt fatisfaction attending a cenfcioufnefs of integrity, to find my conduct approved of, by the wifeft and beft of my fellow-citizens and fellow-fubjects, will ever yield to me the higheft enjoyment.

     I have the honour to be,
        Gentlemen,
        Your moft obliged and obedient fervant,
          TRAVERS HARTLEY.

*Dublin, March* 6, 1782.

---

## BELFAST VOLUNTEER COMPANY.

*At a Meeting of the* Belfaft Volunteer Company, *held at the* Donegal Arms, *on the* 2d *of March,* 1782.

Lieutenant JOHN GALT SMITH in the Chair.

RESOLVED unanimoufly, That the Delegates of the Ulfter Volunteers, who met at Dungannon on the 15th ult. are entitled to our warmeft thanks for their conduct on that day ; and we requeft they may accept of the fame as a tribute juftly due to their wifdom, temper, fpirit and firmnefs on that important occafion ; and that the thanks of this Corps be given to the gentlemen who reprefented us at that meeting, for the propriety of their conduct, fo perfectly coinciding with the fentiments and inftructions of their conftituents.

   Refolved unanimoufly, That the following addrefs to Travers Hartley, Efq; and the Free and Independent Electors of the city of Dublin, be figned by the Chairman, and publifhed

lifhed with thefe refolutions, and that the Chairman do ei.
clofe a copy of faid addrefs to Mr. Hartley.

JOHN GALT SMITH, Chairman.

To Travers Hartley, *Efq; and the Free and Independent Electors
of the City of* Dublin.

*Gentlemen,*

AT a time when the inftructions of conftituents are by fo
many of the reprefentative body treated with contempt,
when the Delegate, on great national queftions, prefumes to
act contrary to the directions of thofe who fent him, and
from whom alone he derives his power; and when the mandate of a minifter, not the intereft of a nation, forms the only
rule of conduct to fo many of thofe who ought to guard the
peoples rights, we rejoice to fee a man of known virtue and
incorruptible integrity chofen a reprefentative in parliament
for the metropolis of the kingdom: we honour the wifdom,
the perfeverance, and the firmnefs of the electors; we revere
the many virtues of the elected; with fanguine hopes we
marked the progrefs of the conteft in which you have been engaged, yourfuccefs has been anfwerable to ourearneft wifhes;
accept then, on the aufpicious occafion, the congratulations
of the Belfaft Volunteer Company, a body of men, whofe
hearts, like your own, beat warm in their country's caufe.
We fincerely congratulate you, ourfelves, and the nation, on
the glorious triumph you have obtained over the undue influence exerted againft you; and we offer you our warmeft
thanks for the noble ftruggle you have made in favour of the
*Freedom of Election;* the fuccefs which has crowned that ftruggle, we hail as a happy omen, and hope your bright example will be followed by all the Electors of Ireland.

We live in a country, which, from its paft conduct, merited
to be well reprefented in the *prefent* parliament, and may we
be no longer admitted among free citizens and free foldiers,
if we do not ftrive to be better reprefented in the *next.*

By order of the Belfaft Volunteer Company,

JOHN GALT SMITH, Chairman.

To the Belfaft Volunteer Company.

*Gentlemen,*

IN your truly patriotic addrefs, you have done me the
honour to connect me with the free and independent Electors
of the city of Dublin, the moft honourable connection I can

poffibly

possibly have, and which, by my conduct, I shall ever be careful to preserve. Those virtuous citizens, as you justly observe, have set a bright example to their fellow-subjects throughout the kingdom, worthy of general imitation; they have manifested their sense of the importance of the *freedom of election*, and their firmness in that great cause has been attended with suitable success—may your future exertions, of a similar nature, be attended with equal success.

It remains now for me to evince, by my parliamentary conduct, that my professions to my fellow-citizens have been sincere, and to maintain in practice that doctrine, which I have always held in opinion, *obedience to the instructions of constituents*, to be the indispensible duty of representatives.

The very favourable opinion you have conceived of me personally, does me great honour; and you may be assured I set a just value on it.

I have the honour to be,

Your obliged and obedient servant,

TRAVERS HARTLEY.

※※※※※※※※※※※※※※※※※※※※※※※※※※※※※

## SLANE VOLUNTEERS.

*At a Meeting of the* Corps *of* Volunteers *of the* Barony *of* Slane, *County* Meath, *assembled on their Parade,* 3d *March,* 1782, *the following Resolutions and Address were Unanimously agreed to:*

RESOLVED, That the members of the House of Commons are the representatives of, and derive their power solely from, the people, and that a denial of this proposition would be to abdicate the representation.

Resolved, That no power on earth can make laws to bind the people of this land but the King, Lords, and Commons of Ireland

Resolved, That the resolutions and address of the Ulster Volunteers, represented at Dungannon the 15th of February last, are such as ought to be adopted by every true friend to this country, and that therefore we will, as soldiers and citizens, support to the utmost of our power, the several Corps whose Delegates met at Dungannon, in every constitutional mode of obtaining a redress of the grievances mentioned in these resolutions.

Resolved,

Refolved, That an addrefs be prefented to John Forbes, Efq; 2nd. Lieutenant of this Corps, and reprefentative in parliament for the Borough of Ratoath.

Refolved, That the above refolutions, and the following addrefs, be publifhed four times in the Dublin Evening Poft, and Faulkner's Journal.

Signed by order, FRANCIS ADAMS, Sec.

### To JOHN FORBES, Efq.

ACCEPT the fincere and hearty thanks, which we, your brother Volunteers, thus unanimoufly prefent to you, for the uniform and upright conduct to which you have fo fteadily adhered fince your entering into parliament, but particularly for your continued, though as yet ineffectual, endeavours to render the judges independent of the crown; and be affured, that the fatisfaction which we feel in offering to you thefe our acknowledgements, is confiderably heightened by being convinced (from a long and thorough knowledge of your principles) that you will perfevere in that line of conduct by which you have fo juftly merited the approbation and confidence of your countrymen.

Signed, FRANCIS ADAMS, Sec.

### To the Corps of Volunteers of the Barony of Slane, in the County of Meath.

*Gentlemen,*

I AM much flattered by the approbation of a Corps, compofed of gentlemen fo peculiarly diftinguifhed by their conftitutional principles and fpirited exertions. I fhall certainly continue to ufe my beft endeavours to obtain a law to render the judges independent of the crown, as the principle and neceffity of this meafure is univerfally felt and acknowledged.

I entertain the moft fanguine expectations, that the general wifhes of the people of Ireland will, in this inftance, be no longer refifted. I beg leave to affure you, that it fhall be my conftant ftudy to perfevere in that line of conduct which may moft contribute to the welfare and profperity of this country, and render me deferving of a continuance of your good opinion and confidence.

I have the honour of being, gentlemen,
Your moft obedient, and
Much obliged humble fervant,
JOHN FORBES.

*Drogheda,*
*March 9, 1782.*

# CLONMEL INDEPENDENTS.

*At a Meeting of the* Clonmel Independents, *on Sunday the 3d of March* 1782.

### Col. BAGWELL in the Chair.

RESOLVED, That the late resolutions of the Delegates from the Ulster Associations, entered into at Dungannon on Friday the 15th of February last, appear to us, to be truly spirited and patriotic, and if adopted by the different volunteer corps of this kingdom, cannot fail of being productive of the happiest consequences.

Resolved therefore, That a meeting of delegates from all the volunteer corps of the county Tipperary, is hereby requested, on Thursday the 14th instant, at Clonmel, in order to declare the sentiments of their constituents, on such resolutions as their wishes, and the exigency of public affairs demand.

Resolved, That these resolutions be inserted in the Dublin Evening Post, and Clonmel Gazettee.

Signed by order,
THOMAS MORTON, Sec.

---

# CORK UNION.

*At a numerous meeting of the* Cork Union, *held the 3d of March, 1782, pursuant to Notice.*

### HENRY HICKMAN, Commandant, in the Chair.

RESOLVED unanimously, That we do highly approve of the resolutions entered into at Dungannon, on the 15th day of February last, by the delegates of the Ulster Volunteers, as they breath the spirit of citizens and soldiers, determined to assert their constitutional righs, and diffuse the liberal sentiments of toleration, so essentially necessary in a free country.

Resolved unanimously, That, as citizens and Volunteers, we will co-operate with them in every constitutional mode of obtaining a redress of the grievances mentioned in their resolutions.

Resolved,

Refolved, That thefe refolutions be tranfmitted to captain
Dawfon by the chairman; and alfo that they be publifhed
in the Freeman's Journal, Dublin Evening Poft, and Cork
papers.

HENRY HICKMAN, C. Union, Chairman.

## DOWN VOLUNTEERS.

*At a full Meeting of the* Down Volunteers, *affembled by public
notice, at the Court-houfe in* Downpatrick, *on Sunday the 3d
of March,* 1782, *to take into confideration the Refolutions and
Addrefs entered into, and publifhed by the Meeting of Delegates
from the* Volunteers *of* Ulfter, *affembled at* Dungannon, *on
the* 15th *Day of February laft,*

Captain HENRY WEST in the Chair.

RESOLVED, That we highly approve of the refolutions
and addrefs entered into by thofe gentlemen; and, as we think
them dictated by the fpirit of moderation, liberality of fentiment and patriotifm, we are determined to fupport and accede
to them, both in our private and public capacities, as citizens
and Volunteers.

Refolved, That our chairman do communicate our approbation of, and acceffion to, faid refolutions, to the fecretary of
the Dungannon meeting, and inform him that we moft willingly embrace the invitation to become members of that affociation.

Refolved, That thefe refolutions be publifhed in the Dublin Evening Poft and Belfaft News-Letter.

Signed by order,
HENRY WEST.

*At a full Meeting of the different Volunteer Corps of the City of*
Waterford, *the Cavalry, Artillery,* No. 1, 2, 3, 4, 5, 6,
*and* 7, *affembled by public Notice on the* 3d *Day of March,* 1782,

Captain HANNIBAL WILLIAM DOBBYN in the Chair.

RESOLVED unanimoufly, That we highly approve of
the refolutions and addrefs of the Ulfter Volunteers, reprefented at Dungannon, on the 15th day of February laft.

D                     Refolved,

Refolved unanimoufly, That as citizens and Volunteers, we will co-operate with the feveral corps whofe delegates met at Dungannon, in every conftitutional mode of obtaining a redrefs of the grievances mentioned in their refolutions.

Refolved unanimoufly, That the members of the Houfe of Commons are the reprefentatives of, and derive their power folely from, the people, and that a denial of this propofition by them, would be to abdicate the reprefentation.

Refolved unanimoufly, That we conceive that the people of this country are now called upon to declare, that the King, Lords, and Commons of Ireland are the only power competent to make laws to bind this kingdom.

Refolved unanimoufly, That we do expect fuch declaration of right from our reprefentatives in parliament, and that we will fupport them with our lives and fortunes in whatever meafures may be neceffary to render fuch declaration an effectual fecurity.

Refolved unanimoufly, That the thanks of this meeting be prefented to captain Hannibal William Dobbyn, for calling this meeting, and for his attention and politenefs of conduct in the chair.

Refolved unanimoufly, That thefe refolutions be publifhed in the Waterford Chronicle, and in the Dublin Evening Poft.

---

## LOYAL SLIGO VOLUNTEERS,

*On Parade affembled the 4th of March, 1782, unanimoufly came to the following Refolution:*

THAT, as citizens and foldiers, we do heartily approve of the Dungannon addrefs to the minority of both houfes of parliament, and do moft chearfully adopt their refolutions of the 15th of February laft, for obtaining a redrefs of grievances; and that we will, to the utmoft of our power, co-operate with them and the feveral volunteer corps of this kingdom, for fo defireable a purpofe.

JOHN ORMSBY, Lieut. Col.

Ordered, That the above refolutions be publifhed in the Dublin Evening Poft, and Sligo Journal.

GAL-

## GALWAY VOLUNTEERS.

*At a general Meeting of the* Galway Volunteers, *held at the* Tholsel *this Day,* March, 4, 1782.

### Major JOHN BLAKE in the Chair.

Came to the following Resolutions :—

RESOLVED unanimously, That we do highly approve of the resolutions and address of the Ulster Volunteers, represented at Dungannon, on the 15th day of February last.

Resolved unanimously, That as citizens and Volunteers, we will co-operate with the several corps whose delegates met at Dungannon, in every constitutional mode of obtaining a redress of the grievances mentioned in their resolutions.

Resolved, That the above resolutions be published in the Dublin and Galway Evening Posts, and Connaught Journal.

Signed by order,
JOHN KERGAN, Sec.

✦•◦✦•◦✦•◦✦•◦✦•◦✦•◦◦✦•◦•✦•◦✦•◦✦•◦✦•◦✦•◦✦•◦✦•◦✦•◦✦

*At a full Meeting of the* Boyne Volunteer Corps *of the City of* Cork, *assembled by public Notice, this* 4th *of* March, 1782.

### Major BASS in the Chair.

RESOLVED unanimously, That we do highly approve of the resolutions and address of the Ulster Volunteers, represented at Dungannon, the 15th February ult.

Resolved, That as citizens and Volunteers, we will co-operate with the several corps, whose delegates met at Dungannon, in every constitutional mode of obtaining a speedy redress of the grievances mentioned in their resolutions.

Resolved, That our chairman do forward to the secretary of the Ulster Volunteers, a copy of these our resolutions, and also a copy to John Bagwell Esq; our Colonel.

Resolved, That the thanks of this corps be presented to our worthy major, for his particular propriety and steadiness of conduct in the chair.

Resolved, That the thanks of this corps be presented to our worthy secretary, lieutenant Charles Willcocks, for his particular propriety of conduct.

Resolved, That these our resolutions be printed in the Cork and Dublin news-papers.

*We*

*We the High Sheriff and Grand Jury of the County of* Weftmeath,
*at a General Affizes held at* Mullingar, *in and for faid County,*
*on Monday the 4th Day of March,* 1782.

RESOLVED unanimoufly, That the King, Lords, and
Commons of Ireland, are the only power competent to make
laws to bind this kingdom.

That the law, vulgarly called Poyning's Law, is unconftitutional, and a grievance, and ought to be repealed.

That a Mutiny Bill, not limited in point of duration, from
feffion to feffion, is unconftitutional, and a *grievance.*

That the independence of the judges of this realm, is
equally effential to the impartial adminiftration of juftice in
Ireland, as in England. That a bill, therefore, for making
the commiffions of judges *Quam diu fe bene jefferint,* is abfolutely neceffary, to render them independent, more efpecially
as their falaries have been lately increafed.

That the numerous abfentees of this kingdom, from the
immenfe fums annually remitted to them, are highly detrimental, and very much contribute to the impoverifhing the
nation, and that the above evil is every day increafing, even
to an alarming degree.

That a tax upon abfentees, would very much contribute
to the profperity, honour and happinefs of this kingdom, and
that the faid tax fhould be appropriated to national purpofes.

That we confider the right of private judgment in matters
of religion, to be equally facred in others as in ourfelves.

That we rejoice in the relaxation of the Penal Laws againft
our Roman Catholic fellow-fubjects ; and that we conceive it
to be a meafure fraught with the happieft confequences to the
union and profperity of the inhabitants of Ireland.

That we do think it now abfolutely neceffary to declare,
that the Commons of Ireland, in parliament affembled, are
the reprefentatives of, and derive their authority folely from,
the people.

That we do think it highly neceffary, for the reprefentatives
of the people, to demand a fpeedy declaration of the rights
of this kingdom.

That we will fupport with our lives and fortunes, our reprefentatives, in conjunction with the hereditary branch of the
legiflature, in every meafure, which may tend to make fo
glorious and neceffary a demand effectual.

That

That, as it is the undoubted right of free and independent electors to inftruct their reprefentatives, fo it is the duty of reprefentatives faithfully to fpeak the fenfe of the people.

We, therefore, as free electors of the county of Weft-meath, do hereby inftruct our reprefentatives, to join in every meafure, which may tend to promote all the objects declared in the above refolutions.

That a copy of the above refolutions be prefented to each of our reprefentatives.

That the above refolutions, together with the anfwers of our reprefentatives, be printed in the Dublin, and Weftmeath Journals, and Dublin, and General Evening Pofts.

| | |
|---|---|
| Wm. Fetherftone, Sheriff | George Clibborn |
| Cuth. Fetherftone, Foreman | Charles Levinge |
| Delvin | Wm. Judge |
| Robert Moore | Peter Delamar |
| James Nugent | John Lyons |
| Lavallin Nugent | Robert Hodfon |
| Guft. R. Hume | Chriftopher Dardis |
| Wm. Smyth | James M. Berry |
| H. Monk | Anthony Nugent |
| James Fetherftone | Nicholas Gay |
| Denis Daly | R. Reynell. |

*To the High Sheriff, and Grand Jury of the County of* Weftmeath.

*Gentlemen,*

WITH the fincereft pleafure, I receive the intimation of your fentiments on all occafions, and fhall always chearfully comply with your defires, as I am convinced they will be founded on principles well calculated to preferve that harmony which fhould ever fubfift through the whole of the Britifh empire.

I fhall never lofe fight of thofe great objects which you now recommend to my attention, and fhall fteadily purfue every meafure to obtain them, that fhall appear to me to be wife, conftitutional, and effectual.

I have the honour to be,

Gentlemen,

Your very obliged, and faithful fervant,

*Bowden-park,*
*6th of March,* 1782.

ROBERT ROCHFORT.

*To the High Sheriff, and Grand Jury of the County of* Westmeath.

*Gentlemen,*

I AM fully convinced of the refpect I owe to the inftructions of my conftituents, and fhall always chearfully cooperate with their fentiments. I fhall obey with particular fatisfaction your commands intimated to me this day, by purfuing fuch a line of conduct in parliament, as I humbly truft, will fully evince my earneft wifhes faithfully to difcharge the duties of that fituation in which your favour has placed,

Gentlemen,

Your moft obliged, humble fervant,

*Mullingar,*
*March 6, 1782.*

BEN. CHAPMAN.

✣⊱⊱✣⊱✣⊱✣⊱⊱✣⊱✣⊱✣⊱✣⊱✣⊱✣⊱✣⊱✣⊱⊱✣⊱✣⊱✣⊱✣⊱✣⊱✣⊱✣

## AUGHNACLOY VOLUNTEERS.

*At a Meeting of the* Aughnacloy Volunteer Light Infantry, *and* Train *of* Artillery *Companies, commanded by* Nathaniel Montgomery, *Efq; on Monday the 4th of March,* 1782.

WILLIAM MOORE, Efq; in the Chair.

WE having deliberately confidered the refolutions entered into and publifhed by the Ulfter meeting at Dungannon, on the 15th of February laft, and it being our unalterable opinion they contain nothing more than what the true reprefentatives of the people in parliament have hitherto in vain moft ardently fought for;

Refolved unanimoufly, That we highly approve of every part of faid refolutions, and pledge ourfelves, as men of honour, that we will give the fame every conftitutional fupport in our power.

Refolved, That our Chairman do communicate our approbation of faid refolutions to captain James Dawfon, Secretary to the Ulfter meeting, and that the fame be publifhed in the Dublin Evening Poft, and Belfaft News-Letter.

WILLIAM MOORE, Efq; Chairman.

*At*

*At a full Meeting of the Corps of* Tipperary Light Dragoons, *and* Tipperary Infantry, *assembled by public notice on Monday the 4th of March,* 1782, *the following Resolutions were proposed, and unanimously agreed to :*

### Lieutenant Colonel BAKER in the Chair.

THAT we do highly approve of the resolutions and address of the Ulster Volunteers, represented at Dungannon on the 15th day of February last, and are happy to declare our concurrence with them in all their sentiments upon civil, religious, and commercial freedom.

That we will co-operate with them in all constitutional modes, to obtain a redress of all the grievances they complain of, and think a thorough communication between the Volunteer Corps of Ireland, a step most materially conducive to that purpose.

That we do appoint Edward Moore, Esq; to be our Delegate in Dublin, in order to communicate with the Ulster, and such other Volunteer Associations as may think proper to come to similar resolutions, and to deliberate with them on the most constitutional means of carrying them into effect.

That the doctrine, that *power* gives *right,* tends to lessen and disjoint the whole frame of civil society, and to introduce universal anarchy and confusion; and that a claim or attempt to govern this kingdom by such an absurd and wicked maxim, is unconstitutional and a *grievance.*

Ordered, that the above resolutions be published in the Dublin Evening Post, the Clonmell Gazette, and Munster Journal.

Signed by order,
ROBERT EVANS, Secretary.

*At a Quarterly Meeting of the Corps of* Independent Dublin Volunteers, *held at the Eagle in* Eustace-street, Dublin, *on* Tuesday, March 5, 1782.

### Major CANNIER in the Chair.

WHEREAS the people of Ireland are a free people, with a parliament of their own, to whose authority alone they are subject: Now, we the corps of

INDE-

## INDEPENDENT DUBLIN VOLUNTEERS,

associated for the defence of the realm, the law, and the constitution, do agree unanimously to the following resolutions for the rule of our conduct, viz.

Resolved, That we do not acknowledge the jurisdiction of any parliament, save only the King, Lords, and Commons of Ireland.

Resolved, That we will, in every capacity, oppose the execution of any statute imposed on us by the pretended authority of the British parliament.

Resolved, That we will support with our lives and fortunes, the parliament of Ireland in declaring and asserting its rights.

Signed by order,

S. CANNIER, Chairman.

## LIMERICK INDEPENDENTS.

*At a full Meeting of the Corps of* Limerick Independents, *assembled at the* Council-Chamber, *on the 6th Day of March,* 1782, *they came to the following Resolutions:*

### Major CALEB POWELL in the Chair.

The resolutions of the Ulster Volunteers represented at Dungannon, the 15th day of February last, being read,

RESOLVED, (with only one dissenting voice) That they meet our warmest approbation, for the truly patriotic sentiments conveyed in them; and that, as volunteers and citizens, we are unalterably fixed in these principles, and are determined to adopt and support every constitutional measure that can promote and secure the rights and liberties of a free people.

Resolved, That the above resolutions be published in the Dublin Evening Post, and Limerick papers.

Signed by order,

JOHN HARRISON, Sec.

AUGHRIM

## AUGHRIM VOLUNTEERS.

*At a full Meeting of the* Aughrim Volunteer Corps *of the City of* Cork, *held the 6th Day of March,* 1782, *pursuant to Notice.*

### EBENEZAR MORRISON, Major, in the Chair.

RESOLVED (with two diffenting voices only) That as Irifhmen and Free Citizens, earneft in the purfuit of, and refolved to protect and defend the civil liberties of our country, and encourage toleration and liberty of fentiment, we highly commend and approve of the refolutions of the Ulfter Volunteers, affembled by their delegates at Dungannon, on the 15th of February laft, and are firmly refolved and agreed, as citizens, volunteers, and free agents, breathing the fpirit of liberty, to co-operate with the volunteer corps reprefented at Dungannon, in every proper and conftitutional mode, to obtain a fpeedy and effectual redrefs of the grievances in their refolutions mentioned.

Refolved, That the above refolutions be forwarded by our chairman to our colonel, Richard Longfield, Efq; and alfo to the fecretary of the Ulfter Volunteers.

Refolved, That thefe our refolutions be publifhed in the Cork News-Papers, the Dublin Evening Poft, and Hibernian Journal.

EBENEZAR MORRISON,
Major Aughrim Volunteers.

◄◄►◄►◄►◄►◄►◄►◄►◄►◄►◄►◄►◄►◄►✕►►◄►◄►◄►◄►◄►◄►◄►◄►◄►

*At a Meeting of the Grand Jury and Freeholders, of the County of* Meath, *at* Trim, *convened by the Sheriff, on Thurfday the 7th of March,* 1782, *the following Refolutions and Addrefs, were unanimoufly agreed to :*

RESOLVED, That no power on earth can make laws to bind the people of this land, but the King, Lords, and Commons of Ireland.

Refolved, That the members of the Houfe of Commons are the reprefentatives of, and derive their power folely from, the people, and that a denial of this propofition by them would be to abdicate the reprefentation.

E

T*

*To* H. L. ROWLEY, and GOR. LOWTHER, *Esqrs.*

*Gentlemen,*

FULLY convinced that Free Trade, and Free Constitution, are inseparably connected, and that nothing can so effectually secure the one, and establish the other in this kingdom, as the independence of our legiflature;

We earnestly intreat you, to use your utmost endeavours in the House of Commons, to procure a declaration of the rights of the parliament of Ireland: and we solemnly pledge ourselves to support, with our lives and fortunes, our representatives in parliament, in whatever constitutional measures may be necessary to render such a declaration a permanent security.

Fully assured, that you will omit no opportunity in parliament of promoting the welfare of your country, we do not at present recommend particularly any other subject to your consideration and attention.

From your knowledge of the interests of Ireland, you cannot be ignorant that, in many instances (exclusive of that already mentioned) the immediate interposition of parliament is absolutely necessary for the relief of the people of this kingdom.

We cannot but observe with concern, that, notwithstanding your virtuous efforts as our representatives, not one of the measures we formerly recommended to your consideration have yet been effectuated.

We have hitherto refrained from repeating our instructions to you, not from any doubt of the propriety of those measures, or any indifference to the success of your exertions, but from a full confidence and daily expectation, that the moment would, before this period, have arrived, when all due efficacy would have been given to the just and ardent wishes of the people of Ireland.

Resolved, That the above resolutions and address, be signed by the chairman, and presented by the sheriff, to our representatives.

Resolved, That the thanks of this meeting be presented to the sheriff, for his readiness in calling this meeting, and also, to Hamilton Gorges, Esq; for the propriety of his conduct in the chair.

Resolved, That the above resolutions and address be printed six times in the Dublin Journal, and General Evening Post.

HAM. GORGES.

*To the Grand Jury and Freeholders of the County of* Meath, *convened by the Sheriff, on Thursday the 7th of March, at* Trim, 1782.

*Gentlemen,*

IT gives me great pleasure to receive your opinions and advice for my parliamentary conduct. Your approbation, and the confidence you place in my proper behaviour in parliament, meet my ardent wishes. I cannot better shew my respectful attention to your unanimous resolutions, and the sentiments expressed in your address to me, than by declaring, I intirely coincide with the principles contained in them; and that from inclination, as well as compliance with your opinions, I shall, as much as possible, endeavour to bring those essential rights of the people of Ireland to be effectually established by every constitutional means.

I have the honour to be,

With the greatest respect and gratitude,

Gentlemen,

Your most faithful and devoted

Friend and servant,

*Dublin,*
11th of March, 1782.     HER. LANGFORD ROWLEY.

➤➤➤➤➤➤◀◀◀◀◀◀

*To the Grand Jury and Gentlemen Freeholders of the County of* Meath.

*Gentlemen,*

I HAVE received, and shall with pleasure observe, your instructions, and am happy to find they coincide with my own sentiments and conduct in parliament; and sorry I am to inform you, that my endeavours have proved hitherto ineffectual.

From your spirit and perseverance, the time cannot be far distant, when the constitutional rights of our country must be acknowledged and established.

You

You may be affured, gentlemen, that I fhall warmly embrace every opportunity that may promote the profperity and welfare of this kingdom, which I fhall ever fupport with my life and fortune.

I have the honour to be,
With the greateft efteem and refpect,
Gentlemen,
Your moft obedient and very humble fervant,
GORGES LOWTHER.

## YOUGHAL VOLUNTEERS and RANGERS.

*At a numerous Meeting of the* Youghal Independent Volunteers, *and* Youghal Independent Rangers, *affembled by public notice on the* 7th of March, 1782.

JOHN SWAYNE, Major of the Youghal Independent Rangers, in the Chair.

RESOLVED unanimoufly, That we highly approve of the refolutions and addrefs of the Ulfter Volunteers, reprefented at Dungannon, on the 15th of February laft.

Refolved unanimoufly, That as citizens and Volunteers, we will co-operate with the feveral Corps whofe Delegates met at Dungannon, in every conftitutional mode of obtaining a redrefs of the grievances mentioned in their refolutions.

Refolved unanimoufly, That the Chairman do tranfmit a copy of thefe our refolutions to captain Dawfon (Secretary to the Dungannon meeting) at Union Lodge, Loughbrickland.

Refolved unanimoufly, That the Chairman do tranfmit copies of thefe refolutions to colonel Uniacke, commanding officer of the Youghal Independent Rangers.

Refolved unanimoufly, That the above refolutions be publifhed in the Cork papers and Dublin Evening Poft.

JOHN SWAYNE, Chairman.

Captain BOLES, of the Youghal Independent Volunteers, having taken the Chair,

Refolved unanimoufly, That the thanks of this meeting be given to Major Swayne, for his very proper conduct this day in the chair.

RICHARD BOLES.

TOWN-HOUSE, BELFAST, March 7, 1782.

*At a very numerous Meeting of the Inhabitants called by a public notice, dated the 4th inftant, and figned by 25 of the principal inhabitants.*

THOMAS SINCLAIR, Efq; in the Chair.

THE requifition calling the meeting, and pointing out the bufinefs propofed for deliberation, was read by the Chairman, after which the refolutions entered into by the Ulfter Volunteers, at Dungannon, on the 15th ult. were read, paragraph by paragraph;

1ft, Refolved unanimoufly, That we highly approve of, and cordially accede to, the faid refolutions, as calculated to promote the juft rights, and no more than the juft rights, of Ireland, as conceived with temper and moderation, yet, animated with a fpirit becoming men determined to be free.

2d, Refolved unanimoufly, That the faid Volunteers are entitled to our warmeft thanks, which we requeft they may accept fas a tribute juftly due to their wifdom, temper, and firmnefs on that important occafion.

3d, Refolved unanimoufly, That it is our decided and unalterable determination, to feek a redrefs of the grievances in faid refolutions mentioned, and to co-operate with the faid Volunteers, and all others who have acceded, or fhall accede thereunto, as with our fellow-electors, and the people at large, by every conftitutional means in our power, to render fuch our purfuit of redrefs fpeedy and effectual.

4th, Refolved unanimoufly, That we will, and we hereby do pledge ourfelves to each other, and to our country, as freeholders, fellow-citizens, and men of honour, that we will at every enfuing election fupport thofe, and thofe only, who have fupported, and will moft folemnly and unequivocally engage to fupport us in our purfuit of fuch redrefs.

5th, Refolved unanimoufly, That the right honourable and honourable the minority in parliament, who have fupported our conftitutional rights, are entitled to our warmeft thanks ; that we honour, efteem and revere them, as the guardians of our liberties and rights ; that we moft cordially approve of the addrefs to them publifhed by the Ulfter Volunteers ; that it fpeaks our thoughts in language which cannot be mended, and therefore we defire to be confidered as fincere fubfcribers to it.

6th,

6th, Refolved unanimoufly, That the members of the Houfe of Commons are the reprefentatives of, and derive their power folely from, the people, and that a denial of this principle by any of them, or a conduct directly contrary thereto, would be to abdicate the reprefentation.

7th, Refolved unanimoufly, That if any Irifhman has been, or fhall be hardy enough to affert, directly or indirectly, that any body of men, other than the King, Lords, and Commons of Ireland had, have, or ought to have a right to make laws to bind this realm, in any cafe whatfoever, every fuch man infults the majefty of the King of Ireland, the dignity of its parliament, and the whole body of its people; is an enemy to this kingdom, and ought to be reprobated as fuch by every friend of Ireland.

8th, Refolved unanimoufly, That it be, and it hereby is, moft earneftly recommended to all the inhabitants of this province, to affemble in their feveral towns and parifhes, to deliberate on thofe matters, and in cafe they fhall approve thereof, to enter into fimilar affociations; as we are fully convinced, that nothing is now wanting to eftablifh and fecure the freedom and profperity of Ireland, but the avowed union of its people.

THOMAS SINCLAIR, Chairman.

## COUNTY of WATERFORD.

*At a Meeting of the Grand Jury of faid County, at the General Affizes held at Blackfryars, in faid County, the 8th Day of March, 1782.*

RESOLVED, That we will not vote for any man to reprefent us in parliament, for any county, city, or borough, who declares, or in actions fupports, that the members of the Houfe of Commons are not the reprefentatives of, and derive their power from, the people.

Refolved, That the King, Lords and Commons of Ireland, are the only power competent to make laws to bind this kingdom.

Refolved, That we will fupport the reprefentatives of the people with our lives and fortunes, in whatever meafures may be neceffary to render the above declaration effectual.

By order of the Grand Jury,
JOHN BERESFORD, Foreman.

## COUNTY of WEXFORD.

Head-Quarters, *Enniscorthy*, March the 8th, 1782.

*At a full Meeting*, *held at the* Bear-Inn, *of the* First Irish Volunteers.

### Lieut. Col. DERENZY in the Chair.

RESOLVED unanimously, That the call of the province of Leinster for the 17th of April next, to consider of the truly spirited and patriotic resolutions of the Ulster Volunteers, may be of the greatest utility to this kingdom, and that therefore a Delegate from our body do attend.

Resolved unanimously, That our worthy Colonel, Sir Vesey Colclough, Bart. be requested to act for us at said meeting.

Resolved unanimously, That we do not think it necessary to instruct our representatives on their parliamentary conduct, their early zeal and attention in the Volunteer cause convincing us, that they will, on every occasion, take a decided part in support of the constitutional rights of their country.

Resolved unanimously, That they merit on any future election our warmest support, and the support of every true friend of this country, for their patriotic, firm, and virtuous conduct in parliament.

Resolved unanimously, That we will support our present representatives with our lives and fortunes, in every measure that may be conducive to the welfare and prosperity of Ireland.

Resolved unanimously, That these resolutions be published in the Dublin Evening Post and Wexford Journal.

Resolved unanimously, That the thanks of this meeting be given to Lieutenant-Colonel Derenzy, for his very proper conduct in the chair this day.     Signed by order,
JAMES FURLONG, Adjutant.

* * *

## WEXFORD INDEPENDENTS.

*At a full Meeting of the* Wexford Independent Corps, *on Friday the 8th of March*, 1782.

RESOLVED unanimously, That as freeholders, freemen, and Volunteers, we will co-operate with the several corps whose Delegates met at Dungannon, in every constitutional mode of obtaining a redress of the grievances mentioned in their resolutions.                         Resolved,

Refolved unanimoufly, That the members of the Houfe of Commons are the reprefentatives of, and derive their power folely from, the people, and that a denial of this propofition by them, would be to abdicate the reprefentation.

Refolved unanimoufly, That we conceive, that the people of this country are now called upon to declare, that the King, Lords and Commons of Ireland are the only power competent to make laws to bind this kingdom.

Refolved unanimoufly, That we expect fuch declaration of right from our reprefentatives in parliament ; and that we will not fupport at any enfuing election, any candidate, who, when in parliament, did not, or will not ufe his utmoft endeavour to obtain it.

Refolved unanimoufly, That we hold the right of private judgment, in matters of religion, to be equally facred in others as in ourfelves.

Refolved, therefore, unanimoufly, That we rejoice in the relaxation of the Penal Laws againft our Roman Catholic fellow-fubjects, and, that we conceive the meafure to be fraught with the happieft confequences to the union and profperity of the inhabitants of Ireland.

Refolved, That the foregoing refolutions be printed three times in the Dublin Evening Poft, and Waxford Journal.

Signed by order,<br>
WILLIAM HUGHES, Adjutant.

*At a Meeting of the* Lowtherftown Independent Volunteers, *the 9th of March,* 1782.

RESOLVED unanimoufly, That the thanks of this company be prefented to William Irvine, Efq; our Colonel, and that the Chairman and Committee of this company be ordered to draw up and prefent the fame.

Refolved, That the faid addrefs, with Colonel Irvine's anfwer, be publifhed in the Freeman's Journal and Dublin Evening Poft.

To WILLIAM IRVINE, Efq.

SIR,

WE, the Officers and Privates of the Lowtherftown Volunteers, under your command, beg leave to approach you with
hearts

hearts over-flowing with gratitude, for the unparalleled hofpitality and attention you have fhewn us upon all occafions,
fince our firft affociation in a military capacity. To you,
Sir, we owe that fteady and exact difcipline for which we
have been fo honourably diftinguifhed, and to your precept
and example alone we owe every thing that conftitute the citizen and foldier. We tender you, therefore, the greateft reward in our power to give, or in yours to receive, the thanks
of men freely and firmly determined, at the rifque of their
lives and fortunes, to follow you to any part of the kingdom, in fupport of their King and the liberties of their country, againft all enemies, foreign or domeftic.

We beheld, with particular fatisfaction, the deliberations of
our brethren of this province, at Dungannon, on the 15th of
February laft, in which you had fo confpicuous and honourable a part. We perfectly approve of every part of their refolutions, as calculated to promote the intereft of Ireland;
and we pledge ourfelves to you, and to each other, as freeholders and men of honour, to ufe every conftitutional means
to carry the fame into effect. Signed by order,
            MATHEW QUIN, Chairman.

*To which Addrefs Col. Irvine returned the following Anfwer:*

*Gentlemen,*

HOWEVER fmall my endeavours have been to merit
your thanks, it has ever been my greateft ambition to deferve
them. You, Gentlemen, from your firft affociation as Volunteers, have always fhewn fuch emulation for difcipline,
good order, regularity, and readinefs to obey when called upon
in the fervice of your country, that I have thought it the
greateft honour of my life to be chofen your commander.

When the liberties of our country, and the freedom of
our conftitution are in danger, I never doubted your fpirit or
firmnefs in their defence.

At the great provincial meeting of Delegates at Dungannon, I was unanimoufly chofen their Chairman: I fhould be
wanting in gratitude, did I not at this time, take the liberty
of returning them my moft fincere and hearty thanks; I am
happy to find that our refolutions have met your concurrence, as well as the moft unanimous approbation of the
whole kingdom, as they muft that of every conftitutional Irifhman in particular.

                        F                              Let

Let us, Gentlemen, perfevere, and our moft gracious Sovereign will, from his goodnefs of heart, in fpight of the pernicious councils of corrupt minifters, fee and redrefs our grievances.

I have the honour to be, Gentlemen,
Your moft faithful, affectionate
Friend and humble fervant,
WILLIAM IRVINE.

*Caftle-Irvine,*
10th *March,* 1782.

*At a Meeting of the United Corps of* Kilkenny Rangers, *and*
Kilkenny Volunteers, *on Saturday the 9th Day of March,*
1782.

Major WEMYS in the Chair.

They came to the following refolutions:

RESOLVED unanimoufly, That we will fupport the refolutions entered into by the Delegates of the Ulfter corps met
at Dungannon, on the 15th day of February laft, in every
conftitutional meafure.

Refolved unanimoufly, That the thanks of this meeting be
given to Major Wemys, for his polite conduct in the chair.

Refolved, That thefe refolutions be publifhed in the Dublin Evening Poft and Leinfter Journal.

Signed by order,
EDMUND BUTLER, Sec.

## GORT LIGHT DRAGOONS.

*At a full Meeting of the* Gort Light Dragoons, *the 9th of*
March, 1782, *purfuant to Notice.*

Major JAMES GALBRAITH in the Chair.

The following refolutions were unanimoufly agreed to:

RESOLVED, That we do highly approve of the refolutions and addrefs of the Ulfter Volunteers, reprefented at
Dungannon, the 15th of February laft.

Refolved, That the members of the Houfe of Commons,
are the reprefentatives of, and derive their power folely from,
the

the people, and that a denial of this proposition by them, would be to abdicate their representation.

Resolved, That it is now very expedient, and we conceive the people of this country are called upon to declare, that the King, Lords and Commons of Ireland are the only power competent to make laws to bind this kingdom.

Resolved, That we do expect such declaration of right from our representatives in parliament, and that we will support them, with our lives and fortunes, in whatever measures may be necessary to render such declaration an effectual security to our rights and liberties.

Resolved, That we will send two Delegates to the meeting at Ballinasloe, the 15th of this month, to confer with the Delegates of the other corps of this province.

Resolved, That the above resolutions be printed in the Dublin Evening Post and Connaught Journal.

Signed by order,

**JAMES O'FLANAGAN, Sec.**

## TRUE BLUE LEGION.

*At a full Meeting of the* True Blue Legion, *held the* 10th *of March,* 1782.

### Lieut. Col. MORRISON in the Chair.

RESOLVED unanimously, That we do highly approve of the resolutions and address of the Ulster Volunteers, represented at Dungannon on the 15th of February last.

Resolved unanimously, That as citizens and Volunteers, we will co-operate with the several Corps whose Delegates met at Dungannon, in every constitutional mode of obtaining a redress of the grievances mentioned in their resolutions.

Resolved, That a copy of the above resolutions be transmitted to our Colonel, the right hon. the earl of Shannon, and to Captain James Dawson, Secretary to the committee of the Ulster Volunteers, by our Chairman, and that the same be published in the Dublin Evening Post, and the Cork news-papers.

**JAMES MORRISON, Chairman.**

*At a Meeting of the* Wexford Independent Volunteers, *on Sunday the 10th of March, 1782.*

## Mr. RICHARD WADDY, Tertius, in the Chair.

RESOLVED unanimoufly, That we highly approve of the refolutions entered into at the laft meeting at Dungannon; that we are determined to be always ready to co-operate with our brother Volunteers of this kingdom, in every conftitutional meafure that may be found conducive to the welfare of our country.

Refolved, That the thanks of this meeting be given to our Chairman.

Refolved, That thefe refolutions be publifhed.

RICHARD WADDY, Tertius, Chairman.

⬥✦⬥✦⬥✦⬥✦⬥✦⬥✦⬥✦⬥✦⬥✦⬥✦⬥✦⬥✦⬥

*At a Meeting of the* Maguire's-bridge Volunteers, *County of* Fermanagh, *affembled the 11th Day of March,* 1782.

## ANDREW JOHNSTON, Efq; in the Chair.

AT this important crifis, when fuch a noble ardour pervades this kingdom, which is at once the aftonifhment of Europe, and a terror to its enemies; a fpirit which arms the citizen in defence of all he holds facred and dear to him, and from every rank of life breathes a determined refolution to fee its juft and legal rights eftablifhed on a fure and permanent bafis; fhould this country, which has at all times ftood fo confpicuous, remain inactive and filent when fuch grand defigns for the general weal are on the carpet, this would derogate from that fpirit which has always actuated us when the calamities of our country required it, and which we are ambitious to think ftill exifts here.

Refolved therefore, with the unanimous confent of this corps, That we moft cordially approve of the refolutions and addrefs entered into by the Delegates of the different corps of Volunteers, convened at Dungannon on the 15th day of February laft, as we confider them dictated by the fpirit of moderation, profound wifdom, liberality of fentiment, and true patriotifm; we perfectly coincide with them, accede to them, and are determined to fupport them by every conftitutional

tutional means, both in our private and public lines, as citizens and Volunteers.

Refolved, That our Chairman do communicate our approbation of, and acceffion to, faid refolutions, to the Secretary of the Dungannon meeting, and inform him, that we moft willingly embrace the invitation to become members of that affociation.

Refolved, That thefe refolutions be pnblifhed in the Dublin Evening Poft, and Belfaft News-Letter.

Signed by order,<br>
GERARD IRWIN, Sec.

✛•◀▶•✛•◀▶•✛•◀▶•✛•◀▶•✛•◀▶•✛•◀▶•✛•◀▶•✛•◀▶•※•✛•◀▶•✛•◀▶•✛•◀▶•✛•◀▶•✛•◀▶•

*At a Meeting of the* True Blue Volunteers *of* L. Derry, *at the Town-hall, on Monday the* 11th *of March,* 1782, *the following Refolutions were agreed to :*

Captain WM. LECKY in the chair.

Resolved unanimoufly, That we highly approve of the refolutions and addrefs entered into by the Volunteer Delegates affembled at Dungannon; and that, as citizens and foldiers, we will moft heartily co-operate with our brother Volunteers, in every conftitutional mode of obtaining a redrefs of the grievances mentioned in faid refolutions.

Refolved unanimoufly, That the members of the Houfe of Commons are the reprefentatives of, and derive their power folely from, the people ; and that a denial of this principle by them, or any of them, would be to abdicate the reprefentation.

Refolved unanimoufly, That we conceive that the people of this country are now called upon to declare, that the King, Lords, and Commons of Ireland are the only power competent to make laws to bind this kingdom.

Refolved unanimoufly, that if any Irifhman has been, or fhall be, hardy enough to affert, that any body of men, other than the King, Lords, and Commons of Ireland, had, have, or ought to have a right to make laws to bind this realm, in any cafe whatfoever, every fuch man infults the majefty of the king of Ireland, the dignity of its parliament, and the whole body of its people ; is an enemy to this kingdom, and ought to be reprobated as fuch by every friend of Ireland.

Refolved

Refolved unanimoufly, That the thanks of this company be given to Capt. Lieut. Moore, for his attendance at Dungannon as our Delegate ; and not only for fupporting our fentiments in that meeting, but alfo for the fpirited fupport he has at all times given the caufe of the Volunteers, his indefatigable attention to this corps, and for the independent and conftitutional principles which have regulated his conduct on all occafions.

Refolved unanimoufly, That the thanks of this company be given to our worthy chairman, for his polite and impartial conduct in the chair.

W. LECKY, Chairman.

*※※※※※※※※※※※※※※※※※※※※※※※※※※※※※※※※

*At a full Meeting of the* Imokilly Horfe, *held at* Middleton, *on Monday the Eleventh of March,* 1782.

### Lieutenant Colonel M'CARTY in the Chair.

T HE feveral refolutions and addrefs of the Ulfter Volunteers reprefented at Dungannon, on the 15th day of February laft, having been read paragraph by paragraph,

Refolved, That we do unanimoufly fubfcribe to refolutions which promife the moft happy confequences to this Kingdom, if profecuted and perfevered in with the fame fpirit and patriotifm by which they have been dictated.

Refolved unanimoufly, That as it is by conftitutional methods alone we hope to arrive at the degree of liberty which is the natural right of mankind, we accede, with particular fatisfaction, to that refolution which is immediately levelled againft the undue influence of a court, and the unequal and corrupt reprefentation of a people.

Refolved unanimoufly, That with the pleafure which liberal minds muft feel at every meafure which is dictated by real patriotifm and true religion, we particularly fubfcribe to that article which promifes a union of interefts and affections, and which we truft will effectually remove that bar, which foreign policy or private intereft has placed between this kingdom and her happinefs.

Refolved unanimoufly, That we will co-operate with our brother Volunteers in the moft fpeedy, effectual, and decifive manner of obtaining a redrefs of grievances.

Refolved,

Refolved, That the chairman be requefted to tranfmit copies of the foregoing refolutions to dward Roche, Efq; our Colonel, and to Captain Dawfon.

Refolved, That the above refolutions be publifhed in the Dublin Evening Poft and Cork papers.

ROBERT M'CARTY, Chairman.

## CARRICKFERGUS VOLUNTEERS.

*At a full Meeting of the* Carrickfergus Volunteer Company, *held on the 12th of March,* 1782.

RESOLVED, That we highly approve of the refolutions and addrefs, entered into at Dungannon on the 15th of February laft, by the Delegates of fo many refpectable corps.

Refolved, That as citizens and Volunteers, actuated by the fame liberal fpirit of freedom and toleration, we will co-operate with the feveral corps, whofe Delegates met at Dungannon, in every conftitutional mode of obtaining a redrefs of the grievances mentioned in their refolutions.

Refolved, That thefe refolutions be tranfmitted to Capt. Dawfon by the Secretary, and publifhed in the Belfaft News-Letter.          Signed by order,

EDWARD CRAIG, Secretary.

*At a Meeting of the* Connor Volunteers, *at* Connor, *on the 12th of March,* 1782.

### The Rev. JAMES BROWN in the Chair.

The Dungannon Refolutions having been read and confidered one by one, the following Refolutions were unanimoufly agreed to:

RESOLVED, That it is the opinion of this company, that the refolutions publifhed by the meeting of Delegates at Dungannon, manifeft fuch wifdom and fpirit, as if univerfally adopted and adhered to by Irifhmen, would not fail of being attended with the happieft confequences.

Refolved, That this company will therefore henceforth confider themfelves as united to the Ulfter affociation of Volunteers; and will, on every future occafion, give all affiftance

ance in their power, that their virtuous defigns may be crowned with fuccefs.

Refolved, That our Secretary fhall tranfmit a copy of thefe refolutions to Captain James Dawfon, Secretary to the Dungannon meeting, and that they be publifhed in the Belfaft News-Letter. Signed,

JAMES BROWN, Chairman.

○○○○○○○○○○○○○○○○○○○○○○○○✕○○○○○○○○○○○○

*Dublin, March* 12, 1782.

## SOCIETY of FREE CITIZENS.

### Mr. WILLIAM WITHERINGTON, Prefident.

RESOLVED unanimoufly, That this fociety, having, fince its firft formation, fupported, upon all occafions, the *Freedom of Election*, and the rights and privileges of their fellow-citizens; and having publicly declared their intention of afferting the right of nomination of the aggregate affembly of citizens, who called upon Travers Hartley, Efq; as a proper perfon to reprefent them in parliament, and in oppofition to one, who, under an affumed appearance of freedom and real independence, was notoriously fupported by the influence of adminiftration. We cannot but confider thofe members who voted for the latter, as deviating from thofe principles, which firft actuated the fociety of Free Citizens; and of courfe incurring the cenfure of our third rule, which declares, that, " any member acting inconfiftent with the patriotie " principles upon which this fociety is founded—fuch perfon " fhall be expelled."

Refolved therefore unanimoufly, That the names of thofe who voted for Alderman Warren on the late election (as now returned by a committee appointed for the purpofe) be erafed from our books, as perfons who have fubfcribed to principles, which, experience has convinced us, they neither fupport nor poffefs.

C L A N-

## CLANRICARDE CAVALRY.

*At a Meeting of the* Clanricarde Cavalry, *at* Loughrea, *the* 12*th Day of March*, 1782.

### Col. PETER DALY in the Chair.

RESOLVED unanimously, That we do highly approve of the resolutions and address of the Ulster Volunteers, represented at Dungannon, on the 15th day of February last.

Resolved unanimously, That as citizens and Volunteers, we will co-operate with the several corps whose Delegates met at Dungannon, in every constitutional mode of obtaining redress of the grievances mentioned in their resolutions.

Resolved unanimously, That the members of the House of Commons are the representatives of, and derive their power solely from, the people, and that a denial of this proposition by them, would be to abdicate the representation.

Resolved unanimously, That we conceive that the people of this country are now called upon to declare, that the King, Lords and Commons of Ireland are the only power competent to make laws to bind this kingdom.

Resolved unanimously, That we do expect such declaration of right from our representatives in parliament, and that we will support them with our lives and fortunes in whatever measure be necessary to render such declaration an effectual security.

Resolved, That we highly approve of the good intentions of parliament towards the Roman Catholics of Ireland.

Signed by order,
CHARLES KELLY, Sec.

-‹-‹-‹-‹-‹-‹-‹-‹-‹ ‹✦✦✦›-›-›-›-›-›-›-›-

### ROBERT FRENCH, Esq; in the Chair.

Resolved unanimously, That Anthony Daly, Esq; be chosen an honorary member of this corps, in testimony of our personal esteem for him, and as a grateful mark of our approbation of his uniform and disinterested conduct in parliament, which for fourteen years has been wholly directed by the true interests and welfare of his country.

Resolved, That the thanks of this meeting be returned to our worthy Chairman, Col. Peter Daly, for his upright conduct in the chair, and his great attention to the discipline and welfare of this corps. Signed by order,
CHARLES KELLY, Sec.

G

# KILKENNY HORSE.

*At a Meeting of the* Kilkenny Horfe, *this 12th Day of March,*
1782.

## Colonel CUFFE in the Chair.

RESOLVED unanimoufly, That we are ready to co-operate with the feveral corps, whofe Delegates met at Dungannon, in every conftitutional mode of fupporting and obtaining the rights of our country.

Refolved unanimoufly, That the above refolution be publifhed in the Dublin Evening Poft, and Leinfter Journal.

Signed by order,
HENRY M'REARY, Sec.

# COUNTY of WICKLOW.

*We, the High Sheriff and Grand Jury, of the County of* Wicklow, *at a General Affizes held at* Wicklow, *in and for faid
County, on Tuefday the 12th Day of March,* 1782.

## Hon. JOHN STRATFORD in the Chair.

RESOLVED unanimoufly, That we will fupport the king
and conftitution of Ireland with our lives and fortunes.

Refolved unanimoufly, That the King, Lords, and Commons of Ireland, are the only conftitutional power competent to bind this kingdom.

Refolved (with three diffentient voices) That we approve
of the fpirit, moderation, and liberality of fentiment, which
appeared in the refolutions entered into' at the Dungannon
meeting.

Refolved unanimoufly, That we are determined to fupport
our representatives in every conftitutional meafure which may
tend to advance the freedom and intereft of Ireland.

Signed, JOHN STRATFORD and Co.

## Colonel WESTBY in the Chair.

Refolved unanimoufly, That we highly approve of the
parliamentary conduct of our reprefentatives, and have hitherto

therto thought unneceffary to exert the undoubted difcre-
tionary power of conftituents to inftruct, relying on their
integrity and fteady perfeverance in the unexceptionable line
of conduct they have purfued.

Refolved, That thefe refolutions be publifhed.

Signed, NICHOLAS WESTBY.

HOPTON SCOTT, Efq; High Sheriff.

GRAND JURORS,

| | |
|---|---|
| Hon. John Stratford, Foreman | Francis Hutchinfon |
| Hon. Benj. Ow. Stratford | William Fairbrother |
| Samuel Hayes | John Ufher |
| Sir James Tynte, Bart. | William Parfons Hoey |
| Nicholas Weftby | Charles Coates |
| James Carroll | George Heighenton |
| Morley Saunders | William Holt |
| Thomas Acton | James Critchly |
| Charles Tottenham | William Ayres |
| William Hume | Pat. Ryan |
| John Smyth | Samuel Faulkener. |
| Laurenzo Nixon | |

*To the High Sheriff and Grand Jury of the County of* Wicklow.

*Gentlemen,*

I AM exceedingly obliged and thankful to you for the very
honourable teftimony of your approbation of me, as one of
your reprefentatives, fignified in your refolutions the 12th
inftant, at Eafter affizes, when the county at large were
affembled. Such approbation muft ever add to my endeavours
to deferve it ; and I feel myfelf the more affected by it, as
being fent free into parliament, without any teft or inftructions. A mark of your good opinion and confidence, I am
happy in this proof of my having merited. Be affured, I
fhall never quit that line of conduct you have thus fanctified ;
and as I fhall, after the recefs, faithfully exprefs your fenfe
in parliament, fo let me entreat, on all momentous and national points, your inftructions and advice. Permit me to beg,
through your favourable indulgence, that any unintentional
omiffions of a private nature, may be atoned for by my
ftrict attention to your public concerns, which fhall ever be
equally near my heart as my own.

I thank

I thank you moſt cordially for an approbation that encourages me to hope for your future favour and confidence, when this trial of me ſhall have an end, in the determination of this preſent parliament; by my paſt, you will judge of my future ſtudy to deſerve it.

   I have the honour to be, with the moſt perfect
     Gratitude, reſpect and eſteem,
      Gentlemen,
   Your moſt obliged and faithful humble ſervant,
      JOHN STRATFORD.

## COUNTY of CAVAN.

*At a Meeting at large of the County of Cavan, convened at the requiſition of the High Sheriff, at Cavan, on Wedneſday, March the 13th, 1782, the following Declaration was unanimouſly agreed to:*

WHEN national claims are mutually acknowledged, explanation is needleſs; when they neceſſarily ſubvert the ſecurity of either nation, it is fruitleſs—but, when nations ſtand bound to each other by every tie of intereſt and principle of conſtitution; when the juſt rights of each ſtrengthen the ſecurity of both, explanation then becomes the bond of indiſſoluble union. Upon this principle, the county of Cavan, aſſembled in its moſt collective capacity, at this intereſting moment of our exiſtence as a free country, feels itſelf called upon to give this ſolemn teſtimony to the reſpective rights of Great Britain and Ireland.

We declare, That we will pay obedience to thoſe laws *only*, which are made by our *own* legiſlature, the King, Lords, and Commons of Ireland, as the very terms of our original compact with Great Britain are, *that we ſhall poſſeſs and exerciſe the full enjoyment of the Britiſh conſtitution.* As external greatneſs and conſtitutional extention were the objects of Great Britain in that compact; as external ſecurity and conſtitutional liberty were the objects of Ireland, whatever leads to ſeparation on the part of the latter, or infringement on the part of the former, is a violation to both.

Upon this principle, we claim, that Great Britain will, in courſe, repeal, or explain every ſtatute that militates againſt the liberties of this kingdom; that our legiſlature
            will,

will, in courfe, adopt and legalize every Britifh ftatute neceffary to preferve the proper intercourfe between the two
nations. But whilft we claim for Ireland every benefit of
the Britifh conftitution, we fhould render ourfelves betrayers
of that truft, if we were not vigilant to prevent and remedy
every abufe of Irifh legiflation.

Juftice, therefore, as well as felf-defence, dictate a repeal
or explanation of the law, commonly called Poyning's Law,
and the explanatory one of the 4th and 5th of Philip and
Mary, which we confider as an unconftitutional facrifice of
the rights and liberties of the people, either in its firft origin,
or fubfequent mifconftruction, which were not in the power
of a parliament to give away, and alfo a conftitutional modification of the Mutiny Bill.

As we feel ourfelves, equally with Great Britain, bound by
every treaty of the King, we feel ourfelves, equally with
Great Britain, entitled to every benefit deriving from them;
we, therefore, claim as free and equal advantages of trade
and commerce with every nation as Great Britain herfelf enjoys, and we pledge ourfelves to our country and to each
other, to exert every conftitutional mean to fupport this our
folemn declaration.

Refolved, That the above be printed in the Dublin Evening Poft, the Freeman's and Faulkner's Journals, and the
Ulfter Journal.

Signed by order,

GEORGE MONTGOMERY, Chairman.

*March* 12, 1782.

✢✦✢✦✦✢✦✢✦✢✦✦✦✢✦✢✦✢✦✢✦✢✦✢✦✦

Market-Houfe, Newton-Ards, March 13, 1782.

*At a Meeting of upwards of three Hundred of the Inhabitants and
Freeholders of the Town and Parifh of* Newtown-Ards, *to
take into Confideration the Refolutions of the* Ulfter Volunteers
*lately met at* Dungannon; *and the fame being read Paragraph
by Paragraph:*

JAMES BRUCE, Efq; in the Chair.

RESOLVED unanimoufly, That we find ourfelves happy
in joining in the applaufes, admiration, and gratitude, which
fo generally prevail over the whole kingdom, and are fo juftly

due

due to a body of men, whose resolutions have exceeded our most sanguine expectations: they are founded in a perfect knowledge of our constitutional rights, and the breaches that from time to time have been made in them; and are framed with so much wisdom, temper and moderation, but, at the same time, with that determined and persevering spirit and firmness, arising from a thorough conviction of the justness of our claims, as must naturally and irresistibly engage every friend to his country in a concurrence with their measures. This operation has already taken place, and is daily encreasing with a rapid pace; so that we have all reason to believe, that this bond of union will prove lasting, and that the voice of the people will at length prevail.

Resolved unanimously, That our warmest thanks be, and are hereby given to that most respectable body of our neighbours and fellow citizens of Belfast, met for a similar purpose the 7th instant, for their manly, spirited, and sensible resolutions (which were also read and acceded to with the greatest pleasure); and to shew our respect for, and attention to every advice and recommendation coming from them, we beg to be admitted into their association, in order to assist in fulfilling every particular declaration in which we so heartily concur. And we do hereby pledge ourselves to our country, to them, and to one another, as freeholders and fellow-citizens, to co-operate with them in every constitutional measure, which may be deemed most effectual for carrying the said resolutions into execution. And we do most earnestly entreat and recommend to all the inhabitants in our neighbourhood to meet together in their several towns, or parishes, in order to form similar associations, and render themselves more respectable by their union. The body of the people is the most essential part of the community, from it are derived the support and strength of the whole; and in every struggle the last appeal must be brought before this great body. How necessary therefore is it, for every individual to know his own rights and those of his country, in order that he may be able to take a decided and conscientious part in endeavouring to transmit them unimpaired to the latest posterity.

Resolved unanimously, That these resolutions be published six times in the Belfast News-Letter and Dublin Evening Post.

JAMES BRUCE, Chairman.

## ENNIS VOLUNTEERS.

*At a Meeting of the* Ennis Volunteers, *held the* 13th *Day of March,* 1782, *purfuant to Notice.*

Lieut. Col. WILLIAM BLOOD in the Chair.

RESOLVED unanimoufly, That we do highly and heartily approve of the feveral refolutions entered into by the Delegates of the Ulfter Volunteers, at Dungannon, on the 15th day of February laft.

Refolved unanimoufly, That as Volunteers, and men firmly and zealoufly attached to the conftitutional rights and commercial intereft of this kingdom, we will exert every effort to co-operate in obtaining fatisfactory and compleat redrefs of the grievances complained of in faid refolutions.

Refolved unanimoufly, That our moft perfect and grateful acknowledgments are due to thofe wife and virtuous men who fo ftrenuoufly demanded, and fo fteadily fought a conftitutional declaration of the rights of Ireland.

Refolved unanimoufly, That to poftpone or evade fuch a declaration, is in effect to deny the right, and that to deny the right, is bafely to betray it.

Refolved unanimoufly, That the thanks of this meeting be given to Sir Lucius O'Brien, Bart. and Edward Fitzgerald, Efq; our reprefentatives in parliament, for their fteady and upright conduct.

Refolved unanimoufly, That a meeting of Delegates from the Volunteer corps of the county of Clare, be requefted at Ennis, on the 7th day of April next.

WILLIAM BLOOD. Chairman.

Colonel Blood having left the chair, it was refolved unanimoufly, That the thanks of this meeting be returned to him, for his upright and impartial conduct therein, and for his conftant and unwearied attention to the corps.

Refolved unanimoufly, That thefe refolutions be printed in the Dublin Evening Poft, and the Clare and Munfter Journals.

Signed by order,
DAVID ENGLAND, Captain and
Secretary.

ROYAL

## ROYAL TRALEE VOLUNTEERS.

*At a Meeting of the* Royal Tralee Volunteers, *held on the* 13th *Day of March*, 1782.

### GEORGE GUN, Major, in the Chair.

The following refolutions were unanimoufly agreed to :

RESOLVED, That we do highly approve of the refolutions entered into by the Ulfter Volunteers, reprefented at Dungannon, the 15th day of February laft.

Refolved, That as the affertion of our rights was one of the great purpofes for which we at firft affociated, we feel ourfelves called upon by that liberal fpirit of our original inftitution, and by every idea of confiftency, to co-operate with them as citizens and Volunteers, in every conftitutional meafure which may be thought conducive to a redrefs of the grievances with which our country is oppreffed.

Refolved, That as friends to humanity, to civil and to religious liberty, we do earneftly wifh the bill for the relief of our Roman Catholic fellow-fubjects, now depending, may meet with the concurrence of the feveral branches of the legiflature, confiding fo far in the wifdom and forefight of parliament, as to be under no apprehenfions, leaft the bill fhould contain any claufe, which may eventually prove detrimental to the ftate, or to the eftablifhed religion.

Refolved, That the thanks of the corps be prefented to Major Gun, for his readinefs in convening this meeting, and for the propriety of his conduct in the chair.

Ordered, That thefe our refolutions be publifhed in the Dublin Evening Poft, and the Kerry Journal, and that they be tranfmitted by the Chairman to Captain Dawfon.

GEORGE GUN, jun. Chairman.

LONDON.

## LONDON-DERRY REGIMENT.

*At a Meeting of the* London-derry Regiment, *held in the* City-hall *the 14th Day of March,* 1782.

### Colonel FERGUSON in the Chair.

RESOLVED unanimoufly, That the Voluntcer Delegates, affembled at Dungannon the 15th day of February laft, have afferted the juft rights, and declared the real grievances, of this kingdom, in temperate and conftitutional language.

Refolved unanimoufly, That it is our decided and unalterable determination, to feek a redrefs of thofe grievances in every conftitutional method; and we pledge ourfelves to each other, and to our country, as freemen, freeholders, and men of honour, that we will, at every enfuing election, fupport thofe only whom we think beft calculated to maintain the true dignity and interefts of this kingdom.

Refolved unanimoufly; That the members of the Houfe of Commons are the only reprefentatives of, and derive their authority folely from, the people; and, that their conduct ought to be conformable to the opinions of their conftituents.

Refolved unanimoufly, That any conduct, therefore, in this branch of the legiflature contradictory of the known fenfe of their conftituents, legally convened, is a breach of truft, and fubverfive of a fundamental principle of our conftitution.

Refolved unanimoufly, That this is the proper time to feek for redrefs of our grievances.

Refolved unanimoufly, That our thanks be, and they are hereby given to the Delegates of this regiment, for their proper conduct at the provincial meeting in Dungannon the 15th of February laft.

JOHN FERGUSON, Chairman.

Refolved unanimoufly, That the thanks of the regiment be given to our worthy Colonel, for his laudable conduct in fummoning the regiment on this occafion, and for his proper and impartial behaviour this day in the chair.

Refolved, That thefe refolutions be publifhed in the Dublin Evening Poft, and London-Derry Journal.

WILLIAM PATTERSON, Sec.

## GOLDSMITHS CORPS,

Commanded by the Right Hon. the Earl of CHARLE-
MONT,

*Affociated in Defence of this Kingdom, and its natural Rights,
have unanimoufly agreed to the following Refolutions:*

RESOLVED, That we will not acknowledge the jurifdiction of any parliament, fave only the King, Lords, and
Commons of Ireland; and that we will, in every capacity,
fupport them with our lives and fortunes, in afferting our
rights againft any pretended authority of the Britifh parliament.          Signed by order,

                                                    J. HARDY, Sec.

＊◆＊◆＊◆＊◆＊◆＊◆＊◆＊◆＊◆＊◆＊◆＊◆＊◆＊◆

*At a Meeting of the Commanders and Deputies of Twenty-five
Volunteer Corps, held at* Downpatrick, *March* 15, 1782..

#### Right Hon. Lord GLERAWLY in the Chair.

RESOLVED, That in order to accommodate the Volunteers in general, there fhall be three reviews in the county of
Down this year, viz. at Newtown-Ards, on Tuefday the 2d
day of July next; at Banbridge, on Wednefday the 10th;
and at Downpatrick, on Thurfday the 18th of fame month.

Refolved, That Lord Glerawly be appointed reviewing general, and the hon. Col. Ward, exercifing officer.

Refolved, That the following gentlemen be a committee
appointed for conducting the review:

| | | |
|---|---|---|
| Capt. Ford, | Capt. Hamilton, | Capt. Aynfworth, |
| Capt. N. Price, | Col. Knox, | Capt. Trotter, |
| Col. Ward, | Capt. Weft, | Capt. Blackwood. |

          Any five to be a quorum.

Committee to meet at Downe, on Eafter Tuefday next, at
ten o'clock in the morning.

Refolved, nem. con. That the ftrength of the Volunteers
depends on their being unanimous, and that the moderate
proceedings at Dungannon, tend to promote union, and meet
with our approbation.

Refolved, That the above refolutions be publifhed in the
Dublin Evening Poft and the Belfaft News-Letter.

                                                    C O N-

## CONNAUGHT VOLUNTEERS.

*At a Meeting of the Delegates from Fifty-nine Volunteer Corps
of the Province of* Connaught, *at* Ballinasloe, *on Friday the
15th of March,* 1782.

The Earl of CLANRICARDE in the Chair.

The following refolutions were entered into unanimoufly:

RESOLVED, That we do highly approve of the refolutions and addrefs of the Ulfter Volunteers reprefented at Dungannon on the 15th of February laft, as they breathe the
genuine fpirit of liberty, loyalty, and toleration, and that
we will co-operate with them, and all other corps who accede to their refolutions, with our lives and fortunes, in obtaining our juft and hereditary rights.

Refolved, That we fhall confider any member of parliament who fhall oppofe the voice of the nation, with refpect
to the grievances complained of in thofe refolutions, as betraying the truft repofed in him by the people, abdicating
his reprefentation, and deferving every ftigma that can be
inflicted on him by his country.

Refolved, That in the prefent critical fituation of this
country, when unlimitted corruption is become the fettled
fyftem of the Minifter, it is neceffary that the people fhould
interpofe, to direct the conduct of their reprefentatives, who,
deriving their power *folely* from them, have no right to difo-
bey their inftructions; as it would be abfurd to call men reprefentatives, who act diametrically oppofite to the fentiments
of thofe whom they are fent to reprefent.

Refolved, That the virtue of the people is a moft effectual
check to the venality of the reprefentatives; and that if counties and independent towns will fend men notorioufly under
the influence of government into parliament, it is abfurd
in them to complain of that corrupt conduct, which experience might have taught them to expect, and of which they
are themfelves the accomplices.

Refolved, That no man ought to be elected to ferve in parliament, who will not previous to his election, pledge himfelf
to exert his utmoft endeavours to obtain a redrefs of the national grievances, and to obey the inftructions of his conftituents.

Refolved,

Refolved, That the idea that private friendſhip and private obligations, are a tie with regard to mens votes for members of parliament, is founded in falſe notions of honour, and fraught with the moſt dangerous conſequences to national virtue, as it is paying a private debt at the public expence; and fulfilling a duty to an individual, by a facriligious violation of that which we owe to the community.

Refolved, That it may be recommended to Grand Juries to enter into ſuch regulations as will facilitate the calling of county meetings, to examine into and direct the conduct of their repreſentatives.

Refolved, That no power on earth has a right to make laws to bind this kingdom, except the King, Lords and Commons of Ireland, and that we will refift, with our lives and fortunes, the execution of any other laws; as we confider to be governed by a foreign legiſlature, over which we have no controul—*abfolute flavery.*

Refolved, That we expect a declaration of our national rights from our legiſlature.

Whereas it has been ſuggeſted to us, that the proceedings of the Iriſh nation at this time has been repreſented in England, as ariſing from a wiſh in the people of this country to ſhake off all connection with Great Britain;

Refolved, That we are perfectly convinced there is not a man in this kingdom, who entertains a wiſh fo ruinous to the profperity of both nations; on the contrary, we declare for ourſelves, and we have the fulleft conviction, of its being the univerfal fentiment of the people of Ireland, that the prefent meafures are intended to remove every object of jealoufy, that we may clafp our fifter nation to our bofom, and cement an indiſſoluble union between us, attached to her by every connection, by every tie of intereſt and affection that cements nations; furrounded as ſhe is by an hoſt of enemies, *we are refolved to ſhare her liberty and ſhare her fate.*

Refolved, That the thanks of this aſſembly by given to the Delegates who met at Dungannon on the 15th of February laſt, for their having fo ſpiritedly ſtepped forward in the caufe of their country, and that our Secretary do ſend a copy of thefe refolutions to Captain James Dawſon, their Secretary.

Refolved, That four members from each of the four counties repreſented at this meeting (feven to be a quorum) be, and are hereby appointed a committee, until the next general meeting, to act for the Volunteer corps here repreſented, and

as

as occasion shall require, to call a general meeting of the province.

Resolved, That the following gentlemen are appointed as said committee, viz.

### County of GALWAY.

Colonel Walter Lawrence,     Major John Kelly,
Colonel William Persse,      Counsellor John Geoghegan,

### County of MAYO.

Colonel Sir H. Lynch Blosse,  Colonel Dominick G. Browne,
    Bart.     Colonel Edmond Jordan.
Colonel Sir Neal O'Donel. Bart.

### County of SLIGO.

Colonel Charles O'Hara,      Colonel Lewis Francis Irwin.
Colonel Sir Booth Gore, Bt.  Lieut. Col. John Ormsby.

### County of ROSCOMMON.

Colonel Denis Kelly,         Colonel John Caulfield,
Colonel Robert Waller,       Major Henry French.

Resolved, That said committee do appoint eight of their members to be a committee in Dublin (any three of whom may act in the absence of the rest) in order to communicate with the Ulster committee, and the Delegates of such other corps, as may think proper to come into similar resolutions, and to deliberate with them on the most constitutional, speedy, and effectual means of carrying them into execution.

In consequence of the above resolution, the committee have appointed the following gentlemen, viz.

Colonel William Persse,      Colonel Lewis Francis Irwin,
Counsellor John Geoghegan,   Colonel Charles O'Hara,
Colonel Sir H. Lynch, Blosse, Colonel John Caulfield,
    Bart.     Colonel Robert Waller.
Colonel Sir Neal O'Donel, Bart.

Resolved, That the thanks of this assembly be presented to the right honourable the Earl of Clanricarde, for his zeal in support of the rights of his country on every occasion, and particularly for his conduct on the present.

Resolved, That the thanks of this assembly be returned to Counsellor Geoghegan, for the well-informed arguments made use of by him, and for his assistance in forming these resolutions.

Resolved,

Resolved, That the thanks of this assembly be returned to Ensign James Joyce, for his conduct as Secretary at this meeting.

It being apprehended that sufficient accommodation cannot be found in a central town, to accommodate the numbers of one provincial review;

Resolved, That there be two reviews, one Northern and the other Southern, in this province, the ensuing summer, the times and places to be hereafter fixed.

Resolved, That the Earl of Clanricarde is hereby appointed reviewing general.

Resolved, That these resolutions be inserted in the Dublin Evening Post, Hebernian Journal, Connaught Journal, and Connaught Advertiser.

Signed by order,

JAMES JOYCE, Secretary.

*At a full Meeting of the* Dunmore Volunteers *on Parade, on Friday the 15th Day of March,* 1782.

RESOLVED, That we highly approve of the resolutions and address entered into, and published by the meeting of Delegates from the Volunteers of Ulster, assembled at Dungannon on the 15th day of February last.

Resolved, That our Secretary do communicate our approbation and accession to the said resolutions, to the Secretary of the Dungannon meeting, and inform him that we most willingly embrace the invitation to become members of the association.

## COUNTY of LEITRIM.

*At a Meeting of the Freeholders of the County of* Leitrim, *at* Carrick-on-Shannon, *convened by the High Sheriff of said County, on Saturday the 16th of March,* 1782, *the following Resolutions were unanimously agreed to:*

RESOLVED unanimously, That the members of the House of Commons are the representatives of, and derive their power solely from, the people, and that a denial of this proposition by them would be to abdicate the representation.

Resolved,

Refolved unanimoufly, That we conceive that the people of this country are now called upon to declare, that the King, Lords, and Commons of Ireland, are the only power competent to make laws to bind this kingom.

Refolved unanimoufly, That we do highly approve of the refolutions, and addrefs of the Ulfter Volunteers reprefented at Dungannon the 15th day of February laft, and are happy to declare our concurrence with them in all their fentiments upon civil, religious, and commercial freedom; and that we will co-operate with them in all conftitutional modes to obtain a redrefs of all the grievances they complain of.

Refolved unanimoufly, That the faid Volunteers are entitled to our warmeft thanks, which we requeft they may accept as a tribute juftly due to their wifdom, temper, and firmnefs, on that important occafion.

Refolved unanimoufly, That the thanks of this meeting be prefented to the High Sheriff, for his readinefs in calling this meeting, and for the propriety of his conduct in the chair.

Refolved, That the above refolutions be printed fix times in the Dublin Evening Poft and Dublin Journal.

| | | |
|---|---|---|
| Morgan Crofton | Rob. Johnftone | John Achefon |
| Peter Latouche | Thomas Hume | John Carter |
| Wm. Gore | Geo. Reynolds | Francis M'Clure |
| H. Nifbit | R. Boyd | John Hamilton |
| L. Lawder | John Johnfton | John Armftrong |
| James Johnfton | Sim. Armftrong | Geo. Crawford |
| R. Cunningham | Wm. Lloyd | Wm. Crawford |
| Thomas Dixon | Geo. Percy | Geo. Wilfon |
| Patt. Carter | Wm. Shanley | Rob. Hamilton |
| Rich. Irwin | B. Cunningham | Rob. Hamilton, jun. |
| J. Armftrong | A. Cunningham | Wm. Hamilton |
| John Cullen | James Murphy | C. Atkinfon |
| John Gore | Tho. Conolly | J. Morrifon |
| And. Johnfton | Char. Waldron | W. Whittaker |
| Harry Seeley | Fran. Waldron | J. Johnfton |
| John Faris | Tho. Waldron | Wm. Keany |
| John Peyton | Fran. Waldron | Wm. Wallace |
| John Carleton | Roger Dodd | James Wallace |
| John Crofton | Rich. Simpfon | Johnft. Wallace |
| Jofeph Moreton | William Lee | Wm. Logheed |
| Duke Crofton | Wm. Armftrong | John Williamfon |
| William Slack | Allen Rutherford | Anth. Civil |
| Walter Peyton | Ad. Rutherford | John Buckard |

Randle

Randle Peyton    Wm. Hamilton    Tho. Armſtrong
Ham. Peyton    Tho. Johnſton    Fran. M'Cawly
George Peyton    Alex. Walker    Lanty Irwin
Wm. Peyton    Rowl. Carter    All. Rutherford,
John O'Brian    Hugh Gilmore    ſen.
Ferd. Keon    Rob. Trumble    All. Rutherford,
Edward Keon    Rob. Cormick    jun.
Wm. Keon    Francis Johnſton    Wm. James
Ambroſe Keon    Lewis Algeo    R. Thompſon
J. Carleton, jun.    Tho. Palmer    Law. Moore
Launcelot Slack    John Palmer    Rich. Portis
Pat. Dundas    Wm. Palmer
Carncroſs Cullen           PAT. CULLEN, Sheriff.

## CALEDON VOLUNTEERS.

*At a full Meeting of the* Caledon Volunteers, *on the* 17*th Day of
March,* 1782.

### JAMES ALEXANDER, Eſq; in the Chair.

RESOLVED unanimouſly, That the reſolutions of the
Ulſter Volunteers, lately met at Dungannon, are ſuch as
ſhould be adopted by every real friend to the freedom of this
kingdom.

Reſolved, That we will, as citizens and freemen, co-operate
with that moſt reſpectable body in every conſtitutional meaſure that may be deemed the moſt effectual for carrying into
execution ſuch wiſe and ſpirited reſolutions.

Reſolved, That our chairman do communicate our approbation of them to captain James Dawſon, Secretary to the
committee of the Ulſter Volunteers.

## NEWMARKET RANGERS.

*At a full Meeting of the* Newmarket Rangers, *County* Cork, *the*
17*th of March,* 1782.

### Colonel BOYLE ALDWORTH, in the Chair.

RESOLVED unanimouſly, That we do highly applaud,
and heartily accede to, the ſpirited and virtuous reſolutions
entered

entered into by the Delegates of the Ulster Volunteers, assembled at Dungannon, the 15th of February last.

Resolved unanimously, That we will most chearfully co-operate with them in every constitutional mode of obtaining a redress of the grievances complained of in their resolutions.

Resolved unanimously, That we reprobate with detestation and contempt, the presumptuous assertion, that *power confers right*, as repugnant to every idea of truth and justice.

Resolved unanimously, That a copy of these our resolutions be forwarded to the Secretary of the Ulster Delegates, and that they be published in the Dublin and Cork Evening Posts.

BOYLE ALDWORTH, Col.

❖◆❖◆❖◆❖◆❖◆❖◆❖◆❖◆❖◆❖◆❖◆❖◆❖

*At the Anniversary Meeting of the* Cork *Cavalry, on the* 17th *of March,* 1782.

Col. CHETWYND in the Chair.

RESOLVED unanimously, That the resolutions of the Delegates of the Ulster Volunteers, assembled at Dungannon on the 15th day of February last, have our warmest approbation, as they are founded on the most spirited and manly attachment to the welfare and honour of Ireland, and as they express those benevolent sentiments of toleration, which must effectually secure unanimity and mutual affection amongst her subjects.

Resolved unanimously, That as citizens and Volunteers, and steadfast friends to our country's interest, we pledge ourselves to make use of every constitutional means in our power, to obtain a redress of those grievances which they so judiciously point out.

Resolved, That the above resolutions be immediately transmitted to captain Dawson, secretary to the Ulster Delegates, at Union-Lodge, Lough-brickland, and published in the Cork newspapers, and Dublin Evening Post.

Signed by order,<br>JOHN SMITH, Secretary.

*At a general Meeting of the* Delegates *of all the* Volunteer Corps *of the County of* Carlow, *convened by public Advertisement, the* 17th *Day of March,* 1782.

Lieut. Col. Sir CHARLES BURTON, Bart. in the Chair.

RESOLVED unanimously, That we do warmly approve of, and most cordially adopt in every respect, as breathing the true spirit of liberty and patriotism, the resolutions and address of the Ulster Volunteers, represented at Dungannon, the 15th of February last; as also the resolutions of the Connaught Delegates, representing their Volunteers at Ballinasloe the 15th of March inst. and that we will co-operate with them, and all other corps who accede to their resolutions, with our lives and properties, in obtaining the just and natural rights of Irishmen.

Resolved, That the thanks of this assembly be given to the Delegates who met at Dungannon the 15th day of February last, for their having so spiritedly stepped forward in the cause of their country, and that our Secretary do send a copy of these resolutions to Capt. Dawson, their Secretary.

Resolved, That the thanks of this assembly be given to the Delegates who met at Ballinasloe, the 15th day of March inst. for their just and constitutional resolutions, and that our Secretary do send a copy of these resolutions to Ensign James Joyce, their Secretary.

Resolved, That although it is almost impossible, at the present period, that any representative of an independent people should mistake the sentiments of his constituents, yet, we think it absolutely necessary thus publicly to declare, that we never will support at a future election, in this or any county, the candidate who shall in the smallest degree oppose the universal sense of the nation.

Beauchamp Bagnal, Esq; William Burton, Esq; Sir Charles Burton, Bart. John Rochfort, Esq; and William Doyle, Esq; are appointed a committee of correspondence with the Delegates of the other Volunteer corps.

CHARLES BURTON, Chairman.

Sir Charles Burton having left the chair,

Resolved, That the thanks of this meeting be returned to our worthy Chairman, for his attentive and proper conduct in the chair. Signed by order,

ROBERT EUSTACE, jun. Secretary
to county Carlow Delegates.

## COUNTY KILDARE.

## ATHY VOLUNTEERS.

*At a full Meeting of the* Athy Volunteers, *March* 17, 1782.

Captain DAKER in the Chair.

The following refolutions were unanimoufly agreed to:

RESOLVED, That the King, Lords, and Commons of Ireland only, are competent to make laws to bind this kingdom.

Refolved, That we highly approve of the refolutions of the Dungannon Delegates, and that we will co-operate with our fellow Volunteers in every conftitutional mode of obtaining redrefs of the grievances complained of in them.

Refolved, That the thanks of this corps be given to Capt. Daker, for his upright conduct in the chair.

Refolved, The thanks of this corps to our Secretary.

Refolved, That thefe refolutions be inferted in the Dublin Evening Poft, and Leinfter Journal.    Signed by order,
THOMAS HAYES, Sec.

✦ ◦ ✦ ◦ ✦ ✦ ◦ ✦ ✦ ◦ ✦ ◦ ✦ ◦ ✦ ✦ ◦ ✦ ✦ ◦ ✦ ◦ ✦ ✦ ◦ ✦ ✦ ◦ ✦ ◦ ✦

## QUEEN's COUNTY.

## CULLENAGH RANGERS.

*At a Meeting of the* Cullenagh Rangers, *at* Ballyroan, *on the 17th of March,* 1782.

Colonel BARRINGTON in the Chair.

IT was unanimoufly refolved, That confidering ourfelves as citizens, armed in defence of the laws and conftitution of our country, and difclaiming every jurifdiction, but that of the King, Lords, and Commons of Ireland, we are firmly determined, with our lives and fortunes, to fupport every meafure which may tend towards a prefervation of that independence, and that we will, in every capacity, oppofe the execution of fuch ftatutes as the ufurped authority of a Britifh

tifh parliament have hitherto enacted, or may hereafter attempt to impofe on a country refolved to be *Free*.

Refolved unanimoufly, That we do approve of the refolutions entered into by the Dungannon affociation, as being the fureft ftep towards a total abolition of thofe ill-advifed meafures, which it was as impolitic in Britain to adopt, as it would be pufillanimous in us to acquiefce in.

Refolved, That a copy of thefe refolutions be inclofed to the Secretary of the Dungannon affociation.

Signed by order,<br>GEO. REILY, Sec.

✦⬥✦⬥✦⬥✦⬥✦⬥✦⬥✦⬥✦⬥✦⬥⬥✦⬥⬥✦⬥⬥✦⬥✦⬥✦⬥✦⬥✦⬥✦

## KILCULLEN RANGERS.

*At a full Meeting of the* Kilcullen Rangers *(affembled by public Notice) on the* 17th *of March,* 1782.

### Captain CARTER in the Chair.

They came to the following refolutions:

RESOLVED, That we do highly approve of the refolutions and addrefs of the Ulfter Volunteers, reprefented at Dungannon, on the 15th of February laft.

Refolved unanimoufly, That as citizens and Volunteers, we will co-operate with the feveral corps, whofe Delegates met at Dungannon, in every conftitutional mode of obtaining a redrefs of the grievances mentioned in their refolutions.

Refolved, That the above be publifhed in the Dublin Evening Poft three times.

Refolved, That the thanks of this meeting be given to our Chairman for his upright conduct in the chair, and his conftant attention to the corps.

Signed by order of the Chairman,<br>C. CROFTON, Adjutant.

G A L-

## GALWAY VOLUNTEERS.

*At a general Meeting of the* Galway Volunteers, *held at the* Tholfel, *in* Galway, *the* 17th *of March,* 1782.

Major JOHN BLAKE in the Chair.

RESOLVED unanimoufly, That it is of the greateft importance (and particularly at this time) that the command of Volunteer corps be entrufted to none but men invariably attached to the rights of Ireland.

Refolved unanimoufly, That Colonel Richard Martin, by fupporting an adminiftration which we confider inimical to the rights of Ireland, has deviated from that line of conduct which induced us to give him the command of this corps.

Refolved unanimoufly, That Richard Martin, Efq; be no longer Colonel of this corps.

Refolved unanimoufly, That this corps will, on Sunday the 31ft inft. at two o'clock in the afternoon, proceed to the election of a Colonel, in the room of Richard Martin, Efq; late Colonel.

Refolved unanimoufly, That any perfon who has invariably fupported the rights and independence of Ireland in parliament, is qualified to be elected Colonel of this corps, though at prefent he is not a member thereof.

Refolved unanimoufly, That thefe refolutions be figned by our Adjutant, and inferted in the Dublin and Galway Evening Pofts, and Connaught Journal.

Signed by order,

J. LYNCH, Adjutant.

## CLANWILLIAM UNION.

*At a Meeting of the* Clanwilliam Union Light Dragoons, *at* Golden, *in the County of* Tipperary, *the* 17th *Day of March,* 1782.

Captain ALLEYN in the Chair.

The following Refolutions were unanimoufly agreed to:

RESOLVED, That we highly approve of the refolutions entered into at Dungannon, on the 15th of February laft, and

and are happy in declaring our warmeſt concurrence with the ſpirited and conſtitutional ſentiments contained therein.

That we will co-operate with our Volunteer brethren in every conſtitutional means, to obtain a ſpeedy and effectual redreſs of the ſeveral grievances ſo juſtly complained of, and think that a thorough communication between the Volunteer corps of this kingdom the moſt conducive to that great end.

That we do appoint our worthy Colonel, the Earl of Clan-william, to be our Delegate in Dublin, in order to communi-cate with the Ulſter, and ſuch other Volunteer aſſociations, as may think proper to come to ſimilar reſolutions, and to deliberate with them on the moſt conſtitutional means of carrying theſe our reſolutions into full effect.

Reſolved, That the above reſolutions be communicated by our Colonel, to Captain Dawſon of the Ulſter Delegates, in Dublin.

Ordered, That the above reſolutions be publiſhed in the Dublin Evening Poſt, and Clonmel Gazette.

Signed by order,

THOMAS RYAN, Secretary.

## CARLOW ASSOCIATION.

*At a Meeting of the* Carlow Aſſociation, *at the County* Court-houſe, *at* Carlow, *on Sunday the* 17th *of March,* 1782.

Sir CHARLES BURTON, Bart. in the Chair.

RESOLVED, That the late reſolutions and addreſs of the Delegates from the Ulſter aſſociations, entered into at Dun-gannon, on Friday the 15th of February laſt, appear to us to be truly ſpirited and patriotic, and that we do highly ap-prove thereof.

Reſolved, That a meeting of Delegates from all the Vo-lunteer corps in the county of Carlow be, and is hereby re-queſted on Sunday the 31ſt day of March, inſt. at ten o'clock in the morning, at the county Court-houſe, at Carlow, in order to take the ſaid reſolutions into conſideration, and to ſpeak the ſentiments of their ſeveral corps in ſuch reſolutions as their wiſhes, and the exigency of public affairs require.

CHARLES BURTON, Chairman.

The

The Chairman having quitted the chair, it was unanimously refolved, That the thanks of this meeting be given to Sir Charles Burton, Bart. for his fpirited and upright conduct in the chair.

Signed by order,<br>
PHILIP WATTERS, Sec.

*At a full Meeting of the* Duhallow Rangers, *held at* Lohort Castle, *on the* 18*th of March*, 1782, *the following Refolutions were unanimoufly agreed to.*

Lieut. Col. WRIXON in the Chair.

RESOLVED, That as Irifhmen, friends to liberty and moderation, we will earneftly purfue fuch meafures as may prove effectual in procuring and preferving our civil and conftitutional rights; and as we approve of the refolutions of the Dungannon corps, we will co-operate with them in every mode which can or may conduce to the removal of our prefent grievances, or any other that fhould in future affect us.

Refolved, That we do fully adopt the idea of reprobating, with deteftation and contempt, the prefumptuous affertion, that *power eonfers right*, as repugnant to every fentiment of truth and juftice.

Refolved, That a copy of thefe refolutions be tranfmitted to our colonel, the honourable Charles George Percival, now in London, and to captain Dawfon, fecretary to the Ulfter Volunteers; and alfo, that they be inferted in the Dublin and Cork Newfpapers.

Refolved, That the thanks of the Duhallow Rangers be prefented to our worthy lieutenant colonel, William Rixon, for his propriety of conduct on this, and every other occafion.

WILLIAM DORE, Secretary.

*At a Meeting of the* Mufkerry True Blue Light Dragoons, *the* Blarney Volunteers, *the* Mufkerry Volunteers, *the* Mufkerry True Blue infantry, *and the* Inchegela Volunteers, *held in* Macromp, *on Monday the* 18*th Day of March*, 1782.

Col. ROBERT WARREN, of the Mufkerry Light Dragoons, in the Chair.

RESOLVED unanimoufly, That we fully approve of the refolutions and addrefs of the Ulfter Volunteers, reprefented at Dungannon on the 15th of February laft.

Refolved

Refolved unanimoufly, That we will co-operate with our brother Volunteers in the moft fpeedy, effectual, and conftitutional means of obtaining a full redrefs of the grievances mentioned in their refolutions.

Refolved unanimoufly, That we will on all future elections, fupport with our votes and intereft thofe only, who we fhall be convinced will be attentive to the inftructions of their conftituents, and will not be biaffed by place, penfion, or honours, from ufing their utmoft endeavours in parliament for the obtaining a redrefs of the grievances mentioned in the refolutions of the Ulfter Volunteers.

Refolved unanimoufly, That a Meeting in the city of Cork, of Delegates from the different Volunteer corps of the county and city of Cork, is highly expedient, and would tend to form the moft perfect union, and thereby more fpeedily and effectually obtain the defired redrefs of grievances.

Refolved, That the fecretary do tranfmit a copy of thefe our refolutions to the fecretary of the Ulfter Volunteers, and that the fame be printed in the Dublin Evening Poft and Cork News-papers.

Refolved, That the thanks of this meeting be prefented to colonel Warren, for his particular propriety of conduct in the chair.

Signed by order,
JAMES DALTERA,
Sec. M. T. B. L. D.

\*\*\*\*\*\*\*\*\*\*\*\*\*\*\*\*\*\*\*\*\*\*\*\*\*\*\*\*\*\*\*\*\*\*\*\*

## COUNTY WATERFORD MEETING.

*At a numerous Meeting of the Gentlemen, Clergy and Freeholders of the County of Waterford, affembled at Dungarvan, on Monday the 18th of March, 1782, purfuant to Notice given by the High Sheriff for that purpofe.*

ROBERT UNIACKE, Efq; High Sheriff, in the chair.

The following refolutions were unanimoufly agreed to :

RESOLVED, that we will not vote for any man to reprefent us in parliament for any county, city or borough, who declares, or in actions fupports, that the members of the Houfe of Commons are not the reprefentatives of, and derive their power folely from, the people.

Refolved,

Refolved, That the King, Lords, and Commons of Ireland are the only power competent to make laws to bind this kingdom.

Refolved, That we will fupport the reprefentatives of the people with our lives and fortunes, in whatever meafures may be neceffary to render the above declarations effectual.

Refolved, That the High Sheriff be requefted to have the above refolutions inferted in the public papers.

ROBERT UNIACKE, High Sheriff.

WHEREAS at a meeting of the Freeholders of the county of Waterford, regularly convened by the High Sheriff at Dungarvan, the 18th of March, 1782, for the avowed purpofe of inftructing their reprefentatives in parliament, the queftion of adjournment was propofed and carried before any inftructions were deliberated on, or even permitted to be read, and though inftructions were offered to their confideration.

Now, We, the undernamed freeholders of the faid county, do enter this our proteft againft fuch irregular and inconfiftent proceedings, as unconftitutional, and as tending to prevent the fenfe of the freeholders from being fairly collected.

| | | |
|---|---|---|
| Chrif. Mufgrave | B. O'Meagher | Wm. Newport |
| John Congreve | Andrew Englifh, jun. | Wm. Morris |
| John Ufher | William Lace | Richard Keily |
| Rich. Power | John Newport | R. Mufgrave |
| John Odell | John Power | James Towell |
| Rich. Mufgrave | Wm. Morrifey | John Bryan |
| Rich. Keily | Ed. Baron Shanna- | Nat. Wigmore |
| Robert Cooke | han | Richard Lee |
| John Mufgrave | Jof. Strangman | Francis Drew |
| A. Englifh | Geo. Hely | John Keily |
| H. W. Dobbyn | Henry Smyth | Sam. Penrofe |
| Rich. Ryland | H. Smyth jun. | Wm. Penrofe, fen. |
| Robert Snow | Rob. Smyth, jun. | R. Shap. Carew |
| Simon Newport | Tho. Kelly | Benj. Morris |
| | | W. Morris, jun. |

## COUNTY FERMANAGH GRAND JURY.

WE the Grand Jury of the county of Fermanagh, being conftitutionally affembled at this prefent affizes, held for the

K                                      county

county of Fermanagh, at Enniſkillen, this 18th day of March, 1782,

Think ourſelves called upon at this intereſting moment, to make our ſolemn declarations relative to the rights and liberties of Ireland.

We pledge ourſelves to this our country, that we never will pay obedience to any law made, or to be made to bind Ireland, except thoſe laws which are, and ſhall be made by the King, Lords, and Commons of Ireland.

2ldy. We claim as free and equal advantages of trade and commerce with every nation as Great Britain herſelf enjoys.

3dly. We declare againſt that law commonly called Poyning's law, as it is generally underſtood, and that at leaſt it requires a full explanation, that ſuch part which may appear to militate againſt the liberties of Ireland may be lopped off.

4thly. We declare the mutiny bill, as it now ſtands, to be an unconſtitutional law, and that as it is dangerous to the liberties of the people, it requires a modification.

And we pledge ourſelves to our country and to each other, to exert every conſtitutional means to ſupport thoſe our ſolemn declarations.

Signed by order,
ARTHUR COLE HAMILTON, Eſq;
Foreman.

✦●✦●✦●✦●✦●✦●✦●✦●✦●✦●✦●✦●✦●✦

## CHARLEVILLE VOLUNTEERS.

*At a Meeting of the* Charleville Volunteers, *commanded by Colonel* Chidley Coote, *held the* 18th *Day of March,* 1782, *for the purpoſe of taking into Conſideration the Reſolutions and Addreſs of the* Ulſter Volunteers, *repreſented at* Dungannon, *on the* 15th *Day of February laſt.*

Major St. GEORGE HATFIELD in the Chair.

The following Reſolutions were agreed to:

Resolved (with one diſſenting voice) That the ſaid reſolutions and addreſs are entitled to, and do meet our warmeſt approbation, as they are dictated with temper and moderation, and animated with a ſpirit becoming men determined to be *free.*

Reſolved,

Refolved, That we will, to the the utmoft of our power, chearfully co-operate with our brethren Volunteers, in every conftitutional mode of reftoring and afferting the rights of our country, and of eftablifhing them on fo fure a bafis, as may fecure them to lateft pofterity.

Refolved, That the chairman be requefted to tranfmit a copy of thefe refolutions to the fecretary of the Dungannon meeting, and to have them publifhed in the Dublin and Cork Evening Pofts.

St. GEORGE HATFIELD, Chairman.

The chairman having left the chair, Refolved, That the thanks of this meeting be prefented to major Hatfield, for his polite and proper conduct in the chair.

C. HOOPER, Secretary.

---

## RAMELTON VOLUNTEERS.

*At a full Meeting,* March 18, 1782.

JAMES WATT, Capt. Lieut. in the Chair.

RESOLVED unanimoufly, That we heartily, and entirely approve of the refolutions entered into at Dungannon, of the meeting at which place we wifh to become members, and hereby teftify our greateft readinefs, to co-operate with them in every conftitutional mode of obtaining redrefs of the feveral grievances there complained of.

Alfo, That a copy of thefe our fentiments be tranfmitted to capt. Dawfon, and publifhed in the L. Derry and Strabane Journals.

By order,<br>ALEX. NESBITT, Sec.

---

*At a Meeting of the Independent and Patriotic Electors of the County of* Leitrim, *convened by their Chairman,* John Peyton, *Efq; at* Carrick-on-Shannon, *on Monday the* 18th March, 1782, *purfuant to Advertifement, the following Refolutions (in Addition to thofe entered into by the High Sheriff and Freeholders of faid County, on Saturday laft) were unanimoufly agreed to :*

RESOLVED, That as it is the undoubted right of free and independent electors to inftruct their reprefentatives, fo it is

the

the duty of reprefentatives faithfully to fpeak the fenfe of the people in parliament.

Refolved, That we (hereby pledging ourfelves to each other, and to our country, as freeholders, and men of honour) will at every enfuing election, fupport thofe, and *only* thofe, who have fupported, and who from their paft conduct, may be expected to fupport every conftitutional mode of afferting the rights of this country, and fecuring and tranfmitting them to pofterity.

Refolved, That we will, at our own expence, employ a clerk to take down the poll at the enfuing general election for this county, whofe bufinefs it fhall be to enter the names and additions of the *Sons of Liberty* in a red lift, and thofe of *venality* in a black lift; printed copies of which, fhall be given to the fupporters of independence, that future ages may honour and revere the one, as much as they fhall execrate and abhor the other.

Refolved, That as feveral gentlemen of the firft confequence and intereft in this county have, from peculiar circumftances and fituation, excufed themfelves from figning our refolutions of the 4th of October laft, but at the fame time declared their approbation of them, and intention of fupporting them with their utmoft ftrength on the day of trial: we think it neceffary to pronounce that fuch affurances have the validity of fignatures to the faid refolutions of the 4th of October laft, and are hereby accepted as fuch by us.

Refolved, That the patriotic and fteady conduct of our worthy Chairman on all occafions, is conformable to our high opinion of his merit, and entitle him to our beft thanks and efteem.

Refolved, That the above refolutions be publifhed in the Dublin Journal, and Dublin Evening Poft.

Signed,

JOHN PEYTON, Chairman,

Leitrim Independent Committee.

PARISH

## PARISH of DRUMBEG.

*At a numerous Meeting of the Inhabitants of the Parish of Drum-*
*beg, convened by public Advertisement, held at Drum Church, on*
*Monday, March 18, 1782.*

WILLIAM STEWART, Efq; in the Chair.

The refolutions of the Ulfter Volunteers, entered into at Dungannon, on the 15th paft, and their addrefs to the minority
in both Houfes of Parliament, being read and deliberated
on,

RESOLVED unanimoufly, That our fentiments perfectly
coincide with faid refolutions and addrefs: that we highly
approve of, and cordially accede to them: that we adopt,
and declare them as our own; and, in the moft folemn manner, engage to co-operate in eftablifhing the feveral conftitutional claims of the people of Ireland, and of feeking a redrefs of the grievances mentioned in faid refolutions.

Refolved, That the virtuous and perfevering ftruggles of
the minority of both Houfes of Parliament, during the courfe
of this feffion, have excited our admiration and efteem; and
we find ourfelves unable to exprefs our grateful fenfe of the
many obligations which their country lies under to them, for
their vigilance, capacity and unfhaken integrity.

We fhall, for the prefent, content ourfelves with the firm
and unalterable purpofe, that none but fuch men fhall, on
future elections, have our votes and intereft; and though it
may be difficult to find equal merit, yet, it fhall ever be our
ftudy and higheft ambition to cultivate kindred principles.

Refolved, That Meffrs. William Stewart, William Hunter,
John M'Clure, John Kelfey, John Malcum, William Johnfon, and William Radcliff, be a committee to convene the
parifh, and to act in concert with any affembly of Delegates
from the freeholders of the feveral towns and parifhes in this
neighbourhood, or in either of the counties of Antrim, or
Down, this parifh being partly in each of faid counties, as
we have no doubt but Delegates for that purpofe will be appointed by the freeholders of every town and parifh, not only
in the province, but throughout the kingdom.

Ordered, That thefe refolutions be publifhed four times in
the Dublin Evening Poft, and four times in the Belfaft News-
Letter.          Signed by order,
                   WILLIAM STEWART, Chairman.

## TOWN of LURGAN.

Lurgan, March 18, 1782.

*At a Meeting of the Inhabitants of the Town of* Lurgan, *and its Neighbourhood, convened by public Notice at the Church.*

### ADAM CUPPAGE, Efq; in the Chair.

The following refolutions were unanimoufly entered into :

1ft. THAT the prefent alarming crifis calls on every man, publicly and unequivocally to declare his fentiments, relative to the rights of this kingdom.

2d. That we are fenfible of our interefts being infeparable from thofe of Great Britain ; but that we do not hold ourfelves bound by, or amenable to any ftatutes, except fuch as are enacted by the King, Lords, and Commons of Ireland, in parliament affembled.

3d. That we will, to the utmoft of our power, fupport each other, and all our fellow-fubjects, in the free exercife of thefe, and all other our juft rights and privileges.

4th. That our Chairman and Secretary, together with John Law, John Greer, Thomas Druitt, Thomas Bowen, Henry Dea, Jofeph Hall and John Gaddas, do, in the name of the freeholders of the Manor of Brownlow's Derry, requeft the High Sheriff of the county to convene the Grand Jury and freeholders, during the enfuing affizes, for the purpofe of enabling our reprefentatives in parliament to declare the united opinion of their conflituents.

Signed by order of the meeting,
RICHARD EUSTACE, Sec.

---

## COUNTY of LOUTH REGIMENT.

*At a Meeting of* Delegates *from the* Dundalk Independent Troop *of* Light Dragoons, *the* Ballymafcanlan Rangers, *the* Ardee Rangers, *and the* Dundalk Train *of* Artillery, *at* Ardee, *the* 18*th of March,* 1782, *purfuant to notice.*

RESOLVED unanimoufly, That the above-mentioned corps do now unite, and take the name of the county of Louth regiment.                                              Refolved,

Refolved unanimoufly, That the Earl of Charlemont be, and he is hereby appointed Colonel of this regiment.

Refolved unanimoufly, That Thomas Read, Efq; be, and he is hereby appointed Lieutenant Colonel; but, Mr. Read being obliged to decline it on account of his prefent bad ftate of health, Thomas Lee, Efq; was unanimoufly chofen in his room.

Refolved unanimoufly, That Robert M'Neale, Efq; be, and he is hereby appointed Major.

Refolved unanimoufly, That the Rev. Edward Hudfon be, and he is hereby appointed Chaplain.

Refolved unanimoufly, That Pullein Spencer, Efq; be, and he is hereby appointed Adjutant; but Mr. Spencer being obliged to decline it, on account of his already being Adjutant to the Dundalk Troop, Mr. Jeremiah Hatch was unanimoufly chofen in his room.

Refolved unanimoufly, That William Lee, Efq; be, and he is hereby appointed Surgeon.

Refolved unanimoufly, That we, from our hearts, approve of the refolutions entered into by the Ulfter Delegates at Dungannon, on the 15th ult. refolutions dictated by that firm, yet temperate fpirit, which, if perfifted in, muft enfure fuccefs.

Refolved unanimoufly, That as we fhall never be wanting in loyalty to our fovereign, fo are we determined to be equally regardful of that duty which we owe to ourfelves and to our pofterity, and that therefore we fhall chearfully co-operate with our fellow-fubjects, in fuch legal and conftitutional exertions as fhall be deemed moft effectual for obtaining a redrefs of thofe grievances under which we labour.

Refolved unanimoufly, That Lieutenant Colonel Lee, and Pullein Spencer, Efq; do wait upon the Earl of Charlemont with the following addrefs, and that the fame, with his Lordfhip's anfwer be publifhed, in the Dublin Evening Poft.

Signed by order,

THOMAS READ, Chairman.

*≻*≻*≺*≺*≻*≻*≺*≺*

*To the Right Honourable the Earl of* Charlemont.

*My Lord,*

AMBITIOUS of being commanded by a nobleman of your Lordfhip's exalted reputation, the county of Louth corps, having formed a regiment, unanimoufly folicit your Lordfhip's acceptance of the command.

Should

Should we be so happy as to succeed, we shall use our best exertions to emulate those truly respectable corps who already enjoy that honour to which we aspire.

Signed by order,

THOMAS READ, Chairman.

Lieutenant Colonel Lee, and Pullein Spencer, Esq; having accordingly waited upon the Earl of Charlemont with the above address, his Lordship was pleased to return the following answer:

*To the Gentlemen of the County of Louth Regiment.*

*Gentlemen,*

THOUGH many cogent reasons, drawn more especially from the various avocations in which I am already engaged, and from my consciousness of the want of sufficient ability, properly to perform the tasks assigned me, concur to dissuade me from accepting the high and singular honour conferred on me by your address, yet, the preference given to me by a body of gentlemen so truly respectable, is too agreeably flattering to every feeling of my heart, to allow me calmly to follow the dictates of a diffidence, which is, I fear, but too well grounded.

I do therefore most gratefully accept of the high office to which you have raised me, hoping and expecting that the same partial goodness which has prompted your choice, will induce you to pardon my deficiencies, and beseeching you to accept my warmest acknowledgments, as the only retribution I can make for so great and so unexpected a favour.

I have the honour to be, gentlemen,
Your most obliged, faithful,
And obedient, humble servant.

*Dublin,*     CHARLEMONT.
*March 23,* 1782.

## CARRICK-ON-SUIRE UNION.

*At a full Meeting of the* Carrick-on-Suire Union, *on the* 19th *Day of March,* 1782.

Capt. EDWARD MORGAN MANDEVILL in the Chair.

RESOLVED, That we will co-operate with our brother Volunteers in every constitutional measure.

Resolved,

Refolved, That the thanks of this meeting be given to the different corps whofe Delegates met at Dungannon, on the 15th day of February laft, for their patriotic and liberal refolutions.

Refolved, That the thanks of this meeting be given to Captain Ed. M. Mandevill, for his upright conduct in the chair.

Refolved, That thefe refolutions be publifhed in the Dublin Evening Poft, and Waterford Chronicle.

Signed by order,

ED. M. MANDEVILL.

✦➤✦➤✦➤✦➤✦➤✦➤✦➤✦➤✦➤➤OO◄◄ ◄◄◄◄◄◄◄◄◄◄◄◄✦➤✦

*At a general Meeting of the Freemen and Freeholders of the City of Dublin, convened by the High Sheriffs, at the Tholfel, on Tuefday the 19th of March, 1782.*

JAMES CAMPBELL, and } in the Chair.
DAVID DICK, Efqrs. }

The following Addrefs was unanimoufly agreed to:

*To Sir Samuel Bradftreet, Bart. and Travers Hartley, Efq; Representatives in Parliament for the City of Dublin.*

*Gentlemen,*

AS men juftly intitled to, and firmly refolved to obtain a free conftitution, we require you, our truftees, to exert yourfelves in the moft ftrenuous manner, to procure an unequivocal declaration, " *That the King, Lords, and Commons of Ireland,* are the *only* power competent to make laws to bind this country." And we folemnly pledge ourfelves to you and to our country, that we will fupport the reprefentatives of the people at the rifque of our lives and fortunes, in every conftitutional meafure which may be purfued for the attainment of this great national object. Be affured, gentlemen, that your zeal upon this occafion, will infure you a continuance of our efteem and regard.

JAMES CAMPBELL, } Sheriffs.
DAVID DICK, }

L                                              The

The Sheriffs having waited on the Representatives, received the following Answers:

*To the Sheriffs, Freemen, and Freeholders of the City of Dublin.*

*Gentlemen,*

IT has ever been my wish to receive with pleasure, and to obey the instructions of my constituents.

You may depend on my using every means in my power to procure an explicit and unequivocal declaration, " That the *King, Lords, and Commons of Ireland,* are the *only* power competent to make laws to bind this country;" and I rely on your solemn engagement to support your representatives, in every constitutional measure which may be necessary for the attainment of this great national object. Permit me to assure you, that my zeal for the accomplishment of your wishes, can be equalled only by my desire to convince you how sacred I esteem the trust you have reposed in me, and how much I value a continuance of the good opinion of my fellow citizens.

I have the honour to be,
With the greatest respect,
Your obliged, and
Faithful servant,
SAMUEL BRADSTREET.

----◄◄-◄◄-◄◄-◄◄-◄◄-◄◄-◄◄-◄✠✠✠►-►►-►►-►►-►►-►►-►►-►-----

*To the Sheriffs, Freemen, and Freeholders, of the City of Dublin.*

*Gentlemen,*

I SHOULD be very unworthy of that honourable and important trust, with which you have so recently invested me, did I not receive with the highest respect, the most perfect satisfaction, and chearful conformity, your instructions, on a subject in which the national honour and security are essentially engaged. To suppose that any power, except that of the " *King, Lords, and Commons of Ireland,* is competent to make laws to bind this kingdom," is utterly inconsistent with the idea of freedom; it is equal liberty alone, which can secure that perfect harmony to the subjects of the same crown, so necessary to the prosperity both of Great Britain and Ireland. You may rely, gentlemen, on every exertion I am capable of, to procure an unequivocal declaration of the sole rights of the legislature of this kingdom, to enact

laws

laws obligatory on the people of Ireland; and I doubt not in this, and every conflitutional meafure, I shall be always fecure of the support of my conflituents. Your inflructions on this occasion will give a dignity to the vote you have intrufted me with, which it must have wanted, if confidered as merely proceeding from my own private judgment.

I have the honour,

Gentlemen, to be,

With the moft perfect refpect,

And fenfe of obligation,

Your faithful and obedient fervant,

**TRAVERS HARTLEY.**

·-‹›· ✦·❖·‹›·❖·‹›·❖·‹›·❖·‹›·❖·‹›·❖· ✦·❖·‹›·❖·‹›·❖·‹›·❖· ✦·‹›·❖·‹›·❖·‹›·

## SKREEN VOLUNTEERS.

Skreen *Corps of* Dragoons *or mounted* Infantry, *March the* 20th, 1782.

Colonel JOHN DILLON in the Chair.

RESOLVED unanimoufly, That we do highly approve of the refolutions of the Ulfter Volunteers, reprefented at Dungannon, the 15th of February laft.

Refolved unanimoufly, That as citizens and Volunteers, we will co-operate with the feveral corps whofe Delegates met at Dungannon, in every conflitutional mode of obtaining a fpeedy redrefs of the grievances mentioned in their refolutions.

Refolved unanimoufly, That no power on earth is competent to make laws to bind Ireland, except the King, Lords, and commons of Ireland, and that we will in every inflance, uniformly and ftrenuoufly oppofe the execution of any ftatutes or laws, except fuch as are made by the authority above mentioned.

Refolved unanimoufly, That our fecretary do forward to the Secretary of the Ulfter Volunteers a copy of thefe our refolutions.

Signed by order,

**JOHN WILKINSON,** Secretary.

Captain JAMES CHENEY in the Chair.

Refolved unanimoufly, That the fincere thanks of this corps be given to our worthy colonel, for convening us at this time,

time, and for his unremitted attention to the Volunteer caufe in general, and to this corps in particular.

Refolved unanimoufly, That thefe our refolutions be printed in the Dublin Evening Poft, and Dublin Journal.

Signed by order,
JOHN WILKINSON, Secretary.

✦●✦●✦●✦●✦●✦●✦●✦✦✦●✦●✦●✦●✦●✦●✦●✦

*At a full Meeting of the* Athy Rangers, *in Athy, on Wednefday the 20th of March,* 1782, *the following Refolutions were unanimoufly agreed to.*

Captain WELDON in the Chair.

RESOLVED That, at a time like this, when queftions of national honour and conftitutional import are generally agitated, the difcuffion of which muft lead to freedom, to be filent in our collective capacity, at fuch a crifis, would, in our opinion, be highly unworthy our characters as Volunteers and Irifhmen.

Refolved therefore, That we do publicly declare our approbation of the refolutions paffed by the meeting at Dungannon, on the 15th of February, expreffive as they are of fuch real liberality of fentiment, both as to civil liberty and religious toleration, and breathing, as we think they do, a free fpirit of freedom and independence well becoming men, confcious of their rights, and determined to affert them : a fpirit, which, if generally adopted and openly avowed, cannot fail to procure for Ireland the full eftablifhment of her legiflative and commercial rights. In the defence of which, we hereby pledge ourfelves to each other and our country, zealoufly to co-operate with our brother Volunteers in every conftitutional exertion, to the utmoft of our lives and fortunes.

Refolved, That our thanks be returned to Stuart Weldon, Efq; for his politenefs and attention to this corps in general, and in particular for his propriety of conduct in the chair this day.

Signed by order,

JOHN B. LEWIS, Treafurer.

BALTIN-

## BALTINGLASS MEETING.

*At a Meeting of* Delegates *assembled at* Baltinglass, *pursuant to public Notice, on the 20th inst. March,* 1782.

The Earl of ALDBOROUGH in the Chair.

The following resolutions were unanimously agreed to:

1st. RESOLVED, That we entirely coincide in sentiments with the wise, liberal, temperate, and spirited resolutions of our Volunteer brethren, the Ulster Delegates, assembled the 15th ult. at Dungannon, and the other corps who already have, or hereafter shall adopt them, and will co-operate with them as fellow-subjects, embarked in the same just and honourable cause, in every constitutional measure, for a redress of the grievances therein expressed, and for the obtaining the perfect and secure establishment of the rights of Ireland.

2dly. That we are determined to resist, with our lives and fortunes, the operation of any law that is dictated by a foreign legislature, as we know and will acknowledge no other but that of the King of Great Britain, and the Lords and Commons of Ireland.

3dly. That being united to the imperial crown of Great Britain, and participating with her in every calamitous event, so likewise we consider ourselves entitled to share in every fortuitous circumstance or prosperity that can attend her—to the same rights and freedom of trade, without which jealousies must ever subsist between the sister kingdoms; for, unless our constitution stands on the same basis, it is impossible our interests should, as we sincerely wish, be inseparably connected and permanent.

4thly. That the thanks of every Volunteer corps in this kingdom are due to those virtuous few in both houses of parliament, and to them only who have made the good of their country their primary object. Such a line of conduct, backed by the voice of the people, must prevail over ministerial influence and corruption, and teach evil administrations how vain and weak is the attempt by prostituted majorities of wretched and servile placemen and pensioners, to triumph over the liberties of a brave, generous, loyal and determined people.

5thly

5thly. That the lavifh mifapplication and unaccounted-for grants of parliament, the profufions of government on worthlefs and unneceffary objects, the increafe of penfions, finecure places, and of the civil and military eftablifhments, and the formation of ufelefs boards, have not only induced the load of debts and taxes this nation labours under, but added to the unconftitutional and oppreffive influence of adminiftration, and are grievances which ought to be redreffed.

6thly. That it is a duty becoming Volunteers who have armed in defence of their country and liberties, to recommend a fyftem of ftrict œconomy to their reprefentatives in the diftribution of the public money, the abolition of all unneceffary employs and penfions, the forbearance of all needlefs expences, and the reduction of the military eftablifhment, as experience hath fhewn (when moft wanted) it was of no fervice to this country ; and when our coafts were braved by the united fleets of France and Spain, and an invafion threatened, we in vain called on government for defence, we were bid to defend ourfelves, as they could not, and that it was owing to the magnanimity, fpirited exertions, and difcipline of the Volunteers, (who, without expence to this country, armed and ftood forth in its defence, and have by their continuance fuperceded the want of any army but themfelves) that the machinations of the houfes of Bourbon againft this kingdom proved abortive.

7thly. That no perfons but the blood-royal, as children of the public, and fuch worthies as have, by fome ftriking circumftance of their life, or of their anceftry, merited well of this country, or whofe fituation render them deferving public confideration, ought to be fuffered to be a burthen to it, and that it is highly difgraceful to fuch, and an impofition on this nation, to have thofe enrolled with them whom public proftitution have rendered infamous.

8thly. That the thanks of this meeting be given thofe officers and Delegates, who, by their attention to their feveral corps, and affiftance upon thefe national points, have contributed their laudable efforts towards their attainment.

9thly. That the thanks of this meeting be given to Colonels the hon. Benjamin O'Neale Stratford, Sir James Stratford Tynte, Bart. and Morley Saunders, Efq; for their attention to, and for the very refpectable appearance of, their refpective corps.

10thly.

1cthly. That the above refolutions be publifhed in the Dublin and General Evening Pofts, Dublin Journal, and be tranfmitted by the Secretary of this meeting to the Secretary of the Ulfter Delegates.

ALDBOROUGH.

The Earl of Aldborough having quitted the chair, and Colonel Saunders having taken it, the following refolutions were unanimoufly agreed to.

Refolved, That the thanks of this meeting be given to the Earl of Aldborough, for his zeal in the fupport of the rights of his country, as well in parliament, as upon every other occafion, and particularly for his conduct on this day.

Refolved, That the thanks of this meeting be given to the hon. John Stratford, and the hon. Benjamin O'Neal Stratford, for their fteady and uniform endeavours to advance the freedom and intereft of Ireland in parliament.

Signed by order,
JOSEPH WINNET, Secretary.

◆◇◆◇◆◇◆◇◆◇◆◇◆◇◆◇◆◇◆◇✕◆◇◆◇◆◇◆◇◆◇◆◇◆◇◆◇◆◇

BIRR MEETING.

*At a Meeting of* Delegates *from* Seventeen Corps of Volunteers, *affembled at* Birr *the* 20th *of* March, 1782.

Sir WILLIAM PARSONS, Bart. in the Chair.

Whereas at a meeting held at Birr the 3d of September laft, previous to the meeting of parliament, Colonel Rolefton in the chair, the following refolutions were agreed to:

" RESOLVED, That Ireland is an independent kingdom, and can only be bound by laws enacted by the King, Lords and Commons of Ireland.

" Refolved, That a perpetual mutiny bill is a meafure of the moft dangerous tendency, as it vefts a power in the crown, inconfiftent with the liberties of the fubject.

" Refolved, That the law paffed in the tenth of Henry the Seventh, commonly called Poyning's Law, is unconftitutional, as the parliament in which it was enacted, was a partial reprefentation of the people ; and alfo, as it prefumed to give away their rights, which we apprehend exceeds the power of parliament.

" Refolved,

" Refolved, That for the more impartial diftribution of
juftice, it is proper that the commiffions of Judges fhould be
during good behaviour."

And as it appears to us, That thefe refolutions have not
been productive of thofe beneficial confequences we had reafon to expect,

Refolved unanimoufly, That we view the virtuous endeavours of this kingdom, to afcertain and eftablifh her juft
rights and privileges, with fincere joy, flowing from hearts
inviolably attached to its true intereft and happinefs.

Refolved unanimoufly, That we have every reafon to expect, that the liberal fpirit of parliament towards the Roman
Catholics of this kingdom, by emancipating them from reftraints which we are happy to think no longer neceffary, will
be attended with the moft beneficial confequences to this
country, as nothing can contribute fo much to encreafe the
profperity and fecure the independency of this kingdom, as
a cordial union among its inhabitants of every religious denomination.

Refolved unanimoufly, That actuated by the moft fincere
loyalty to our Sovereign, it is our duty to declare our determined refolution to fupport his Majefty with our lives and
fortunes againft the natural enemies of Great Britain and
Ireland, and to defend this his Majefty's kingdom of Ireland
againft the enemies of our King and conftitution.

Refolved unanimoufly, That we will co-operate with the
other Volunteer affociations in fuch meafures, as, guided by
prudence, and fupported with firmnefs, we conceive may
moft effectually tend to reftore and confirm the conftitution
and commerce of this kingdom.

Refolved unanimoufly, That the thanks of this meeting
be prefented to our worthy Chairman, Sir William Parfons,
Bart. for his propriety of conduct, and polite attention
throughout the proceedings of this day.

Signed by order,

THOMAS BERRY, Sec.

MEATH

## MEATH VOLUNTEERS.

*At a Meeting of* Delegates *from the* Volunteer Corps *of the County of* Meath, *at* Trim, *March* 21, 1782, *convened at the requifition of Colonels* Rowley *and* Lowther, *who were both prefent.*

The Earl of MORNINGTON in the Chair.

The following refolutions were unanimoufly agreed on :

RESOLVED, That we do highly approve of the fpirited, and in thefe times neceffary refolutions, adopted by the Ulfter Volunteers, at Dungannon, on the 15th of February laft.

Refolved, That we will, in every capacity and fituation of life, co-operate with our fellow-citizens and fellow-foldiers, the Ulfter Volunteers, affembled at Dungannon, in all con-ftitutional efforts towards a redrefs of the grievances, and an eftablifhment of the rights of Ireland.

Refolved, That a common participation in every advan-tage of the Britifh conftitution, being not only the unaliena-ble right of Ireland, but alfo, the fole tie which can attach the interefts and affections of this kingdom to Great Britain. It were equally injurious to the generofity and wifdom of the Britifh character, to fuppofe that our fifter country can look with a jealous eye upon that truly conftitutional fpirit, which now fo happily pervades Ireland ; a fpirit, which by promot-ing a temperate and feafonable affertion of the freedom of this kingdom, tends to fecure the union, ftrength, and ho-nourable tranquility of the Britifh empire.

Refolved, That the thanks of this meeting be prefented to Captain Finlay, and the Trim corps, for their very refpecta-ble attendance under arms this day.

MORNINGTON.

Refolved, That the thanks of this meeting be prefented to the Earl of Mornington, for his fpirited efforts in the fupport of the rights of his country in parliament, and for his very proper conduct this day in the chair.

Refolved, That the above refolutions be publifhed three times in the Dublin Evening Poft, the Dublin Journal and General Evening Poft.    Signed by order,

E. MALONE, Sec.

*At*

*At a Meeting of the* Glendermot Battalion, *in* Glendermot, *the* 21*st of March,* 1782.

### Colonel GEO. ASH in the Chair.

RESOLVED unanimously, That the principles on which we associated ourselves as Volunteers, were the support of our King, and the defence of our country and constitution.

Resolved unanimously, That we will most chearfully co-operate with our Volunteer brethren of Ireland, in asserting and maintaining the constitutional rights of this kingdom, by every means which we shall judge most proper and effectual.

Resolved unanimously, That firmness and moderation are the most eligible means of obtaining and securing our civil and commercial rights.

Resolved unanimously, That the only bond and cement of the Volunteer corps is *union*.

Resolved unanimously, That the thanks of this corps be given to our worthy Chairman, for the marked attention, which he has paid us as Soldiers in the defence of, and as freemen, in our exertions to ascertain the unequivocal rights of Ireland.

Resolved unanimously, That these resolutions be published in the Belfast News-Letter, the Liberty Journal, and the Dublin Evening Post.　　　GEO. ASH, Col. Chairman.

### LIBERTY VOLUNTEERS.

*At a numerous Meeting of the* Liberty Volunteers, *commanded by Sir* Edward Newenham, 21*st March,* 1782.

### Captain GEORGE SLATER in the Chair.

RESOLVED unanimously, That it appears to this corps that a *Non-Importation Agreement* is the only means that can be devised to preserve this kingdom from utter ruin.

Resolved unanimously, That we do pledge ourselves to each other, and to the public, not to purchase or wear any other cloath but the manufacture of Ireland.

Resolved, That in our opinion similar resolutions throughout the kingdom would greatly serve the trade thereof.

Ordered, That the Secretary do sign these resolutions, and that the same be published three times in the Hibernian Journal and Dublin Evening Post. · Signed by order,
　　　　　　ROBERT WALKER, Sec.

*At a Meeting of all the* Volunteer Corps *of the County and City of* Limerick, *22d March*, 1782.

### Major CROKER in the Chair.

The refolutions and addrefs of the Ulfter Volunteers, affembled at Dungannon on the fifteenth day of February laft, being read, paragraph by paragraph;

RESOLVED unanimoufly, That we do moft highly approve of thefe refolutions and addrefs, and that we will co-operate with the Ulfter and other Volunteer corps of this kingdom, in every conftitutional mode of carrying the fame into effect.

Refolved unanimoufly, That the members of the Houfe of Commons are the reprefentatives of, and derive their power folely from the people, and that to act contrary to the general fenfe of their conftituents, would be to deny this pofition.

Refolved unanimoufly, That the affertion, that *power conftitutes right*, is repugnant to every principal of law, reafon and common fenfe.

Refolved unanimoufly, That nine Delegates from the corps here reprefented (three to be a quorum) be and are hereby appointed a committee, until the next general meeting, to act as occafion fhall require, for the Volunteer corps of this county and city, and communicate with the Ulfter committee and the Delegates from the other Volunteer corps, and to deliberate with them on the moft conftitutional, fpeedy and effectual means of carrying our refolutions into execution.

| | |
|---|---|
| Major Croker, | Colonel Ryves, |
| Colonel Odell, | Major Lloyd, |
| Colonel Maffy, | Colonel Smyth, |
| Colonel Haffet, | Colonel Monfell. |
| Colonel Waller, | |

Refolved unanimoufly, That our Chairman fign and tranfmit the above refolutions to the Secretary of the Ulfter Volunteers, and that they be publifhed in the Dublin Evening Poft, and the Limerick papers.

Refolved unanimoufly, That the idea of a perpetual ftaff, is inconfiftent with the fpirit and inftitution of Volunteers.

Refolved unanimoufly, That the appointment of a ftaff for the Volunteer corps of the county and city of Limerick, except in cafes of emergency, is inexpedient.

Refolved,

Refolved, That there be a general review in the courfe of the enfuing fummer.

Refolved, That fuch Volunteer corps of this and the neighbouring counties, as would with to appear at faid review, be, and are hereby requefted, to fend a Delegate each, to meet on the 10th day of April next, at the Exchange of Limerick, in order to appoint the time and place for faid review, and elect a reviewing General, by ballot.

Refolved unanimoufly, That the thanks of this meeting be given to the right hon. Lord Mufkerry, Colonel Croker, Colonel Smyth, Colonel Brown, Lieutenant Colonel Harte, and Major Burgefs, for their uniform attention to the Volunteer fervice of this county.

Refolved unanimoufly, That the warmeft thanks of this meeting be given to Major Croker, for his polite, fpirited, and manly conduct in the chair.

EDWARD CROKER, Chairman.

❁─✦─✦─✦─✦─✦─✦─✦─✦─✦─✦─✦─✦─✦─✦─✦─✦─✦─✦─✦─❁

## MALLOW INDEPENDENT VOLUNTEERS.

### JOHN LONGFIELD, Efq; in the Chair.

*At a Meeting of faid Corps, held the 22d Day of March, 1782.*

RESOLVED unanimoufly, That we highly approve of, and heartily accede to, the fpirited and conftitutional refolutions of the Dungannon and Ulfter Volunteers, reprefented at Dungannon the 15th of February laft.

Refolved unanimoufly, That we will moft chearfully co-operate with them in every conftitutional mode of obtaining redrefs of the grievances complained of in their refolutions.

Refolved unanimoufly, That we will, on all future elections, fupport with our votes and intereft thofe only who we fhall be convinced will be attentive to the inftructions of their conftituents, and will not be biafed by *place, penfion,* or *honours,* from ufing their utmoft endeavours in parliament, for obtaining a redrefs of fuch grievances.

Refolved unanimoufly, That a copy of thefe our refolutions be forwarded to the Secretary of the Ulfter Delegates, and that they be publifhed in the Cork and Dublin Evening Pofts.

JOHN LONGFIELD, Chairman.

## KILKENNY INDEPENDENTS.

*At a Meeting of the* Five Companies *of* Kilkenny Independents, *held the* 22d *Day of* March, 1782.

### Major ROCHE in the Chair.

The following refolutions were unanimoufly agreed to, and ordered to be publifhed:

RESOLVED, That the King, Lords, and Commons of Ireland are the only power competent to make laws to bind this kingdom.

Refolved, That we do folmnly pledge ourfelves to fupport this exclufive right of the parliament of Ireland with our lives and fortunes.

Refolved, That Great Britain and Ireland are, and ought to be infeparably connected, by being under the dominion of the fame king, and enjoying equal liberty and fimilar conftitutions.

Refolved, That we approve of the conduct of our brother Volunteers, and will co-operate with them in fupporting the conftitutional rights of Ireland.

Signed by order,
VAL, COGHLAN,

*At a Meeting of the Officers of the* Dungiven *Battalion,* March 22, 1782.

### Major BOND in the Chair.

THE refolutions of the Ulfter Volunteers, whofe Delegates met at Dungannon the 15th of February, were read and confidered, after which it was unanimoufly refolved,

1ft. That as faid refolutions appear to us, calculated to promote the juft rights, and no more than the juft rights, of Ireland, they juftly merit our approbation.

2d. Refolved, That it is our fixed purpofe to co-operate with faid Volunteers, in every conftitutional mode to accomplifh the important end propofed by their meeting.

3d. Refolved, That major Bond do communicate our fentiments to captain James Dawfon, fecretary to the Dungannon meeting.                                                          4th.

4th. Resolved, That the thanks of this corps be presented to the right hon. Edward Cary, for his particular attention to the good order and discipline of the battalion, his desire to see them on a respectable footing, and his generous and liberal contribution to promote that end.

Resolved, That the above resolutions be printed in the Belfast news-papers, and Londonderry Journal.

*◆●◆●◆●◆●◆●◆●◆●◆●◆●◆●◆●◆●◆●◆*

*At a Meeting of the Inhabitants of the Town and Neighbourhood of* Monaghan, *convened by public Notice, signed by twenty-eight of the principal Inhabitants,* March 22, 1782.

Mr. FORSTER in the Chair.

RESOLVED, That we do most heartily approve of the resolutions of the Volunteer Delegates, assembled at Dungannon the 15th of February last, particularly that which declares, that the King, Lords, and Commons of Ireland are the only power competent to make laws to bind this kingdom. To no other laws will we submit; and it is with astonishment we behold our sister kingdom retaining claims of a contrary tendency: claims which are and must be useless to her, and insulting to us.

We will at the ensuing election, support those, and those only, who we are convinced will support the constitutional and commercial rights of Ireland; but from the unequal representation of the people, we have too much reason to dread our efforts will be ineffectual. Should any well-judged attempts be made to remedy the evil, and bring the constitution to its first principles, our zealous support shall not be wanting.

We have heart-felt pleasure in that resolution, which tends to exempt from penalty our brethren, for following the dictates of conscience. Lovers of freedom—we wish to diffuse its blessings through every breast; convinced, that in this enlightened age, it is the only policy capable of producing lasting peace, harmony, and prosperity.

WM. FORSTER, Chairman.

*At a Meeting of the Nobility, Representatives, Freeholders, and Inhabitants of the County of* Tyrone, *at* Omagh, *convened by the Sheriff the* 22*d of March,* 1782, *the following Declaration and Resolutions were unanimously agreed to.*

### Right Hon. Lord BELMORE in the Chair.

WE the nobility, representatives, freeholders, and inhabitants of the county of Tyrone, thinking it now particularly necessary to declare our sentiments, respecting the fundamental and undoubted rights of this nation; and desirous, by a seasonable application, to terminate any anxious jealousy, and to prevent the possibility of any future contest, do declare we will, in every situation of life, and with all the means in our power, assert and maintain the constitutional rights of this kingdom, to be governed by such laws only, as are enacted by the King, Lords, and Commons of Ireland; and that we will in every instance, uniformly and strenuously, oppose the execution of any statutes, except such as derive authority from said parliament; pledging ourselves to our country, and to each other, to support with our lives and fortunes, this our solemn declaration. And further, we bind ourselves, that we will at all times renew this necessary vindication of our rights, till such time as they shall be explicitly acknowledged, and firmly established by the authority of parliament. • Finally, we declare, that it is our wish to remove every jealousy between Great Britain and Ireland, and to prove to the world, our unalterable affection to our sister kingdom; surrounded as she is by an host of enemies, we are determined to share her liberty and share her fate.

Resolved unanimously, That the thanks of this meeting be given to our worthy representatives in parliament, James Stewart and Nathaniel Montgomery, Esqrs. for their steady, upright, and uniform good conduct in parliament.

Signed by order,
BELMORE, Chairman.

### Col. Wm. IRVINE in the Chair.

Resolved, That the thanks of this meeting be presented to the Right Hon. Lord Belmore for his conduct in the chair.

Resolved, That the thanks of this meeting be given to the Sheriff for his readiness in calling this meeting.

Resolved,

Refolved, That thefe declarations and refolutions be publifhed in the Dublin Evening Poft, Strabane Journal, and
Belfaft News-Letter.

Signed by order,

W. IRVINE, Chairman.

## ANTRIM MEETING.

*At a Meeting of the High Sheriff and Grand Jury of the County
of* Antrim, *at an Affizes held at* Carrickfergus, *March* 22,
1782.

The following refolutions were unanimoufly agreed to:

THAT we think it expedient and indifpenfably neceffary
now to exprefs our fentiments on certain points of undoubted
fundamental juftice, and rights due to the fubjects of this
kingdom; defirous by a feafonable explanation of our minds
to terminate every anxious jealoufy, and to prevent the poffibility of any future conteft between our fifter kingdom of
Great Britain and us, with whom we defire to live on the
pureft terms of amity and moft cordial friendfhip, our intereft being infeparable, being the fame blood and people,
and having the fame charters of liberty and conftitution
granted to our anceftors when they removed from England
to Ireland; and being convinced that fuch a unity of rights
will encreafe and eftablifh the ftrength of the whole Britifh
empire; we therefore do declare, that we will, in every fituation of life, by every conftitutional means in our power, affert and fupport the independence of this nation, on any
other legiflative body than the King, Lords, and Commons of Ireland: we will endeavour to procure our free and
equal commerce to be confirmed, and the army raifed and
paid by Ireland to be regulated by a limited law of that
kingdom, during the time they are provided for by the Irifh
parliament and no longer: we will endeavour to have the
liberty of the fubject fecured, the adminiftration of juftice
impartially promoted by the independence of the Judges,
holding their employments upon a better and more certain
tenure; fully determined, by every conftitutional means, to
fupport the legal rights of Ireland.

Refolved,

Refolved, That we pledge ourfelves to our country, and to each other, to renew our endeavours to accomplifh thefe neceffary and defirable claims, until they fhall be explicitly obtained and acknowledged by authority of parliament.

Refolved, That when thefe our inherent rights are obtained, we will fupport with our lives and fortunes our conftitution, in *all its parts*, unaltered and unimpaired, under a Prince of the illuftrious houfe of Hanover, as by law eftablifhed.

Refolved, That we think that an infeparable connection between this country and Great Britain, but a diftinct legiflation, is effentially neceffary not only for the profperity of this kingdom; but for that of the empire at large.

Refolved, That we do recommend it in the ftrongeft manner to the independent Volunteers of Ulfter, to perfevere in that fpirit of moderation and fteady adherence to the laws and conftitution of their country, which has hitherto done them fo much honour, and has been of fo effential fervice to preferve the internal peace of Ireland.

A. Mc. Manus, Sheriff.

| | | | |
|---|---|---|---|
| 1 | Barth. Mc. Naughten, Foreman, | 12 | John Hunter, |
| 2 | James Leflie, | 13 | Stewart Banks, |
| 3 | Ez. D. Boyd, | 14 | Jackfon Wray, |
| 4 | Her. Rowley, | 15 | Jofeph Hardy, |
| 5 | Roger Moore, | 16 | John Allen, |
| 6 | William Legg, | 17 | |
| 7 | John Cromie, | 18 | Clotworthy Rowley, |
| 8 | Alexander Mc. Aulay, | 19 | Francis Shaw, |
| 9 | Andrew Todd, | 20 | James White, |
| 10 | John Brown, | 21 | |
| 11 | Thomas Thompfon, | 22 | George Black, |
| | | 23 | Waddel Cunningham. |

Refolved unanimoufly, That the above refolutions, with the names annexed, be given to the High Sheriff, and that he be requefted to have them publifhed three times in the Dublin Evening Poft, Dublin Journal, and Belfaft News-Letter.

COUNTY

## COUNTY of WEXFORD.

## ENNISCORTHY LIGHT DRAGOONS.

*At a Meeting of the* Enniſcorthy Light Dragoons, *held in* Enniſcorthy, *on Saturday,* March 23, 1782.

Captain CHARLES DAWSON in the Chair.

RESOLVED unanimouſly, That any laws made to bind this kingdom, by any other power, except the King, Lords, and Commons of Ireland, are unconſtitutional, and a grievance.

Reſolved unanimouſly, That as from long experience we can repoſe unbounded confidence in our repreſentatives, we will ſupport them with our lives and fortunes, in whatever declaration of rights they may make in parliament for the ſalvation of the conſtitution and the good of this kingdom.

Reſolved unanimouſly, That we highly approve of the Dungannon reſolutions, and that we will, to the utmoſt of our abilities, co-operate with the corps whoſe Delegates met on the 15th day of February, at Dungannon, in every conſtitutional effort to ſupport our juſt rights and properties; and that we will ſend a Delegate to attend any meeting that may hereafter be held in Dublin, for the purpoſe of ſupporting theſe our reſolutions, and communicating with our brethren Volunteers of this kingdom.

Reſolved unanimouſly, That it gives us particular pleaſure, that the parliament of this kingdom have thought proper to relax the Penal Laws againſt our Roman Catholic brethren, as we conſider thoſe reſtraints no longer neceſſary on a body of men, who have ſhaken off the influence of an eccleſiaſtical prince in temporals, and joined with us to diffuſe the bleſſings of unanimity in civil government, through this kingdom, under our moſt gracious Sovereign, and that we hope that the bill now depending for that purpoſe may, without any obſtruction or delay, be carried into a law.

Reſolved unanimouſly, That a copy of theſe reſolutions be tranſmitted to Captain James Dawſon, by our Chairman.

Reſolved unanimouſly, That our thanks be given to Colonel Phaire, for convening this meeting, and for his letter this day addreſſed to the Chairman.

Reſolved

Refolved unanimoufly, That the thanks of this meeting be given to Captain Charles Dawfon, Chairman, for his very proper conduct this day.

Refolved unanimoufly, That thefe refolutions be printed fix times in the Dublin Evening Poft and Wexford Journal.

CHARLES DAWSON, Chairman.

Bangor, March 23, 1782.

*At a numerous Meeting of the Inhabitants of the Town and Parifh of* Bangor, *convened by a public Advertifement, figned by feveral of the principal Freeholders.*

Rev. JAMES HAM. CLEWLOW in the Chair.

The refolutions and addrefs of the Ulfter Volunteers, reprefented at Dungannon, being read paragraph by paragraph,

RESOLVED, That the faid refolutions and addrefs fully and perfectly exprefs our fentiments, and that we will cooperate with all the friends of Ireland, with our lives and fortunes, in obtaining our national rights.

Refolved, That we will vote for no candidate at any future election, who fhall not enter into the moft folemn engagement, that he will endeavour to procure redrefs of all the grievances mentioned in the Dungannon refolutions; that he will regularly attend his duty in parliament, and obey the inftructions of his conftituents.

Refolved, That the perfons who fhall be thought worthy of our fupport, fhall not be fubjected to any expence on our account.

Refolved, That a freeholder is anfwerable only to God for his vote, and that whofoever fhall attempt to influence him by any other means than that of argument, is an enemy to the freedom of election, and confequently to the real intereft of his country.

Refolved, That James Hamilton Clewlow, John Crawford, Pat. Clevland, William Nicholfon, Don. Nicholfon, James Hull, John Blackwood, William Blackwood, James Gray, James Johnftone, Hugh Jackfon, Robert Dunn and Alexander Reid, be appointed a committee to call the next meeting of the parifh, and till then to communicate with fimilar committees,

mittees, which may be appointed in other parishes of this county, five to be a quorum.

Resolved, That these resolutions be published in the Dublin Evening Post, and Belfast News-Letter.

Signed by order,
**JAMES HAM. CLEWLOW.**

✧·◦·✦·◦·✧✦·◦·✧✦·◦·✧✦·◦·✧✦·◦·✦✦·◦·✧✦·◦·✦✦·◦·✧✦·◦·✦

## DUNLAVAN MEETING.

*At a Meeting of the* Dunlavan Light Dragoons *and* Battalion, *held at* Dunlavan *in the County of* Wicklow, *the* 23d *day of March,* 1782.

Colonel Sir **JAMES STRATFORD TYNTE**, Bart. in the Chair.

R ESOLVED unanimously, That the spirit, moderation, and liberality of sentiment, expressed in the resolutions entered into at Dungannon, by the Delegates of the province of Ulster, merit the approbation and support of this corps.

Resolved unanimously, That we do highly approve of the conduct of our representatives in parliament for this county, whose endeavours, though ineffectual, to procure us their constituents a redress of grievances, merit our sincere and warmest thanks.

Resolved unanimously, That the thanks of this corps be returned to our worthy colonel Sir James Stratford Tynte, for his unremitted attention to the order and discipline of this corps, and his upright conduct in the chair.

Resolved, That the above resolutions be published in the Dublin Evening post, and in Faulkner's and the Carlow Journals.

By order,
**JOHN HALL**, Secretary.

## KINSALE VOLUNTEERS.

*At a Meeting of the* Kinſale Volunteers, *this 24th Day of March,* 1782.

### Captain LEARY in the Chair.

RESOLVED unanimouſly, That as citizens and Volunteers, we highly approve of the truly patriotic reſolutions of that very reſpectable meeting of the Delegates, convened at Dungannon, the 15th day of February laſt.

Reſolved unanimouſly, That we will co-operate with our brother Volunteers in every conſtitutional meaſure that ſhall be judged neceſſary for obtaining a redreſs of national grievances, and for ſupporting our undoubted, unalienable rights, as freemen.

Reſolved unanimouſly, That in entering into theſe reſolutions jointly with the other Volunteers, we are convinced that we are taking the moſt effectual means in our power for removing all future cauſe of jealouſy between Great Britain and Ireland, and for cementing that union of hearts and ſentiments between our fellow-ſubjects in Great Britain and us, now ſo indiſpenſably neceſſary for the ſafety of both.

Reſolved, That the thanks of this meeting be preſented to Colonel Kearny, for his great attention and care of the corps, and that he will forward theſe reſolutions to the Secretary of the Ulſter Volunteers, and that the ſame be publiſhed in the Dublin Evening Poſt, and the Cork papers.

F. LEARY Chairman.

---

## CORK UNION.

*At a numerous Meeting of the* Cork Union, *held on Sunday the* 24th Day of March, 1782.

### HENRY HICKMAN, Captain-commandant, in the Chair.

RESOLVED, That as we perfectly coincide with the ſeveral corps aſſembled at Macromp, on Monday the 18th day of March inſt. on the expediency of a general meeting of Delegates from the Volunteer corps of this county and city, to
carry

carry their late resolutions into effect, we submit to them the propriety of appointing Sunday the seventh of April next, as the most convenient day for that purpose.

Resolved, That Delegates from this corps shall be appointed to attend on the said seventh of April, at the county Court-house, at one o'clock, to confer with the Delegates of such other corps as shall agree in the necessity of such a meeting.

Published by order,

JAMES GREGG, Secretary.

---

## COUNTY of MAYO.

*At a Meeting of the Gentlemen, Clergy, and Freeholders of the County of Mayo, convened by the High Sheriff, and of the Grand Jury of said County, at Spring Assizes at* Castlebar, *on Sunday the 24th of March,* 1782.

CHARLES COSTELLO, Esq; High Sheriff, in the Chair.

The following resolutions were enter into unanimously:

RESOLVED, That representatives are sent into parliament to serve the people, and not themselves; and that any man whose parliamentary conduct inverts this proposition, deserves the indignation of his constituents.

Resolved, That the very word Representative, implying a delegated, not a personal right; men who are elected into that office ought, like trustees in private life, be subject to the controul of those for whose benefit they were entrusted.

Ordered, That a people who could suffer their most sacred rights to be bartered for the emolument of an individual, would deservedly become objects of contempt, as they would be the accomplices of his guilt, without even the excuse of his temptation.

Resolved, That although it may in general be expedient to leave members of parliament open to the conviction of debate, yet, as long experience has evinced that few proselytes are made by reason, when opposed to the conclusive arguments of places and pensions, it becomes necessary for the people in great national questions to interpose, that their voice may strengthen the honest, and awe the corrupt representative.

Resolved,

Refolved, That the prefent important period calls loudly upon every man in this country, to take an active and decided part in the public caufe. It is not now the conteft of different factions for power, it is the ftruggle of our conftitution for exiftence and emancipation; at fuch a moment, to be filent, is to be criminal. Impreffed with thefe fentiments, and determined to fupport them, We

Refolved, That no power on earth has a right to make laws to bind this kingdom, but the King, Lords, and Commons of Ireland; and that any Irifhman, who directly or indirectly dares to· deny that pofition, is an enemy to his country, and can only be fheltered from its refentment, by the contemptibility of his character.

Refolved, That we expect a declaration of our national rights from our legiflature, and that we will fupport them therein, with our lives and fortunes.

. Refolved. That a bill limitting placemen and penfioners in parliament to a very fmall number, would be the moft effectual means of plucking up corruption by the roots.

Refolved, That this kingdom ought to equalize its expences to its revenues. It appears to us equally ruinous in a nation as in an individual, to engraft prefent extravagance upon future and contingent wealth.

Refolved, That the following refolutions and addrefs be prefented to our reprefentatives in parliament.

That our duty to our country is paramount to all private obligations, and fo percedes every tie inconfiftent with the public welfare : We, therefore, pledge ourfelves to each other, and to our country, as freemen and men of honour, that neither private virtues, private friendfhips, or connections, fhall influence our votes for members of parliament, if in oppofition to the interefts of our country, but that the public conduct of the candidate fhall alone be the teft by which we will guide our fuffrages.

✦•◆•✦••◆••✦•◆•✦•✦

To the Hon, George Browne, and James Cuffe, Efqrs.

Gentlemen,

A NATION, emerging from oppreffion by the nobleft exertions which the hiftory of mankind can record, has called upon her legiflature to affert her rights, and vindicate its own privileges. The Grand Jury and freeholders of this county (one of the largeft and moft confiderable in the kingdom)

dom) fnould blufh, if they did not join their fellow-fubjects in the call. A fingular concurrence of circumftances has given us an opportunity of eftablifhing our conftitution, and our commerce, which once loft, may perhaps never be regained. As we have not until now regularly inftructed you, we fhall not impeach your paft parliamentary conduct, however diffonant from our fentiments.

But we have a right to expect, if you value the approbation and fupport of your conftituents, that you will in future act conformable to their inftructions. We do not however, at prefent, wifh to embarrafs the great national queftions, by objects that may be digefted and adopted at more leifure next feffion of parliament. We therefore, on this occafion, fhall confine ourfelves to the following meafures, which we call upon you, as our reprefentatives, to fupport, viz. *A declaration of our national rights; an ademption of the affumed power of the Privy Council to ftop or alter bills; a mutiny bill limited in its duration; and a bill rendering the Judges independent of the Crown.*

Although this is not a moment for compliment to individuals, we cannot conclude this addrefs, without paying a juft tribute to thofe virtues which have won you the affection and efteem of your countrymen in private life.

Refolved, That the thanks of this meeting be given to Sir Henry Lynch Bloffe, Bart. for his fpirited and uniformly upright conduct in parliament, in the fupport of the rights of his conntry.

Refolved, That the thanks of this meeting be given to Richard Martin, Efq; for having fpiritedly pledged himfelf to this meeting, that his parliamentary conduct fhall be exerted in the fupport of thefe refolutions in general, and particularly refpecting the four great national queftions; a declaration of rights; Poyning's law; a limited mutiny bill, and the independence of our Judges.

Refolved, That the thanks of this meeting be given to the Delegates who met at Dungannon and Ballinafloe, for their fpirited refolutions and addrefs, and that the Chairman be requefted to forward a copy of thefe refolutions to their Chairman.

Refolved, That the thanks of this meeting be given to Charles Coftello, Efq; High Sheriff of this county, for having fo readily convened this meeting, and for his proper conduct in the chair.

Refolved, That the thanks of this meeting be given to Anthony Brabazon and Edmond Jordon, Efqrs. for their fpirited conduct, in framing and prefenting thefe refolutions.

Refolved,

Resolved, That these resolutions be signed by our worthy chairman, and also presented to the Grand Jury and freeholders of this county for that purpose.

Resolved, That these resolutions be published in the Dublin Evening Post, Connaught Journal, and Connaught Advertiser.

Charles Costello, Sheriff.

Valentine Blake, foreman,
Dennis Browne,
Henry Browne,
Henry Bingham,
William Bermingham,
Anthony Brabazon,
James Browne,
William Orme,

Thomas Ormsby,
John Browne,
Neal O'Donnel,
Dominick Geoffry Browne,
George Fitzgerald,
Edmond Jordon,
George O'Maly,
George Jackson,
John Ormsby,

And six hundred and fourteen freeholders.

Sir Roger Palmer, Bart. and member of parliament, though present, and assenting to those resolutions and address, was the *only* man in the county, who declined signing them!

* * * * * * * * * * * * * * * * * * * * * * *

*At a General Meeting of the* Hanover Society *of Clough-jordan, on the* 25th day *of* March, 1782.

Col. HUNGERFORD *in the Chair.*

The following Resolutions were unanimously agreed to:

RESOLVED, That we highly applaud the meeting of the Delegates at Dungannon on the 15th of February last, and that we will co-operate with our brethren Volunteers, in every constitutional mode of obtaining a redress of the grievances of this kingdom.

Resolved, That as soldiers and freemen, we will ever stand forth in defence of our liberties, and support (as far as lies in our power) the rights of the parliament of Ireland.

Resolved, That we are happy at the prospect of having these jealousies (which hitherto created a distrust between a part of our fellow-subjects) removed by the liberal spirit of our parliament.

Resolved, That the above resolutions be printed in the Dublin and Cork Evening Posts, and a copy thereof be transmitted to major Dawson, secretary to the Ulster Volunteers.

RICH. HUNGERFORD, Colonel.

O

## COUNTY of WEXFORD.

## ENNISCORTHY ARTILLERY,

*At a Meeting of the* Enniscorthy Train *of* Artillery, *on Monday the 25th Day of March,* 1782.

### Major WILLIAM BENNETT in the Chair.

RESOLVED unanimously, That we will in every sense, and in every capacity, support the resolutions entered into at Dungannon, on the 15th of February last, and that we are happy in having it in our power thus publicly to express our approbation of such spirited and patriotic resolutions.

Resolved unanimously, That we think no power under Heaven competent to make laws to bind this kingdom, except the King, Lords, and Commons of Ireland.

We embrace this opportunity (which affords us particular pleasure) to return our warmest thanks to George Ogle, Esq; and Sir Vesey Colclough, Bart. our representatives, for their spirited and upright conduct in parliament; they having hitherto, on all occasions, been ready, zealous, and forward in supporting every constitutional mode of restoring to this kingdom its rights and privileges, and as there remains no doubt but such men must persevere in the same line hereafter, we shall with pleasure use our utmost efforts to support them in it.

Resolved unanimously, That the thanks of this corps are justly due to Joshua Pounden, Esq; our colonel, for his unwearied attention to this corps.

Resolved unanimously, That the thanks of this meeting be returned to major William Bennett, for his very proper conduct in the chair.

Resolved unanimously, That these resolutions be signed by our chairman, and published in the Dublin Evening Post and Wexford Journal.

Signed by order.
WIL. BENNET, Chairman.

DRU.

# DRUMAHARE BLUES.

*At a full Meeting of the* Drumahare Blues, *assembled the 25th of March,* 1782.

### Lieut. ARMSTRONG in the Chair.

The following Resolutions were unanimously agreed to:

RESOLVED, That we steadily adhere to the original principles of our association, the defence of our country against
foreign invasion, and the preservation of our internal peace.

Resolved, That our political sentiments are already so fully
described in the Dungannon and Ballinasloe assemblies of
Delegates, that they leave us no words adequate to express
our warmest approbation: and we therefore request they
will consider this corps as perfectly coinciding with their spirited and loyal determination.

Resolved, That a copy of the above resolutions be trans-
mitted to the Secretaries of the Dungannon and Ballinasloe
Delegates, and that the same be published in the Dublin
Evening Post, and Sligo Journal.

Signed by order,

**WILLIAM BARTLY, Sec.**

✦✦✦✦✦✦✦✦✦✦✦✦✦✦✦✦✦✦✦✦✦✦

# BANDON MEETING.

*At a Meeting of the* Volunteer Corps of Bandon Cavalry, *and*
Bandon Independent Company, *convened by their respective
commanding Officers at* Bandon, *the 25th of March,* 1782.

### FRANCIS BERNARD, Esq; Colonel of the Bandon In-
dependent Company, in the Chair.

The resolutions and address of the Ulster Volunteers, at a
meeting holden by their representatives at Dungannon, on
the 15th day of February, 1782, being read,

RESOLVED unanimously, That the said resolutions and
address are conceived with a spirit of patriotism and liberality
of sentiment, which deserves our admiration and praise, and, as
they

they are calculated to remove grievances under which this kingdom labours, and directed to a constitutional mode of redressing those grievances, meet with our full approbation.

Resolved unanimously, That as it is our duty, so it is our determination, to give every possible encouragement to the manufactures of Ireland, and we do recommend this as a proper object of the consideration and adoption of every patriotic Irishman in general, and of our brother Volunteers in particular, as the most likely means of alleviating the present, and of obviating the future distresses of our manufacturers, and of compensating in some measure to Ireland, for the specious, though hitherto ideal and delusive, advantages of a *Free Trade*.

Resolved unanimously, That the enormous list of pensions which are now paid by this country, and many of them to the most worthless and undeserving, is a grievance.

Resolved unanimously, That we look upon religious toleration as highly advantageous to society, as powerfully aidant to civil liberty, as necessary for the strength and happiness of a state, and that we feel the greatest joy at the relaxation of those severe laws which affected the Roman Catholic inhabitants of this kingdom; a measure most wise, most political, most necessary, and which must be attended with the happiest consequences, and produce a perfect union among all the people of Ireland.

Resolved unanimously, That we are attached to our most gracious Sovereign with the most zealous and unshaken loyalty, and that our firm resolution is to risk our lives and properties in defence of his crown, person, and dignity.

Resolved unanimously, That we regard our fellow-subjects of Great Britain with the most sincere affection, and wish always to maintain the closest connection with them, convinced that such is absolutely necessary for the strength and preservation of both kingdoms; but as we are willing to share their fate in the extremities of danger, we are resolved to enjoy the free constitution they boast, and to which we are equally entitled, and resolve, that no power on earth can make laws to bind Ireland, except the King, Lords, and Commons thereof.

Resolved unanimously, That the doctrine of *power conferring right*, is erroneous, contrary to all systems of natural law, founded upon principles which are absolutely false, and tending towards the subversion of the natural rights of mankind.

Resolved

Resolved unanimously, 'That we do think it now absolutely necessary to declare, That the Commons of Ireland, in parliament assembled, are the representatives of, and derive their power solely from, the people.

Resolved, With six dissenting voices, (five being of the Cavalry, and one of the Independent Company) That corruption in the representatives of the people is the great obstacle to any redress of grievances, and that we will not aid or assist by suffrage, influence or otherwise, any man, who will not use every endeavour to obtain a redress of the grievances enumerated in the resolutions of the Ulster Volunteers, at the meeting holden the 15th of February, at Dungannon.

Resolved, That the above resolutions be signed by the commanding officers of each corps, and transmitted by the Secretary to Captain Dawson, Secretary to the meeting at Dungannon, and be also published in the Dublin Evening Post, and Cork Newspapers.

S. STAWELL, Colonel Bandon Cavalry.

F. BERNARD, Colonel Bandon Independent Company.

The Chairman having left the chair,

Resolved unanimously, That the thanks of this meeting be, and is hereby returned to Colonel Bernard, for his upright, manly, and truly patriotic conduct in parliament, and also for his peculiar propriety of conduct in the chair.

Resolved, That the thanks of this meeting be returned to Captain Sealy, for his readiness in accepting the office of Secretary.

❖✿❖✿❖✿❖✿❖✿❖✿❖✿❖✿❖✿❖✿❖✿❖✿❖✿❖✿❖✿❖✿❖

### KILLYMOON VOLUNTEERS.

Killymoon Battalion *and* Artillery Company, *on Parade, March the 26th,* 1782.

THE several companies now assembled, having already, on their separate parades, expressed their approbation of the proceedings of the Delegates of the Ulster Volunteers, at Dungannon, on the 15th of February last;

Resolved unanimously, at this our first general meeting since that time, That the Killymoon Battalion and Artillery Company do highly approve of, and fully accede to, the resolutions and address of the Ulster Volunteers, and that our Adjutant be ordered to send a copy of this resolution to Captain Dawson, Secretary to their committee.

ROBERT WHITE, Adjutant.

## CASTLEDERMOTT VOLUNTEERS.

*At a full Meeting of the* Castledermott Independent Horse, *on the 26th of March,* 1782.

### Captain ROBERT POWER in the Chair.

RESOLVED unanimously, That as a free-born people, we have a right to enjoy every advantage in trade that the good situation of our country affords, without further controul than what the King, Lords, and Commons of Ireland may think proper, and that we will co-operate with our brethren Volunteers in procuring a redress of such grievances as our country justly claims, and that we will hold ourselves in readiness, at all times, to assist our sister kingdom of Great Britain in subduing her natural enemies.

Resolved, That the above resolutions be printed in the Dublin Evening Post.

Resolved, That the thanks of this corps be given to our Captain, Robert Power, Esq; for his constant attention to this corps.

❂×❂×❂×❂×❂×❂×❂×❂×❂×❂×❂×❂×❂×❂

## BALLINROBE MEETING.

*At a Meeting of Delegates from the following Volunteer Corps, commanded by* James Cuff, *Esq; viz.* Kilmain Horse *and* Infantry, Crossmolina Infantry *and* Artillery, Killala Infantry *and* Tyrawly Rangers.

### Major JOHN D'ARCY in the Chair.

RESOLVED, That we highly approve of the resolutions and address of the Ulster Volunteers, represented at Dungannon, on the 15th of February last, and that we will co-operate with them in every constitutional measure which can tend to obtain a redress of the grievances complained of in those resolutions.

JOHN D'ARCY.

*Ballinrobe, March* 26, 1782.

CORPO-

## CORPORATION of WEXFORD.

*At an Assembly of the Mayor, Bailiffs, Burgesses, and Freemen of the Corporation of Wexford, convened at the Request of a great number of the Burgesses and Freemen thereof, on Wednesday the 27th Day of March, 1782, pursuant to public Notice, the following Address and Declaration were unanimously agreed to.*

To RICH. NEVILL and RICH. LE HUNT, Esqrs.
Reprefentatives in Parliament for faid Borough.

*Gentlemen,*

WE deem it highly neceffary to declare that you poffefs our entire confidence, and that we are fo thoroughly convinced of your unalterable attachment to the conftitutional rights and commercial interefts of this kingdom, as to make us hope for your reprefentation in a future parliament.

We entertain fo juft a fenfe of your integrity and abilities, that it is by no means our intention to inftruct you on particular points ; but as it has been alledged by defigning men, for their own unconftitutional purpofes, that the minority in parliament have fpoken language not perfectly approved of by their conftituents, we think it peculiarly our duty thus publicly to declare, that we will, in every fituation of life, and with all the means in our power, affert and maintain the conftitutional rights of this kingdom, to be governed by fuch laws only as are enacted by the King, Lords, and Commons of Ireland ; and that we will, in every inftance, uniformly and ftrenuoufly oppofe the execution of any ftatutes, except fuch as derive authority from faid parliament, pledging ourfelves to our country, and to each other, to fupport with our lives and fortunes this our folemn declaration. And further, we bind ourfelves, that we will yearly renew this neceffary vindication of our rights, till fuch time as they fhall be explicitly acknowledged, and firmly eftablifhed.

We think it neceffary to add, that if any thing fhould prevent our prefent worthy reprefentatives ftanding candidates at the next general election, we will not then, or at any other time, vote for any perfon who poffeffes place or penfion, or who will not give his folemn promife that he will not accept of either while in parliament.

We are, gentlemen,

With refpect and regard,

Your obliged,

And obedient fervants.

*Wexford,*                    Signed by order,

*March* 27, 1782.          THOMAS JONES, Town-Clerk.

Refolved, that the above addrefs be fix times printed in the Dublin Evening Poft, and Wexford Journal.

❮❮❮❮❮❮❮❮❮❮❯❯❯❯❯❯❯❯❯❯❯

*To the Mayor, Bailiffs, Burgeffes, and Freemen of the Corporation of* Wexford.

*Gentlemen,*

NOTHING could have been more flattering, than the addrefs I have had now the pleafure of receiving from you. The fentiments contained in it reflect the higheft honour on men fo glorioufly determined to affert and maintain their rights, to attain which, you fhall ever have my moft zealous endeavours.

Permit me to affure you of my warmeft gratitude, for the very ftrong proof you have given of your approbation of my conduct, by wifhing to repofe a further truft in me, which I fhall always receive from your hands with the trueft heartfelt fatisfaction, as it convinces me of the rectitude of my paft proceedings, and the neceffity of the friends of Ireland adhering ftrenuoufly to principles fo juftly calculated to promote and confirm their emancipation.

I have the honour to be,

Gentlemen,

Your moft obliged,

And moft faithful,

Humble fervant,

*Furnace, April* 3, 1782.          RICHARD NEVILL.

❮❮❮❮❮❮❮❮❮❮❮✦✦❯❯❯❯❯❯❯❯❯❯❯

*To the Mayor, Bailiffs, Burgeffes, and Freemen of the Corporation of* Wexford.

*Gentlemen,*

I HAVE received your addrefs, which contains fo marked a proof of the continuance of your kind difpofition towards me,

with

with the most heartfelt satisfaction. To make vain professions of principles which I have not for some time had an opportunity of carrying into action, might appear rather ostentatious than becoming. I shall therefore only, on the present occasion, solemnly declare my thorough coincidence of opinion with yours, and that the same constitutional principles which have repeatedly been honoured with your approbation shall continue to possess my breast, while I have existence.

My ill state of health might, perhaps, have discouraged me from soliciting a continuance of your confidence in me; but I can never suffer myself to be so far depressed, as not to meet the wishes of my constituents, from whom I have received so many and such important obligations.

You, gentlemen, have a right to judge for yourselves, and to call for the services of any citizen; to you, therefore, I chearfully commit myself, and if you shall think proper to honour me at the general election with a continuance of your representation, I shall do my utmost to discharge the duties of it. My abilities may be weakened, but my zeal never shall.

I am peculiarly happy to find my worthy colleague joined with me in your address, as the greatest unanimity has ever prevailed between us; and it has been our constant study to unite our efforts in the service of the public.

I am, gentlemen,

With respect and gratitude,

Your faithful servant,

*Artramont, April* 1, 1782.              RICH. LE HUNT.

✦◗●◗●◗●◗●◗●◗●◗●◗●◗● ◗●◗●◗●◗●◗●◗

*At a Meeting of the Officers of the* First Donegall Regiment,
*held at* Lifford, *March* 27, 1782

### Lieut. Col. HAMILTON in the Chair.

RESOLVED, That we do highly approve of the resolutions and address of the Ulster Volunteers, represented at Dungannon on the 15th of February, 1782.

Resolved, That as citizens and Volunteers, we will co-operate with the several corps whose Delegates met at Dungannon, and with the other volunteer corps who shall pursue the same line of conduct, in every constitutional mode of obtaining redress of grievances mentioned in their resolutions.

P

Resolved,

Refolved, That we are determined, with our lives and fortunes, to fupport our natural and conftitutional rights, that of being governed only by fuch laws as may be enacted by the King, Lords, and Commons of Ireland.

Refolved, That it is our earneft wifh, that all jealoufies which may fubfift between us and our fifter kingdom, might be removed, as we fhould be ready and willing to fhare with her in every fate, and happy at every opportunity of proving our loyalty and attachment to our fovereign.

JAS. HAMILTON, Chairman.

## LONDONDERRY MEETING.

*At a Common-hall, held purfuant to public Notice, March 28, 1782.*

ROBERT FAIRLY, Efq; Mayor, in the Chair.

Refolved unanimoufly, That the following declaration be publifhed:

WE, the Mayor and freemen of Londonderry, convinced that at this period, it is incumbent on all the people of Ireland publicly to affert the unalienable rights of this nation, and that a feafonable exertion may produce fuch explanation as will remove the poffibility of future conteft with Great Britain, do declare, That we will, in every fituation of life, and with all the means in our power, maintain the right of this kingdom, to be governed only by the King, Lords, and Commons thereof; and that we will in every inftance, uniformly and ftrenuoufly oppofe the execution of any ftatutes which do not derive their authority from the King, Lords, and Commons aforefaid, pledging ourfelves to our country, and to each other, to fupport, with our lives and fortunes, this our folemn declaration; and further, as men fenfible of the excellence of the Britifh conftitution, and refolved to affert our right to a full enjoyment thereof, as fubjects of the fame King, and entitled to equal freedom, we muft reprobate the powers exercifed by the Privy Council under cover of Poyning's law, a mutiny bill unlimited in point of duration, and the dependence of our Judges on the pleafure of the Crown: thefe are fhackles upon the freedom of our conftitution, which are unknown to the Britifh, and grievances which it is

the

the duty of the reprefentatives of the people to redrefs. To exert the influence we conftitutionally poffefs is our duty: we do therefore now ftrictly bind ourfelves, by every tie of honour, to oppofe the re-election of any member of the Houfe of Commons, who will not on every occafion fupport a parliamentary declaration of rights, a conftitutional modification of Poyning's law, a limitation of the mutiny bill, and every exertion neceffary to eftablifh the independence of the Judges.

Whereas it has been fuggefted, that the proceedings of the Irifh nation, have been reprefented in England, as arifing from a wifh in the people of this country to fhake off all connection with our fifter kingdom;

Refolved unanimoufly, That it is our earneft wifh to preferve, and by removing all jealoufies, perpetuate an intimate and conftitutional connection with Britain, and that, furrounded as fhe is by an hoft of enemies, we are determined to *fhare her liberty and fhare her fate.*

Refolved unanimoufly, That a copy of our declaration, and the above refolution, be tranfmitted to our reprefentatives.

Refolved unanimoufly, That the warm thanks of this meeting be given to James Alexander, Efq; for his uniform exertions in fupport of the rights of Ireland, and for his conftitutional declaration to us this day.

Refolved unanimoufly, That the proceedings of this meeting be publifhed in the Dublin Evening Poft, the Derry Journal, and the Belfaft News-Letter.

ROBERT FAIRLY, Mayor.

Refolved unanimoufly, That the thanks of this meeting be given to our worthy Mayor, for his readinefs in convening the citizens, and for his proper conduct in the chair.

JAMES ATCHESON,

Secretary to the meeting.

LOYAL

## LOYAL·BALLINA and ARDNAREE VOLUNTEERS.

*At a full Meeting of the* Ballina *and* Ardnaree Volunteers, *af-fembled by public Notice, on the 28th of March*, 1782.

### Lieut. ROBERT JONES in the Chair.

WHEREAS a very great and decided majority of the peo-ple of Ireland are unanimoufly determined to obtain a re-drefs of the grievances ftated at large in the Dungannon re-folutions, the exiftence of which is fo apparently evident; Now, we the Loyal Ballina and Ardnaree Volunteers, affo-ciated from the beginning, as well to protect the conftitution of our country from illegal encroachments, as to defend it from hoftile invafion, do accord unanimoufly to the follow-ing refolutions:

Refolved, That the voice of that great and decided majo-rity of the people of Ireland, is the voice of the people of Ireland.

Refolved, That animated with a manly fenfe of our coun-try's wrongs, we moft cordially accede to the refolutions of the fpirited and patriotic Delegates affembled at Dungannon: when thofe refolutions are fanctified by the opinion of a corps, which has made the fcience of Law and the Irifh conftitution their particular care, ftudy, and attention, a redrefs of grie-vances will neceffarily be expected.

Signed by order,

T. MULLOY, Secretary.

✦◀◦✦◀◦✦◀▶✦◀▶✦◀▶✦◀▶✦◀▶✦◀▶✦◀▶✦◀※▶◦✦▶◦◀◦✦◀▶✦◀▶◦◀◦✦◀◦✦◀▶◦✦◀▶◦

*At a very numerous Meeting of the Freeholders and other Inhabi-tants of the Parifh of* Carmony, *convened by public Notice the 28th of March*, 1782.

### RICHARD BATESON, Efq; in the Chair.

The refolutions of the Delegates affembled at Dungannon, on the 15th of February laft, were confidered, and the fol-lowing refolutions entered into not only with unanimity, but zealous affection.

1ft. RESOLVED, That we highly approve, and cordially accede to faid refolutions, as breathing the genuine fpirit of *moderate* patriotifm, loyalty and liberty.

2d. Re-

2d. Refolved, That as the body of the people is the moft effential and important part of the community, the fupport and ftrength of government; and as it is the duty of *every individual* to know and affert his own rights and thofe of his country, fo we, as a part of this great body, are earneftly defirous to co-operate with the real friends of Ireland, in every conftitutional meafure which may tend to fecure its freedom and profperity, and procure a fpeedy and effectual redrefs of national grievances.

3d. Refolved, That private friendfhip, and private obligations ought, in reafon, to yield to the love and duty we owe to our country, and that the contrary idea is pregnant with the moft dangerous confequences to *national virtue*, as it is paying a private debt at the public expence, and facrificing to individuals the duty we owe to the community at large.

4th. Refolved, That the virtue of the people is the moft effectual check to the venality of the reprefentative; that confequently to elect men of a doubtful character, or notorioufly under the influence of government, is to be accomplices in their guilt, acceffary to any evil confequences which may enfue from fuch a choice, and traitors to our country.

5th. Refolved, That we will virtuoufly difcharge the facred truft repofed in us by the conftitution, in fupporting, by every effort in our power, at any enfuing election, him, and him only, whofe former fidelity or future folemn and unequivocal declarations fhall render worthy of a call fo honourable, and a truft fo important; and we pledge ourfelves to our country and each other, to exert every conftitutional means to carry into effectual execution thefe our folemn refolutions.

6th. Refolved, That Richard Batefon, Efq; Rev. Mat. Garnet, Rev. John Thompfon, Meffrs. William Batefon, Nicholas Grimfhaw, John Cairns, William Anderfon, John Ruffel and Robt. Mc. Creight be, and they are hereby appointed a committee, to convene from time to time, as they fhall judge neceffary, a general meeting of this parifh; and in the interim, to act in concert with any affembly of Delegates from the neighbouring towns and parifhes, in promoting and fecuring the important ends of the Dungannon meeting.

7th. Refolved, That the thanks of this meeting be given to our worthy Chairman, Richard Batefon, Efq.

Refolved, That thefe refolutions be thrice publifhed in the Belfaft News-Letter, and Dublin Evening Poft.

Signed by order,

RICHARD BATESON, Chairman.

*At a Meeting of the Freemen and Freeholders of the County of the City of* Waterford, *at the* Tholsel *in said City, constitutionally convened this 28th Day of March,* 1782, *pursuant to Notice from the Sheriffs.*

WILLIAM BARRETT and JAMES RAMSEY, Esqrs.
Sheriffs, in the Chair.

The following instructions were unanimously agreed to:

*To* Cornelius Bolton *and* Robert Shapland Carew, *Esqrs. representatives of the City of* Waterford.

> *Gentlemen,*

AT a crisis the most momentous which Ireland has ever experienced, when every class of men through this kingdom zealously concur in demanding those constitutional privileges which are the unalienable birth-right of a free people (notwithstanding the misrepresentations of open and secret enemies, who would insinuate that it is the wish and aim of this kingdom to dissolve that union which has subsisted for six centuries with Great Britain) conscious that friendship and social affection will be most effectually secured between the sister kingdoms, by a perfect enjoyment of equal liberties and equal privileges, we should consider ourselves as guilty of the most criminal negligence, as highly deficient in that sacred duty which we owe to our country and ourselves, did we delay for a moment to declare to you, our representatives, to whom we have delegated our dearest trusts, our unalterable sentiments on those great constitutional questions, which, in their decision, must involve our existence as a free people.

We call upon you to exert your utmost endeavours to procure a full and explicit parliamentary declaration of the rights of this country, that no man, or body of men, other than the King, Lords, and Commons of Ireland, had, have, or ought to have a right to make laws to bind this kingdom; on this basis alone can the constitutional privileges of this realm rest in permanent security.

We instruct you, as far as in you lies, to endeavour to procure a repeal of that law of Poyning's, under colour of which, powers are exercised by the Privy Council, inconsistent with, and inimical to the rights of a free people.

We

We have beheld, with the utmost concern, a mutiny bill enacted, which, not being limited in duration, like the English law, has created a perpetual standing army, peculiarly dangerous in this country, where a large hereditary revenue has greatly encreased the power of the Crown. To a repeal of this law we would direct your warmest exertions.

That the fountain of justice may be pure and unpolluted, the independence of Judges should be firmly established and carefully guarded ; and we cannot but express our surprise, that a bill tending to so laudable a purpose, has not yet been granted to the wishes of a loyal people.

In these points, most essentially affecting the rights of a free nation, we demand your attention, convinced by experience, that you will persevere in that line of conduct, which you have hitherto pursued with honour to yourselves, and satisfaction to your constituents.

These our instructions are not founded in any distrust, but to add weight and energy to your parliamentary exertions.

Resolved unanimously, That a copy of the instructions now agreed to by this meeting, be presented to each of our representatives in parliament.

Resolved unanimously, That the Sheriffs be requested to have the instructions to our representatives, with their answers, published in the Waterford papers, and General Evening Post.

WILLIAM BARRETT, } Sheriffs.
JAMES RAMSEY,

Resolved unanimously, That the thanks of this meeting be given to William Barrett and James Ramsey, Esqrs. Sheriffs of this city, for their ready compliance with the requisition, by calling this meeting, and their very proper conduct in the chair this day.

··◄·▶►·▶►·▶►·▶►·◄◄·◄◄·◄◄·◄◄·◄‹·◄‹·►··

*To* William Barrett, *and* James Ramsey, *Esqrs. Sheriffs, and to the Freemen and Freeholders of the County of the City of* Waterford, *convened at the* Tholsel, *by the Sheriffs, on the 28th of March,* 1782.

Gentlemen,

I RECEIVED your instructions, and am happy to find that I you approve the part I have taken in parliament.

Since

Since I have had the honour of reprefenting you, I have endeavoured to purfue that line of conduct, which appeared to me moft conducive to the public welfare; your defiring me to perfevere in it, convinces me I acted right.

I fhall pay particular attention to the great conftitutional queftions you have pointed out.

I am, Gentlemen,

Your moft obedient,

And devoted fervant,

*Ballycanvan,*
*March* 29, 1782.

CORN. BOLTON.

*To* William Barrett, *and* James Ramfey, *Efqrs. Sheriffs, and to the Gentlemen, Freemen, and Freeholders of the County of the City of* Waterford, *affembled at the* Tholfel *in faid City, on the* 28th *Day of March,* 1782.

*Gentlemen,*

THE moment is at hand when the unalienable rights of this free nation, and the independence of its legiflature muft for ever be eftablifhed ; when the union between Great Britain and this country (the only firm bafis of whioh is equal liberty) will be infeparably cemented. The univerfal voice of a fpirited, enlightened, and determined people demands it, and the voice of the people *muft* prevail.

Uninfluenced by connection, independent in principle, the public good has been the fole rule of my parliamentary conduct. Happy am I to find that it has met the fanction of your unanimous approbation.

I have heretofore, from private opinion, promoted, as far as was in my power, the objects you now recommend to my attention, my indifpenfable duty to obey the inftructions of my conftituents, will determine me to purfue the fame line, and to perfevere fteadily until fuccefs, anfwerable to the general wifhes of the nation, fhall be obtained.

I have the honour to be,

Gentlemen,

Your much obliged, moft obedient,

And faithful humble fervant,

ROBERT SHAP. CAREW.

GLAN-

## GLANMIRE UNION.

*At a monthly Meeting of the Glanmire Union, on the 28th of March, 1782.*

#### Colonel MANNIX in the Chair.

RESOLVED unanimously, That the people of Ireland are a free people, with a parliament of their own, to whose authority alone, they are subject; now, we the Glanmire Union, associated for the defence of the realm, the laws, and the constitution, do agree to the following resolutions:

Resolved unanimously, That we do not acknowledge the jurisdiction of any parliament, save only the King, Lords and Commons of Ireland, and that we think the people of this country are at this time particularly called upon to make such declarations.

Resolved unanimously, That we will, in every capacity, oppose the execution of any statute imposed upon us by the pretended authority of the British parliament.

Resolved unanimously, That we expect a full declaration of rights from our representatives, and that we will support with our lives and fortunes the parliament of Ireland, in declaring and asserting its rights.

Resolved, That as we are convinced the ties of private friendship should yield to the juster claims of national virtue, and our country's good, so we are unalterably determined, on every future election, to support those only, of whose steady attachment to the constitutional rights and commercial interests of this country, we have or shall receive the most solemn assurances.

Resolved unanimously, That we will co-operate with the other Volunteer corps of this kingdom, in every constitutional mode of obtaining a redress of our grievances.

Resolved unanimously, That as we do approve the sending Delegates to the meeting in Cork, as advertised by the Muskerry True Blues, &c. we appoint Colonel Mannix, and Captain Dring, for that purpose.

Resolved unanimously, That these our resolutions be published in the Dublin Evening Post, and Cork Newspapers.

Signed by order,
HENRY MANNIX, Colonel.

Q

The

The Chairman having quitted the Chair,

Refolved, That the thanks of this fociety be returned to Colonel Mannix, for his conftant attention to the interefts of this corps, and his active and fpirited conduct as a magiftrate in this country.

‑‑‑‑‑‑‑‑‑‑‑‑‑‑‑‑‑‑‑‑‑‑‑‑‑‑‑‑‑‑‑‑‑‑‑‑‑‑‑‑

## GRANARD VOLUNTEERS.

*At a Meeting of the* Granard Volunteers, *on Thurfday the 28th Day of March*, 1782.

### Lieut. ROBERT HOLMES, Efq; in the Chair.

Resolved unanimoufly, That we highly approve of the refolutions and addrefs of the Delegates from the 143 corps, convened at Dungannon on the 15th day of February laft, as they feem to breathe nothing but the pureft fpirit of patriotifm, toleration and loyalty, void of all party prejudices, and confequently muft be pleafing to all perfons endowed with liberal fentiments ; we therefore pledge ourfelves to each other, and to the Volunteers in general, that we will always be ready, and will chearfully co-operate in any conftitutional meafure that may be adopted for the redrefs of our national grievances.

Refolved, That the thanks of this corps be given to the Ulfter Volunteers, who fo nobly ftepped forth, and fo fpiritedly afferted their country's rights, and that a copy of thefe refolutions be tranfmitted to Captain James Dawfon, their Secretary.

Refolved, That the thanks of this corps be given to the right hon. the Earl of Granard, our Colonel, for the great attention he has always fhewn to our corps.

Refolved, That our thanks be given to Lieut. Robert Holmes, for the propriety of his conduct this day in the chair.

Refolved, That thefe refolutions be printed three times in the Dublin Evening Poft.

Signed by order,

ANDREW AUNG. M'CALLY, Sec.

LAGAN

# LAGAN VOLUNTEERS.

*At a Meeting of the* Lagan Volunteers, *March* 28, 1782.

### Lieut. Col. WALKER in the Chair.

The Dungannon refolutions of the 15th of February laft
being read, and feverally propofed :

RESOLVED unanimoufly, That we agree to the refolutions
in the whole, and in every part, and that we hereby become
a part of the Ulfter affociation.

Refolved unanimoufly, That we pledge ourfelves to each
other, and to our country, to perfevere in every conftitutional
means of obtaining a redrefs of the grievances mentioned in
the Dungannon refolutions, and until the independence of
Ireland, under the King of Great Britain, be firmly eftablifhed, and unequivocally explained.

Refolved unanimoufly, That thefe refolutions be figned by
our Chairman, and tranfmitted to the Secretary of the Ulfter committee, and publifhed in the Londonderry Journal,
and Dublin Evening Poft.

Lieutenat Colonel Walker having left the Chair, and Lieut.
Brown taken it ;

Refolved, That the thanks of the company be given to our
Chairman, for his polite and proper conduct in the chair, and
alfo for his unremitting attention to the company on every
occafion.

# WESTPORT VOLUNTEERS.

*At a General Meeting of the* Weftport Volunteers, *at* Weftport,
*on Friday the* 29th *of March*, 1782.

### EDMOND JORDAN, Efq; in the Chair.

RESOLVED unanimoufly, That we do highly approve of
the whole and every part of the refolutions entered into by
the Connaught meeting at Ballinafloe, on Friday the 15th
inftant, as calculated to promote the juft rights of Ireland,
and animated with a fpirit becoming men determined to be
free.                                                    That

That we moſt heartily approve the conduct of our worthy Delegate on that important occaſion, and now return him our warmeſt thanks accordingly.

That the ports of this kingdom are, by right, open to all foreign countries not at war with the king. That we conſider this right as the gift of heaven alone. That our honeſt induſtry ſhall be exerted in availing ourſelves of it, by all and every means in our power; and that we will ſupport it at the utmoſt hazard of our lives.

That theſe reſolutions be publiſhed in the Dublin Evening Poſt and Connaught Advertiſer.

EDMOND JORDAN, Chairman.

## COUNTY of CORK.

### BLACKWATER VOLUNTEERS.

*At a full Meeting of the* Blackwater Volunteers, *held the 29th of March,* 1782.

RICHARD ALDWORTH, Eſq; in the Chair.

RESOLVED unanimouſly, That we as Volunteers, and independents, chearfully concur in the ſpirited and virtuous reſolutions and addreſs of the Ulſter Volunteers, repreſented at Dungannon, on the 15th of February laſt, as they breathe the genuine ſpirit of liberty, loyalty, and toleration, and we pledge ourſelves to each other, and to all the other armed aſſociations who have, and ſhall approve the ſaid reſolutions, that we will heartily co-operate with them, in every conſtitutional meaſure, until the grievances ſo juſtly complained of be done away.

Reſolved unanimouſly, That a copy of theſe our reſolutions be forwarded to the Secretary of the Ulſter Delegates, and that they be publiſhed in the Dublin and Cork Evening Poſts.

RICHARD ALDWORTH.

The Chairman having left the Chair;

Reſolved unanimouſly, That the thanks of this meeting be preſented to our worthy Colonel, for his truly patriotic and upright conduct in the chair.

Lieut. Col. STANNARD.

## KILMORE LIGHT INFANTRY.

*At a Meeting of the* Kilmore Light Infantry, *March* 29, 1782.

### MATT FORDE, Jun. Esq; in the Chair.

RESOLVED unanimously, That we highly approve of, and heartily accede to, the spirited, yet moderate resolutions entered into at Dungannon, by the Ulster Volunteers, and that we thankfully accept of their invitation to become members of so respectable a body.

MATT FORDE, jun.

⬦—✦—⬦—✦—⬦—✦—⬦—✦—✦—✦—✦—⬦—✦—⬦✦✧✦⬦✦—⬦—✦—✦—⬦—✦—✦—⬦—✦—✦—⬦—⬦—⬦

## COUNTY of LONDONDERRY.

*We, the High Sheriffs and Grand Jury of the City and County of* Londonderry, *assembled at an Assizes held the* 29th *Day of* March, 1782, *in the* Town-hall *of the City of* Londonderry,

THINKING it now peculiarly necessary to declare our sentiments, respecting the fundamental and undoubted rights of this nation, and desirous, by a seasonable explanation, to terminate an anxious jealousy, and to prevent the possibility of any future contest, do declare, That we will, in every situation of life, and with all the means in our power, assert and maintain the constitutionl rights of this kingdom to be governed by such laws, only, as are enacted by the King, Lords, and Commons of Ireland: and that we will, in every instance, uniformly and strenuously oppose the execution of any statutes, except such as derive their authority from said parliament; pledging ourselves to our country, and to each other, to support, with our lives and fortunes, this our solemn declaration: and further, we bind ourselves that we will yearly renew this necessary vindication of our rights, 'till such time as they shall be explicitly acknowledged, and firmly established, by the authority of parliament.

Michael Ross,  } Sheriffs
Will. Lenox,   }
Edw. Cary, Foreman
James Alexander,
John Richardson,

James Scott,
Rich. Charleton,
Thos. Bateson.
Alexander Lecky,
John Ferguson,
Clotworthy

Clotworthy Rowley,
Richard Lloyd,
Alexander Stewart,
William Lecky,
George Afh,
Robert Alexander,
Paul Canning,
Hugh Lyle.

David Rofs,
George Lenox,
William M'Clintock,
William Rofs,
Conolly M'Caufland,
Dominick M'Caufland,
James Patterfon.

*At a numerous and refpectable Meeting of the Gentlemen Clergy, and Freeholders of the City and County of* Londonderry, *affembled purfuant to public Notice at* Londonderry *the 29th Day of March,* 1782.

MICH. ROSS, and WM. LENOX, High Sheriffs, in the Chair,

The foregoing declaration being read,

Refolved unanimoufly, That the faid declaration merits our warmeft approbation, as being fpirited, moderate, and fpeaking the language of freemen.

Refolved, That copies of the faid declaration fhall be immediately tranfmitted to the feveral parifhes in this county, for the approbation of the freeholders and inhabitants thereof.

Refolved, That the thanks of this meeing be given to the reprefentatives of this county for their declaration, *" That they will fupport the rights of Ireland."*

Refolved, That the thanks of this meeting be given to our worthy High Sheriffs, for their ready compliance in convening the county, and for their polite and impartial conduct in the chair.

Refolved, That the foregoing declaration and refolutions be publifhed in the Londonderry Journal, Dublin Evening Poft, and Belfaft News-Letter.

Signed by order of faid meeting,

MICH. ROSS, } Sheriffs.
WM. LENOX, }

MITCHEL-

## MITCHELSTOWN INDEPENDENT LIGHT DRA-
## GOONS.

*At a Meeting of the* Mitchelstown Independent Light Dragoons, *held at* Mitchelstown, *the 29th of March*, 1782.

### LORD KINGSBOROUGH, Colonel, in the Chair.

RESOLVED, That Lord Kingsborough, our colonel,
Henry Cole Bowen, Esq; our lieutenant-colonel, and James
B. Thornhill, Esq; our major, be appointed Delegates from
this corps, to attend the meeting of Delegates of the county
and city corps, at Cork, on the 7th of April.

Resolved, That it is our instructions to our Delegates above
mentioned, to signify at that meeting, our most hearty concurrence in any resolutions of a similar spirit to those adopted
by the two provincial meetings of Dungannon and Balinasloe.

KINGSBOROUGH, Colonel.

### ARRAN PHALANX MEETING.

*At a Meeting of the* Arran Phalanx, *the 30th of March*, 1782.

### The Earl of ARRAN in the Chair.

RESOLVED unanimously, That we do highly approve of
the resolutions entered into at Dungannon on the 15th day of
February last, by the Ulster Volunteers, as they breathe the
spirit of citizens and soldiers determined to assert their constitutional rights, and diffuse the liberal sentiments of toleration, so essentially necessary in a free country.

Resolved unanimously, That as citizens and Volunteers, we
will co-operate with them in every constitutional mode of obtaining a redress of the grievances mentioned in their resolutions.

Resolved, That these resolutions be transmitted to Captain
Dawson, Secretary to the Ulster Delegates, and published in
the Dublin Evening Post, Freeman's Journal and Wexford
Journal. Signed by order,

G. HORAN, Secretary.

*At a Meeting of the* Loyal Newberry Mufqueteers, *March* 30, 1782, *it was refolved,*

THAT we highly applaud the liberal, tolerating fpirit and conftitutional zeal, with which the Ulfter Volunteers have ftood forth, in behalf of the rights, freedom and trade of this kingdom ; being convinced, the afcertaining thofe points, at this critical period, will be the moft firm and permanent foundation of chearful unanimity and future happinefs between this nation and Great Britain. We will, therefore, moft heartily co-operate in every legal and conftitutional mode for eftablifhing the rights of this nation, and forming the moft honourable and perfect union with our fifter kingdom.

Refolved, That being attached to our gracious fovereign by the moft unfhaken loyalty, we will, at the utmoft hazard of all we hold dear to us, fupport his crown, perfon and dignity.

Refolved, That we feel the utmoft fatisfaction at the relaxation of the fevere laws againft our Roman Catholic brethren, whofe good conduct and behaviour for feveral years have eradicated old prejudices, and from which we expect the happieft confequences and moft perfect union among the people of this country.

*At* Lent Affizes, *March* 30, 1782.

WE the High Sheriff and Grand Jury of the county of Carlow, affembled, think the duty we owe to our country and ourfelves, calls upon us to declare unanimoufly,

That the members of the Houfe of Commons, are the reprefentatives of, and derive their power folely from, the people, and that to act contrary to the fenfe of their conftituents would be to deny this pofition. .

That the King, Lords and Commons of Ireland, are the only power competent to make laws to bind this kingdom, and that every attempt by any other body of men to exercife this right is unconftitutional, illegal, and a grievance.

That we do expect fuch declaration of right 'from our reprefentatives in parliament, and that we will not fupport at any enfuing election any Candidate, who when in parliament, will not ufe his utmoft endeavours to obtain it.

Ordered, That thefe our refolutions be publifhed fix times in the Dublin Evening Poft, and Carlow Journal.

RICHARD MERCER, Sheriff.
ROBERT POWER, Foreman.

*At a Meeting of the Corps of* Tullow Rangers (*Light Dragoons*) *March* 30, 1782.

Captain WHELAN in the Chair.

The following refolutions were all unanimoufly agreed to:

RESOLVED, That we do highly and warmly approve of the refolutions and addrefs of the Ulfter Volunteers, reprefented at Dungannon the 15th day of February laſt.

Refolved, That as citizens, and Volunteers, we will co-operate with the feveral corps whofe Delegates met at Dungannon, in every conftitutional mode of obtaining redrefs of the grievances mentioned in their refolutions.

Refolved, That we will at the enfuing election, in either county, city, or borough, fupport thofe, and thofe only, who have hitherto fupported, or who we are convinced will fupport the conftitutional and commercial rights of Ireland.

Refolved, That the thanks of this corps be prefented to the virtuous minority of both houfes of parliament, for their noble, though hitherto ineffectual, efforts in favour of the rights and conftitution of Ireland.

Refolved, That the following addrefs be prefented by our Captain, to Beauchamp Bagenal, Efq; our worthy reprefentative in parliament.

S I R,

WE the corps of Tullow Rangers, beg you will accept of our fincere thanks for your conduct in parliament; affuring you that it meets our wifhes, and merits our higheſt approbation. We hope that, although the exertions of gentlemen, who, animated by the fame fentiments that directed you, have ſtruggled hard for a declaration of the conftitutional and commercial rights of this kingdom, have hitherto been unfuccefsful; yet, truth will, at laſt, prevail, and we fhall eftablifh, on firm grounds, that liberty to which, by nature and by law, we are entitled.

Refolved, That Captain Whelan be appointed our Delegate. to attend at the county meeting to-morrow at Carlow.

Refolved, That a copy of the two firſt refolutions be tranfmitted to James Dawfon, Efq; Secretary to the Ulfter Volunteers.

R                                                      Captain

Captain Whelan having left the Chair,

Refolved, That the thanks of this corps be prefented to Thomas Whelan, Efq; our worthy Captain, for his great attention to this corps fince its firft eftablilhment.

Refolved, That there be a general meeting of this corps on Tuefday the 16th day of April, to dine together at the houfe of Mr. Richard Magill in Tullow, in commemoration of the day, and that the diftant members of the corps be requefted to attend.

Refolved, That the foregoing refolutions and addrefs, be publifhed in the Carlow Journal, and Dublin Evening Poft.

Signed by order of the corps,

ROBERT ROBINSON, Secretary.

*To the* Tullow Rangers.

*Gentlemen,*

IT will always give me the greateft fatisfaction, whenever I am fo fortunate as to meet the approbation of fo refpectable and fpirited a body of the inhabitants of the county of Carlow; it has always been my intention to deferve the approbation of the friends of Ireland, and perhaps if I had not fometimes given a vote with a deferving adminiftration, which my conftituents never difapproved of, and which I can vindicate to the world, I could never have any merit in uniformly oppofing thofe under whom we receive no benefit.

I will only beg leave to obferve, that the late change of Englifh minifters, amongft whom we have fome infatuated enemies, makes this the moft critical period that Ireland ever faw. It is abfolutely neceffary for us to be unanimous.

*To Be—or not to Be, is now the Queftion.*

I have the honour to be,

With the greateft refpect and efteem,

Your faithful and obliged

Humble fervant,

B. BAGENAL.

KILDARE.

## K I L D A R E.

At a full Meeting of the Kildare Infantry, at Kildare, March 31, 1782.

JAMES SPENCER, Efq; Capt. in the Chair.

RESOLVED unanimoufly, That the King, Lords, and Commons of Ireland, are the only power competent to make laws to bind Ireland.

Refolved unanimoufly, That we will in every capacity, as citizens, and Volunteers, co-operate with our fellow citizens and Volunteers, in all conftitutional meafures, towards a re-drefs of grievances, and an eftablifhment of the rights of Ireland.

Refolved, That the above refolutions be publifhed three times in the Dublin Journal, and Dublin Evening Poft.

Signed by order,

G. HETHERINGTON, Sec.

✤-◇-✤ ◇-✤-◇-✤ ◇-◇-✤-◇-✤-◇-✤-◇ ✤-◇-✤-◇-✤-◇ ✤-◇-✤-◇-✤-◇-✤-◇-✤

At a Meeting of the Kanturk Volunteers, holden at Kanturk, in the County of Cork, March 31, 1782.

JAMES PURCELL, Efq; in the Chair.

The following refolutions were unanimoufly agreed to :

RESOLVED, As loyal fubjects to our moft gracious fove-reign we ought, and do adopt, and warmly approve of, the refolutions entered into by the Ulfter Volunteers, on the 15th day of February laft.

Refolved, That the pofition of *power conferring right*, is repugnant to every fentiment of juftice and humanity, and though relying on his Majefty's wifdom and our own loyalty, we do not at prefent fear the alarming confequences of fuch a doctrine, it muft remind us of the hiftory of former times in this kingdom, when the fervants of the crown, by tyranny and oppreffion, drove the people firft to defpair, and then to take up arms, in order to accummulate fortunes for them-felves by plunder and forfeiture.

Refolved, That copies of thefe refolutions be tranfmitted to our Colonel, the right hon. the Earl of Egmont, and to Capt.
Dawfon,

Dawfon, Secretary to the Ulfter Volunteers, and that they
be publifhed in the Cork News-papers, and Dublin Evening
Poft.                                    JAMES PURCELL.

SPRING ASSIZES, 1782.

*At a full Meeting of the Grand Jury, Gentlemen, Clergy, and
Freeholders of the County of Galway, affembled purfuant to public
Notice from the High Sheriff, at the County-hall, in Galway,
March 31, 1782.*

The following refolutions were unanimoufly entered into:

JOHN KELLY, of Caftlekelly, Efq; in the Chair.

(The High Sheriff being indifpofed.)

RESOLVED, That a feat in parliament was never intended
by our conftitution as an inftrument of emolument to individuals; and that the reprefentative who perverts it to fuch a
purpofe (particularly at fo momentous a period as the prefent)
is guilty of betraying the truft repofed in him by the people,
for *their*, not *his* benefit.

Refolved, That the people who could tamely behold their
fuffrages made the tool of private avarice or ambition, are
ftill more criminal than the venal reprefentatives, as they become the pandors without even the wages of proftitution.

Refolved, That when we daily fee the mandate of the Minifter fupercede all conviction in debate; when placed and
penfioned members of parliament notorioufly fupport in public, meafures which they condemn in private; when the hirelings of corruption avow, and Government have exemplified
in recent inftances of diftinguifhed public characters, that to
vote according to confcience, amounts to a difqualification to
hold any office in the fervice of our country, it is time for the
people to look to themfelves, and in great national queftions
to affert their right to controul thofe who owe their political
exiftence to *their* breath, and may be annihilated by *their* dif-
pleafure.

Refolved, That, at an æra when every thing that can be dear
to a nation is at ftake, we are called upon by our duty to ourfelves, to our country, and to pofterity, to ftand forth, and
by the moft unremitting exertions ftem the returning torrent
of

of corruption at home, and resist usurpation from abroad, that all mankind may see we are determined to preserve the purity, while we vindicate the rights of our legislature.

Resolved therefore, That we do hereby solemnly pledge ourselves to each other, and to our country, by every tie of honour and religion which can be binding to man, that, as the sacred duty which we owe to the community supercedes all ties and obligations to individuals, we will not suffer private friendship or private virtues, to ward our settled determination not to vote for any man, at a future election, either for county, town, or borough, who shall act in opposition to our instructions, and who will not subscribe a test to obey them previous to the election, or who shall absent himself when those questions on which we instruct him, are agitated in parliament.

Resolved, That the King, Lords, and Commons of Ireland are the only power competent to make laws to bind this kingdom, and that we will resist the execution of any other laws with our lives and fortunes.

Resolved, That if *force constitutes right*, the people of this country have a right to *use force* against the man who *dares* to maintain doctrines subversive of their constitution ; but as the object is beneath the dignity of the national resentment, we shall only bid such a man beware how he hereafter trifles with the rights of his country, and provoke the vengeance of a people determined to be *free*.

Resolved, That we highly approve of the resolutions of the Volunteer Delegates, assembled at Dungannon and at Ballinasloe.

Resolved, That the thanks of this county be returned to the minority in parliament, and particularly to our countrymen Anthony Daly, Sir Henry Lynch Blosse, and Robert Dillon, Esqrs.

Resolved, That the thanks of this county be returned to John Kelly, Esq; our worthy Chairman.

Resolved, That the thanks of this county be returned to our High Sheriff, for his readiness in convening this meeting.

Resolved, That the thanks of this county be returned to Counsellor Geoghegan for his conduct at this meeting, and for framing these resolutions, and the following addresses.

Resolved, That the following addresses be presented to the right hon. Denis Daly, and W. P. Keating Trench, Esqrs. representatives in parliament for this county.

*To*

## To Denis Daly, *Esq.*

SIR,

THERE is a moment in the affairs of nations as well as of individuals, which if feized and happily improved, may lead to profperity, if neglected, may terminate in the rivetting of its oppreffions. Such a moment is the prefent: the eyes of Europe are upon us, and pofterity will read our conduct with applaufe or execration, according to the ufe we make of the opportunities, which a providential combination of events has afforded us. When the rights of a nation become objects of public queftion or difcuffion, not to affert is to relinquifh, to hefitate is to betray. The die is caft; if we advance with a manly and determined ftep, we enfure fuccefs; if we recede or divide, we fink for ever; in fo awful an hour, who is the man that however unwilling to provoke the queftion, will not at the day of trial be found in his poft. Your private opinion, Sir, muft give way to the national voice; the affemblage of qualities which formed and elevated your character, raifed you to one of the moft exalted fituations a fubject could arrive at. Your abilities remain, we have relied on your integrity; yet, we cannot but lament, that at the moment we ftood in need of all the influence of fuch a character, its brightnefs fhould have been fhaded, and its weight loft to the nation, by being placed in a ftation in which, however chafte, it may at leaft be fufpected. But waving at prefent the confideration of this fubject, we now call upon you, as one of our reprefentatives, as you value our future approbation and fupport, to give your fulleft affiftance to the following meafures, whenever they fhall be propofed in parliament, viz. *A declaration of our national rights; an ademption of the affumed power of the Privy Council to ftop or alter bills; a mutiny bill limited in its duration; a bill rendering the Judges independent of the Crown; and a bill to reduce the expences of the nation to a level with its revenues,* as we cannot conceive a conduct more infane, than for a people fcarce emerging from ruin, like a profligate heir, to anticipate its funds, and ground *certain* extravagance on *uncertain* profperity.

### To W. P. Keating Trench, *Esq.*

SIR,

THE prefent period calls upon every man in this country to take an active and decided part in the common caufe. The nation is not now to be trifled with. Upon our conduct at this eventful hour, depends the eftablifhment of our conftitution, and the liberties of unborn generations. We fhall not, Sir, fuffer our attention to be drawn from the great objects in which we are engaged by a retrofpect into your paft parliamentary conduct, however diffonant in many points from our opinions; but we call upon you, if you value our future approbation, to give your fulleft fupport to the following meafures whenever they fhall be agitated in parliament, viz.

A declaration of our national rights.

An ademption of the power of the Privy Council to ftop or alter bills.

A mutiny bill limited in its duration.

A bill to render the Judges independent of the Crown,

And a bill to reduce the national expences to a level with its revenues.

Signed by our Chairman, the Grand Jury, and all the freeholders prefent, and ordered to be engroffed, and copies left at the principal towns of the county to be figned.

Refolved, That thefe refolutions be publifhed in the Dublin Evening Poft, and Connaught Journal.

❖✦❖✦❖✦❖✦❖✦❖✦❖✦❖✦❖✦❖✦❖✦❖✦❖✦

## COUNTY of the CITY of WATERFORD.

*We the Grand Jury of the County of the City of* Waterford, *at Spring Affizes,* 1782, *affembled, think the Duty we owe to our Country and Ourfelves, calls upon us at this time to declare,*

THAT the members of the Houfe of Commons are the reprefentatives of, and derive their power folely from, the people; and that a denial of this pofition, by them, would be to abdicate the reprefentation.

That the King, Lords, and Commons of Ireland, are the only power competent to make laws to bind this kingdom, and that every attempt, by any other body of men, to exercife this right, is unconftitutional, illegal, and a grivance.

That

That we do expect such declaration of right from our representatives in parliament, and that we will support them with our lives and fortunes in whatsoever measures may be necessary to render such declaration an effectual security.

That the powers exercised by the Privy Councils of both kingdoms, under, or under colour or pretence of the law of Poyning's, are unconstitutional, and a grievance.

That the ports of this country are, by right, open to all foreign countries not at war with the King, and that any burthen thereupon, or obstruction thereto, save only by the parliament of Ireland, are unconstitutional, illegal, and a grievance.

That a mutiny bill not limited in point of duration from session to session, is unconstitutional, and a grievance.

That the independence of Judges is equally essential to the impartial administration of justice in Ireland, as in England; and that the refusal or delay of this right to Ireland, makes a distinction where there should be no distinction, may excite jealousy where perfect union should prevail, and is in itself unconstitutional, and a grievance.

That it is our decided and unalterable determination to seek a redress of those grievances, and we pledge ourselves to each other, and to our country, as freemen, fellow-citizens, and men of honour, that we will, at every ensuing election, support those only who have supported, and will support us therein; and that we will use all constitutional means to make such our pursuit of redress speedy and effectual.

Resolved, That the Foreman be requested to have these resolutions inserted in the Dublin Evening Post, the Waterford papers, and Clonmel Gazette.  (Signed)

Simon Newport, Foreman.

| | | |
|---|---|---|
| Js. Henry Reynett, | David Jones, | Edward Phair, |
| Sim. John Newport, | Henry Tandy, | Richard Drapes, |
| John Jones, | Herman Zurhurst, | David Wilson, |
| Henry Bolton, | John Brown, | Hugh Cormack, |
| Benjamin Morris, | John King, jun. | John Cormack. |
| William Bell, | Charles Dobbs, | |

## COUNTY of WEXFORD.

*We the High Sheriff, Foreman, and Grand Jury of the County of Wexford, this Day assembled,*

THINKING it now peculiarly necessary to declare our sentiments respecting the fundamental and undoubted rights of this nation, and desirous, by a seasonable explanation, to terminate an anxious jealousy, and to prevent the possibility of any future contest, do unanimously declare, That we will, in every situation of life, and with all the means in our power, assert and maintain the constitutional rights of this kingdom, to be governed by such laws *only* as are enacted by the King, Lords, and Commons of Ireland ; and that we will, in every instance, uniformly and strenuously oppose the execution of any statutes, except such as derive authority from said parliament, pledging ourselves to our country and to each other, to support with our lives and fortunes this our solemn declaration ; and further, we bind ourselves, that we will yearly renew this necessary vindication of our rights, until such time as they shall be explicitly acknowledged and firmly established.

Resolved unanimously, That these declarations be published in the Dublin Evening Post, and Wexford Journal.

**HENRY BROWNRIGG**, Sheriff.
**HEN. THO. HAUGHTON**, Foreman and Fellows.

✶✳✶✳✶✳✶✳✶✳✶✳✶✳✶✳✶✳✶✳✶✳✶✳✶✳✶✳✶✳✶✳✶✳✶

## COUNTY of LIMERICK.

*We the Grand Jury of the County of Limerick, at Spring Assizes, 1782, assembled, think the Duty we owe to our Country and ourselves, makes it indispensably necessary for us unanimously to declare,*

THAT the members of the House of Commons derive their power solely from, and are the only representatives of, the people, and that a denial of this position, would be to abdicate the representation.

That the King, Lords and Commons of Ireland, are the only power competent to make laws to bind this kingdom, and that an attempt of any other to usurp such right, is subversive of our constitutional liberties, illegal, and a grievance.

S                                                            That

That we do expect our reprefentatives in parliament will exert their moft ftrenuous endeavours to have immediately paffed,

Bills explanatory and declaratory of our rights.

A proper modification of Poyning's law.

A *real* Free Trade. And

A better confideration of the pernicious mutiny bill.

That we hold the right of private opinions in religious matters to be inherent to all mankind, and that we do congratulate our countrymen of the Roman Catholic perfuafion, on the late relaxation of the penal laws, fatisfied that fuch a meafure muft enfure union and harmony among us.

That we do abhor and execrate that prefumptious doctrine, *That power makes right*, and rejoice that the public fpirit of our brave Volunteers prevents men, who dare advance fuch defpotic maxims, from carrying them into execution.

And leaft it fhould be fuggefted, that our proceedings arife from a defire to fhake off all communication with Great Britain; we thus publicly declare, That we are convinced there is not a man in this kingdom, who entertains a wifh fo ruinous to both; but on the contrary, our fincere intention is to remove every object of jealoufly from the eyes of either nation, that we may embrace our fifter with the warmeft feelings of affection, and cement fo indiffoluable a connection between us, as will enfure an equal liberty to both; what we are convinced we are doubly entitled to, as we are ready *to fhare any equal fate with her*.

We do hereby moft folemnly engage ourfelves to each other, and to our country, as freemen, men of honour and public fpirit, that we will on every enfuing election, fupport *thofe only* who have exerted, or will exert themfelves, to put *thofe* our *fixed* refolutions into fpeedy and effectual execution.

Refolved, That the above refolutions be inferted in the Dublin Evening Poft, and Limerick Papers.

| | | |
|---|---|---|
| 1 John Grady, junior, | | 13 John Fitzgerald, |
| 2 Hugh Maffy, | | 14 Hugh Maffy, jun. |
| 3 John Thomas Waller, | | 15 Edward Croker, |
| 4 Wm. W. Newenham, | | 16 Michael Furnell, |
| 5 William Ryves, | | 17 William Fitzgerald, |
| 6 John Croker, | | 18 Richard Bourke, |
| 7 Charles Coote, | | 19 Darby O'Grady, |
| 8 Ger. Blennerhaffet, | | 20 Benjamin Frend, |
| 9 William Odell, | | 21 James Gubbins, |

10 John

10 John Tuthill,                    22 William Wilfon,
11 Thomas Odell,                    23 Richard Taylor.
12 James Ellard,

❂×❂×❂×❂×❂×❂×❂×❂×❂×❂×❂×❂×❂×❂×❂

## COUNTY of CORK.

*Refolutions of the Grand Jury of the County of* Cork, *Spring Affizes,* 1782.

RESOLVED, that we think it neceffary to declare, That no power has a right to make laws for this kingdom, fave only the King, Lords, and Commons of Ireland, and that we fhall not confider ourfelves to be bound by any other, and that we will, with our lives and fortunes, maintain and defend the Irifh parliament in fuch a declaration of rights, and in any meafure that they may think proper to fupport it.

Refolved, That confidering ourfelves as a loyal and free people, we fhall be ever ready to manifeft the principles upon which that opinion is founded, by fupporting, in every conftitutional manner, the juft rights and liberties of the fubject, and fhewing a warm zeal in loyalty to our King.

Refolved, That we think it effentially neceffary to the intereft of this kingdom, that the moft cordial intercourfe, and good underftanding between the fifter kingdoms of Great Britain and Ireland, be kept up on our parts, as neceffary to the commercial interefts of each refpectively.

Refolved, That as we conceive all men are entitled to an abfolute freedom in their religious opinions, we highly approve of all acts of toleration, as by removing caufes of complaint they tend to unite the people, and make them happy.

Refolved, That we highly approve of an increafe of falaries to, and the independence of the Judges, as we are fatisfied it will ftrengthen the hands of juftice, and give an additional fecurity to the rights of the people.

Refolved, That the power affumed by the Privy Council under colour of Poyning's law, to detain or alter the heads of bills of the Irifh parliament, is unconftitutional, and a grievance.

1 Richard Townfend, Fore.    13 Auguftus Warren,
2                            14 Rob. Uniacke Fitzgerald,
3 James Bernard,             15 Thomas Hungerford,
4 Richard Longfield,         16 James Purcell,

5 William

| | |
|---|---|
| 5 William Tonfon, | 17 William Chetwynd, |
| 6 Francis Bernard, | 18 Hewit Poole, |
| 7 Rd. Boyle Townfend, | 19 Daniel Connor, |
| 8 Richard O'Brien Boyle, | 20 John Bowen, |
| 9 Abraham Devonfher, | 21 John Gilman, |
| 10 William Connor, | 22 Roger Conner, junior, |
| 11 John Townfend, | 23 John Atkin. |
| 12 Henry Baldwin, | |

WE the undernamed members of the Grand Jury, are of opinion, that a perpetual mutiny law is unconftitutional, dangerous to the liberties of the people, and ought to be repealed. We alfo think it incumbent on us to publifh our fentiments on a meafure which appears to require public cenfure, and to enter into the above refolution, though not agreeable to the other gentlemen of the Grand Jury.

| | |
|---|---|
| Kingfborough, | Francis Bernard, |
| James Bernard, | Auguftus Warren. |

## CITY of KILKENNY.

*We the Grand Jury of the County of the City of Kilkenny, at Spring Affizes, 1782, affembled, confcious that every Citizen who wifhes to fupport the glorious Caufe of Liberty, fhould, at this critical Juncture, declare his Sentiments, have unanimoufly entered into the following Refolutions :*

RESOLVED, That the King, Lords, and Commons of Ireland, are the only power that have a right to make laws to bind Ireland ; and that we will, to the utmoft of our power, refift the execution of any other laws.

Refolved, That the members of the Houfe of Commons are the reprefentatives of the people, and that fuch members as fupport meafures contrary to the opinion of their conftituents, betray the truft repofed in them.

Refolved, That we will not, on any future election, vote for any member to reprefent us in parliament, who will not (previous to his election) folemnly promife to obey the inftructions of his conftituents ; that he will not only give his vote, but exert his utmoft endeavour to obtain for this kingdom its conftitutional rights.

Refolved,

Refolved, That the relaxation of the penal laws againſt our Roman Catholic fellow-citizens and ſubjects, gives us the higheſt fatisfaction, convinced that it will more ſtrongly cement the bond of union between us.

Refolved, That we are, and ever will be ready to ſupport our Sovereign againſt his natural enemies, and ſhare the *liberty* and *fate* of our ſiſter kingdom.

Refolved, That the attempt againſt the tenantry of this kingdom, holding leaſes for lives, was a moſt injurious meaſure, and fraught with many ruinous and dangerous confequences: we, therefore, pledge ourſelves, that we will not, on any future election, ſupport the intereſts of, or vote for any member to ſerve in parliament, who voted againſt the tenantry bill.

Refolved, That theſe reſolutions be publiſhed three times in the Leinſter Journal, and Dublin Evening Poſt.

| | | |
|---|---|---|
| T. Butler, Forem. | Richard Butler, | Tho. Shearman, |
| Edmund Butler, | Henry Birch, | Richard Treſham, |
| John Helſham, | Edward Oldfield, | Val. Coughlan, |
| James Cooke, | Thomas Bibby, | Henry M'Creary, |
| Edward Hunt, | Jn. M'Cloughry, | John M'Creary, |
| John Boyde, | Wm. Robertſon, | Richard Empſom. |
| W. Knareſborough, | | |

Refolved, That the thanks of this Grand Jury be given to our worthy Foreman, Colonel Thomas Butler, for his ſpirited conduct on this and every occaſion.

✦❀✦◈✦◈✦◈✦◈✦◈✦✦◈✦◈✦◈✦◈✦◈✦◈✦

## COUNTY of KILKENNY.

*At a Meeting of the High Sheriff and Grand Jury of the County of* Kilkenny, *at Lent Aſſizes,* 1782.

### PRESENT,

| | | |
|---|---|---|
| Js. Kearney, Sheriff, | James Wemys, | Eland Moſſom, |
| H. Blunt, Forem. | Thomas Boyce, | Will. Barton, |
| George Agar, | Edward Hunt, | Luke Roche, |
| John Butler, | Patt Walſhe, | John Mitchell, |
| Hon. P. Butler, | Rich. W. D. Cuffe, | Clayton Bayly, |
| Sir R. St. George, | Benj. Kearney, | Richard Lower, |
| Bart. | Benj. Morris, | Henry La Rive, |
| John Flood, | Robert Snow, | Francis Flood. |
| Gerv. P. Buſhe, | | |

Refolved

Refolved unanimoufly, That we conceive that it is now neceffary, in the fulleft manner, to affert the rights of this country:

We do declare for ourfelves, That we deny the authority
of the Britifh parliament to make laws to bind this kingdom;
and that we will not obey but refift the execution of any laws
fo made; and that we are ready to fupport our parliament, in
declaring its exclufive rights, with our lives and fortunes.

Refolved unanimoufly, That Great Britain and Ireland are
and ought to be infeparably connected, by being governed by
the fame King, and enjoying equal liberty and fimilar conftitutions.

Refolved, That no man ought to be elected to ferve in parliament, who will not, previous to his election, pledge himfelf to exert his utmoft endeavours to obtain a redrefs of the
national grievance.

HENRY BLUNT, Foreman and Fellows.

Refolved unanimoufly, That the above refolutions be publifhed in the Dublin Evening Poft, and Leinfter Journal.

--◆-◆-◆-◆-◆-◆-◆-◆-◆-◆-◆-◆-◆-◆-◆-◆-◆-◆-◆-◆-◆-◆-◆--

## COUNTY of KILDARE.

### LENT ASSIZES, 1782.

AT this critical and momentous period, when our fellow
fubjects throughout the kingdom have thought it neceffary, by
public declarations, to affert the independence of their country, we think it incumbent on us, the Sheriff and Grand Jury
of the county of Kildare, to exprefs our determination on the
fame important fubject; and we do therefore unanimoufly declare, That no power on earth hath right to make laws to bind
Ireland, fave only the King, Lords, and Commons of Ireland; profeffing at the fame time, that we hold it to be effentially neceffary to the profperity of both kingdoms, that
the imperial crown of Great Britain, and the imperial crown
of Ireland, fhall be for ever infeparably united. And we are
confident, that a repeal of that Britifh ftatute, which declares
a power in the Britifh parliament to make laws of fufficient
force to bind Ireland, would remove all grounds of jealoufy
between the two kingdoms, and would cement that harmony
and affection which ought to fubfift between them for ever.
And we do declare, that we will firmly fupport, to the utmoft

of

of our ability, our reprefentatives in parliament, in every
conftitutional means of obtaining the defired object of a fpirited and unanimous people.

ROBERT POWER, Sheriff.
R. BROOKE, Foreman.

## COUNTY of MONAGHAN.

*We the High Sheriff, Foreman, and Grand Jury, of the County
of Monaghan, this Day affembled,*

THINKING it now peculiarly neceffary to declare our fentiments refpecting the fundamental and undoubted rights of
this nation, and defirous, by a feafonable explanation, to terminate an anxious jealoufy, and to prevent the poffibility of
any future conteft, do unanimoufly declare, That we will, in
every fituation of life, and with all the means in our power,
affert and maintain the conftitutional rights of this kingdom,
to be governed by fuch laws only as are enacted by the King,
Lords, and Commons of Ireland, and that we will, in every
inftance, uniformly and ftrenuoufly oppofe the execution of
any ftatutes, except fuch as derive authority from faid parliament; pledging ourfelves to our country, and to each other,
to fupport, with our lives and fortunes, this our folemn declaration; and further, we bind ourfelves, that we will yearly renew this neceffary vindication of our rights, until fuch time
as they fhall be explicitly acknowledged and firmly eftablished.

Refolved unanimoufly, That thefe declarations be publifhed
in Faulkner's Journal, the Evening Poft, and Ulfter Journal.

THOMAS CORRY, Sheriff.
SAMUEL MADDEN, Foreman and Fellows.

## DONEGALL MEETING.

WE the High Sheriff, Grand Jury, Reprefentatives, Burgeffes, Freeholders, and Inhabitants of the county of Donegall, thinking it now peculiarly neceffary to declare our fentiments, refpecting the fundamental and undoubted rights of
this nation, and defirous, by a feafonable explanation, to
terminate

terminate an anxious jealoufy, and to prevent the poffibility of any future conteft, do declare, That we will, in every fituation of life, and with all the means in our power, affert and maintain, that it is the conftitutional right of this kingdom to be governed by fuch laws only as are enacted by our parliament, the King, Lords, and Commons of Ireland; and that we will, in every inftance, uniformly and ftrenuoufly oppofe the execution of any ftatutes, except fuch as derive authority from parliament; pledging ourfelves to our country, and each other, to fupport with our lives and fortunes this our folemn declaration. And further, we bind ourfelves, that we will at all times renew this neceffary vindication of our rights, until fuch time as they fhall be explicitly acknowledged, and firmly eftablifhed.

Refolved unanimoufly, That the thanks of this meeting be given to our worthy High Sheriff, for his readinefs in convening the county, and for his proper conduct in the chair.

Refolved unanimoufly, That the thanks of this meeting be given to our worthy reprefentative, Alexander Montgomery, Efq; for his conftant attention to the inftructions of his conftituents, and his fpirited conduct in parliament.

Refolved unanimoufly, That the thanks of this meeting be prefented to Sir Annefly Stewart, Bart. and Henry Brooke, Efq; for their fpirited and upright conduct in parliament.

Refolved, That the Sheriff be requefted to publifh the above refolutions in the Dublin Evening Poft, and Derry Journal.

Signed by order,

RICH. CHARLETON, Sheriff, Chairman.

✠·◦··✠✠·◦··✠✠··◦··✠✠··◦··✠✠··◦··✠✠··◦··✠✠··◦··✠✠··◦··✠✠··◦··✠✠··◦··✠✠··◦··✠✠··◦··✠

## COUNTY of TIPPERARY.

*We, the Grand Jury of the County of Tipperary, at Spring Affizes, 1782, affembled, think the duty we owe to our Country and ourfelves, calls upon us at this time to declare,*

THAT the members of the Houfe of Commons are the reprefentatives of, and derive their power folely from, the people, and that to act contrary to the fenfe of their conftituents, would be to deny this pofition.

That the King, Lords and Commons of Ireland are the only power competent to make laws to bind this kingdom; and that every attempt by any other body of men to exercife this right, is unconftitutional, illegal, and a grievance.

That

That we do expect such a declaration of right from our representatives in parliament, and that we will support them with our lives and fortunes, in whatever measures may be necessary to render such declaration an effectual security.

That the power exercised by the Privy Council of both kingdoms, under, or under colour or pretence of the law of Poyning's, is unconstitutional, and a grievance.

That the ports of this country are by right open to all foreign countries not at war with the King, and that any burthen thereupon, or obstruction thereto, save only by the parliament of Ireland, are unconstitutional, illegal, and a grievance.

That a Mutiny Bill, not limited in point of duration from session to session, may be dangerous to the constitution, and is a grievance.

That the independence of judges is equally essential to the impartial administration of justice in Ireland as in England, and that the refusal or delay of this right to Ireland, makes a distinction where there should be no distinction, and may excite jealousy where perfect union should prevail, and is a grievance.

That it is our decided and unalterable determination to seek a redress of these grievances; and we pledge ourselves to each other, and to our country, as freemen, fellow-citizens, and men of honour, that we will use all constitutional means to make such our pursuit of redress speedy and effectual.

| | |
|---|---|
| 1 | 13 |
| 2 Henry Prittie, | 14 Minchin Carden, |
| 3 | 15 Robert Nicholson, |
| 4 | 16 Edward Moore, |
| 5 | 17 John Power, |
| 6 John Bagwell, Marlfield, | 18 Samuel Jacob, |
| 7 John Bagwell, Kilmore, | 19 Gamahel Fitzgerald Magrath, |
| 8 Wray Pallifer, | |
| 9 | 20 William Baker, |
| 10 Daniel Gahan, | 21 Samuel Alleyn, |
| 11 Anthony Parker, | 22 |
| 12 William Perry, | 23 John Lap Judkins. |

Resolved, That the thanks of this Grand Jury are justly due, and are hereby given to Richard Butler Hamilton Lowe, Esq; for his upright and impartial conduct, as High Sheriff of this county, since his commencement in office.

FRANCIS MATHEW, Foreman

T                                    CER-

CERTAIN refolutions having been propofed to the confideration of the Grand Jury of the county of Tipperary,
at Spring Affizes affembled, which were approved of, and
figned by many of the faid Jury, and were ordered by them
to be printed; and certain other refolutions having been alfo
propofed, which feveral of the Jury thought more unexceptionable than the above-mentioned, equally firm, but more
moderate.

In order therefore to ftrengthen and confirm the people in
the maintenance of their juft and undoubted rights, to prove
to the world that, although it was not found practicable to
obtain unanimity, the difference of opinion was not in the
great or effential articles; that in thofe every man of the Jury
was unanimous; that the whole Jury declared with one voice,
That the commerce of this kingdom was, and of right ought
to be free from every reftraint, fave only fuch as were impofed
by the parliament of Ireland; that the independence of Judges
was a great national point, never to be relinquifhed; and
that the King, Lords, and Commons of Ireland only, and
no other power upon earth, were competent to make laws for
the people of this kingdom. For thefe reafons, therefore,
the gentlemen who diffented from their brethren on the Grand
Jury, think it incumbent on them to fubmit the following refolutions to the public, to which they have affixed their names,
and which contain their decided and unalterable fentiments.

Refolved, That the members of the Houfe of Commons
are the reprefentatives of, and derive their power folely from,
the people; and that a denial of this pofition would be to
abdicate the reprefentation.

That the King, Lords and Commons of Ireland are the
only power competent to make laws to bind this kingdom;
and that we will oppofe every attempt by any other body of
men to exercife this right, or to impofe laws on the people
of Ireland.

That we will fupport, with our lives and fortunes, any
meafures, which our reprefentatives in parliament may deem
expedient to adopt, in order to prevent any fuch encroachment on our conftitution.

That the ports of this country are by right open to all foreign countries not at war with the King; and that any burthen thereupon, or obftruction thereto, fave only by the parliament of Ireland, are unconftitutional, illegal, and a grievance.

That

That the independence of Judges is equally effential to the impartial adminiftration of juftice in Ireland as in England; and we recommend it ftrenuoufly to our reprefentatives in parliament, not to lofe fight of this great national object, but to ufe every means in their power for the attainment of it.

Thefe are our decided and unalterable fentiments; and we pledge ourfelves to each other, and to our country, to ufe all conftitutional means, to carry fuch our determinations into fpeedy and effectual execution.

Francis Mathew,     R. H. Hutchinfon,   Wm. Armftrong,
Corn. O'Callaghan,  Theob. Butler,      James Fogarty.
Rich. Pennefather,

ooooooooooooooooooooXooooooooooooooooooooooo

## SLIGO MEETING.

*At a Meeting of the Gentlemen Freeholders of the County of Sligo, convened by the High Sheriff, April 1, 1782.*

GEORGE DODWELL, Efq; High Sheriff, in the Chair,

The folloiwng Refolutions were unanimoufly agreed to:

1ft. THAT the refolutions entered into by the Delegates affembled at Dungannon and Ballinafloe, by the Volunteer affociations, and fince approved of by the different meetings of feveral other corps and counties of this kingdom, are fuch as ought to be adopted by every friend to the liberties and commerce of Ireland.

2d. That we will fupport, with our lives and fortunes, all the juft rights and privileges of this kingdom, and that we will ufe our utmoft endeavours to promote peace, harmony, and good order in this county; and that we will co-operate with all the other counties in this kingdom, in any meafures that may tend to the accomplifhing fo falutary an end.

3d. That the thanks of this meeting be given to the different Delegates from the Volunteer corps of this county, who attended the meeting at Ballinafloe, on the 15th of March laft.

4th. That thefe refolutions, unanimoufly approved of, be publifhed three times in the Dublin Evening Poft, and Sligo Journal.

5th. That the thanks of this meeting be given to the high Sheriff, for his chearful compliance with our requeft, in convening the county, and for his polite and candid conduct in the chair.

GEORGE DODWELL, Sheriff.

## COUNTY of KILKENNY.

## IVERK VOLUNTEERS,

Commanded by the Right Hon. *John Ponfonby*, Colonel.

*At a full Meeting of the* Iverk Volunteers, *at* Befborough, *on Eafter Monday*, 1782.

### Major OSBORNE in the Chair.

The following refolutions were unanimoufly agreed on, and ordered to be publifhed in the Waterford Chronicle, Leinfter Journal, and Dublin Evening Poft:

RESOLVED, That we conceive it to be a duty we owe our King, our country, and ourfelves, to concur, at this important crifis, with our countrymen, and fellow Volunteers, in fuch temperate, but firm exertions, as may eftablifh the freedom of this kingdom upon permanent foundations, according to the principles of our moft excellent conftitution.

Refolved, That we conceive the firft ftep now neceffary for this great purpofe, to be a folemn, and recorded declaration in parliament, of the legiflative rights of this free nation, and that no body of men have any power or authority to make laws to bind this ancient and independent kingdom, fave only the King, Lords, and Commons of Ireland.

Refolved, That we pledge ourfelves to fupport, in concurrence with our virtuous countrymen and brother Volunteers, fuch a parliamentary declaration of our rights, with our lives and properties, and that in every other conftitutional meafure, that may be found neceffary for the further fecurity of our liberties, we are convinced the people of Ireland will difplay zeal and perfeverance, united with loyalty and moderation.

Refolved, That as it is the mutual intereft of Great Britain and Ireland always to poffefs the clofeft degree of liberal connection, we are perfuaded, that, from this motive, as well as from partiality, affinities, and affections, it is the univerfal and fincere defire of our countrymen, that the two kingdoms, by having the fame King, equal liberty, and fimilar conftitutions, fhould remain infeparably connected for ever.

Refolved, That our thanks are peculiarly due to two members of this corps, our Colonel, the right hon. John Ponfonby,

by, and our Lieutenant-colonel, Richard Cox, Efq; for having given their fupport in parliament, to the attempts which
were made in the prefent feffion, to reftore the ancient conftitution of this realm, by preventing the Privy Council (an affembly not known to that ancient conftitution) from *fuppreffing*
or *altering* fuch bills, or heads of bills, as the deliberative wifdom of an Irifh parliament may think proper to be offered to
the confideration of the Sovereign of Ireland.

Refolved, That we highly applaud the fpirit, and the liberality of fentiment concerning religious toleration, expreffed
in the refolutions entered into by the Volunteer Delegates at
Dungannon and Ballinafloe, and that we moft cordially and
fincerely join them, and all the other Volunteers of Ireland,
in the warmeft affection for our countrymen of every religious
denomination. Signed by order,

PETER WALSH, Secretary.

After all the above refolutions were agreed on, Major Of-
borne left the chair ; and then the unanimous thanks of the
corps were voted to him for his conduct as Chairman ; and
for his conftant zeal and attention to this corps on all occafions. And the unanimous thanks of the corps were then alfo
voted to Mr. Walfh.

---

*At a Meeting of the* Caftle-Durrow Light Dragoons, *purfuant
to Adjournment, April* 1, 1782, *to appoint a Major.*

Lieutenant-colonel RIDGE in the Chair.

When John Barrington, of Caftlewood, Efq; was unanimoufly
appointed Major, vice Ridge.

R ESOLVED unanimoufly, That we are ready to co-
operate with every Volunteer corps in the fupport of, and obtaining the conftitutional rights of our country.

Refolved, That we will not vote for any member to ferve
in parliament, who will not pledge themfelves to fupport their
conftituents.

Refolved, That the above refolutions be publifhed in the
Leinfter Journal, and Dublin Evening Poft.

Signed by order,

THOMAS KING, Secretary.

MOUNT-

## MOUNTMELICK VOLUNTEERS.

*At a Meeting of said Volunteers, at* Mountmelick, *April* 1, 1782.

Lord Viscount CARLOW in the Chair.

RESOLVED unanimously, That the King, Lords, and Commons of Ireland, are the only power who have, or ought to have any right to make laws to bind this kingdom ; and that we will not obey or give operation to any laws, except those enacted by them.

Resolved unanimously, That Great Britain and Ireland are inseparably connected by every tie that can cement an union between two nations, and should enjoy equal liberty and similar constitutions.

Resolved unanimously, That we approve of the patriotic spirit of our brother Volunteers; and that we will co-operate with them, in supporting the constitutional rights of Ireland with our lives and fortunes.

Resolved unanimously, That the thanks of this meeting be given to our right hon. Chairman, for his spirited conduct on this occasion.

Resolved, That these resolutions be published in the Dublin Evening Post, and Leinster Journal.

Signed by order,<br>
JOHN SHAW, Secretary.

## CURRAGHMORE RANGERS.

*At a full Meeting of said Troop at* Newtown, *on Monday, April* 1, 1782.

Captain SHEE in the Chair.

The following resolutions were unanimously agreed to :

RESOLVED, That we are ready to assist and co-operate with the several corps whose Delegates met at Dungannon, on the 15th of February last, in every constitutional measure for supporting the rights, and promoting the interests and prosperity of Ireland.

Resolved,

Refolved, That union and mutual confidence between all denominations of Irifhmen will effectually contribute to render Ireland a free, flourifhing, and profperous nation.

Refolved, That we conceive the interefts of Great Britain and Ireland to be infeparable.

Refolved, That we will fupport our gracious Sovereign, with our lives and fortunes, againft any defigns or attempts of his natural enemies.

Whereas numbers of Irifh manufacturers, particularly in the woollen branch, are in the utmoft diftrefs for want of employment;

Refolved, That it is our wifh that the Irifh Volunteers fhould be cloathed in the manufactures of their own country only.

Refolved, That we are fully determined not to wear any uniform in future but what is entirely of Irifh manufacture.

Refolved, That thefe refolutions be immediately tranfmitted to the Secretary of the Ulfter Delegates.

Refolved, That thefe refolutions be printed in the Dublin Evening Poft, and Ramfey's Waterford Chronicle.

Refolved, That the thanks of this troop be given to Captain Shee for his great attention on all occafions, and proper conduct in the chair.

Signed by order,

JOHN HATCH JENKIN, Sec.

✦✦❖✦❖✦✦❖✦✦❖✦✦❖✦✦❖✦✦❖✦✦❖✦✦❖✦✦❖✦✦❖

## WESTMEATH.

*At a Meeting of the* Fertullagh Rangers, *held at their Parade, on Monday, April* 1, 1782.

Colonel ROCHFORT HUME in the Chair.

RESOLVED unanimoufly, That we will fteadily maintain the principles of our original inftitution, the defence of our country, againft foreign enemies, and, the prefervation of the internal peace of the kingdom.

Refolved unanimoufly, That the Dungannon refolutions, entered into on the 15th of February laft, do fo fully exprefs
and

and coincide with our thoughts, on their several subject matters, that it is needless to say more than declare, that they have our entire approbation ; and that they do perfectly comprehend our sentiments, in every respect, and that we will firmly adhere to them.

Resolved, That these resolutions be printed in the Dublin Journal, Westmeath Journal, and Dublin Evening Post.

Signed by order,

JOHN JONES, Secretary.

## COUNTY of KILKENNY.

### CASTLE-DURROW VOLUNTEERS.

*At a full Meeting of the* Castle-Durrow Volunteers, *held at the* Market-house *in* Durrow, *April* 1, 1782.

Major FITZPATRICK in the Chair.

RESOLVED, That at this important crisis, when such noble ardour pervades this kingdom, we contemplate with admiration the virtuous efforts of our dear countrymen, to ascertain and establish our commercial and constitutional rights ; we therefore judge it a duty incumbent on us now to declare our sentiments :

Resolved, That no power on earth has a right to make laws to bind this kingdom, save only the King, Lords, and Commons of Ireland, and that we will, in every instance, uniformly and strenuously oppose the execution of any statute or laws, except such as are formed by the authority aforesaid.

Resolved, That we do expect a declaration of rights from our representatives in parliament, and we pledge ourselves to them and each other, that we will, in every capacity and situation of life, co-operate with our brother Volunteers in all constitutional efforts to procure a redress of our grievances, and a permanent establishment of the rights of our country.

Resolved, That the ports of this kingdom should be by right open to all foreign countries not at war with the King, and that any restriction laid on, or obstruction thereto, except

by

by the parliament of Ireland, are unconstitutional and a grievance.

Resolved, The thanks of this meeting to the different corps,
whose Delegates met at Dungannon the 15th of February,
for their patriotic and liberal resolutions.

Resolved, The thanks of this meeting to our worthy Chairman, for his polite and spirited conduct in the chair.

Resolved, The above resolutions be published in the Dublin Evening Post, and Leinster Journal.

Signed by order,
JOHN B. RIDGE, Secretary.

✦·◦·✦✦·◦·✦·✦◦·◦·›·›·✦·◦·✦✦✦✦·◦·✦·◦·✦·◦·✦◦·◦·✦·◦·✦·◦·✦

## TYRERIL TRUE BLUES.

*At a Meeting of the* First Tyreril True Blues, *held at* Colloony, *April* 1, 1782, *pursuant to Notice.*

The Rev. JOHN LITTLE in the Chair.

Rᴇꜱᴏʟᴠᴇᴅ unanimously, That we do, from our hearts,
approve of the resolutions entered into by the several Delegates of the Ulster Volunteers, at their meeting, held at Dungannon, on the 15th of February last.

Resolved, That we do also highly approve of the moderate,
loyal, and spirited resolutions entered into by the Delegates
of the several corps of Connaught Volunteers, held at Ballinasloe, on the 15th of March last, which last-mentioned
meeting we had appointed a Delegate, but from an unfore-
seen accident, the effects of which (though unavoidable) we
must still consider as a great misfortune, that said Delegate
could not attend the said meeting.

Resolved, That considering ourselves as free citizens, armed
in defence of ourselves, the laws and constitution of our
country, and disclaiming any jurisdiction whatsoever, but of
the King, Lords, and Commons of Ireland, we are firmly
determined, with our lives and fortunes, to support every
measure which may tend towards a preservation of that independence; and we also declare, that we will, in every capacity, oppose the execution of all such statutes as the (at present to us seemingly) usurped authority of a British parliament has hitherto enacted, or may hereafter attempt to impose on a country, whose great wishes are to be *Free;* at the
U                                                          same

same time that we declare, in almost the words of our worthy brethren, the Delegates of the Connaught corps, That the chief wish of our hearts is to clasp our sister nation to our bosom, and cement an indissoluble union between us; attached to her by every tie of affection and interest that can unite nations, surrounded as she is by an host of enemies, we are resolved *to share her liberty, and share her fate.*

Resolved, That copies of these resolutions be sent to the Secretaries of the Ulster and Connaught Volunteers.

Resolved, That these resolutions be published in the Dublin Evening Post, and the Sligo Paper.

JOHN LITTLE, Chairman.

*At a respectable Meeting of privates of the* Royal Larne Volunteers, *April* 2, 1782.

Mr. THOMAS MOORE in the Chair.

RESOLVED unanimously, That the Volunteer army of this kingdom hath been the salvation thereof, by protecting our coasts from foreign invasion, securing domestic tranquility, and (we hope) procuring to us a restoration of our constitutional rights; and that these salutary purposes could not have been effected, unless the several corps of which it is composed, had collected themselves together, for their improvement in military discipline, and declared their sentiments freely on national affairs; for without the former, they could not have been qualified to take the field for real action; and without the latter, they could not have been assured of their unanimity.

Resolved, That means have been used, not only to prevent this corps from joining any neighbouring corps, but even to shackle our minds, by forbidding us to publish our sentiments on public measures! Such ignominious restraint, we deem fitter for the stalls of asses, or beasts of burden, than the ranks of Freemen or Volunteers; and it is with no less astonishment than regret, that in this land of liberty, and at this important crisis, when the spirit of the nation seems roused to a proper sense of its own dignity, that we yet find any individuals capable of tamely submitting to such base restraint: for our parts we are *determined* to be free, and therefore consider fider ourſelves no longer members of the Royal Larne Volunteers.

Reſolved, That a new company be formed under the name of the Larne Independents, and that any gentleman of independent principles, ſhall be eligible to command ſaid corps.

Reſolved, That we have ſeen with heart-felt pleaſure, the truly noble reſolutions of the Ulſter Delegates; and it being our unalterable opinion, that they contain no more than what every real friend to this country ſhould uſe his utmoſt efforts to obtain, we, therefore, pledge ourſelves to our country, and to one another, that as citizens and Volunteers, we will perſevere in our preſent line of conduct, until theſe great ends are obtained and ſecured to us, upon a permanent foundation.

Reſolved, That the Chairman do tranſmit theſe reſolutions to the Secretary of the Dungannon meeting, and that they be publiſhed in the Belfaſt News-Letter.

THOMAS MOORE.

❦❦❦❦❦❦❦❦❦❦❦❦❦❦❦❦

*At a Meeting of the* Kinnilea *and* Kirrikurihy Union, *convened April 2, 1782.*

Colonel ROBERTS in the Chair.

IT was unanimouſly reſolved, That we do moſt chearfully accede to the truly virtuous and patriotic reſolutions and addreſs of the Ulſter Delegates, aſſembled at Dungannon on the 15th of February laſt, and that we will, to the fulleſt extent, co-operate with them in every conſtitutional mode of obtaining the moſt ſpeedy and effectual redreſs of thoſe grievances, they ſo judiciouſly point out.

Reſolved unanimouſly, That we feel the moſt perfect ſatisfaction at the relaxation of the ſevere laws againſt our Roman Catholic fellow-ſubjects.

Reſolved, That the perſon who, in a free ſtate, advances the abomniable doctrine *of power conferring right,* is an enemy to his King and country.

Reſolved, That as we approve of the expediency of ſending Delegates to the meeting at Cork, as advertiſed by the Muſkerry and other ſocieties, we appoint Lieut. Col. Herrick, and Major Roberts for that purpoſe.

Reſolved, That theſe our reſolutions be tranſmitted to Capt. Dawſon, Secretary to the Ulſter Volunteers, and publiſhed in the Cork and Dublin Evening Poſts.

THOMAS ROBERTS, Col.

The Chairman having left the chair,

Refolved, That the thanks of this fociety be returned to Col. Roberts, for his peculiar propriety of conduct in the chair.

* * * * * * * * * * * * * * * * * * * * *

## MOYCASHEL.

*At a Meeting of the* Moycafhel Affociation, *at the Houfe of* Anthony Miller, *in* Killbeggan, *on* Tuefday, *April* 2, 1782.

The Hon. ROBERT ROCHFORT, Col. in the Chair.

RESOLVED unanimoufly, That the power of making laws to bind this country, is vefted folely in the King, Lords, and Commons of Ireland, and that we will not put any other laws into execution.

Refolved unanimoufly, That a modification, by a partial repeal of Poyning's law, would be highly beneficial to the conftitution of this country.

Refolved unanimoufly, That making the Judges commiffion *quam diu fe bene gefferint*, would greatly tend to the impartial diftribution of juftice in this kingdom.

Refolved unanimoufly, That we will join our brother Volunteers of Ireland, united with the conftitutional branches of legiflature, in every legal and proper meafure, to promote and bring into effect, the fpirit of the above refolution.

Refolved unanimoufly, That the immenfe fums of money, annually remitted to the abfentees of this kingdom, greatly contribute to impoverifh the nation.

Refolved unanimoufly, That the idea of repealing thofe laws reftrictive on the property and religion of the Roman Catholics of this country, are (fo far) properly liberal and highly commendable; and, that a removal of thefe reftrictions which prevent their being called to the bar, on taking the oath lately formed for Roman Catholics, would greatly tend to lead them into a line of information, which at prefent they have no inducement to feek for.

ROBERT ROCHFORT, Chairman.

Colonel

Colonel Rochfort having left the chair:

It was unanimoufly refolved, That the thanks of this meeting be prefented to the hon. Colonel Rochfort, for his great propriety of conduct in the chair.

Refolved unanimoufly, That the foregoing refolutions be inferted three times, in the Dublin and Weftmeath Journals, and the Dublin Evening Poft.

Signed by order,

SAM. W. HANDY, Secretary.

## BURRASSAKANE VOLUNTEERS.

*At a Meeting of the* Burraffakane Volunteers, *April* 2, 1782.

Major THOMAS STONEY in the Chair.

The following refolutions were unanimoufly agreed to:

RESOLVED, That we fincerely congratulate our brother Volunteers on the refolutions entered into by the Ulfter Delagates, reprefented at Dungannon, on the 15th of February laft, and that we highly approve of the fame, and will co-operate with them in every conftitutional mode of obtaining a fpeedy and effectual redrefs of the grievances fo juftly complained of throughout the kingdom.

Refolved, That the virtuous efforts of the minority of both houfes of parliament claim our warmeft thanks, and truft their endeavours will be crowned with fuccefs.

Refolved, That our thanks is juftly due to Henry Prittie, Efq; our worthy reprefentative, for his fteady, upright, and uniform conduct in parliament.

Major Stoney having quit the chair,

Refolved, That the thanks of this corps be given to him for his unwearied attention to us, and convening this meeting.

Signed by order,

JOS. ABBOTT, Secretary.

PORTAR.

## PORTARLINGTON INFANTRY.

*At a Meeting of the* Portarlington Infantry, *assembled by notice on Tuesday, April 2, 1782.*

### Major LEGRAND in the Chair.

RESOLVED unanimously, That mutual and inseparable interests should unite Great Britain and Ireland. As citizens and Volunteers, we will never lose sight of that grand object. We took up arms to support his Majesty against the enemies of Great Britain and Ireland, to protect ourselves, and to maintain, by every constitutional mode, the freedom and independence of this kingdom, bound only by laws enacted by the King, Lords, and Commons of Ireland, whose rights and liberties we jointly and severally are determined to support with our lives and properties.

### WILLIAM HENRY LEGRAND.

Resolved unanimously, That the thanks of this Meeting be presented to Major Legrand, for his particular propriety of conduct in the chair.

Signed by order,

### JOHN BROWN, Secretary.

## QUEEN's COUNTY, LENT ASSIZES, 1782.

*At a Meeting of the Grand Jury of said County, at* Maryborough, *Tuesday, April 2, 1782.*

### GEORGE BURDETT, Esq; Foreman, in the Chair.

The following resolutions were unanimously agreed to:

RESOLVED, That the period is now arrived, when it is necessary unequivocally to ascertain the constitutional rights of this kingdom; and that a speedy, determined, and unanimous declaration of the same by the nation in general (conformable to those just and spirited resolutions heretofore entered on the journals of both houses of parliament on that head) will tend to the tranquility of our common empire, and be productive of many salutary consequences.

Resolved,

Refolved, That the King, Lords, and Commons of Ireland, being fully and alone competent to enact laws to bind the fame, the interference of any other legiflature is inconfiftent, injurious, and oppreffive; and that we will ever refift the execution of any fuch pretended laws, at the hazard of our lives and fortunes.

Refolved, That any idea of feparation from the imperial crown of Great Britain, is abfurd, extravagant, and runions; that attached by loyalty and duty to his majefty's perfon and government, and by affection and intereft united to Great Britain, we will ftand and fall by her; but, that being bound to fhare her diftreffes, we are entitled to a full participation of her liberty; and we hope the candour of her legiflature will remove every ideal ground of future jealoufy or cavil.

Refolved, That the prefent well-eftablifhed internal police of Ireland, and the rank fhe now holds in the political world, is principally owing to the Volunteer affociations; and that they be requefted to perfevere in a line of conduct fo honourable to themfelves, and fo beneficial to their country.

GEORGE BURDETT, Foreman, in the Chair.

Sir Robert Staples, Bart. having taken the Chair,

Refolved, That the thanks of this meeting be given to our worthy Chairman, George Burdett, Efq; and that thefe our refolutions be inferted in the Dublin and Kilkenny Newfpapers.

Signed by order,

RICHARD EVANS, Secretary.

✦•◦✦•◦✦•◦✦•◦✦ ◦✦•◦✦•◦✦•◦✦ ◦✦•◦✦•◦✦✦ ◦✦•✦ ◦✦•✦•◦✦•◦✦ ✦ •◦✦•◦✦•◦✦

## STRABANE MEETING.

*At a Meeting of the Inhabitants of the Town of Strabane, on the 3d Day of April, 1782, in order to take into Confideration the prefent flate of public affairs.*

JOHN SPROULL, Efq; Provoft, in the Chair.

1. RESOLVED, That as it is the undoubted right, fo we think it the indifpenfable duty of every man, at this important crifis, publicly and unequivocally to declare his fentiments relative to the rights of Ireland.

2. Refolved, That in common with our countrymen, we warmly approve and admire the temper, and patriotic fpirit,

by

by which the Dungannon refolutions are fo confpicuoufly
diftinguifhed.

3. Refolved, That we will, in every fituation of life, and
with all the means in our power, affert and maintain the conftitutional right of this kingdom, to be governed by fuch laws
only as are enacted by the King, Lords, and Commons of
Ireland; and that we will, in every inftance, uniformly and
ftrenuoufly oppofe the execution of any ftatute, except fuch
as derive authority from faid parliament.

4. Refolved, That we will not, at any future election,
vote for, or fupport any man who has oppofed a parliamentary declaration of the independent rights of the Irifh legiflature.

JOHN SPROULL.

At this meeting, the inhabitants of Strabane being unanimous in favour of the above refolutions, and I thinking it
my duty, as Chairman, to announce the fentiments of the
people then affembled, did fubfcribe my name; yet, notwithftanding, I difapprove of the 4th refolution, as it may tend to
difcourage fuch reprefentatives, as on former occafions have
oppofed the fenfe of the nation in parliament, but may in future be able to prove, by their conduct, that they intend to
fupport the intereft of Ireland.

JOHN SPROULL.

*At a general Meeting of the Delegates from the feveral Volunteer
Corps of the Queen's County, viz. 5 of Cavalry and 15 of
Infantry, held at Maryborough, April 3, 1782.*

The Vifcount CARLOW in the Chair.

The following refolutions were unanimoufly agreed to:

RESOLVED, That it is now neceffary unequivocally to
afcertain the conftitutional rights of this kingdom; and that
a general declaration of our national and natural independence,
and the moft determined refolutions to fupport the fame, will
be productive of many advantages, and preferve tranquility
to our common Empire.

Refolved, That the King, Lords, and Commons of Ireland, are fully and alone competent to enact laws to bind the
fame;

same ; and that we will resist the execution of any other pretended laws, at the hazard of our lives and fortunes.

Resolved, That any idea of separation from the imperial crown of Great Britain, is absurd, extravagant, and ruinous ; that enjoying similar constitutions, we are entitled to equal liberty ; and we hope the prudence of the British legislature will remove every ideal ground of future jealousy and discontent, and that no meer cavil in words may prevent that affectionate and perfect amity and union we ever wish to preserve.

Resolved, That the House of Commons, as representatives of the people, from them derive their sole consequence and existence : That freemen and freeholders, peaceably assembled, have a constitutional right, respectfully to convey their sentiments to any or every branch of the legislature ; and that they are answerable for consequences, who neglect seasonable admonition.

Resolved, That the internal order and peace of this kingdom, and the respectable rank she now holds, is principally owing to the Volunteer associations ; and that we are convinced a conduct so honourable to themselves, and so very serviceable to their country, will most chearfully be persevered in by them.

Resolved, That the warmest acknowledgements of this nation are most deservedly due to the association assembled at Dungannon, for their early, spirited, and liberal declarations on this great and constitutional question ; and that the Chairman do forthwith transmit to their Secretary, Captain Dawson, the thanks of this meeting.

CARLOW, Chairman.

Sir Robert Staples, Bart. having then taken the Chair,

Resolved, That the thanks of this meeting be given to the Viscount Carlow, for his very proper conduct this day in the chair ; and that these our resolutions be published in the Dublin Evening Post, and Leinster Journal.

ROBERT STAPLES, Chairman.

X                                    UNIVER-

## UNIVERSITY MEETING.

*At a Meeting of the Electors of the* University, *convened on Wednesday the 3d of April, by public Notice.*

### Mr. WILLIAM BAKER in the Chair.

The following addrefs was unanimoufly agreed to, and ordered to be prefented to their reprefentatives:

*To the Right Honourable* WALTER BURGH, *and* JOHN FITZGIBBON, *Efq;* Reprefentatives in Parliament for the Univerfity *of* Dublin.

*Gentlemen,*

WHEN the murmurs of a people, ftruggling for their rights, have been heard even in the quiet retreat of fcience, we fhould deem it a breach of duty to our countrymen and ourfelves, did we neglect to fecond their virtuous exertions: we are never forward in political contefts; we fhall always be decided and fteady; although we have not been the firft to complain of, yet, we have not been the laft to feel the repeated injuries this country has fuffered, not only from thofe who may have feparate duties and feparate interefts, but from men who are bound by the ftrongeft duty, and the deareft intereft, to vindicate its rights, and cherifh its profperity.

The power of binding Ireland by acts of a foreign legiflature, is what nothing but a fpirit of arrogance or oppreffion would infift upon; nothing but the moft abject fervility fubmit to; for we cannot fuppofe, that the appearance of a claim which iritates the whole body of the people, would be retained, unlefs there was an intention of enforcing this claim hereafter; we are therefore convinced, that an exprefs declaration of rights, is the only meafure upon which this country can build its legiflative independence, and that a reluctance to affert the conftitution of the land, may furnifh Great Britain with a pretence for denying the juftice of our requifition.

We do not think the prefent fituation of Great Britain to be any objection againft fuch a declaration, as we can never fuppofe that fhe could derive ftrength from our weaknefs, or any fecurity to her liberties from the oppreffion of ours; and *that* time is undoubtedly to be preferred for the affertion of

our

our rights, when the object is likely to be obtained with the leaft ftruggle.

The infecure attachment of Ireland to the crown of England at a former period, furnifhed a pretext for divefting the houfes of parliament of their right to originate bills, unlefs previoufly certified into England under the great feal of this kingdom; now, as the loyalty of this country for feveral centuries paft, fo often tried, and fo often acknowledged, has removed every caufe of diftruft, we conceive that this injurious and humiliating reftriction fhould alfo ceafe.

The dependance of the judges of Ireland on the will of the fovereign, may, in the hands of an afpiring monarch, prove a powerful inftrument of oppreffion; now, holding ourfelves entitled to every conftitutional fecurity which our fifter kingdom poffeffes, we confider it neceffary that the judges of this kingdom fhould be made equally independent with thofe of Great Britain.

But fince every advantage which could refult from thefe reformations muft be precarious, as long as a perpetual mutiny bill exifts, by which, force may be made to fupercede right, and the foldiery of Ireland are fubjected to trial and punifhment by any future articles of war, which the king and privy council of Great Britain may think proper to adopt; we are perfuaded, that every conceffion muft be imperfect, unlefs accompanied with the repeal of fo dangerous a law.

We therefore expect you will exert your moft ftrenuous efforts, to obtain a declaration of the rights of Ireland; a repeal or fatisfactory explanation of the law of Poyning's; an act for making the tenure of the judges independent of the crown; and a repeal of the perpetual mutiny bill.

We declare, That thefe are our fixed and unalterable fentiments, and we are convinced that nothing fhort of the requifitions herein contained, can be, in any degree, fatisfactory to the people of Ireland.

It is our wifh to render the connection between this country and Great Britain, as clofe and permanent as poffible, and we are perfuaded that this is only to be accomplifhed by abolifhing all ufurped authority of the one over the other, and removing every invidious diftinction between the conftitutions of two countries, equally entitled to be free.

Signed,
WIL. BAKER, Chairman.
*To*

*To the* Electors *of the* University, *convened on Wednesday the* 3d *of April,* 1782.

Gentlemen,

WHEN I reflect on my past parliamentary conduct, it affords me the highest satisfaction, to find that it entirely corresponds with the tenor of your instructions. Whenever the objects that you recommend have come into discussion, I have given them my uniform and decided support. My conduct has been founded upon principles, which no motives of interest or ambition have been able to shake, and in which I shall persevere unto the last hour of my life.

I have the honour to be,
With the greatest respect,
Gentlemen,
Your most faithful,
Humble servant,
WALTER BURGH.

*To the* Electors *of* Trinity College.

Gentlemen,

I AM just now honoured with your instructions, which have been forwarded to me by post. Be assured, that I shall always feel the utmost satisfaction in receiving the instructions of that very great and respectable body which I have the honour to represent, and that you shall ever find me ready, to the best of my ability, to vindicate your rights.

I have always been of opinion, that the claim of the British parliament to make laws for this country, is a daring usurpation on the rights of a free people, and have uniformly asserted this opinion both in public and in private. When a declaration of the legislative right was moved in the house of commons, I did oppose it, upon a decided conviction that it was a measure of a dangerous tendency, and withal inadequate to the purpose for which it was intended. However, I do, without hesitation, yield my own opinion upon this subject to yours, and will, whenever such a declaration shall be moved, give it my support.

With

With refpect to an explanation of the law of Poyning, I confefs, the more I confider the fubject, the more difficult it appears to me. Allow me to remind you, that the Univerfity did, upon a very recent occafion, experience that this law, in its prefent form, may operate beneficially. A total repeal of it, will I hope, on confideration, appear to you to be not, by any means, a defireable object—You may reft affured, that the beft attention which I can give to the fubject fhall be exerted; and I truft and doubt not, that upon a communication with you upon this topic, I fhall be able to give you full fatisfaction.

I agree with you moft warmly, that any advantage which we may derive from reformation muft be precarious, fo long as the articles of war fhall continue to be a permanent and eftablifhed branch of municipal law, which they certainly are under the prefent act for regulating the king's army in Ireland. I have not a doubt in my mind, that a perpetual mutiny law lays the foundation of a military government in this country; upon this principle I did oppofe it as ftrenuoufly as I could, from the firft moment it was introduced into the houfe of commons, and upon this principle I will, whilft I live, make every effort within my power to procure a repeal of it. The adminiftration of juftice in this country is certainly an object of the firft importance, and therefore I will, at all times, concur in any meafure which can be propofed to make the judges of the land independent and refpectable.

I have the honour to be,
Gentlemen,
'With great refpect,
your moft obedient, and
Very humble fervant,
JOHN FITZGIBBON.

*Mount-Shannon, April* 11, 1782.

## COUNTY WEXFORD VOLUNTEERS.

*At a Meeting of the Delegates of* Nineteen Corps, *convened by the Commander in Chief, at the requeft of their refpective corps, at the* Bear-Inn, Ennifcorthy, *April* 4, 1782.

### Colonel PHAIRE in the Chair.

RESOLVED unanimoufly, That at a time when there is a want of public fpirit in parliament, and when the patriotic
and

and ſtrenuous efforts made there, have been thoſe of a minority, and of courſe inſufficient to give effect to their own and the nation's ſentiments, by a parliamentary declaration of rights, it becomes the people at large, to aſſert and declare their conſtitutional rights, on which the happineſs of themſelves and their poſterity ſo materially depends ; and as great objects can only be obtained by unanimity and perſeverance, we think it incumbent on us to unite our voices with that of our fellow-citizens and Volunteers, at this critical and important period.

Reſolved unanimouſly, That both intereſt and inclination prompt us to a firm and indiſſoluble connection with England ; and, in our opinion, nothing can ſo much contribute to this end, as the ſettling our conſtitution on a firm baſis, by preventing the revival of thoſe queſtions which have already ſevered from England the moſt extenſive part of her dominions, and involved her in the greateſt calamities.

The well-known loyalty of the people of Ireland, and the recent offer of the whole Volunteer army, to enter into the ſervice of government, on the alarm of an invaſion, are facts ſufficient to refute the calumnies thrown out in England, againſt the juſt, neceſſary and public-ſpirited meaſures, which this kingdom at preſent ſo laudably purſues.

Reſolved unanimouſly, That we do entirely approve of the reſolutions and addreſs of the Ulſter Volunteers, entered into at Dungannon, on the 15th day of February laſt.

Reſolved unanimouſly, That as citizens and Volunteers, we will co-operate with the ſeveral corps, whoſe delegates met at Dungannon, in every conſtitutional mode of obtaining a redreſs of the grievances mentioned in their reſolutions.

Reſolved unanimouſly, That the Secretary of our commander in chief be requeſted to communicate our approbation of, and acceſſion to the ſaid reſolutions, to the Secretary of the Ulſter Volunteers.

ROBERT PHAIRE, Chairman.

ROCK-

## ROCKINGHAM VOLUNTEERS.

*At a Meeting of the* Rockingham Volunteers, *at the Court-house of* Coollattin, *April* 4, 1782.

### Major CHAMNEY in the Chair.

RESOLVED unanimously, That we highly approve of the principles declared in the resolutions of the Ulster Volunteers assembled at Dungannon, the 15th of February last.

Resolved unanimously, That we will co-operate with the several Volunteer corps of Ireland, in every constitutional mode of obtaining a redress of grievances, and establishing the rights of Ireland.

JOSEPH CHAMNEY, Chairman.

Resolved, That the thanks of this meeting be presented to our Chairman, Major Chamney, for the propriety of his conduct this day in the chair.

Resolved, That these resolutions be printed in the Dublin Evening Post three times.     Signed by order,

JOHN SYMES, Sec.

❁×❁××❁××❁××❁×××❁××❁××❁××❁××❁××❁×❁

## ARMAGH MEETING.

*At a numerous Meeting of the Freeholders of the County of* Armagh, *convened by public Notice from the High Sheriff of said County, on Thursday, April* 4, 1782.

### WILL. RICHARDSON, Esq; in the Chair.

The Dungannon resolutions being read,

RESOLVED unanimously, That the said resolutions be adopted as the resolutions of this meeting.

Resolved unanimously, That the following address be signed by the Chairman, and presented to our worthy representatives :

*To the Right Hon.* William Brownlow *and* Tho. Dawson, *Esq.*

WE approve of your past, and look up with unbounded confidence to your future conduct.   The Dungannon resolutions

tions are, by adoption, ours ; fupport them, it will be honour-able to you, juftice to us, and effential to the freedom and profperity of Ireland.

WILLIAM RICHARDSON.

William Richardfon, Efq; having left the chair, and Thomas Townly Dawfon, Efq; taken it,'

Refolved unanimoufly, That the thanks of this meeting be prefented to William Richardfon, Efq; for his proper con-duct in the chair.

Refolved unanimoufly, That the thanks of this meeting be prefented to Francis Dobbs, Efq; and that we highly ap-prove of his patriotic zeal and fpirited conduct at this meet-ing.

Refolved unanimoufly, That thefe refolutions and addrefs, together with the anfwer of our reprefentatives be publifhed in the Dublin Evening Poft, the Belfaft News-Letter, and the Newry Chronicle.

THO. TOWNLY DAWSON.

To the Freeholders of the County of Armagh.

*Gentlemen,*

I AM happy in your approbation, as it adds ftrength to our efforts for the public fervice. Your fentiments were well known to me, and I have anticipated your commands. The united voice of the people coincides with yours, and calls loudly from all parts of the kingdom, for a vindication of their conftitutional rights. Such union and firmnefs muft prevail, and the happy æra cannot be remote. I confider the refolu-tions of Dungannon as the cement of that union, and I ap-plaud them. Your confidence in me is not mifplaced—I ne-ver will betray you. Yours, faithfully,

W. BROWNLOW.

*At a Meeting of the* Cumber Battalion, *April* 4, 1782.

Colonel DAVID ROSS in the Chair.

1ft. RESOLVED unanimoufly, That an equal diftribution of juftice is both the glory and ftrength of every empire.

2d. Refolved

2d. Refolved unanimoufly, That to affert or maintain, that this kingdom is to be governed by any other power except the King, Lords, and Commons of Ireland, is an unequal diftribution of juftice, a fubverfion of the rights of this kingdom, and detrimental to the real happinefs of the whole empire.

3d. We unanimoufly approve of the refolutions entered into by the Delegates of the Ulfter Volunteers, who met at Dungannon the 15th of February; and do pledge ourfelves, as foldiers, and men of fpirit, that we will, with our lives and fortunes, fupport our brethren, the Volunteers of Ireland, in every conftitutional effort to effect the fame.

Laftly, Refolved, That thefe refolutions be publifhed in the Londonderry Journal, and Dublin and Belfaft papers, and tranfmitted to the Secretary, Capt. Dawfon.

D. ROSS, Colonel, Chairman.

✦◦✦✦◦✦◦✦✦◦✦✦◦◦✦✦◦◦✦✦◦◦✦✦◦◦✦✦◦◦✦◦✦

*At a full Meeting of the* Ormond Independents, *affembled the 5th Day of April,* 1782.

ACTUATED as we are by loyalty to our Sovereign, and impreffed with a juft fenfe of thofe rights which we hold as citizens and Volunteers, the prefent critical fituation of affairs feems to us a proper occafion, for thus publicly declaring our fentiments; fully determined to affert our rights, yet anxious to preferve that unanimity and cordial friendfhip, which we fincerely hope may always fubfift between Great Britain and Ireland.

Refolved, That by learning the ufe of arms, we are not the lefs intitled to make a declaration of our rights.

Refolved, That the refolutions of the Ulfter Volunteers, affembled at Dungannon on the 15th day of February laft, and of the Connaught Volunteers, affembled at Ballinafloe on the 15th day of March laft, are fo fully expreffive of thofe rights, as to render any declaration on our part unneceffary, further than that they meet our hearty and unanimous approbation, and that we are determined to co-operate with the Volunteer corps of Ireland, in every conftitutional mode of redrefs.

Y                                              Refolved,

Refolved, That the thanks of this meeting be prefented to Colonel Toler, our worthy Chairman, for his zeal in fupport of the public good, and his upright conduct as Chairman.

Refolved, That thefe refolutions be printed in the Dublin Evening Poft, and the Clonmel Gazette.

Signed by order,

WM. GREENSHIELDS, Lieut. and Sec.

00000000000000000Y00000000000000000

*At a full Meeting of the* Firft *and* Independent Killinchy Volunteer Company, *April* 6, 1782.

## Captain GAWIN HAMILTON in the Chair.

RESOLVED unanimoufly, That the fpirited, manly, and moderate refolutions of the Ulfter Volunteers met at Dungannon, have our warmeft approbation, and that we do moft chearfully accede to them; with pleafure we accept of their invitation, and think ourfelves honoured by being admitted members of fo refpectable a body.

*At a Time when Refolutions and Addreffes of the moft ferious Confequences are daily multiplying from all Quarters of the Kingdom, where either Volunteer Corps, or other fpirited Friends to the true Interefts of Ireland exift, the* Lemavady Battalion, *confifting chiefly of Freeholders in this County* (Londonderry) *on Parade affembled, April* 6, 1782,

### Came to the following refolutions:

THAT it is our opinion, that the right hon. Edward Cary, is entitled to the warmeft returns of gratitude from every friend to this country, whether we confider him as a Volunteer, for his generous treatment to Volunteers, or, as a reprefentative of this county, for his parliamentary conduct, a conduct, we hereby declare we will, to our utmoft, fupport on every future occafion.

An entire change of men and meafures having taken place in our fifter kingdom, the county of Derry reprefentatives will, we truft, ftand foremoft on the lift of friends to Ireland, as we will, on every fuch occafion, give them public teftimonies of our gratitude and affection.

That

That the warmeſt thanks of this battalion be returned to General Cary, and the inhabitants of Dungiven, for their hoſpitality on Friday the 5th inſt. to the officers and privates of theſe corps.

That theſe reſolutions be publiſhed.

Signed by order,

RICH. GRAY, Adjt. Gen.

━━━━━━━━━━━━━━━━━━━━━━━━━━━━━━━

## CLARE MEETING.

*At a general Meeting of the Gentlemen, Clergy, and Freeholders of the County of* Clare, *convened by the High Sheriff at* Ennis, *April 6, 1782, purſuant to public Notice,*

POOLE HICKMAN, Eſq; High Sheriff, in the Chair.

The following Reſolutions were unanimouſly agreed to :

RESOLVED, That it appears to us to be obſolutely ne ceſſary to declare, That no power on earth has any right to make laws to bind this kingdom, ſave the King, Lords, and Commons of Ireland.

Reſolved, That a claim of any body of men, other than the King, Lords, and Commons of Ireland, to make laws to bind this kingdom, is unconſtitutional, illegal, and a grievance.

Reſolved, That it is at this time abſolutely neceſſary, that the Iriſh parliament ſhould enact a law declaratory of their ſole and excluſive right to make laws to bind Ireland.

Reſolved, That the powers exerciſed by the Privy Council of both kingdoms under, or under colour of the law of Poyning's, are unconſtitutional, illegal, and a grievance.

Reſolved, That we are determined to render the Engliſh claim of legiſlation in Ireland ineffectual, by every conſtitutional reſiſtance.

Reſolved, That a mutiny bill, not limited in point of du- ration, is unconſtitutional and a grievance.

Reſolved, That the ports of this country are by right open to all foreign countries, not at war with our Sovereign, and that any reſtriction on our trade, or obſtruction thereto, ſave only by the parliament of Ireland, is illegal, unconſti- tutional, and a grievance.

Reſolved,

Refolved, That the independence of Judges is effential to the impartial adminiftration of juftice in Ireland, and that the refufal or delay of this right, may excite jealoufy and difcontent, and is a grievance.

Refolved, That the thanks of this meeting are due to thofe wife and virtuous men, who fo firmly demanded, and fo ftrenuoufly contended for declarations of our rights, and re-drefs of our grievances.

Refolved, That to poftpone or delay fuch declarations of our rights, and compleat and fatisfactory redrefs of our grie-vances, is in effect to deny the rights, and to deny them, is bafely to betray them.

Refolved, That it is our unalterable determination to feek a redrefs of thefe grievances; and we pledge ourfelves to each other, and to our country, as freeholders, fellow-citi-zens, and men of honour, that we will at every enfuing elec-tion for our county, fupport thofe only, who will fupport us therein; and that we will ufe all conftitutional means to make fuch our purfuit of redrefs, fpeedy and effectual.

Refolved, That our reprefentatives in parliament, Sir Lu-cius O'Brien, Bart. and Edward Fitzgerald, Efq; have ful-filled the truft repofed in them, and deferve the warmeft ap-probation of their conduct, which is peculiarly praife-wor-thy and difinterefted, at a time when venality and corruption influence fo many members of parliament, and conftitutes the minifterial fyftem of government in this country.

Refolved, That the thanks of this meeting be given to our worthy High Sheriff, for his ready compliance with the re-queft made to him for convening the county, and for his im-partial conduct in the chair.

Refolved, That thefe refolutions be figned by the Chair-man, and printed in the Dublin Evening Poft, and in the Clare and Munfter Journal.

POOLE HICKMAN, High Sheriff, and Chairman.

---

## CITY of CORK.

*Council Chamber, April 6,* 1782.

WE, the Grand Jury of the county of the city of Cork, at Spring affizes affembled, firmly convinced, that an explicit and timely avowal of the decided fentiments of the Irifh na-tion, will be the moft effectual means of preventing all future jealoufy between us and our fifter kingdom, and, that it will
beft

best tend to cement that union of hearts and sentiments between the subjects of the two countries, so devoutly to be wished for by every friend to either, and so indispensably necessary to the real happiness and prosperity of both, have thought it necessary to make the following solemn and unanimous declarations, to which we have affixed our names, and by which we will abide:

That the people of Ireland are a *Free People*, firmly attached by every tie of interest and of duty, to the maintenance of their constitutional rights, zealously loyal to the King, and sincerely affectionate to their British fellow subjects.

That it is the undoubted privilege, and unalienable right of a free people to make laws for themselves, and to be bound by no laws but only such, to which, by their representatives in parliament, they have given consent.

That the exercise of the power of legislation by any foreign legislature, is degrading to the country over which such power is exerted, subversive of its liberties, calculated to break down the spirit of its people, and sufficient to reduce a great kingdom to the contemptible situation of a tributary province.

That the King, Lords, and Commons of Ireland are the legislature thereof, competent solely, and in exclusion of every other power upon earth, to make laws to bind this kingdom; and that every attempt by any other body of men to exercise this right, is unconstitutional, and ought to be resisted.

That the claim of the British parliament to bind this kingdom by laws, is a claim disgraceful and unproductive; disgraceful to us, because it is an infringement of our constitution; unproductive to Great Britain, because the exercise of it will not be submitted to by the people of Ireland.

That the members of the house of commons are the representatives of, and derive their power solely from, the people. That it is their indispensable duty to redress the grievances, and to gratify the wishes of the people. That in this firm persuasion, we do expect from them a declaration of right; we recommend this great object to them as the humble, but earnest request of an unanimous nation, whose liberty they are delegated to protect, and at whose tribunal they are accountable for their conduct; and we pledge ourselves to them, and to each other, to support with our lives and fortunes, any measures which they may deem expedient to adopt in support of these our undoubted rights.

That

That the independence of Judges is equally effential to the impartial adminiftration of juftice in this kingdom as in Great Britain; that it is a national object of the firft importance, and of which we recommend it ftrenuoufly to our reprefentatives in parliament, never to lofe fight; and that we look up with peculiar confidence for the attainment of this valuable acquifition to the fame Irifh Minifters, to whofe faithful reprefentations and fuccefsful efforts we are indebted, for that other bulwark of our conftitution and liberties, the habeas corpus act.

That, as the Grand Jury of this city were among the foremoft in expreffions of gratitude for the commercial favours conferred upon the people of Ireland, by the liberal hand of their fifter kingdom, fo fhould they confider themfelves wanting in that duty which they owe to their fellow-citizens and their country, if they failed to affert their commercial rights, if they did not declare that the ports of this kingdom are of right open to all foreign countries not at war with the King; and that any burthen thereupon, or obftruction thereto, fave only by the parliament of Ireland, is unconftitutional, illegal, and a grievance.

That a mutiny bill not limitted in point of duration, from feffion to feffion, may be dangerous to the conftitution, and is a grievance.

That we cannot fufficiently applaud the liberal fpirit which has dictated to our reprefentatives in parliament the emancipation of their Roman Catholic brethren, from perfecution in a land of liberty, and from vaffalage in the bofom of their country, which has reftored them to their common rights, and has confirmed to the ftate the loyalty and the affections of a great majority of its people; thofe affections which injuries could not eradicate, and that loyalty, which the oppreffion of a century was infufficient to extinguifh.

That we contemplate with pleafure the happy confequences of this enlarged policy; that mutual confidence has taken root amongft us, and that the public ftrength has rifen in proportion; that Ireland is united, and that therefore fhe muft be *Free*.

R. H. Hutchinfon, Foreman.

| | | |
|---|---|---|
| Aylmer Allen, | John Travers, | Kevan Izod, |
| John Pedder, | Wm. Jamefon Wm. | Henry Wrixon, |
| Richard Perry, | John Lindfay, | Ben. Bousfield, |
| E. Jamefon, | Jofeph Witherall, | M. R. Weftropp, |
| Thomas Waggett, | Samuel Mayler, | Charles Denroch, |
| John Shaw, | Hugh Lawton, | Chriftopher Lawton, |
| William Cormack, | John Harding, | James Kingfton. |
| Phil. Allen, | | |

# ULSTER VOLUNTEERS.

*By the Subscribing Members of the Committee.*

*To the* Electors *of* Members *of* Parliament, *in the Province of* Ulster.

*Gentlemen,*

DELEGATED by the Volunteers assembled at Dungannon, we call on you to support the constitutional and commercial rights of Ireland; to exert the important privileges of freemen at the ensuing election, and to proclaim to the world that you at least deserve to be *Free.*

Regard not the threats of landlords or their agents, when they require you to fail in your duty to God, to your country, to yourselves, to your posterity. The first privilege of a man is the right of judging for himself, and now is the time for you to exert that right. It is a time pregnant with circumstances, which revolving ages may not again so favourably combine. The spirit of liberty is gone abroad, it is embraced by the people at large, and every day brings with it an accession of strength. The timid have laid aside their fears, and the virtuous sons of Ireland stand secure in their numbers. Undue influence is now as despised as it has ever been contemptible; and he who would dare to punish an elector for exerting the rights of a freeman, would meet what he would merit, public detestation and abhorrence.

Let no individual neglect his duty. The nation is an aggregate of individuals, and the strength of the whole is composed of the exertions of each part; the man, therefore, who omits what is in his power, because he has not more in his power, and will not exert his utmost efforts for the emancipation of his country, because they can, at best, be the efforts of but one man, stands accountable to his God and to his country, to himself and to his posterity, for confirming and entailing slavery on the land which gave him birth.

An upright House of Commons is all that is wanting, and it is in the power of the electors to obtain it. Vote only for men whose past conduct in parliament you and the nation approve, and for such others as will solemnly pledge themselves to support the measures which you and the nation approve. Do your duty to your country, and let no considera-

tion

tion tempt you to facrifice the public to a private tie, the greater duty to a lefs.

We entreat you, in the name of the great and refpeƈable body we reprefent; we implore you, by every focial and honourable tie; we conjure you as citizens, as freemen, as Irifhmen, to raife this long infulted kingdom, and reftore to her her loft rights. One great and united effort will place us among the firſt nations of the earth, and thofe who fhall have the glory of contributing to that event, will be for ever recorded as the Saviours of their country. *April 6,* 1782.

| | | |
|---|---|---|
| Wm. Irvine, | Alex. Stewart, | James Dawfon, |
| Rob. M'Clintock, | Fran. Dobbs, | James Atchifon, |
| John Fergufon, | Jas. M'Clintock, | Tho. Dickfon, |
| C. P. Leſlie, | John Harvey, | David Bell, |
| Fran. Lucas, | Rob. Campbell, | John Corelfon, |
| T. M. Jones, | Jof. Pollock, | Rob. Brack, |
| And. Thompfon, | W. Cunningham, | Wm. Crawford, |
| Charles Nifbitt, | Fran. Evans, | Rob. Thomfon. |

## MUNSTER VOLUNTEERS.

*At a Meeting of the Delegates from the following Volunteer Corps of the County and City of Cork, holden at the County Courthoufe of Cork, on Sunday the 7th Day of April,* 1782.

The Right Hon. Lord KINGSBOROUGH in the Chair.

1. *Kanturk Volunteers.*
James Purcell, Efq.

2. *Mufkerry Volunteers.*
Tho. Barter, Efq; Capt. Commandant.

3. *Cork Union.*
Henry Hickman, Efq; Capt. Commandant,
Richard Moore, Efq;
John Egan, Efq;
Richard Fitton, Efq;
Benjamin Swayne, Efq;

4. *Inchegeelagh Volunteers.*
Jafper Mafters, Efq; Capt. Commandant,
John Boyle, Efq; Lieut.

5. *Boyne Society.*
John Bagwell, Efq; Colonel,
John Bafs, Efq; Major,
Tho. Chatterton, Efq; Capt. Lieut. 1ſt company.

6. *Culloden Volunteers.*
Benjamin Boufield, Efq; Col.
Henry Newfom, Efq; Capt. Lieut. 1ſt company,
Sampfon Jervais, Efq; Capt. grenadiers,
Ifaac Jones, Efq; Capt. battal.

7. *Mallow Independent Volunteers.*
Jir J. Conway Colthurft, Bart.
Geo. Stawell, Efq; privates.

8. *Black-*

8. *Blackpool Affociation.*
John Harding, Efq; Colonel,
Tho. Barry, Efq; Lieut. Col.
Bradfhaw Popham, Efq; Lieut.
Cavalry.

9. *Bandon Independent Company.*
Francis Bernard, Efq; Colonel,
Robert Sealy, Efq; Captain.

10. *Cork Independent Artillery.*
Richard Hare, Efq; Captain,
Francis Jones, Efq; Lieut.

11. *Youghal Independent Rangers.*
Meade Hobfon, Efq; Lieut. Col. Commandant;
John Swayne, Efq; Major.

12. *Bandon Cavalry.*
John Travers, Efq; Major,
Auguftus Warren, Efq; priv.

13. *Glanmire Union.*
Henry Mannix, Efq; Colonel,
Simon Dring, Efq; Capt.

14. *Charleville Volunteers.*
Chrif. Sanders, Efq; Lieut.

15. *Imokilly Horfe.*
Edw. Roche, Efq; Colonel,
Rob. M'Carty, Efq; Lieut. Col.
Bartho. Hoare, Efq; private.

16 *Mallow Boyne.*
Rogerf. Cotter, Efq; Captain Cavalry,
Wm. Gallwey, Efq; Captain Infantry.

17. *Mufkerry True Blue Light Dragoons.*
Robert Warren, Efq; Col.
Rob. Hutchinfon, Efq; Lt. Col.
Sam. Swete, Efq; Major.

18. *Blackwater Volunteers.*
Rich. Aldworth, Efq; Col.
Rob. Stannard, Efq; Lt. Col.

19. *Newmarket Rangers.*
Boyle Aldworth, Efq; Col.

Wm. Allen, Efq; Major.

20. *True Blue Legion.*
The right hon. the Earl of Shannon, Colonel,
Jas. Morrifon, Efq; Lt. Col.
Mich. Weftropp, Efq; Major.

21. *Aughrim Volunteers.*
Rich. Longfield, Efq; Col.
Edw. Jamefon, Efq; Capt.

22. *Imokilly Blues.*
Rob. Uniacke Fitzgerald, Efq; Colonel,
Edw. Hoare, Efq; }
John Uniacke, Efq; } privates

23. *Mitchelflown Independent Dragoons.*
The right hon. Lord Kingfborough, Col.
Henry Cole Bowen, Efq; Lt. Col.
James Badham Thornhill, Efq; Major.

24. *Blarney Volunteers.*
Daniel Gibbs, Efq; Lt. Col.
Edw. O'Donnoghue, Efq; Capt.

25. *Kinnalea and Kirrikurihy Union.*
Tho. Herrick, Efq; Lt. Col.
John Roberts, Efq; Major.

26. *Cork Cavalry.*
Abraham Morris, Efq; High Sheriff of the county of Cork,
John Gillman, Efq; Major,
John Smith. Efq; Capt.

27. *Innifkillen Volunteers.*
Jofhua Connor, Efq; Major.

28. *Carbery Independent Company.*
John Townfend, Efq; Captain Commandant.

Z

1. RE.

1. Resolved unanimously, That as Delegates from our respective corps, we think the grievances enumerated in the Dungannon and Ballinasloe resolutions *real* and *substantial*.

2. Resolved unanimously, That no sincere or permanent connection can subsist between the kingdom of Ireland and the kingdom of Great Britain, without a full and unrestrained enjoyment of all their respective commercial and constitutional rights.

3. Resolved unanimously, That we consider ourselves connected with Great Britain, by all the nearest and dearest ties, our interests inseperable, our King the same, to whom it is the pride of Irishmen to be loyal ; that it is our determined resolution to be *Free*; and that our warmest wish is to meet an honourable opportunity of convincing our Sovereign of our duty, and our British brethren of our sincerest affection.

4. Resolved unanimously, That a provincial meeting of Delegates from the different Volunteer corps of Munster, would be highly advantageous to the public cause; and we therefore request Delegates from the different corps who have acceded, or shall accede to the Ulster resolves, to meet us the second day of May next, at Mallow, as being the town nearest to the centre of the province, where proper accommodations may be had for their reception.

5. Resolved unanimously, That as Ireland may furnish a sufficiency of manufactures of every kind for the consumption of its inhabitants, we ought and do bind ourselves to prefer the manufactures, and by preferring them, give subsistence to the manufacturers of our own country.

6. Resolved unanimously, That the thanks of this meeting be given to James Bernard, Esq; one of the representatives of this county, the right hon. Lord Kinsborough, and Francis Bernard, Esq; for their upright and virtuous conduct in parliament.

Resolved, That the thanks of this meeting be given to the right hon. Lord Kingsborough, for his impartial and proper conduct as Chairman.        By order,

HENRY NEWSOM, Secretary.

--◄◄{◄•}►◄{◄•}►◄{◄•}►◄{◄•}►►►►►--

*To the Delegates of the County and City of* Cork Volunteer Corps, *assembled on the* 7th *inst.*

Gentlemen,

THE very honourable and public manner, in which you have been pleased to express your approbation of my parliamentary conduct, demands my warmest thanks.        I have

I have ever been defirous to fupport the meafures, which I knew to be the general fenfe of the people of this kingdom, and I fhall, in every fitnation of life, endeavour to merit your efteem and confidence, having the honour to be,

Gentlemen,

With the greateft refpect,

Your moft obliged,

And obedient humble fervant,

KINGSBOROUGH.

To the Delegates of the Volunteer Corps of the County and City of Cork, convened in Cork, the 7th inft.

Gentlemen,

I FEEL myfelf under the greateft obligation to you for exprefling your public approbation of my conduct in parliament.

When I undertook to reprefent this county, I refolved to make the public good the fole object of my purfuit, to ufe every endeavour to ferve my country ; that the mode I have purfued has met with your applaufe, muft give me the greateft fatisfaction ; that I may continue to deferve it fhall be my future unremitted ftudy.

I have the honour to be,

With the greateft gratitude,

Gentlemen,

Cork, April 11, 1782.   Your obliged and humble fervant,

JAMES BERNARD.

To the Delegates of the Volunteer Corps of the County and City of Cork, convened the 7th inft. in Cork.

Gentlemen,

THE approbation of my parliamentary conduct, with which you have been pleafed to honour me, deferves my warmeft acknowledgements ; calls forth my public thanks.

My endeavours have been always directed by a zeal for the public good, an attention to the voice of the people : to you, as the reprefentatives of fo refpectable a part thereof, as the Volunteer corps of the county and city of Cork, I look up as the moft juft diftributors of cenfure and praife : as I have

been

been rewarded with the latter, I truft never to forfeit your
good opinion, or appear unworthy of the honour you have
conferred upon me. I have the honour to be, with the greateft refpect, gratitude, and efteem,

Gentlemen,<br>
Your obedient,

*April* 11,
1782.

And moft humble fervant,<br>
FRANCIS BERNARD.

## NEWPORT VOLUNTEERS.

*At a Meeting of the County* Tipperary Newport Volunteer *Corps,
on parade, affembled the 7th Day of April,* 1782, *purfuant to
notice.*

Captain WALLER in the Chair.

RESOLVED unanimoufly, That we do from our hearts
moft highly approve of the wife, liberal, and fpirited refolutions entered into by the Delegates of the Ulfter Volunteers,
at Dungannon, on the 15th day of February laft.

Refolved unanimoufly, That as citizens and Volunteers, as
men firmly attached to the rights of this kingdom, we will
fteadily co-operate with the feveral corps, whofe Delegates
met at Dungannon, in every conftitutional mode of obtaining
compleat redrefs of the grievances mentioned in their refolutions.

Refolved unanimoufly, That we will, at every future election
in this county, fupport with our free votes, thofe only whom
we find, by their virtuous conduct, beft calculated to maintain
the juft rights and commercial interefts of this country.

Refolved unanimoufly, That our moft grateful acknowledgments are due to the wife, fteady, and virtuous men,
who fo ftrenuoufly and perfeveringly fought a conftitutional
declaration of the rights of this kingdom, and that to refufe
or evade fuch declaration, is to betray the people, and high
treafon againft the conftitution.

Refolved unanimoufly (Captain Waller having left the
chair) That the thanks of this meeting be given to him, for
his upright conduct therein, and for his activity and conftant
attention to the corps.

Refolved, That thefe refolutions be printed in the Dublin
Evening Poft, and Munfter Journal.

Signed by order,<br>
RICHARD WALLER, Captain.

*At a full Meeting of the* Lower Iveagh Legion, *at* Dromore, *on the 7th of April,* 1782,

The following refolutions were propofed, and unanimoufly agreed to :

RESOLVED, That the ftrength of the Volunteers depends on their being unanimous.

Refolved, That the moderate proceedings at Dungannon tend to promote union, and meet with our approbation.

✦✦✦✦✦✦✦✦✦✦✦✦✦✦✦✦✦✦✦✦✦✦✦

## CLANE RANGERS.

*At a Meeting of the* Clane Rangers, *held at* Clane, *in the County of* Kildare, *the 7th of April,* 1782.

Captain SAMUEL MILLS in the Chair.

RESOLVED unanimoufly, That we entirely coincide in opinion with the refolutions of the Delegates held at Dungannon, the 15th of February laft.

Refolved, That we will co-operate with our brethren Volunteers in every conftitutional meafure, to fupport faid refolutions.

Refolved unanimoufly, That the thanks of this corps be given to Captain Mills, for his conftant attention to this corps.

Signed by order,
SAMUEL MILLS.

✦✦✦✦✦✦✦✦✦✦✦✦✦✦✦✦✦✦✦✦✦

*At a Meeting of the* Paffage Union Volunteers, *April* 7, 1782.

RESOLVED, That no power has a right to make laws to bind Ireland, but the King, Lords, and Commons thereof.

Refolved, That we will co-operate with our brother Volunteers in every conftitutional meafure, that fhall be judged neceffary for obtaining redrefs of real national grievances.

Refolved, That we are moft loyally attached to our Sovereign, and will, to the utmoft of our power, fupport his perfon, crown and dignity ; and that we wifh moft ardently to have
the

the bonds of friendſhip indiſſolubly united between our fellow-ſubjeĉts of Great Britain and us, as nothing can tend more to the welfare of both.

Signed by order,
DAVID THOMPSON, Secretary.

*At a numerous Meeting of the* Tallow Blues, *held the 7th of April*, 1782.

GEORGE BOWLES, Capt. Commandant, in the Chair.

RESOLVED unanimouſly, That we do highly approve of, and moſt heartily accede to, the patriotic and ſpirited reſolutions of the Ulſter Volunteers, repreſented at Dungannon, the 15th of February laſt; and that we will chearfully co-operate with our brother Volunteers in ſuch conſtitutional meaſures, as ſhall appear moſt expedient for obtaining a redreſs of the grievances mentioned in their reſolutions.

Reſolved, That a copy of the above reſolutions be tranſmitted by our Chairman, to the Secretary of the Ulſter Delegates, and be publiſhed in the Dublin and Cork Evening Poſts.

Signed by order,
GEORGE BOWLES, Capt. Commandant.

The Chairman having quitted the Chair,

Reſolved unanimouſly, That the thanks of this meeting be returned to Captain Bowles, for his upright conduĉt, and great attention to the diſcipline and welfare of this corps.

Signed by order,
ANTHONY HAYLES, Lieut. Tallow Blues.

## COUNTY of WICKLOW.

## BARONY of TALBOTSTOWN.

*At a Meeting of this* Barony Corps, *the 7th of April*, 1782.

WILLIAM HUME, Eſq; in the Chair.

RESOLVED unanimouſly, That we moſt heartily approve of the patriotic and ſpirited reſolutions entered into by the

Delegates

Delegates of the Ulster Volunteers, assembled at Dungannon, on the 15th of February, and of the Connaught Volunteers, assembled at Ballinasloe, the 15th of March last; and that we will most chearfully co-operate with our brother Volunteers, in asserting and maintaining the constitutional rights of this kingdom.

Resolved unanimously, That a Delegate do attend from this corps in Dublin, at the Royal Exchange, on the 17th instant, and that our worthy colonel, Nicholas Westby, be, and he is hereby appointed to represent us there that day.

Resolved unanimously, That copies of these our resolutions e transmitted to the secretaries of the Ulster and Connaught Volunteers, and that they be published in the Dublin Evening Post.

W. HUME, Chairman.

Resolved unanimously, That the thanks of this meeting be returned to our worthy chairman, Lieut. Col. Hume, for his upright conduct in the chair.

Resolved, That the above resolutions be published.

Signed by Order,<br>Rev. JOSEPH PASLEY, Secretary.

*At a Meeting of* Knox's Independent Troop *of* Light Horse, *at* Dromore, *on the* 7th *inst. the following Resolutions were proposed, and unanimously agreed to :*

RESOLVED, That the strength of the Volunteers depends on their being unanimous.

Resolved, That the moderate proceedings at Dungannon tend to promote union, and meet with our approbation.

*At a Meeting of the* Castlecomer Hunters, *and* Light Infantry, *held at* Castlecomer, *the* 8th *Day of* April, 1782.

Colonel Lord WANDESFORD in the Chair.

RESOLVED unanimously, That we highly approve of the Resolutions entered into at the Dungannon meeting, on
Friday

Friday the 15th of February laft, and are ready to co-operate
with our brother Volunteers in fupport of every conftitutional
meafure.

Refolved, That the thanks of this meeting be given to our
worthy chairman, for his attention to thefe corps.

Signed by Order,

ALEXANDER BRADLY, Secretary.

* * * * * * * * * * * * * * * * * * * * * * * * * *

## UNION REGIMENT.

*At a Meeting of the Reprefentatives of the feveral Corps of this
Regiment held at the* Market-houfe *in* Moira, *on Monday
the 8th Day of April,* 1782, *in order to take into confideration
the Dungannon Refolutions.*

### Lieut. Col. SHARMAN in the Chair.

RESOLVED, That in the prefent general appeal to the
people, we think ourfelves called on, as part of the civil body,
to make a public declaration of our principles.

Refolved, That his majefty's loyal fubjects of this regiment, entertain a fincere and unfeigned attachment to his
majefty's perfon and government.

Refolved, That his Majefty's people of Ireland are a free
people, inheritors of a free conftitution defcended to them
from their anceftors.

Refolved, That his Majefty's kingdom of Ireland is a diftinct kingdom, giving a diftinct title to an Imperial crown;
with a parliament of its own, the fole legiflature of the ftate.

Refolved, That it is the undoubted right of this free people (a right which they value as their lives) to be governed
folely by their own laws: That the King, Lords, and Commons of Ireland, are the only reprefentatives of this crown
and people, and that the interpofition of any other body
of men with the legiflature of this country, is incompatible
with our fundamental laws and franchifes.

Refolved, That next to our liberties, we value our connection
with Great Britain as a blefling, on which the happinefs of
both kingdoms depends; we fhall look forward, therefore, with a
pleafing conviction, that the juftice of Great Britain will fhake

hands

hands with the liberties of Ireland : and that a liberal renun-tiation of claims, fo ufelefs to the claimants, to us the caufe of difcontent, and to others of fatal calamities, will fecure the peace of the prefent, and the attachment of the fucceeding generations.

Refolved, That our fellow-citizens at Dungannon have fet an example of public fpirit, controuled by moderation, declaratory uf our rights, to the fatisfaction of our underftandings, and explanatory of our grievances, without inflaming our difcontents.

We affure them, therefore, of our approbation, and that we fhall join with them in every falutary application which may heal the conftitution; and adopt every conftitutional mode which may tend to eftablifh our rights, and obtain a redrefs of our grievances.

Refolved, That we return them our fincere thanks for, and embrace the invitation held out in their two laft refolutions, of becoming members of the faid meeting, and hereby requeft Captain Dawfon to lay thefe refolutions before the committee.

Capt. PATTON in the Chair;

Refolved, That the thanks of this meeting be returned to Lieut. Col. Sharman, for his particular propriety and politenefs of conduct in the chair.

Signed by order,
WILLIAM BATEMAN, Secretary.

✦●✦●✦●✦●✦●✦●✦●✦●✦●✦●✦●✦●✦●✦●

## R O S C R E A  B L U E S.

*In full Body affembled on Monday the 8th Day of April,* 1782.

### Capt. EDWARD BIRCH in the Chair.

THINK it would be at this time highly criminal in them, as independent Volunteers and freeholders, to remain filent, and have therefore come to the following refolutions :

Whereas, it has been afferted, *that the Volunteers, as fuch, cannot debate or publifh their opinions on political fubjects, or on the conduct of parliament, or on men in public employments.*

A a                                    Refolved

Refolved unanimoufly, That a freeholder, by learning the ufe of arms does not abandon any of his civil rights.

Refolved unanimoufly, That we highly approve of the fpirited and conftitutional refolutions of the Ulfter Delegates affembled at Dungannon, on the 15th day of February laft; and alfo, the refolutions entered into at Birr, on the 20th of March laft, at which meeting our Delegate, Col. Vaughan, attended.

Refolved unanimoufly, That the thanks of this corps be prefented to the majority of the Grand Jury at the laft Lent Affizes in Clonmel, for their truly fpirited declarations, and that we perfectly coincide in opinion with them, and will ufe every conftitutional means in our power to obtain a redrefs of the grievances therein mentioned.

Refolved unanimoufly, That, connected as we are with Great Britain by every tie of intereft and affection, we are determined to fhare her liberty and fhare her fate.

Refolved unanimoufly, That at every enfuing election we are determined to fupport thofe only, who have made the good of their country the primary object.

Refolved unanimoufly, That the thanks of this corps be prefented to Henry Prittie, Efq; one of our reprefentatives, for his fteady and upright conduct in parliament, and while he continues to perfevere (which we have not the leaft doubt of) in maintaining the rights of his country, he fhall meet with our warmeft fupport.

Refolved unanimoufly, That it appears to us, that from the unequal reprefentation of the people, we have reafon to apprehend that the endeavours of the virtuous part of our Houfe of Commons to obtain a redrefs of grievances may prove abortive; we, therefore, pledge ourfelves, fhould any well judged conftitutional attempts be made to bring our parliament to its priftine purity, our zealous fupport will not be wanting.

Captain BIRCH having left the chair,

It was unanimoufly refolved, That the thanks of this corps be prefented to him, for his propriety of conduct in the chair.
By Order,
JOHN FRANCK, Secretary.

*At*

*At a numerous Meeting of the Freeholders and principal Inhabitants of the Parish of* Dondonald, *on Monday the 8th of April,* 1782.

ANDREW CUMMING, Efq; in the Chair.

The following refolutions were unanimoufly agreed to:

RESOLVED, That in the prefent critical fituation of our affairs as a nation, in which we have fo much at ftake, and in which every individual is of fome weight, we confider it as an indifpenfable duty we owe to ourfelves, and to our country, to join with our fellow-citizens in demanding thofe conftitutional privileges, which are our unalienable birth-right as a free-people.

Refolved, That we highly admire, and adopt in their fulleft latitude, the wife, fpirited, and patriotic refolutions of the Ulfter Volunteers reprefented at Dungannon; and we do, in the moft folemn manner, declare, That we will co-operate with all the true friends of Ireland, in every meafure that may feem beft calculated for obtaining a full redrefs of our grievances—the eftablifhment of the independence of our legiflature, and the fecuring the conftitution of our country againft every illegal encroachment.

Refolved, That as the members of the Houfe of Commons are the reprefentatives of the people, and derive their power folely from them, every member of that houfe, who contemptuoufly neglects the inftructions of his conftituents, or acts in oppofition to the declared fenfe of the people, betrays his truft, and abdicates his reprefentation: it being the groffeft abufe of language, to call that man the reprefentative of him whofe known fentiments he directly oppofes.

Refolved, That we will not be acceffary to the greater miferies of our country, or the future guilt of thofe men, who in the prefent parliament oppofed a redrefs of our grievances and the eftablifhment of our rights, by giving them our fupport on any future election; but will ftrenuoufly exert ourfelves to procure a return of fuch men, as we have reafon to believe are men of real integrity and true patriotifm; and who will folemnly engage to attend their duty, and to make the public good the fole rule of their parliamentary conduct.

Refolved,

Refolved, That, as it is effential to the very being of parliament, that elections fhould be abfolutely free, and as we
owe above all things juftice to our country, we pledge ourfelves, as freeholders, to one another, and to our country,
by every tie that can bind men, that we will, on every enfuing
election in this county, give our votes to fuch men only, as we
are convinced will faithfully difcharge the duties of the important truft committed to them ; and that we will difcounte-
nance every fpecies of undue influence and corruption, not
admitting the fmalleft favour from thofe to whom we give our
fupport, that they may have no pretence of right to fell us,
having firft bought us.

Refolved, That Andrew Cumming, Robert Lambert,
Daniel Blow, John Glenhome, James Stewart, John Boyd,
David Mc Nall, John Cumming, John Cumming, jun. and
James Caldwell, be appointed a committee to call the next
meeting of the parifh, and to act in concert with the other
committees of the county, appointed for fimilar purpofes.

Refolved, That the above refolutions be publifhed three
times in the Dublin Evening Poft, and in the Belfaft News-
Letter.

Signed by Order,
ANDREW CUMMING.

---

## LONDONDERRY REGIMENT.

*In Committee, 8th of April,* 1782.

### Colonel FERGUSON, Chairman.

RESOLVED, That the following addrefs be publifhed in
the L. Derry Journal.

*To the* Inhabitants *of the* City *and* Liberties *of* Londonderry.

IN the feafon of national diftrefs and danger, the Volunteers of Ireland, affociated for its relief and protection, the
corps which form this regiment, early entered into this neceffary and honourable fervice ; they, in common with their
fellow-fubjects, have had the fatisfaction of feeing the diftreffes
of their country relieved ; but have, at the fame time, feen
the

the enemies of the empire encrease, and its danger become still more imminent. The principles on which they originally associated must therefore, now, more than ever, engage them to continue their exertions; for, at no time hath the exertions of the Volunteer army been so necessary to the peace and security of Ireland. The Londonderry regiment, sensible of this truth, are determined to persevere in perfecting their discipline, compleating their appointments, and providing every necessary to enable them to serve their country with effect.

In consequence of this determination, we, the regimental committee, have taken measures to provide the regiment with artillery, so absolutely essential to the success of all military operations. This provision must, however, be attended with considerable expence, and, therefore, a subscription has been opened in the regiment; but, as the benefits are general, and the cause common, so ought to be the exertions; and hence we are led to observe, that those who are not personally engaged, are in justice, peculiarly called upon to shew their attachment to the cause by their contributions.

We mean to make a general application, and we doubt not the zeal and public spirit of our fellow-citizens.

Signed by order,

WM. PATTERSON, Secretary.

## CITY of DUBLIN MEETING.

*At Meeting of the Sessions Grand Jury, for the County of the City of Dublin, held at the Tholsel on Monday, April 8, 1782, the following Resolutions were unanimously agreed to:*

RESOLVED, That we hold it to be repugnant to common sense, as well as incompatible with every idea of freedom, that Ireland should be governed by two separate and distinct legislatures.

Resolved, That every attempt of the British parliament to restrain or limit the trade, or to frame laws for the government of this kingdom, is illegal and unconstitutional.

Resolved, That we most cordially, and without any reserve, assent to the resolutions delivered at Dungannon on the 15th of February last, by the very respectable assembly of Delegates

from

from the Ulſter corps of Volunteers; and that we will, upon every enſuing election, ſupport thoſe only who have and will maintain the independence of Ireland; and that we will alſo co-operate with our patriotic countrymen, in all legal and conſtitutional meaſures, to liberate our country from every oppreſſion and illegal reſtraint.

| | |
|---|---|
| 1 Pat. Bride, Foreman | 12 Alan Bellingham |
| 2 William Humfrey | 13 John Decluzeau |
| 3 Alex. Kirkpatrick | 14 William Dickſon |
| 4 Arthur Stanley | 15 George Lunell |
| 5 Henry Gudgeon | 16 Samuel Canier |
| 6 Hugh Trevor | 17 Montfort Green |
| 7 Samuel Read | 18 Samuel Holmes |
| 8 John Carleton | 19 George Sall |
| 9 Henry Lyons | 20 Peter Wilkenſon |
| 10 Francis Armſtrong | 21 James Lecky |
| 11 Arch. Armſtrong | 22 Lundy Foot. |

The Foreman having left the Chair, and the Treaſurer having taken it, the following Reſolution was agreed to:

Reſolved unanimouſly, That the thanks of this Jury be given to our worthy Foreman, Patrick Bride, Eſq; for his ſteady, upright, and impartial conduct in the chair, and that this reſolution be ſigned by the Treaſurer, and publiſhed.

JOHN CARLETON, Treaſurer.

✦✧✦✧✦✧✦; ✦✧✦✧✦✧✦✧✦✧✦✧✦✧✦✧✦✧✦

*At a Meeting of the Freemen, Freeholders, and Citizens of Cork, on the 9th of April, purſuant to Notice given by Robert Hutchinfon, Eſq; one of the Sheriffs of the City, in the public Papers of the 5th and 8th inſt.*

ROBERT HUTCHINSON, Eſq; Sheriff, in the Chair.

Resolved unanimouſly, That a national bank, on the eſtabliſhment and principles propoſed in the heads of a bill for the regulation thereof, appears to be a ſcheme, deviſed to give an additional temporary value to the public debt of this kingdom: That the intended ſtock being of fictitious, not real value, no additional coin will be thrown into circulation, and no advantage can ariſe to the mercantile intereſt. That as the paper currency may be encreaſed in an unlimited manner, on a limited ſecurity, danger to the induſtrious part of the community is to be apprehended, and a ſudden check to the trade and commerce of this country expected: and that

such

such measure must tend to encrease the influence of the crown ; and by encreasing it, endanger the rights of the people.

Resolved (with one dissenting voice) That a test be tendered to every person who shall, in future, offer himself a candidate to represent this city in parliament.

ROBERT HUTCHINSON, Chairman.

*The Chairman being required to attend immediately in Court, and Mr.* Stawell *being placed by him in the Chair, the following resolutions were proposed and agreed to :*

RESOLVED unanimously, That the test to be tendered to each candidate, be in the underwritten form and words, viz.

Will you solemnly promise to vote for a declaration of the independence of the King, Lords and Commons of Ireland, and oppose, to the utmost of your power, as a member of the legislature, the usurped claim of the parliament of Great Britain, to make laws to bind this kingdom.

To which, the candidate (who expects to be returned) will answer, should I be elected, I solemnly promise so to do.

Will you solemnly promise to vote for a repeal, or for such an amendment of the law, called Poyning's, as. may destroy the unconstitutional power exercised by the Privy Council of either kingdom ?

To which, &c. &c.

Will you, to the utmost of your power, as a member of the legislature, oppose any burthen on, or obstruction to the trade of this kingdom, save only by the parliament of Ireland ?

To which, &c. &c.

Will you solemnly promise to vote for limiting the present perpetual mutiny bill two years ?

To which, &c. &c.

Will you solemnly promise to vote for making the tenure of the judges, *Quam diu se bene jefferint ?*

To which, &c. &c.

Will you in all other things, act as a good and honest representative ?

To which, &c. &c.

The candidate shall then say,

The things which I have before promised, I pledge my sacred word of honour to perform.

Resolved unanimously, That the thanks of this meeting be given to Sheriff Hutchinson, for so readily complying with the desire of the gentlemen assembled on the 4th, for his very proper conduct this day in the chair ; and that he be requested to publish the transactions of this day.

S. STAWELL, Chairman.

## COUNTY of WEXFORD.

*At a Meeting of the Gentlemen, Clergy, and Freeholders of the County of* Wexford, *convened by the High Sheriff, at the County* Court-house, *on Tuesday the 9th Day of April,* 1782, *pursuant to public Notice.*

RESOLVED, That the late spirited and successful efforts of the parliament of Great Britain to assert their own rights, and support their own constitution against the undue influence of the crown, is an example well worthy the imitation of the parliament of Ireland.

Resolved, That Great Britain and Ireland ought to enjoy equal liberty and the same constitution, and that we will, in every situation of life, and with all the means in our power, support this position.

Resolved, That we deny the authority of the British parliament, to make laws to bind this kingdom, and that we will not obey any laws that shall be so made.

Resolved, That a mutiny law, not limited in point of duration from session to session, is unconstitutional, alarming, and a grievance that requires redress.

Resolved, That the assumed legislative authority of the Privy Council of Great Britain and Ireland, are unconstitutional, and a grievance, and that there ought to be a proper modification of Poyning's law.

Resolved, That Ireland is entitled to a real and perfect free trade.

Resolved, That the virtues of the people are the great basis upon which alone the government of any country can, or ought to stand, and that the means by which Providence raises a nation to greatness, are the virtues infused into its inhabitants, and that to withhold from those virtues (which the Volunteer associations of Ireland possess in an eminent degree, the tribute of esteem and veneration) is to deny ourselves the means of happiness and honour.

Resolved, That Mr. Izod's address to his countrymen, ought to be written in indelible characters on the heart of every Irishman, that he deserves not our thanks alone, but the grateful acknowledgments of the whole nation, and that we offer ours to him with the highest sense of his virtue, his zeal for the public good, and his disinterested motives.

Resolved, That we will not at the next, or any future election, vote for any person to represent us in parliament, who

shall

ſhall then hold or enjoy any place or penſion, or ſhall not, previous to his election, aſſure us, that during his continuance
in parliament, he will not accept of either, directly or indirectly.

Reſolved, That we will not vote for any perſon poſſeſſed of
a borough, that ſells or diſpoſes of that borough to any perſon,
who does not promiſe not to accept any place or penſion from
government.

Reſolved, That we think it peculiarly neceſſary now to declare, that all Judges ſhould be appointed during good behaviour.

Reſolved, That as Great Britain has thought it neceſſary
to make a general reform, no partial reform will anſwer for
Ireland, and that it is impoſſible this kingdom can exiſt under
the preſent ſyſtem of corruption, and the profligate expenditure of its revenues.

Reſolved, That we highly approve of the late relaxation
of the penal laws againſt our countrymen of the Roman Catholic perſuation, ſatisfied that ſuch a meaſure will inſure harmony and union amongſt us, and be the means of making them
happy.

Reſolved, That the intereſt of Great Britain and Ireland
are inſeparably connected, and we take this opportunity of
declaring for ourſelves, and we have the fulleſt confidence and
conviction of its being the univerſal ſentiment and wiſh of
the people of Ireland, that the preſent meaſures are intended
ſeaſonably to remove and terminate all anxious jealouſies, to
prevent future conteſts, and cement the ſtrongeſt union between us and our ſiſter kingdom, attached to her, as we are,
by every tie of intereſt and affection, and reſolved *to ſhare her
liberty and her fate.*

Reſolved, That we do moſt highly approve of the parliamentary conduct of our repreſentatives, George Ogle, Eſq;
and Sir Veſey Colclough, Bart.

Reſolved, That we have been long and well acquainted
with, and have the moſt perfect confidence in their zeal for the
welfare of their country. We think it altogether unneceſſary
to offer them any inſtructions, further than to add weight to
their exertions.

B b

*At the above Meeting, the following Address of the Gentlemen,
Clergy, and Freeholders, convened at said Meeting, was read
and ordered to be presented to* George Ogle, *Esq; Representative in Parliament for said County.*

### S I R,

THE sentiments we have just now expressed, are such as
require a representative of consummate abilities, and the most
incorruptible integrity, to carry them into execution. ,

Many years experience have fully convinced us, that no
person is more capable to discharge this high and important
trust than you are. We, therefore, intreat you to stand forth
a candidate to represent this county in parliament, at the next
ensuing general election.

We should blush at making this request, if we were not
ever ready to acknowledge, with the most lively gratitude,
that the public good has been invariably the rule of your
conduct, and particularly, that your exertions to establish the
constitutional rights and commercial interests of Ireland, on
the most settled and permanent foundation, have been great
and unremitting.

We also esteem ourselves exceedingly fortunate in your
having a colleague, who has, at all times, uniformly supported
the rights and privileges of his country; and we return him
our thanks for the polite offer of his services, and do assure
him that a steady perseverance in the same line of conduct,
will be the surest and certain foundation of our future suffrages. Be assured, you have our warmest approbation, and
that we are, with respect and regard,

Your most obliged, and
Most faithful servants,
Signed by order,
HENRY BROWNRIGG, Sheriff.

Resolved at said meeting, That our thanks be given to
Henry Brownrigg, Esq; the High Sheriff, for his ready compliance in convening the county, and for his candour, impartiality. and propriety of conduct in the chair.

Resolved, That the above resolutions and address be inserted six times in the Dublin Evening Post, and Wexford
Journal.

*To*

*To the Gentlemen, Clergy, and Freeholders of the County of*
Wexford.

*Gentlemen,*

I HAVE this day had the pleasure to receive your address; the honourable testimony it bears to my past conduct in parliament, and the generous confidence it reposes on my future exertions, cannot fail to impress my mind with such sentiments, as a heart, conscious of its own rectitude, and resolved to persevere, must naturally feel.

Though I have not canvassed your county, though I have not declared myself a candidate, be assured, I will never decline any post of honour or of public trust, to which you shall please to appoint me; and that it is impossible to entertain a stronger sense of obligation and gratitude than I do, at the very distinguishing manner in which you have called upon me to become, at the ensuing general election, the guardian of your rights and liberties.

Dispose of me as you judge I shall be of the most advantage to you; my life is devoted to your service; I have no ambition above the confidence and esteem of my constituents; I have no object in my public view beyond the glory and welfare of my country.

Depend upon it, no effort of mine shall be wanting to carry the measures you advise into the fullest execution; the decided opinion of so great and powerful a county, must give the greatest weight to the exertions of your representatives. I shall be happy on all occasions to learn your sentiments; I shall always receive your instructions with pleasure, and will ever pay them the highest respect, and most scrupulous attention. I have the honour,

Gentlemen, to be,
Your most obedient,
And faithful humble servant,

GEORGE OGLE.

*Merrion-square,*
*April 15, 1782.*

## COUNTY of LONGFORD.

*At a Meeting of the Gentlemem, Clergy, and Freeholders of the County of* Longford, *convened at the Requisition of the High Sheriff, on the 9th of April,* 1782.

The following resolutions and declarations were agreed to:

RESOLVED, That we have hitherto delayed making any declaration of our sentiments, or communicating our instructions to our representatives, in order that we might obtain the general sense of the unbiassed, unprejudiced, and independent constituents of this united kingdom, and are more happy in declaring our concurrence with the universal voice of the nation.

That the King, Lords, and Commons of Ireland, only, are competent to make laws to bind this kingdom; that the commerce of this kingdom was, and of right ought to be free from every restraint, except such as are imposed by the parliament of Ireland. That the power of the Privy Council exercised under the pretence of the law of Poyning's, is an unconstitutional grievance.

That a mutiny bill, not limited, may be dangerous to the liberties of Ireland.

That the independence of Judges is essential to the impartial administration of justice, as well in Ireland as in England.

Resolved, That the thanks of this meeting be presented to the virtuous minority of the House of Commons, who have uniformly supported the great constitutional and commercial rights of this kingdom, and we expect their steady perseverance in the same.

Resolved, That it is our deliberate and unalterable determination, and we pledge ourselves to our country, as freemen and fellow-citizens, that we will use every constitutional means to render our pursuit of redress effectual.

Resolved, That a copy of these resolutions and declarations be transmitted to our representatives, assuring them that their steady support of these measures, will be the effectual means of receiving our future confidence and support.

LEWIS MONTFORT, Sheriff.

The

The Sheriff having left the chair, the following refolutions were unanimoufly agreed to:

Refolved, That the thanks of this meeting be prefented to the High Sheriff, for his readinefs in convening the freeholders upon this occafion.

Refolved, That the thanks of this meeting be prefented to Lau. H. Harman, Efq; for his upright conduct in parliament, and we lament, that the infirm ftate of health of our other reprefentative, Henry Gore, Efq; has hitherto deprived us of his affiftance.

Refolved, That the above refolutions and declarations be publifhed in the Dublin Evening Poft, and Dublin Journal.

WM. SANDYS, Efq; Chairman.

## COUNTY KERRY MEETING.

*We the Gentlemen, Clergy, and Freeholders of the County of* Kerry, *convened at* Tralee, *on Tuefday the 9th Day of April,* 1782, *purfuant to Notice given by the High Sheriff,*

Do unanimoufly declare,

THAT we acknowledge no other power, fave the King, Lords, and Commons of Ireland, as competent to make laws to bind this kingdom; that we conceive the interference of any other body for that purpofe, to be a wanton and unwarrantable encroachment, and an infringment of our rights; and that we do expect fuch declaration from our reprefentatives in parliament.

Refolved unanimoufly, That the members of the Houfe of Commons are the reprefentatives of, and derive their power folely from, the people.

That every member is fent into parliament for the purpofe of making known the fenfe of his conftituents.

That therefore any member who does not, on all occafions, pay implicit obedience to the inftructions of his conftituents, is a betrayer of the truft repofed in him.

That a perpetual mutiny bill is unconftitutional, and highly dangerous.

That Ireland is equally entitled with England to trade to foreign countries; and that an exclufive right, affumed by the latter in any inftance, is an unjuft monopoly.

That

That the independence of the Judges is equally effential to the impartial administration of justice in Ireland as in England, and that a refusal or delay of this right to us is a partial and unjust distinction.

That the proceedings of the people of Ireland at this time, are dictated by no other spirit than that of a sincere wish to render indissoluble the bonds by which the sister countries are united, by removing every object of jealousy which subsists between them, thus to insure their mutual affections, their interests being one.

That we return our warmest acknowledgments to the minority of the House of Commons, for their spirited efforts to vindicate the constitution of this kingdom, and trust that in the end, a steady perseverance in such conduct will produce the desired effect ; and we pledge ourselves, that we shall ever be ready to devote our lives and fortunes to the establishment of our rights.

DENIS MAHONY, Sheriff.

The Sheriff having left the chair, it was unanimously resolved, That the thanks of this meeting be given to the High Sheriff, for his readiness in convening the county, and for his proper conduct in the chair.

---

*At a Meeting of the* Moycashel Affociation *at* Mullingar, *on the 9th of April,* 1782.

Captain JOHN LYONS in the Chair.

RESOLVED, That the King, Lords and Commons of Ireland, are the only power competent to make laws to bind this kingdom.

That the members of the House of Commons are the representatives of, as they derive their power only from the people.

That we highly approve of the spirited toleration, lately manifested in our legislature, by a relaxation of certain penal laws, which cannot fail to render the Roman Catholics of this kingdom happy.

That we will co-operate with our countrymen Volunteers, in support of our constitutional rights, by every means consistent with the strict observance of the laws of this kingdom.

Resolved,

Resolved, That the thanks of this association be given to captain Lyons, for his great attention to the corps.

Signed by Order,

JOSEPH BEARD, Adj. and Sec.

Ordered, That the above resolutions be printed in the Westmeath Journal, and Dublin Evening Post.

<hr />

## COUNTY of DOWN.

*At a Meeting of the Inhabitants of the Parish of* Seapatrick, *in the County of* Down, *at the* Market-house *of* Banbridge, *the* 10th *Day of April,* 1782, *pursuant to Notice given.*

The Rev. HENRY JACKSON in the Chair.

The resolutions and address of the Delegates at Dungannon, the 15th day of February last, and the address from the committee by them appointed, dated the 6th of April inst. to the electors and members of parliament of the province of Ulster, being read,

RESOLVED unanimously, That the said resolutions and addresses do meet with our warmest approbation, and that we will, with our lives and fortunes, co-operate with our fellow-citizens, in rendering those resolutions and addresses effectual.

Resolved, That these resolutions be signed by our Chairman, and published in the Dublin Evening Post, and in the Belfast and Newry papers.        By order,

HENRY JACKSON, Chairman.

<hr />

*At a Meeting of the* Ida Light Dragoons, *on the* 10th *Day of April,* 1782.

Major FITZGERALD in the Chair.

The following resolutions were unanimously agreed to:

RESOLVED, That it is our indispensible duty, as Irishmen and Volunteers, to declare our approbation of the resolutions agreed to by the Delegates assembled at Dungannon.

Resolved,

Refolved, That we will co-operate with our brother Volunteers, in maintaining the conftitutional rights of Ireland, and in procuring redrefs of our national grievances.

Refolved, That a parliamentary declaration of the rights of Ireland is now abfolutely neceffary, as a foundation and fecurity for obtaining a bill of rights.

Refolved, That it is the duty of the reprefentatives of the people, in great conftitutional and national queftions, implicitly to obey the inftructions of their conftituents, and to attend to the voice of the nation.

## COUNTY of WESTMEATH.

## FORE INFANTRY LOYALISTS.

*At a Meeting of the Barony of* Fore Infantry Loyalifts, *held at* Caftle-Pollard, *on Wednefday the* 10th *of April,* 1782.

### Major WILLIAM POLLARD in the Chair.

The following Refolutions were unanimoufly agreed to, viz.

RESOLVED, That the King, Lords, and Commons of Ireland are the only power competent to make laws to bind Ireland.

Refolved, That the fubjects of Ireland, having the fame King, and a conftitution exactly fimilar, are entitled to the fame rights and privileges with the Britifh fubjects.

Refolved, That we will moft firmly and chearfully co-operate with our fellow-citizens and Volunteers in every conftitutional and loyal meafure to obtain, not only thofe rights and privileges, and confequently a redrefs of grievances, but alfo to give them a permanent fupport and eftablifhment.

Major William Pollard having quit the Chair,

Refolved, That the thanks of this meeting be prefented to Major William Pollard, for his fpirited and upright conduct in the chair this day.

Refolved, That the thanks of this corps be given to Capt. Nugent, for his unwearied attention to the difcipline and good order of this corps.

Refolved, That the above refolutions be publifhed in the Dublin Evening Poft, and Weftmeath Journal.

JOHN ORFORD, Secretary.

# RATHDOWN CARABINEERS.

*At a Meeting of the* Rathdown Carabineers, *at* Powerscourt, *in the County of* Wicklow, *April* 10, 1782.

Major EDWARDS in the Chair.

The following resolutions were unanimously agreed to :

RESOLVED, That we do highly approve of the resolutions lately entered into at Dungannon.

Resolved, and we do pledge ourselves to be ready to co-operate with the other Volunteer corps, in every constitutional measure for the support of the rights and liberties of this kingdom.

Signed by order,

THO. DOWSE, Sec.

## CALLAN UNION.

*At a Meeting of the* Callan Union, *held at* Callan, *on W-day, the* 10th *of April,* 1782.

Captain POE in the Chair.

RESOLVED unanimously, That the Dungannon Volunteer resolutions, entered into on the 15th of February last, entirely meet our approbation, and fully comprehend our sentiments, and that we will, at all times, most chearfully co-operate with our fellow-citizens and Volunteers, in obtaining a redress of all national grievances, and an establishment of the rights of Ireland.

Resolved unanimously, That the thanks of this meeting be given to our worthy Colonel, George Agar, Esq; for his patriotic conduct in parliament.

Resolved, That the above resolutions be printed in the Dublin Evening Post, and the Freeman's Journal.

T. TAYLOR, Secretary.

C c

DUN-

## DUNGARVAN VOLUNTEERS.

*At a Meeting of the* Dungarvan Volunteers, *No.* 1, *No.* 2, *at the* Town-house *in* Dungarvan, *the* 10th *of* April, 1782.

### Captain BOATE in the Chair.

RESOLVED unanimously, That the King, Lords, and Commons of Ireland are the only power competent to make laws to bind this kingdom.

Resolved, That we will support the representatives of the people with our lives and fortunes, in whatever measures may be necessary to render the above declaration effectual.

Resolved, That we will co-operate with our brother Volunteers in every constitutional measure, for the emancipation of our country from all foreign legislation.

Resolved, That it is our earnest wish that all jealousies that may subsist between us and our sister kingdom might be removed, as we should be ready and willing to share with her in every fate, and happy, at every opportunity, of proving our loyalty and attachment to our Sovereign.

Resolved, That the thanks of this meeting be given to our worthy Chairman, for his attention to the corps, and upright conduct in the chair.

Resolved, That these resolutions be published in the Dublin Evening Post, and Waterford papers.

Signed by order of the corps,
JOHN WILKINSON, Sec.

### COUNTY of WESTMEATH.

*At a full Meeting of the* Farbill Light Dragoons, *held at* Killucan, *the* 10th *Day of April,* 1782.

### Captain ROBERT COOK in the Chair.

The following Resolutions were agreed on:

RESOLVED, That as our original institution was for the internal peace of this county, as well as for the defence of this kingdom in general, from foreign enemies, that we will maintain the same with our lives and fortunes.

Resolved,

Refolved, That it is the inherent right of his Majefty's free-born fubjects of Ireland, to give their opinion on fuch laws, as may be thought neceffary for the intereft and welfare of this kingdom.

Refolved, That no power on earth is competent to make laws to bind Ireland, except the King, Lords, and Commons thereof.

Refolved, That we do recommend it moft ftrenuoufly to our brethren Volunteers, to perfevere in the fpirit of moderation and firmnefs, which have already done them fo much honour.

Refolved, That we will not fupport any candidates to reprefent us in parliament, that will not give the moft apparent proofs of the brilliantcy of their integrity, relative to the falvation of the conftitution of their country; and that any landlord who ufes his influence contrary to the freedom of fentiment of his tenantry, upon any election, fhall be confidered as an enemy to his country.

ROB. COOK, Chairman.

Refolved unanimoufly, That the fincere thanks of this corps be given to our worthy captain, for convening us at this time, and for his attention to the Volunteer caufe in general, and to this corps in particular.

Refolved, That our thanks be given to Edward Purdon, fen. Efq; for his fteady adherence to the intereft of this corps fince its formation.

Refolved unanimoufly, That thefe our refolutions be printed in the Dublin Evening Poft, and Dublin Journal.

Signed by Order,

JOHN PURDON, Sec.

✦✦●✦✦●✦✦●✦✦●✦●✦✦●✦✦●✦✦●✦✦●✦✦

## RATHDOWN LIGHT DRAGOONS.

### COUNTY OF DUBLIN.

*At a Meeting of this Corps, on Wednefday the 10th of April, 1782.*

Col. Sir JOHN ALLEN JOHNSON, Bart. in the Chair.

The following refolutions were unanimoufly agreed to.

RESOLVED, That we do highly approve of, and accede to, the refolutions entered into by the Delegates of the Ulfter

corps

corps affembled at Dungannon, and feveral other county corps, and that we will co-operate with them in every conftitutional meafure, to preferve our rights and liberties, and obtain a redrefs of grievances.

Refolved, That the King, Lords, and Commons of Ireland are alone competent to make laws to bind this kingdom.

Refolved, That we will not, on any election for a reprefentative to ferve in parliament in this kingdom, vote for any candidate who has not uniformly fupported the rights and liberties of his conftituents.

Refolved, That we feel the fincereft fatisfaction at the relaxation of the penal laws againft our fellow-fubjects and brethren, the Roman Catholics of this kingdom, and confider it as fraught with wifdom and humanity.

Refolved, That a Delegate from this corps do attend the provincial meeting, at the Royal Exchange, on Wednefday the 17th of April, inft.

Refolved, That the above refolutions be publifhed in the Hibernian Journal, Saunders's News-Letter, and the Dublin Evening Poft.

J. A. JOHNSON, Chairman.

Refolved, That the thanks of this meeting be given to our chairman, for his particular attention to this corps, and upright conduct this day in the chair.

JOHN FARRAN, Secretary.

## CITY of LIMERICK.

Limerick, April 11, 1782.

AT a time when religious prejudices feem intirely laid afide, and a fpirit of liberty and toleration breathes unanimoufly through all fects, we fee with concern fo loyal and refpectable a part of our brethren, as the Roman Catholics, ftand idle fpectators of the glorious exertions of their countrymen in the Volunteer caufe: Actuated by thefe principles, the Limerick Independents think themfelves called upon to ftep forward, and invite their fellow-citizens of the Roman Catholic perfuafion to unite in the common caufe, and enrol themfelves under their ftandard. By order,

JOHN HARRISON, Secretary.

Such

Such gentlemen as wish to join the corps, are requested to send in their names to any of the officers or committee, that they may be ballotted for.

The Roman Catholics of the city of Limerick, impressed with a just sense of the honour conferred upon them by the Limerick Independents, are happy in this public testimony of their acknowledgements to the corps, for the very liberal invitation of associating themselves with so respectable a body of their fellow-subjects. Whilst they feel a most grateful sense of the late removal of many of their restraints, and look forward with pleasure to the approaching period of emancipation, it is their most earnest wish to maintain those principles of virtue and loyalty, which are the glory of a free people, and have so eminently distinguished the character of Irish Volunteers. *Limerick, April* 10, 1782.

MARTIN HARROLD, Esq; in the Chair.

## COUNTY of DUBLIN.

*At a Meeting of the High Sheriff and Grand Jury of the County of* Dublin, *assembled in the Court-house, at* Kilmainham, *on Thursday the* 11th *of April,* 1782.

The following Resolutions were agreed to:

THOMAS BAKER, Esq; Foreman, in the Chair.

RESOLVED, That no power on earth, but the King, Lords and Commons of Ireland, can in right, make laws to bind the people of this land.

Resolved, That the members of the House of Commons are the representatives of, and derive their power solely from, the people; and that a denial of this proposition by them would be to abdicate the representation.

The following Address was then read by the Chairman, and agreed to:

*To the Right Hon.* Luke Gardiner, *and Sir* Edward Newenham, *Knight.*

Gentlemen,

WE, the High Sheriff and Grand Jury of the county of Dublin, warmly coinciding with that determination respecting the

the conftitutional rights of Ireland, with which the mind of every man in this nation is deeply impreffed, think it our duty to exprefs thofe feelings in the ftrongeft terms.

As you have already evinced your intention to. fupport the fole and undoubted authority of the legiflature of Ireland to make laws for its government, we confidently hope and expect, that you will perfevere in purfuing the moft decifive and im- mediate meafures that may effectually carry that great object into execution, by a folemn ratification of our rights.

Though this is, at the prefent crifis, the principle matters under the confideration of parliament, we have no doubt but that you muft confider it your duty to act, in all things that affect the freedom of our conftitution, in fuch manner as may become the reprefentatives of a great and independent country.

Refolved, That copies of the above refolutions and addrefs, figned by the high Sheriff and Foreman, be prefented to the right hon. Luke Gardiner, and Sir Edward Newenham, Knight, and that the fame, together with their anfwers, be publifhed.

Refolved, That the thanks of this Grand Jury be pre- fented to our worthy high Sheriff, William Fortick, Efq; for his chearfully concurring with us in the above refolutions.

THOMAS BAKER, Foreman.

The Sheriff having taken the chair, it was refolved, That the thanks of this meeting be prefented to Thomas Baker, Efq; our Foreman, for his great propriety, and impartial conduct in the chair.

WM. FORTICK, Sheriff.

-◄►-◄►-◄►-◄►-◄►-◄-◄-◄-◄-◄◄-◄◄-◄◄-◄◄-►-

*To the High Sheriff and Grand Jury of the County of* Dublin.

*Gentlemen,*

IT gives me very fincere fatisfaction, that my conduct, re- lative to the fole and undoubted authority of the legiflature of Ireland, has merited your approbation. You may be affured, that I fhall perfevere in giving my warmeft fupport to that great and important object; as I confider it fo decifively founded in right, that no man, who loves to be free, can hefi- tate to aknowledge and to affert it.

With refpect to any other matter that may affect the freedom of our conftitution, I am fo confcious of my intentions to promote the perfect contentment of this country, that I have.

no

no doubt I shall, in every particular, deserve that confidence with which you have hitherto honoured me.

I am very glad that you have given me an opportunity of declaring my sentiments thus publicly at this crisis; as I think that the time is now come which demands an explicit and a permanent settlement of the constitution of Ireland, as the certain means of establishing the tranquility of this country, and of perpetuating the harmony which ought to subsist between us and Great Britain.

I have the honour to be, gentlemen,
With the greatest respect,

*Henrietta-street,*      Your very obliged humble servant,
*April* 13, 1782.         LUKE GARDINER.

*To the High Sheriff, Foreman, and Grand Jury of the County of*
Dublin.

*Gentlemen,*

I ALWAYS receive your instructions with respect and pleasure, for it is equally my duty and inclination to obey them; if I did not, I should betray that delegated trust with which you have honoured me.

In respect to those great objects in which you desire " I will " persevere," I assure you, I will most faithfully pursue that line of conduct marked out by you; confident that his Majesty cannot, in justice to this independent kingdom, refuse his royal assent to such acts, as may be deemed by the Irish parliament " a solemn ratification of our rights." I flatter myself that no Irish Minister should be found so presumptuous, as to impede the total annihilation of foreign usurpation; if such a Minister should be found, the parliament of Ireland, supported by the general voice of the people, *ought to do* their duty. Though effectual impeachments have been too long neglected, and thereby our sister kingdom has nearly fallen a martyr to the corruption and wickedness of its ministry, the spirit of this nation is too high, to submit patiently to national insults.

You are also pleased to direct me " to act in all things that affect the freedom of our constitution, as may become the representative of a great and independent county;" in order to accomplish that object, I have frequently introduced heads of a bill to secure the freedom of parliament, by limiting the number of placemen, and totally excluding pensioners from sitting therein; a hostile band of parliamentary placemen and
pensioners

penfioners is the foundation of internal and external corruption.

Every meafure tending to maintain the freedom, or promote the trade and manufactures of your great, refpectable, and independent county, fhall meet my warmeft fupport in every ftation of life.

I have the honour to be,<br>
With the greateft refpect,

*Dumcondra,*      Your moft obliged,<br>
*April* 13, 1782.      And faithful truftee,<br>
EDWARD NEWENHAM.

## MULLINGAR VOLUNTEERS.

*At a Meeting of the* Mullingar *Corps,* on Friday, *April* 12, 1782.

### WILLIAM JUDGE, Efq; Colonel, in the Chair.

The following Refolutions were unanimoufly agreed to :

THAT the King, Lords, and Commons of Ireland are the only power competent to make laws to bind this kingdom, and that we will not affift in the executing of any, but thofe enacted by the legiflature aforefaid.

That we highly approve of the wife, fpirited, and liberal refolutions of the gentlemen of the county Galway, on the 31ft of March laft, and that we will co-operate with them, and our Volunteer brethren, in every conftitutional meafure for obtaining the moft perfect unequivocal eftablifhment of the juft rights of Ireland.

That we highly approve of, and rejoice in the relaxation of the penal Popery Laws of this kingdom.

Refolved, That the above refolutions be inferted three times in the Dublin Evening Poft, and Weftmeath Journal.

WM. JUDGE, Chairman.

Colonel Judge having left the chair, the Rev. Robert Rofs was voted in,

When it was unanimoufly refolved, That the thanks of this corps be given to our worthy Colonel, William Judge, Efq; for his great attention to the corps, and for his prefent of an elegant ftand of colours.

*At*

*At an Assembly held at the* Tholsel *of the City of* Dublin, *on Friday the 12th Day of April,* 1782.

The following Resolutions were agreed to:

RESOLVED unanimously, That the members of the House of Commons, are the representatives of, and derive their power solely from, the people, and that a denial of this proposition by them, would be to abdicate the representation.

Resolved unanimously, That we conceive that the people of this country, are now called upon to declare, that the King, Lords, and Commons of Ireland, are the only power competent to make laws to bind this kingdom.

Resolved unanimously, That we do hope and expect such declaration of rights, from our representatives in parliament, and that we will support them, with our lives and fortunes, in whatever measure may be necessary to render such declaration an effectual security.

Resolved unanimously, That the present critical and declining state of the manufactures of Ireland, requires the particular attention of the legislature.

Resolved unanimously, That a copy of the above resolutions be presented to our worthy representatives in parliament, Sir Samuel Bradstreet, Bart. and Travers Hartley, Esq.

Resolved, That the above resolutions be published in the Freeman's and Dublin Journals.

Signed by order,
TAYLOR and LAMBERT, Town Clerks.

---

## RAKENNY VOLUNTEERS.

*At a Meeting of the* Rakenny Independent Volunteers, *on the 12th of April,* 1782.

Colonel THEOPHILUS CLEMENTS in the Chair.

The following resolutions were unanimously agreed to:

RESOLVED, That we admire and highly approve of the resolutions and address of that virtuous and truly patriotic meeting of Delegates, assembled at Dungannon, on the

D d

15th

15th of February laſt, and that we, as freemen, citizens and Volunteers, pledge ourſelves to co-operate with them, and our brother volunteers, in every conſtitutional mode of obtaining a redreſs of the grievances by them mentioned.

Reſolved, That our warmeſt acknowledgments are due to that generous aſſembly, whoſe liberality allowed us, as one of the county of Cavan corps, a participation of the honour of the meeting, and permitted us to join that aſſociation, though not repreſented.

Reſolved, That we think it neceſſary to declare, that we greatly regret we had not the honour of being repreſented at Dungannon, on the 15th of February laſt, as we had reſolved upon it, and appointed our Delegates on the 9th, but that this our good intention was defeated, by a ſubſequent meeting of the county Delegates.

Reſolved, That the members of the Houſe of Commons are the repreſentatives of, and derive their power ſolely from, the people, and as ſuch are in duty bound, upon every momentuous queſtion, to aſk for, and obey the inſtructions of their conſtituents.

Reſolved, That the repreſentative only who obeys the inſtructions of his conſtituents, and not the mandate of the miniſter, is worthy of eſteem and ſupport.

Reſolved, That as the ſacred duty which we owe to the community, ſupercedes all ties and obligations to individuals, we will not ſuffer private friendſhip or private virtues to warp our ſettled determination, not to vote for any man at a future election, who ſhall act in oppoſition to the inſtructions of his conſtituents, and who will not ſubſcribe a teſt previous to the election, or who ſhall abſent himſelf when thoſe queſtions, on which he is inſtructed, are agitated in parliament.

Reſolved, That freedom in election is the baſis of our liberties, and the bulwark of our conſtitution.

Reſolved therefore, That any perſon who attempts to deprive the elector of this glorious privilege, by any corrupt means or undue influence, ſuch as bribery and corruption, or public entertainments, (the worſt ſpecies thereof) or who ſhall make uſe of threats or promiſes to warp any elector from his duty, does what in him lies, to ſubvert the conſtitution, and is conſequently an enemy to his country.

Reſolved, That our chairman do communicate theſe our reſolutions to captain James Dawſon, Secretary to the committee of the Ulſter Volunteers, and inform him, that we

cordially

cordially accept of the invitation to become members of that affociation.

Refolved, That the addrefs publifhed in the Evening Poft, &c. figned James Fleming, importing to be the addrefs of the county of Cavan electors, is furreptitious; as freeholders we difavow it.

Refolved, That the county was not convened by the Sheriff, and that the freeholders at large knew nothing of fuch a meeting or addrefs being intended.

THEO. CLEMENTS, Chairman.

John Forfter, Efq; in the Chair.

Refolved, That the thanks of this corps be returned to our worthy Colonel, for his upright and proper conduct upon this and every other occafion, in the chair.

Refolved, That thefe our refolutions be publifhed three times in the Dublin Evening Poft.

Signed by Order.

JAMES DEANE, Sec.

- - - - - - - - - - - - - - - - - - - - - - -

*At a Meeting of the united Parifhes of* Killinchy, Killmud, *and* Tollynakill, *at the* Diffenting Meeting-houfe *of* Killinchy, *in the Barony of* Duffrin, *convened by public Notice, the* 13th *of April,* 1782.

The following refolutions were unanimoufly agreed to:

HAMILTON MOORE, Efq; in the Chair.

(Prefent and fubfcribed by 335.)

THAT the Dungannon refolutions are founded in wifdom and juftice, and breathe the true fpirit of toleration and independence; we, therefore, pledge ourfelves to join with them, in every meafure that may tend to eftablifh our rights, and promote the happinefs of the people.

That we will not fupport any man, on the enfuing election, but fuch as are of approved integrity, and friends to the conftitution of Ireland.

That we confider any member of parliament who may oppofe the voice of the nation, a betrayer of the truft repofed

in

In him, and of courfe unworthy the fupport of independent electors.

We cannot but lament, that indifpenfable bufinefs, for fome time paft, has prevented our members from paying that ftrict attention to their parliamentary duty, our fanguine expectations might have hoped for; yet, we now are happy with the pleafing profpect of their return, and of their immediate refidence among us; being perfectly convinced, their utmoft endeavours have been ufed to eftablifh the real welfare of Ireland.

Refolved, That any man or body of men, actuated by any party-fpirit (except that of promoting unanimity and the happinefs of the people) are enemies to religious and civil fociety.

Refolved, That the underneath perfons are appointed a committee for thefe parifhes (five to be a quorum) to call us together, and to act as occafion may require.

Refolved, That the thanks of thefe parifhes be given to our chairman, for his particular attention to us at this period.

| For the parifhes at large, | Hamilton Moore. |
|---|---|
| Ballymacreely, | Samuel Cuffy, |
| | Samuel Hay, |
| | James Anderfon. |
| Ballow, | Geore Logan, jun. |
| Ballymacafhan, | David Lowry, |
| | Samuel Lowry. |
| Drumreagh, | Thomas Hazlet, |
| | James Hazlet. |
| Rafrey, | William Cars, |
| Carrickrufkey, | John Cars. |
| | William Mattear. |
| Ballyminiftragh, | James Bailie. |
| Tullynagee, | James Neill, |
| | Alexander Johnfton. |
| Lifban, | Andrew Lowry. |
| Ballygleghom, | William Douglafs. |
| Caftle-efpie, | James Dickfon. |
| Ringireel, | Ham. Jelly. |
| Killinchy, | William Smyth. |
| Ballydrain, | John Berry. |
| Ballymartin, | William Carlifle. |
| Ardmillen, | Robert Hamilton. |
| Carrigullen, | John Hewit. |
| Ballybreagh, | James Smyth. |

Bally

| | |
|---|---|
| Ballygeegan, | Francis Morrow. |
| Lesbarnet, | Samuel Johnston. |
| Curraghadoes, | Anthony Smyth. |
| Tullynakell, | Andrew Lowry. |

By order,
**HAMILTON MOORE**, Chairman.

✦•◆✦•◆✦•◆✦•◆✦•◆✦•◆✦•◆✦•◆✦•◆✦•◆✦•◆ ✦ ◆

## DONERAILE RANGERS.

*At a Meeting of the* Doneraile Rangers, *at* Doneraile, *on Sunday the 14th of April,* 1782.

Captain NICHOLAS GRREEN EVANS in the Chair.

RESOLVED, That the resolutions entered into by the Ulster Delegates, assembled at Dungannon, on the 15th day of February last, are spirited and rational, and that the gentlemen who formed them deserve our praise, our thanks, and our imitation.

Resolved, That we will, at the hazard of our lives and fortunes, endeavour, by every constitutional means, to obtain a declaration of the rights, and a redress of the grievances set forth in said resolutions.

Resolved, That copies of these our resolutions be transmitted to our Colonel, the Right Honourable Lord Doneraile, in Dublin, and to captain Dawson, Secretary to the Ulster Delegates, and that they be published in the Cork and Dublin Evening Posts.

Resolved, (on his leaving the chair) That our thanks be given to captain Evans, for his readiness and zeal in convening us on this occasion.

Signed by Order,

JAMES HENNESSY, Sec.

COUNTY

## COUNTY of DUBLIN LIGHT DRAGOONS.

*At a Meeting of the County* Dublin Light Dragoons, *on Parade,*
*April the 14th,* 1782.

The Right Hon. LUKE GARDINER, Colonel, in the
Chair.

RESOLVED unanimoufly, That the King, Lords, and
Commons of Ireland, are the only power competent to make
laws to bind this kingdom.

Refolved unanimoufly, That until the indifputable rights
of the different branches of the legiflature of this kingdom
fhall be fully recognized, harmony between Great Britain and
Ireland can never be compleatly eftablifhed.

Refolved unanimoufly, That any man or body of men in
either kingdom, who, at this crifis, can hefitate at a recognition of our rights, muft be confidered as holding fentiments
tending to feparate Great Britain and Ireland, and inimical
to the tranquility of both countries.

Refolved unanimoufly, That we highly approve of the
fpirit and unanimity which have been fo decifively manifefted
by all ranks of men in this country, as well armed as unarmed,
in the affertion of our natural rights, and we pledge ourfelves
to purfue every meafure which fhall moft effectually, and moft
fpeedily tend to the perfect freedom and eftablifhment of the
conftitution of Ireland.

Signed, LUKE GARDINER, Colonel.

Refolved unanimoufly, That the thanks of this corps be
given to Colonel Gardiner, for his indefatigable attention to
the corps, and his zealous conduct this day in the chair.

WILLIAM BROOME, Major.

## COUNTY of LONGFORD.
## EDGWORTHSTOWN BATTALION.

*At a Meeting of the* Edgworthftown Battalion, *April* 14, 1782.

Captain SLATOR in the Chair.

RESOLVED unanimoufly, That Ireland is an independent
kingdom, and that we conceive ourfelves called on, at this
interefting

interesting crisis, by the duty we owe ourselves, and our country, publicly to declare, That the King, Lords, and Commons of Ireland, are the only power competent to make laws to bind Ireland; and that we cannot admit the interference of any foreign legislature whatever, without a manifest violation of our unalienable rights.

Resolved unanimously, That as men of honour, and Volunteers, we will ardently co-operate with the patriot sons of Ireland, in every constitutional mode of emancipating our country from impolitic restraints, and establishing on a firm and permanent basis, unequivocal freedom.

Resolved unanimously, That a declaration of rights from our legislature is expedient and necessary, as tending in its operation to prevent future innovations on the part of England, and future jealousies on the part of Ireland, and consequently to unite the sister nations in the indissoluble bands of reciprocal interest and affection.

Resolved unanimously, That the powers claimed by the Privy Council of England and Ireland, under, or under colour and pretence of a law passed in 10 Henry 7, commonly called Poyning's Law, are inimical to the constitutional rights Ireland, and require immediate and effectual redress.

Resolved unanimously, That a mutiny bill, not limited in point of duration from session to session, is, or may be a dangerous instrument in the hand of the executive power, and of militates against the constitutional security of the laws.

Resolved unanimously, That as the fountain of justice is liable to taint and pollution from the dependence of Judges, which may gradually corrupt and overspread the body politic, the appointment of Judges should be during good behaviour, which would infuse a new portion of vigour into the constitution, and enable it to bear those infirmities, if such there are, which elude a remedy.

Resolved unanimously, That the virtuous *few* in both houses of parliament, who have uniformly supported the great constitutional and commercial rights of Ireland, deserve our warmest and most heartfelt thanks, which we request they may receive, as a testimony of our love and admiration. for those worthies, who spurn the corruption and venality of the times, and dare to tread the neglected path of public virtue.

Resolved unanimously, That in the genuine spirit of liberty, sound policy, and toleration, we contemplate with peculiar satisfaction, the relaxation of the penal laws against our Ro-

man

man Catholic fellow-subjects, for which we conceive the
causes have long since ceased to operate, and joyfully hail
the dawn of national prosperity when Ireland, aided and in-
vigorated by the united virtues of commercial, political, and
religious freedom, shall raise her head among the nations,
and reign the queen of arts and arms.

Resolved unanimously, That as freeholders and electors,
we have a right to an unbiassed choice of representatives, and
that the exigencies of the times call loudly for the honest
exertion of this right; we therefore pledge ourselves to each
other, and to our country, that private friendship and connection shall not influence our choice of representatives, at
the ensuing election; and that no candidate shall have our
countenance and support, who does not solemnly engage to
defend the rights of his country with unwearied effort, and
faithfully adhere to the instructions of his constituents, from
whose delegated power, his senatorial power and consequence
are solely derived.

Resolved unanimously, That we are attached by every tie
of interest and affection to England, our sister kingdom; are
loyal to our gracious Sovereign, and devoted to the service of
our country; and that we will defend the King of Ireland,
his crown and dignity, from every attempt of his natural
enemies, with unshaken resolution, and with an animated
glow of sentiment and spirit, which those only know and
feel, who have souls capable of venerating freedom, and are
determined to be free.

Resolved unanimously, That a copy of these resolutions
be transmitted by the Chairman to our Colonel, Sir William
Gleadowe Newcomen, Bart. accompanied by our most grateful and cordial thanks, for his steady and persevering attention to this corps.

W. H. SLATOR, Chairman.

Resolved unanimously, That the thanks of this corps be
presented to Captain Slator, for his propriety of conduct in
the chair, and for his general activity and vigilance, as an
officer in the Edgworthstown Battalion.

Resolved unanimously, That these resolutions be published
in the Dublin Evening Post, and Westmeath Journal.

Signed by order,
ALEX. BOND, Secretary, &c.

COUNTY

# COUNTY of CORK MEETING.

*At a Meeting of the Gentlemen, Clergy, and Freeholders of the County of Cork, convened pursuant to Advertisement, at the County Court-house, on Monday the 15th Day of April, 1782.*

ABRAHAM MORRIS, Esq; High Sheriff, in the Chair.

RESOLVED unanimously, That national and independent legislation, being the fundamental right of the subject, without the establishment of which we can never hope for security to our persons or our properties, is an object of great national importance ; and that we will assert, promote, maintain, and defend, this and all other our natural and inherent rights, by every constitutional means ; solemnly declaring, That no power or state whatsoever, hath any right to make laws to bind this kingdom, save only the King, Lords, and Commons of Ireland.

Resolved unanimously, That the independence of the Judges, by holding their appointments *quam diu se bene gesserent,* would be an additional security to this kingdom, for the impartial administration of justice.

Resolved unanimously, That any restriction on the commerce of this kingdom, imposed by proclamation, particularly during the sitting of parliament, is injurious to the spirit of our constitution, hath been pernicious, and may be fatal to our trade.

Resolved unanimously, That we recommend such a modification or explanation of the law called Poyning's law, as will entirely destroy that power assumed by the Privy Council, of altering or suppressing the bills of the Irish parliament.

Resolved unanimously, That a mutiny bill, not limitted in point of duration, is repugnant to every idea of liberty, unconstitutional, and a grievance.

Resolved unanimously, That as we hold the interests and connections of Great Britain and Ireland to be inseparable, so we also declare their legislatures to be distinct and independent of each other ; and that the security and firmness of the former, can only be maintained by the establishment of the latter.

Resolved, That the immense sums of which this country is annually drained, by remittances to the absentees of this kingdom,

E e

dom, conftitute a grievance worthy the confideration of the legiflature.

Refolved unanimoufly, That the commons of Ireland are the keepers of the purfe of the nation, and as fuch ought to deal out the public money with frugality and œconomy; and that a prodigal expenditure of the public money, in unmerited penfions and unneceffary places, is unconftitutional and a grievance.

Refolved unanimoufly, That the debt of this nation amounts to an enormous fum; the revenue not being adequate to the public expences, œconomy and retrenchment are effentially neceffary to prevent new burdens being impofed on the fubject.

Refolved unanimoufly, That the encreafing the falaries annexed to old and ufelefs places, and the creation of new ones with large falaries, tend to augment the undue influence of the crown, by encreafing the power of corruption in the hands of government.

Refolved unanimoufly, That we will not vote for any perfon as our reprefentative in parliament, who will not zealoufly fupport thefe our refolutions, and perfevere in feeking a conftitutional redrefs of thefe our grievances.

Refolved unanimoufly, That we rejoice in the fpirit and religious toleration which now prevails through all ranks of people, and contemplate with fatisfaction the national advantages likely to arife from the liberal indulgences which that fpirit has extended to our Roman Catholic brethren.

Refolved unanimoufly, That we are fully determined to give every encouragement and every proper preference to the manufactures of our country, but that fuch encouragement and fuch preference fhall be proportionable to the induftry, the integrity and good conduct of our manufacturers.

Refolved, That the thanks of this meeting be given to James Bernard, Efq; for his fteady and conftant, though unfuccefsful, exertions in feeking redrefs for thofe our grievances.

Refolved, That the thanks of this meeting be given to the right hon. Lord Kinfborough, James Kearney, and Francis Bernard, Efqrs. for their fteady and conftant, though unfuccefsful, exertions in feeking redrefs for thofe our grievances.

Refolved, That the above refolutions be tranfmitted by the High Sheriff of this county, as inftructions to our reprefentatives for their conduct in parliament.

ABRAHAM MORRIS, High Sheriff.

The

The High Sheriff having left the Chair.

Rofolved, That the thanks of this county meeting be given to Abraham Morris, Efq; our high Sheriff, for his readinefs in convening the county, and for his very impartial and proper conduct in the chair.

-( *)- *)- *)- *)- *- (- (- (- (- (-( )- -

*To the* Gentlemen, Clergy, *and* Freeholders *of the County of* Cork, *convened purfuant to Advertifement by the High* Sheriff, *at the County* Conrt-houfe, *on Monday the* 15th *of April,* 1782.

THERE is no event of my life has given me more fatisfaction, nor can any honour be fo flattering to me, as that I have now received; your public approbation of my parliamentary conduct (more particularly fo, as the period is now approaching when you will have it in your power to confer further obligations on thofe whofe principles you approve). Be affured I fhall never lofe fight of that duty, which I confider myfelf bound by every tie to fupport, I mean the juft reprefentation of the wifhes of my countrymen. And though hitherto all efforts to recover our national rights, and to obtain redrefs of the grievances we labour under, have proved ineffectual, the time, I hope, is now arrived, when corruption, overawed by the virtue of the people, fhall no longer dare to oppofe their unanimous voice. And I truft, I may foon have it in my power to congratulate you, on the full enjoyment of all your conftitutional and commercial privileges.

I have the honour to be,

Gentlemen,

With the greateft refpect,

Your much obliged,

And devoted humble

Servant.

KINGSBOROUGH.

LORHA RANGERS.

*At a Meeting of the* Lorha Rangers, *held at* Lorha, *in the County of* Tipperary, *on the* 16th *Day of April,* 1782.

Captain WALSH in the Chair.

RESOLVED unanimoufly, That the perfect emancipation of this country, ought to be the primary object of each individual

vidual, and fhould not only be wifhed, but fought for, by every patriotic and conftitutional mode.

Refolved, That we conceive it a duty we owe to our country, to difavow the authority of any body of men, to make laws for this independent kingdom, fave only, the King, Lords, and Commons of Ireland ; and we pledge ourfelves to our brother Volunteers, to co-operate with them in every effectual meafure, for the eftablifhments of our rights on the moft permanent bafis.

Refolved, That we fhall be always ready to affift our Sovereign againft his natural enemies.

Captain Walfh having left the Chair ;

Refolved, That our moft grateful thanks be returned to captain Walfh, for the propriety of his conduct as chairman, and to him and the other officers for their attention to the corps.

Signed by order,
ROB, PURCELL, Secretary.

❀❀❀❀❀❀❀❀❀❀❀❀❀❀❀❀❀❀❀❀❀❀❀

# KING's COUNTY.

## BARONY of KILCOURSEY UNION,

*At a Meeting of the* Barony *of* Kilcourfey Union, *held at* Horfeleap, *on* Tuefday *the* 16th *of* April, 1782.

Major BAGOT in the Chair.

The following refolutions were unanimoufly entered into :

RESOLVED, That we highly approve of the virtuous and patriotic refolutions of the Ulfter Delegates, affembled at Dungannon, on the 15th of February laft.

Refolved, That the King, Lords, and Commons of Ireland, are the only power competent to make laws to bind this kingdom, and that we will refift, with our lives and fortunes, the execution of any other laws, fave thofe only that are enacted by the authority aforefaid.

Refolved, That we expect a full declaration of rights from our reprefentatives in parliament.

Refolved, That we will co-operate with the Volunteer corps of this kingdom, in every conftitutional mode of obtaining a redrefs of grievances.

Refolved,

Refolved, As it was originally our wifh, that the moft li
beral indulgence fhould be extended towards our Roman Catholic Brethren, we feel the moft cordial fatisfaction, at the
removal of thofe penal reftrictions they fo long laboured
under.

Signed by order,
JOSEPH HENDERSON, Sec.

*At a Meeting of the* Independent Freeholders *at* Dundonald,
*on Tuefday the 16th of April,* 1782.

ROBERT LAMBERT, Efq; in the Chair.

The following with many other patriotic toafts were drank,

THE King, Lords, and Commons of Ireland ; The Irifh
Volunteers; The friends of Ireland in the Britifh parliament;
The independent electors of the county of Antrim, and may the
electors of the county of Down follow their patriotic example ;
Robert Stewart, Efq; only reprefentative of the county of
Down ; equal liberty and commerce to Great Britain and
Ireland.

Refolved, That this meeting be, and is hereby adjourned
to the 18th of June next.

R. LAMBERT, Chairman.

Mr. Lambert having left the chair, and Mr. John Glenholme having taken it,

Refolved, That the thanks of this meeting be given to
our chairman, for his politenefs of conduct in the chair.

JOHN GLENHOLME.

*At a Meeting of the* Ouzle Galley, *at* Dublin, 16th *of April,*
1782.

THEO. THOMPSON, Efq; Captain, in the Chair. ¦

The following refolutions were unanimoufly agreed to:

RESOLVED, That the King, Lords, and Commons of
Ireland, are folely competent to make laws for the government

ment thereof, and that we will pay obedience to such laws only as have received, or shall receive their sanction.

Resolved, That the captain, officers, and crew of this Galley, will co-operate with their countrymen, in every conftitutional effort, to support the just rights of Ireland, and to oppose the interference of any other legiflature.

Resolved, That we view with the utmost satisfaction the late proceedings of the British House of Commons, which we conceive manifest a disposition to acknowledge the unquestionable rights of this country, and may happily afford the strongest cement to that connection of interests and warm affection between the two kingdoms, which we trust will have an uninterrupted and perpetual existence.

Resolved, That said resolutions be published in the Dublin Evening Post, Saunders's and Faulkner's papers, and the Hibernian Journal.

Signed by order,
CHRIST. DEEY, Secretary.

<hr>

## CLONLONAN VOLUNTEERS.

*At a Meeting of the* Clonlonan Light Infantry, *at* Moate, *on Tuefday the 16th of April,* 1782.

The following refolutions were unanimoufly agreed to:

Colonel GEORGE CLIBBORNE in the Chair.

RESOLVED, That we will steadily maintain, and strenuoufly support the principles of our original institution, the defence of our country against foreign enemies, the prefervation of the public peace, and the protection of our conftitutional freedom, rights, and privileges.

Resolved, That the sole power of enacting laws to bind this kingdom, is vested in the King, Lords, and Commons of Ireland only, and that we will not, as Volunteers, or in any other capacity, enforce the execution of any laws, except such as have received that constitutional sanction.

Resolved, That it is essentially necessary, to repeal that part of the ftatute, commonly called Poyning's law, which
uncon-

unconftitutionally vefts a fupreme legiflative power in a Privy Council, compofed of perfons who do not derive their authority from the nobility of their birth, or the free fuffrages of the people.

Refolved, That as it is highly expedient, to fecure the dignity and independence of thofe, who are intrufted with the adminiftration of juftice, a law ought to be enacted, limitting the duration of the Judges commiffions, by their good behaviour, and not by the arbitrary will of the crown.

Refolved, That fince confiderable fums of money, are annually remitted out of this kingdom to abfentees, reafon and juftice require, that thofe who draw fo much wealth out of the nation, fhould, by a tax, be obliged to contribute their proportion to the fupport and defence of it.

Refolved, That a repeal of thefe penal ftatutes, that opprefs our brethren, the Roman Catholics of Ireland, would be a juft, as well as neceffary meafure.

Refolved, That as a perpetual ftanding army muft ever be confidered as a very dangerous inftitution in a land of liberty, that a claufe in our mutiny bill ought to be repealed, which unconftitutionally makes the military force, thereby eftablifhed in this kingdom, perpetual.

Refolved, That we will on all occafions, co-operate with our brethren Volunteers, and with our countrymen in general, in every meafure that our laws and conftitution may authorife, and that may be judged requifite and neceffary, in order to obtain a redrefs of grievances, with a full and explicit declaration and acknowledgment of the rights and privileges of this kingdom.

Refolved, That the above refolutions be publifhed in the Weftmeath Journal, the Dublin Evening Poft, and Dublin Journal.

Signed by order,

J. ADAMSON, Secretary.

The Chairman having left the Chair,

Refolved unanimoufly, That the thanks of this corps, be prefented to our worthy Colonel, for his unwearied attention to us, and his truly patriotic, and upright conduct in the chair.

Signed by order of the corps,

J. ADAMSON, Secretary.

QUEEN's

# QUEEN's COUNTY.

## BORRISS-IN-OSSORY MEETING.

*At a Meeting of the* Borriſs Rangers, *29 Members preſent,* April 16, 1782.

JAMES STEPHENS, Eſq; Captain Commandant, in the Chair.

RESOLVED unanimouſly, That we will, on every future election of members to ſerve in parliament, vote for ſuch men, and thoſe only, who, by their conduct in and out of parliament, give us ſufficient reaſon to be convinced they will ſupport the true intereſt of this nation, without being influenced by any honours or emoluments from government, and that they will attend to ſuch inſtructions as they may receive from their conſtituents.

Reſolved unanimouſly, That the thanks of this corps be given to our worthy member, John Warburton, Eſq; for his conduct in parliament, by voting on every queſtion for the true intereſt of his country.

Reſolved (nine diſſentient, and the Chairman not having poled) That the thanks of this corps be given to our worthy member, Charles Henry Coote, Eſq; for his virtuous conduct in parliament, in ſupport of his country.

JAMES STEPHENS, Chairman.

Captain Stephens having quit the Chair,

Reſolved unanimouſly, That our thanks be given to him for ſo ſpiritedly expreſſing our ſentiments, by propoſing the firſt reſolution above-mentioned, at a meeting of Delegates of the Queen's County Volunteers, at Maryborough, the 3d of April inſtant.

Reſolved unanimouſly, That our thanks be given to the Offerlane Blues, Oſſory True Blues, Cullina Rangers, Palmer's Rathdowny Volunteers, Roſenallis Volunteers, and Stradbally Volunteers, who ſupported ſaid reſolutions by their Delegates on ſaid day.

Reſolved, That theſe reſolutions be publiſhed in the Dublin Evening Poſt, and Leinſter Journal.

Signed by order,

SAMUEL ODLUM, Secretary.

## COLERAINE VOLUNTEERS.

*At a general Meeting of the* Coleraine Battalion, *the 16th of April*, 1782, *in* Coleraine, *commanded by Colonel* Richardfon.

### Lieut. Colonel CANNING in the Chair.

RESOLVED unanimoufly, That we ftrictly adhere to the principles of our firft affociation, the defence of our King and country, and moft excellent conftitution, againft all foreign and domeftic enemies.

Refolved, That we highly approve of the refolutions entered into by the Delegates of the Ulfter Volunteers, met at Dungannon the 15th of February laft, which affert the conftitutional rights of this kingdom, and that we will ftrenuoufly co-operate with our fellow-citizens and Volunteers, to obtain an explicit acknowledgment, and fecure the full enjoyment of thofe rights.

Refolved, That the refolutions of the Grand Jury and freeholders of the city and county of Londonderry, affembled by the High Sheriffs at the laft affizes, deferve our approbation, and fhall have our firm fupport.

Refolved, That being united to Great Britain by blood and affection, and attached to our gracious Sovereign by the pureft loyalty, we wifh ever to continue fo, confident, that upon fuch a union depends the ftrength and happinefs of both kingdoms.

Refolved, That thefe our unanimous refolutions be communicated by our Chairman, Paul Canning, Efq; to James Dawfon, Efq; Secretary of the Dungannon affociation, and that he do inform him, that we heartily accept of their invitation to become members of that refpectable body; and alfo that thefe refolutions be publifhed in the Dublin Evening Poft, and Belfaft News-Letter.

Refolved unanimoufly, That the thanks of this meeting be tranfmitted to Colonel Richardfon, for affembling the battalion this day, and for his conftant politenefs and attention to it.

PAUL CANNING.

Lieutenant Colonel Canning having left the Chair, and Major Lyle taken it;

Refolved unanimoufly, That the thanks of this meeting be alfo given to our worthy Chairman, for his polite and very proper behaviour in the chair.

COUNTY

## COUNTY of WESTMEATH.

*At a Meeting of the* Barony *of* Fore Cavalry, *and* Finae Rangers, *on Wednesday the* 17th *of April,* 1782.

Colonel WILLIAM GORE, of the Finae Rangers, in the Chair.

The following refolutions were unanimoufly agreed to:

RESOLVED, That as freeholders and Volunteers, highly approving of the patriotic and liberal refolutions, entered into by the Delegates affembled at Dungannon and Balinafloe, we will chearfully co-operate with them in every conftitutiónal ‡ mode of obtaining an effectual redrefs of thofe grievances complained of therein.

Refolved, That we will with zeal and firmnefs, in our feveral capacities, maintain the juft rights of this kingdom, and promote the peace, harmony, and good order of this county.

Refolved, That we will fupport fuch gentlemen only, as candidates to reprefent this county in parliament, as have, and will continue uniformly to maintain the independency and commercial rights of Ireland.

Colonel Gore having left the chair, and Major Webb having taken it;

Refolved unanimoufly, That the thanks of this meeting be prefented to colonel Gore, for his very proper conduct in the chair.

Refolved, That the above refolutions be publifhed in the Weftmeath Journal, and Dublin Evening Poft.

Signed by order,
GEORGE KERR, Secretary.

✦❖✦❖✦❖✦❖✦❖✦❖✦❖✦❖✦❖✦❖✦❖✦❖✦❖✦

## HOLLYWOOD VOLUNTEERS.

*At a Meeting of the* Firft Hollywood Company *of* Volunteers, *at* Cultra, *on the* 17th *of April,* 1782.

### Captain KENNEDY in the Chair.

RESOLVED, That we think it neceffary to adopt the refolutions of the Delegates, affembled at Dungannon on the

15th

15th of February laſt, in as much as they breathe ſentiments of ſuch conſtitutional importance as claim our warmeſt approbation, and that we will co-operate with the ſaid aſſociation, in eſtabliſhing, on a permanent baſis, the juſt rights of Ireland.

Reſolved, That a copy of the above reſolution be tranſmitted to the Secretary of the Dungannon meeting, and publiſhed three times in the Dublin Evening Poſt, and Belfaſt News-Letter.

Signed by order of the company,

JOHN KENNEDY, Captain.

---

## LEINSTER MEETING.

*At a Meeting of the Delegates from* One Hundred and thirty-nine *Corps of Volunteers of the Province of* Leinſter, *at* Guild-Hall, *in the* Tholſel, Dublin, *the* 17th *Day of* April, 1782, *purſuant to public Notice.*

### Colonel HENRY FLOOD in the Chair.

RESOLVED unanimouſly, That the thanks of this meeting be preſented to our patriotic and worthy brethren who met at Dungannon on the 15th of February laſt, for having originated, and alſo, to the provincial meeting of Connaught, and to the reſt of our brethren, for having adopted that mode of redreſs for the national grievances, which, through the virtue and perſeverance of our independent repreſentatives, we now confide, will be fully and ſpeedily carried into effect.

Reſolved unanimouſly, That we feel ourſelves called upon to declare our ſatisfaction in the unanimous ſenſe of the Houſe of Commons, expreſſed in favour of the rights of Ireland, in their addreſs to the King, yeſterday, as amended by Col. Grattan ; and, that we will ſupport them therein with our lives and fortunes.

Reſolved unanimouſly, That the thanks of this meeting be given to Colonel Grattan, for his extraordinary exertions and perſeverance in aſſerting the rights of Ireland.

Reſolved unanimouſly, That the following thirteen commanders of corps be appointed a ſtanding committee of Delegates from this province, to correſpond and commune with the

the other provincial committees or Delegates of Ireland, to wit:

| | |
|---|---|
| Earl of Granard, | Col. Montgomery Lyons, |
| Earl of Aldborough, | Col. Parnell, |
| Sir Wm. Parfons, Bart. | Lieut. Col. Lee, |
| Col. Flood, | Capt. Richard Neville, |
| Col. Grattan, | Capt. W. T. Smyth, |
| Col. Talbot, | Capt. H. Gorge. |
| Col. Burton, | |

Refolved unanimoufly, That the firft review of fuch corps of this province, as choofe to attend, be at Dublin on Monday the 3d of June next: and Delegates from forty corps having agreed to attend at faid review, they then proceeded to ballot for a reviewing General, when the right hon. General Earl of Charlemont was elected; at the fame time, Major Gudgeon was chofen exercifing officer of the infantry, and Major Broom of the cavalry.

Refolved unanimoufly, That we recommend it, that the fecond review in this province be at Ballewftown, on Monday the 15th day of July next; and, the third review at Carlow, on Monday the 12th of Auguft next.

Refolved unanimoufly, That all the corps who have fent Delegates to this meeting, and have ballotted for a reviewing General for the review at Dublin, fhall receive inftructions from Lord Charlemont, as to all matters relative to the faid review.

Refolved unanimoufly, That an officer's guard from each corps in the city and county of Dublin, be mounted at Lord Charlemont's, in rotation, at ten o'clock each morning, for fourteen days preceding the review, and two days after.

Refolved unanimoufly, That the thanks of this meeting be given to the feveral Volunteer corps of the city and county of Dublin, who lined the ftreets for the Delegates this day, and to Major Monk, and the Light Infantry of the Dublin Volunteers, who mounted guard at Guild-hall during the fitting of the Delegates therein.

Refolved unanimoufly, That the thanks of this meeting be returned to John Talbot Afhenhurft, Efq; for the great trouble he has been at as Secretary to this meeting, and the attention always paid by him to the Volunteer caufe in general.

HENRY FLOOD, Chairman.

The Earl of Arran having taken the chair, it was refolved unanimoufly, That the thanks of this meeting be prefented

to

to Colonel Henry Flood, for the propriety of his conduct this day in the chair, and for the virtuous and patriotic exertions of his great abilities in support of the rights of Ireland.

Signed by order,

J. T. ASHENHURST, Secretary,

Affociated Corps, Province of Leinfter.

Colonel Flood, and the Delegates, having fince waited upon the right hon. the Earl of Charlemont, and acquainted him of his being chofen reviewing General for the 3d day of June next, his Lordfhip was pleafed to return the following anfwer:

*Gentlemen,*

WITH renewed and redoubled gratitude, I moft chearfully accept the new honour which your goodnefs has conferred upon me, alluring you, that however flattering this repetition of your favours muft necefsarily be to every feeling of my heart, it is principally dear to me, when I confider it as an affurance of the continuation of that which confticutes one chief happinefs of my life, *your approbation.*

I have the honour to be,

Gentlemen,

Your moft obliged, moft faithful, and,

*April* 18,    Moft obedient humble fervant,

1782.    CHARLEMONT.

❖•◇•❖•◇•❖•◇•❖ ◆◇•❖•◇•❖•◇•❖◇• ❖❖ ◇•❖ ◇•❖•◇•❖•◇•❖•◇•❖ ◇•❖•◇•❖

## DELVIN VOLUNTEERS.

WE, the Delvin Volunteers, think it necefsary to concur with our brethren of other independent corps, in declaring, That the King, Lords, and Commons of Ireland, are the fole power competent to make laws to bind this kingdom.

In fupport of this great conftitutional principle, we pledge ourfelves to each other, firmly to unite, trufting at the fame time, that, in the prefent difpofition of public affairs, fuch prudent, liberal meafures will be adopted, as may promote a lafting harmony between Great Britain and Ireland, two nations, which an equal participation of conftitutional rights would infeparably connect.

Signed by order of faid corps,

*April* 18, 1782.    THO. SMYTH, Colonel,

STRAD-

## STRADBALLY VOLUNTEERS.

*At a Meeting of the* Stradbally Horse, *held on the 18th Day of April,* 1782.

### Lieut. Col. COSBY in the Chair.

IT was unanimously resolved, That we do most chearfully accede to the truly virtuous and patriotic resolutions and address of the Ulster Delegates assembled at Dungannon, on the 15th of February last, and that we will, to the fullest extent, co-operate with them in every constitutional mode of obtaining the most speedy and effectual redress of those grievances they so judiciously point out.

Resolved unanimously, That we feel the most perfect satisfaction at the relaxation of the severe laws against our Roman Catholic fellow-subjects.

THOMAS COSBY.

### Captain Purcell in the Chair.

Resolved unanimously, That the thanks of this meeting be returned to Lieut: Col. Cosby, for his great attention to the corps on this and every occasion, and for convening this meeting.            Signed by order,

P. WALLIS, Secretary.

## COUNTY of FERMANAGH.

*At a Meeting of the* True Blue Battalion, *commanded by* Colonel Archdall, *April* 19th, 1782.

### Captain LENDRUM in the Chair.

RESOLVED, That we highly approve of the resolutions of the Dungannon meeting, and do declare, such spirited and constitutional measures shall always have our warmest support, and request our worthy colonel will communicate these our resolutions to captain Dawson.

Resolved, That the thanks of this battalion be presented to the virtuous minority of the house of commons, who have supported the great constitutional rights of this kingdom.

Resolved,

Refolved, That his Majefty's gracious meffage to the
Houfe of Commons of Ireland, fignifying his royal pleafure,
that all complaints and jealoufies of his loyal Irifh fubjects
fhould be removed, meets our warmeft thanks, and that we
will fupport him againft all his natural enemies, with our lives
and fortunes.

Signed by order,
ROBERT COWAN, Secretary.

## WICKLOW FORESTERS.

*At a Meeting of the* Reprefentatives *of the* Independent Wicklow Forefters, Cavalry, *and* Infantry, *at* Wicklow, *the* 20th
*of April,* 1782,

Colonel HAYES in the Chair.

RESOLVED unanimoufly, That though we had conceived
the general voice of this county in the unanimous refolutions paffed at laft lent affizes, had fully fpoken our fentiments,
yet, perceiving that feveral refpectable corps have thought it
proper to remove every poffible doubt of their principles, by
fpeaking particularly for themfelves; and being fully perfuaded, that fubjects, by acquiring a knowledge in the ufe of
arms, do in no refpect relinquifh their right to a free difcuffion of public meafures we do now declare, That no power
on earth, has a power to make laws to bind this kingdom,
but the King, with the Lords and Commons of Ireland.

Refolved, That we approve of and admire the fpirit, moderation, and liberality of fentiment, which appear in the
refolutions of the Ulfter Delegates, affembled at Dungannon the 15th of February, and will co-operate with them
and the other affociated corps, in every conftitutional mode
of redreffing the grievances of this kingdom; felicitating at
the fame time, our brother Volunteers, in the profpect of
fpeedily obtaining thefe defirable ends, from the unanimous
refolution of our fenate, on Mr. Grattan's fpirited and truly
patriotic motion; from the parental attention his Majefty has
gracioufly fhewn his loyal fubjects of Ireland, in his meffage
to both houfes of parliament, and, from his choice of a miniftry, who appear to be the friends of the people.

SAMUEL HAYES.

Colonel Hayes having quit the chair, Captain Foulkes was voted in.

Refolved unanimoufly, That colonel Hayes be appointed our Delegate, to appear for us the next provincial meeting in Dublin, and to correfpond with the Ulfter affociation.

Refolved, That the thanks of this meeting be given to colonel Hayes, for his very proper and fpirited conduct in the chair, and for his unremitting attention at all times, to the honour of our affociated corps.

Refolved, That thefe refolutions be publifhed in the Dublin Journal, and the Dublin Evening Poft, and copies of them be tranfmitted to the Secretaries of the Ulfter and Leinfter Delegates.

ARCH. HAMILTON FOULKES.

## CLONMEL INDEPENDENTS.

*At a full Meeting of the* Clonmel Independents, *the 2·ft of April,* 1782.

### Colonel BAGWELL in the Chair.

RESOLVED unanimoufly, That the unfeigned and moft heartfelt thanks of this corps be given to Henry Grattan, Efq; for the fteady and invariable exertion of his diftinguifhed abilities, for the purpofe of obtaining a redrefs of the feveral grievances under which Ireland has long laboured, which we now truft will be fpeedily effected, to the utmoft of our wifhes, in the eftablifhment of all our conftitutional rights.

Refolved unanimoufly, That in a particular degree we conceive ourfelves called upon to render him every poffible acknowledgment for his motion in parliament, on Tuefday the 16th inft. whereby he has glorioufly obtained meafures that will for ever perpetuate the name of GRATTAN in the annals of this kingdom, and in the hearts of a grateful people.

Refolved, That the above refolutions and following addrefs be tranfmitted to Mr. Grattan, by the Chairman, and publifhed in the Dublin Evening Poft, and Clonmel Gazette.

JOHN BAGWELL, Chairman.

*Clonmel, April* 21, 1782.

S I R,

WI1H inexpreffible fatisfaction, we took the earlieft opportunity of returning you our unfeigned thanks, for that unremitting ardour, and unfhaken perfeverance you manifefted on every occafion, in fupport of the liberty of your country, and by which, we hope, you have compleatly emancipated it.

Every thing to form a perfect character, the 16th of April, 1782, has fhewn in the perfon of a Grattan, whofe name the prefent, and after ages, mult revere as the redeemer of his country.

JOHN BAGWELL., Chairman.

*To the* Clonmel Independents.

*Gentlemen,*

THIS teftimony of your approbation is perhaps much more than I have deferved, but what, I think, I will not forfeit.

I hope our conftitutional rights will be fpeedily eftablifhed; it will be our own fault if they are not fo; as the eftablifhment is to be final, fo muft it be full.

I need not add more words to affure you of my regard and refpect for your fentiments and your privileges.

  I am, Gentlemen,
   With many thanks,
    Your humble and
     Obedient fervant,
      HENRY GRATTAN.

*To* John Bagwell, *Efq.*

S I R,

I RECEIVED your moft obliging and flattering letter, accompanied with the refolutions of the Clonmel Independents.

I fend my anfwer, unequal to exprefs my fenfe of the honour they have done me. Permit me to return you my moft particular thanks.

  I am, Sir, with much refpect,
   Your moft obedient
    And humble fervant,
     HENRY GRATTAN.

G g

## ÉYRÉCOURT BUFFS.

*At a full Meeting of the* Eyrecourt Buffs, *held the 21st of April,* 1782.

### Col. WALTER LAWRENCE in the Chair.

The following addrefs was unanimoufly agreed on, and ordered to be prefented by Peter Lawrence, Efq; Captain of a company in faid corps, to that diftinguifhed citizen, Henry Grattan, Efq.

*To* Henry Grattan, *Efq.*

SIR,

HISTORY, both facred and profane, informs us, that there have been men born to perplex and fcourge the human race ; but we likewife know, that all-bounteous Heaven has often, in pity to our fufferings, bleffed us with affertors of our rights ; bleffed us with thofe, who, fraught with Heaven-born virtue, and endowed with extraordinary talents, have boldly ftepped forward in behalf of the people of this kingdom, and unmafked that fatal fpecies of tyranny, which, affuming the awful veil of law, has for a century paft not only broke through all the barriers of juftice, but in defiance of fenfe and reafon, pretended to bind the people of this country by acts of a foreign legiflature, thus falfely and imperioufly legalifing oppreffion.

Such a man, Sir, has Ireland found in Henry Grattan. Born to be the inftrument of your country's falvation, you met corruption on her own ground, who, coward like, hid her guilty head, and fhrunk from the fplendor, dignity, and irrefiftible force of your eloquence and virtue.

That army of patriots, Sir, the Volunteers of Ireland, who ftand unrivalled in the hiftory of mankind, have declared the rights of Ireland.

Led by their glorious example, and influenced by their fupport, her parliament has declared them ; the whole kingdom has, with one voice, declared them ; who then, or what can deny them?

The torch of freedom is lighted, and illumines the Irifh nation, from the peer to the pooreft peafant; nor is it ever to be quenched, but in the blood of its inhabitants.

All

All Europe, Sir, the friends of legal liberty in every part of the globe, have seen and admired the settled, calm, but determined resolution of a brave people, in behalf of that first of sublunary blessings, and will rejoice in that spirit and unanimity which has put a period to the bondage of a century, and given justice a decisive victory over wrongs; a victory, which by restoring us to our ancient, and unalienable rights, and re-establishing our constitution on its true principles, must raise these kingdoms to the highest point of happiness and glory.

And here, Sir, permit us to congratulate, not only you and the people of this country, but those of every part of the British empire, on the choice of servants, which our beloved Sovereign has been lately pleased to make; as they appear determined (so far as we are hitherto enabled to judge) to make justice, equality, and œconomy, the settled basis of their administration, disdaining those mean, evasive, and temporising arts, and disdaining that abominable system of corruption and boundless extravagance, which reduced the people to indigence, by supporting a numerous host of mercenary hirelings, and sycophants of power, at their expence; engines of infamy, who, having no will of their own, sacrificed honour, liberty, and every thing that was dear to men, at the altar of the ministerial high-priest. But enough of such noxious beings. May you, Sir, live long to enjoy the most perfect felicities the human mind can possess—the consciousness of having done right, and the blessings of the people; and may they, on their parts, regardless of any other consideration but their country's good, ever prove themselves worthy of the blessings of a free constitution, rejecting on every occasion, with becoming indignation, those miscreants, those slavish tools, who have, on former occasions, betrayed their interests; and may they send those, and those only, to future parliaments, who, however inferior to you in abilities, will yet imitate your virtues.

WALTER LAWRENCE, Chairman.

Colonel Lawrence having left the chair, and Chapt. Charles Groome taken it,

Resolved, That our sincere thanks be presented to our worthy Chairman, Colonel Walter Lawrence, not only for his constant attention to this corps, and his attendance as our Delegate at the meeting at Ballinasloe, the 15th of last March, but also for the zeal which he has uniformly manifested in support of the rights and liberties of this country.

Ordered,

Ordered, That the above refolutions and addrefs, with Mr.
Grattan's anfwer, be publifhed in the Dublin and Galway
Evening Pofts.

✦➤✦➤✦➤✦➤✦➤✦➤✦◄✦◄✦◄✦◄✦◄✦◄✦◄

*To the* Eyrecourt Buffs.

*Gentlemen,*

THE warmth, generofity, and force with which you exprefs your fentiments ; that firm and undifguifed manner in
which you affert your rights; the liberality with which you
encourage one who among others has endeavoured to ferve
you, demand, on my part, the warmeft acknowledgments.

A generous country overpays her advocates, and binds them
to her fervice for ever.

You ought to have many friends, for your caufe is juft and
your fentiments exalted.

I do entirely coincide with you in the moft fanguine expectations from thofe councils which his Majefty has called to
his affiftance; a government that fhall found itfelf on privilege, an adminiftration that fhall ftand on reduction, muft be
univerfally popular, and irrefiftably powerful.

Europe has feen with approbation our efforts for freedom ;
when we fhall have obtained that freedom, fhe will behold the
fame nation raifing her government above the neceffity of corruption, by an emulation of independent fupport,—and thus
fhall we prove that privilege is the foundation of order, and
purity the ftrongeft engine of power.

I am, Gentlemen,
Your moft humble, and
Obedient fervant,
HENRY GRATTAN.

✦➤✦➤✦➤✦➤✦➤✦➤✦➤✦➤✦➤✦➤✦➤✦OO◄✦◄✦◄✦◄✦◄✦◄✦◄✦◄✦◄✦◄✦◄

# WATERFORD UNION.

*At a Meeting of the* Waterford Union, *April* 21, 1782.

Secretary SAMUEL DRAPES in the Chair.

RESOLVED unanimoufly, That we conceive the great
mental abilities of Henry Grattan, Efq; guided as they have
been by immutable integrity of heart, and exercifed folely
for the advantage of this kingdom, are likely to prove the
primary

primary caufe of meafures fraught with the beft of confequences to us, and to our lateft pofterity.

Therefore, refolved unanimoufly, That this troop (as Irifhmen interefted in favour of their deareft rights) do return
their moft grateful and unfeigned thanks to Henry Grattan, Efq; for his fteady and uniform parliamentary conduct
in fupport of thofe meafures.

Refolved unanimoufly, That Henry Grattan, Efq; be admitted an honorary member of this troop.

Refolved unanimoufly, That a copy of thefe refolutions
be tranfmitted to Thomas Chriftmas, Efq; our Captain, and
that he be requefted to prefent them to Mr. Grattan.

Refolved unanimoufly, That our Secretary be ordered to
have thefe refolutions publifhed in the Dublin Evening Poft,
and in the Waterford Chronicle.

Signed by order,
SAM. DRAPES, Sec. and Chairman.

## INDEPENDENT DUBLIN VOLUNTEERS.

*At a full Meeting of the Corps of* Independent Dublin Volunteers, *April* 21, 1782.

Major CANIER in the Chair.

The following Addrefs was unanimoufly agreed to:

To Colonel HENRY GRATTAN.

SIR,

AT a time when every voice is raifed to thank you, who
ever ftood foremoft in the caufe of liberty and your country,
we, who have the honour of ferving under your command,
would ill deferve fo high a diftinction, were we not to add
our fuffrages to thofe of an applauding and grateful people,
who prefs forward with a jealous emulation, to exprefs their
feelings to you, who have fo often, and at length fo fuccefsfully combated for the rights of this injured nation.

Permit us, therefore, Sir, to fay, that we are truly fenfible
of the many obligations we are under to you, for fo nobly
introducing, and with fuch manly eloquence, unequivocally
defending the rights of this country; and beg leave to affure

fure you, that, as citizens and foldiers, we fhall ever remember your unceafing exertions with pleafure.

We know your heart too well to urge you to perfevere; all we have to hope is, that your life may long be fpared to your country, to watch over that liberty you were fo honourably diftinguifhed in afferting.

SAMUEL CANIER, Chairman.

Refolved, That our Chairman and a committee do wait on Colonel Grattan with the above addrefs, and that it be publifhed, with his anfwer, in the Dublin Evening Poft, Saunders's News-Letter, and Hibernian Journal.

The Rev. Mr. Miller having taken the Chair,

Refolved unanimoufly, That our thanks be given to Major Canier, for his conftant attention to the difcipline of the corps, and his proper conduct in the chair.

Signed by order,

C. B. KIPPAX, Secretary.

The committee having waited upon Col. Grattan, he returned the following Anfwer:

*To the* Independent Dublin Volunteers.

*Gentlemen,*

THE principles which are now likely to become law and conftitution, are thofe which have ever diftinguifhed your corps: I have many reafons which incline me to a perfonal, as well as a political predilection in favour of the Independent Dublin Volunteers; my knowledge of your fentiments, makes your approbation particularly acceptable.

I think I will not forfeit your efteem; I am fure you will always command mine; and that we both fhall continue in thefe fentiments towards each other, is my ardent wifh, and fincere opinion.

I am, gentlemen,

With great refpect and thanks,

Your moft obedient fervant,

HENRY GRATTAN.

DOWN

# DOWN MEETING.

*At a Meeting of the Inhabitants and Freeholders of the Parish of* Saintfield, *and part of the Parishes of* Killinchy *and* Killeny, *County of* Down, *assembled at* Saintfield *the* 22d *of April,* 1782, *pursuant to public Notice.*

## FRANCIS PRICE, Esq; in the Chair.

The following Resolutions were unanimously agreed to:

1. RESOLVED, That we highly approve of, and cordially accede to the resolutions of the Delegates assembled at Dungannon, on the 15th of February last, as breathing the genuine spirit of moderate patriotism, loyalty and liberty.

2. Resolved, That as the body of the people is the most essential and important part of the community, the strength and support of government, and as it is the duty of every individual to know and assert his own rights, and those of his country, so we, as a part of this great body, are earnestly desirous to co-operate with the real friends of Ireland, in every constitutional measure which may tend to secure its freedom and prosperity, and procure a speedy and effectual redress of national grievances.

3. Resolved, That we will not support any man at the ensuing election, but such as are known to be men of real integrity, and friends to the King and constitution of Ireland.

4. Resolved, That Francis Price, Esq; Nicholas Price, Esq; Rev. Thomas Birch, John Barnett, Andrew Todd, John Todd, Alexander Gordon, James Wallace, Samuel M'Burney, John Coffey, John Broadley, Samuel Broadley, and James Magee, be appointed a committee, who are empowered to call future meetings to act in concert with other associations.

5. Resolved, That these resolutions be twice published in the Dublin Evening Post, and Belfast News-Letter.

FRANCIS PRICE.

Mr. Price having left the chair, and Mr. Barnett taken it,

Resolved, That the thanks of this meeting be given to our worthy Chairman, Francis Price, Esq; for his very polite and impartial conduct in the chair.

JOHN BARNETT.

COUNTY

## COUNTY of DOWN.

*At a Meeting of a very considerable Number of Freeholders and principal Inhabitants of the Parishes of* Tullylish *and* Donaghclony, *on Tuesday the 23d of April,* 1782.

The Rev. JOHN SHERRARD in the Chair.

The following resolutions were unanimously agreed to :

RESOLVED, That at the present alarming and very important situation of public affairs, we consider it as a duty of the first magnitude which we owe to our country, ourselves, and to posterity, to join with our virtuous countrymen and fellow-citizens, in every constitutional measure, which may be deemed most effectual to obtain, secure and perpetuate our civil and religious liberties.

Resolved, That it is with particular pleasure, and heartfelt joy, we behold the unexampled spirit, the virtuous deportment, and the temper and steady exertions of the Volunteers of Ireland at large in behalf of their country ; and though we have not the honour of being enrolled in their number, yet we are ready to stand or fall by their side, as long as they continue to pursue the same line of conduct which they have hitherto done.

Resolved, That the resolutions agreed upon, and entered into by the Delegates of the Ulster Volunteers, at Dungannon, the 15th of February last, and the subsequent address from the committee by them appointed, do meet with our warmest approbation and support ; and that the tribute of our thanks is due, and is hereby given to the gentlemen who first planned and convened that meeting, to the Delegates who composed it, and to every other approving corps.

Resolved, That our warmest thanks are due, and are hereby given to our worthy representative, Robert Stewart, Esq; for his former steady and upright conduct in the honourable House of Commons.

Resolved, That it is a reproach to so respectable a county as that of Down, as well as a public loss, to have but one representative in the House of Commons ; and that, in order to remove this reproach, and redress this grievance, we hold ourselves ready, the first proper opportunity, to invite and support any gentleman who may be deemed properly qualified

to

to reprefent us, and will engage to attend upon his duty, to hearken to our inftructions, and at all times to fupport the conftitutional rights of the nation at large.

Ordered, That the above refolutions be figned by our Chairman, and publifhed in the Dublin Evening Poft, and Belfaft News-Letter.

Signed by order,

JOHN SHERRARD.

+·o·+↓·o··+↓·o·+↓·o·+↓·o·+↓·❖··↓↓↓·❖·+↓·❖·o·+↓·o··↓↓·o··↓↓·o·+↓·o·↓·o·+

*At a Meeting of the Freeholders and other principal Members of the ancient Congregation of Broad Ifland, held at Ballycarry, in the County of Antrim, on Tuefday the 23d of April, 1782.*

The Rev. JOHN BANKHEAD in the Chair.

The following refolutions were agreed to, without a diffenting voice:

1ft. THAT we are fully convinced, that indifference to the profperity of the nation, ill becomes any individual or body of individuals; with heart-felt pleafure therefore, we behold the exertions of our fellow-fubjects in this kingdom, to reftore and fecure our national rights. And that, notwithftanding the chimerical and ambitious dreams of fovereignty over us as a nation, which darken the underftandings, chill the affections, and fetter the policy of fome of the inhabitants of Britain, we think it our duty to love and regard all the inhabitants of Britain as our fellow-fubjects, and no more than our fellow-fubjects; and we think it their duty to love and regard the inhabitants of Ireland, as their fellow-fubjects, and no lefs than their fellow-fubjects.

2d. That as fubjects of Britain and Ireland's King, we feel a joy, which patriotifm and loyalty, by their combined power, excite; upon learning that his Majefty, by a late aufpicious and moft gracious meffage to the commons of Ireland, hath expreffed his concern for, and required a ftatement of our national grievances; his royal and paternal heart anxioufly wifhing their removal.

3d. That a late ftatement of national grievances; in the Commons Houfe of Parliament, by that honour to his coun-

H h

try,

try, Mr. Grattan, appears to us a full and well timed state-ment—well timed, for it was immediate; and full, for their removal brings Irish policy within the reach of Hibernia's arm.

4th. That the thanks of this meeting be, and hereby are most respectfully offered to Mr. Grattan, for his statement of the grievances of the people of Ireland; to Mr. Brownlow, for seconding the amendment; and to all the other members present for their unanimous support.

5th. That an upright parliament is, at all times, a blessing to the community.

6th. That uprightness in electors, as it merits, so it bids fair for an upright representation.

7th. That, as a part of the freeholders and inhabitants of the county of Antrim, we pledge ourselves to each other, and to our country, to use our best endeavours to have representatives in the next parliament; and with this view, our Chairman, with Messrs. James Steel, James Sillyman, Thomas Horsborough, James Yule, Roger Carally, John Lusk, William Taylor, John Horsborough, James Graham, James Farle, John Campbell, Alexander Neilson, and James Hoey, are hereby appointed a committee (five to be a quorum) to call meetings as occasion shall require, and to communicate with other committees in neighbouring parishes: this meeting having it much at heart to serve, in our small circle, the important ends of the Dungannon meeting, to which we conceive the publications of their committee of the 6th and 16th inst. not a little subservient.

Signed by order,<br>
JOHN BANKHEAD, Chairman.

## SAINTFIELD LIGHT INFANTRY.

*At a Meeting of the* Saintfield Light Infantry, *April* 24, 1782.

The following Resolutions were unanimously agreed to:

RESOLVED, That we highly approve of, and heartily accede to the spirited resolutions entered into by the Delegates, assembled at Dungannon on the 15th of February last.

Resolved,

Refolved, That our thanks are due to thofe men who have
fo ftrenuoufly fupported and maintained our rights in parliament.

Refolved, That the above refolutions be publifhed in the
Dublin Evening Poft, and the Belfaft News-Letter.

NICHOLAS PRICE, Captain.

✦✦✦✦✦✦✦✦✦✦✦✦✦✦✦✦✦✦✦✦✦

## COUNTY of CAVAN VOLUNTEERS.

*At a Meeting of the Reprefentatives of the Corps of the County of
Cavan Volunteers, convened by order of Colonel Enery, their
Commanding Officer, at Cavan, the 24th of April, 1782.*

### THEO. CLEMENTS in the Chair.

RESOLVED unanimoufly, That the thanks of this meeting be returned to the Chairman and Delegates affembled at
Dungannon, the 15th of February laft, for admitting us a
part of that body, though not reprefented at that meeting,
and for their very polite letter in anfwer to one they received
from the Volunteers of this county, dated the 12th of faid
month ; and for their particular attention, in having communicated to us the refolutions entered into at faid meeting.

Refolved unanimoufly, That we do entirely approve of the
refolutions and addrefs of the Ulfter Volunteers entered
into at the Dungannon meeting, the 15th of February laft.

Refolved, That Colonel Enery, Colonel Stuart, Colonel
Montgomery, and Colonel Theophilus Clements, are appointed Delegates to meet and confult with the Delegates of
the Dungannon meeting, and thofe of the different corps of
Volunteers of this kingdom, on all legal and conftitutional
methods of obtaining the end propofed by that meeting.

Refolved, That a copy of thefe refolutions be tranfmitted
by our Secretary, to Captain James Dawfon, Secretary to
the Ulfter Volunteers, and publifhed in the Dublin Evening
Poft, and Ulfter Journal.

THEO. CLEMENTS, Chairman.

The Chairman having left the Chair,

Refolved, That the thanks of this meeting be prefented to
our worthy Chairman, Colonel Theo. Clements, for his polite
and proper conduct at faid meeting.

Signed by order,

JOHN BALL, Secretary.

# LOUGHAL MEETING.

*At a numerous Meeting of the Freeholders and Volunteers of the Manor and Parish of* Loughal, *assembled in the* Parish Church, *on Thursday the 25th Day of April,* 1782, *pursuant to Notice.*

ARTHUR GRAHAM, Esq; in the Chair.

The following resolutions were unanimously agreed to:

RESOLVED, That at this important crisis, it is the duty of all descriptions of men, to declare publicly and unequivocally their sentiments, touching the grand fundamental and constitutional rights of this kingdom.

Resolved, That notwithstanding the iron hand of power, hath long oppressed and degraded the inhabitants of this kingdom, they have, nevertheless, been distinguished, not more by their unexampled exertions for the peace and defence of their country, than for their unshaken attachment and loyalty to his majesty's sacred person and government.

Resolved, That we highly approve of the spirit and moderation of the resolutions of the Ulster Delegates, assembled at Dungannon on the 15th of February last, and that we shall at all times be ready, at the hazard of our lives and fortunes, to co-operate with them, and our fellow-subjects, in every constitutional measure, for carrying the purposes of the said resolutions into full effect.

Resolved, That these resolutions be signed by our Chairman, and published three times in the Dublin Evening Post and Belfast News-Letter, and a copy transmitted by the captain of the Loughal Volunteers, to James Dawson, Esq; Secretary of the Ulster Delegates.

ARTHUR GRAHAM, Chairman.

Arthur Graham, Esq; having left the chair, and Joshua M'Geough, Esq; having taken it,

Resolved unanimously, That the thanks of this meeting be given to our worthy Chairman, for the propriety of his conduct in the chair.

JOSHUA M'GEOUGH.

*At a Meeting of the* Mullingar Volunteers, *on Friday, the 26th of April,* 1782.

WILLIAM JUDGE, Efq; Lieut. Col. in the Chair.

RESOLVED unanimoufly, That our thanks be prefented to the Earl of Granard, for his great goodnefs and liberality to us, fince he has done us the honour to accept the command (as Colonel) of this corps.

Refolved, That we will at all times, moft chearfully co-operate with his Lordfhip, in all fuch meafures as he fhall deem eligible, for the purpofe of carrying into execution, thofe neceffary and fpirited refolutions, entered into by our Volunteer brethren, affembled at Dungannon and Ballinafloc.

Refolved, That our worthy Lieut. Col. William Judge, be requefted to tranfmit the above refolutions to his Lordfhip.

Ordered, That the above refolutions be inferted in the Weftmeath Journal, and Dublin Evening Poft.

Signed by order,
JOSEPH BEARD, Lieut. and Sec.

*At a numerous Meeting of the Freeholders, and Volunteers of the Manor and Liberty of* Mountnorris, *affembled in the Meeting-houfe, on Friday the 26th Day of April,* 1782, *purfuant to Notice.*

Mr. JOHN M'CAMON in the Chair.

The following refolutions were unanimoufly agreed to :

RESOLVED, That at this important crifis, it is the duty of all defcriptions of men to declare publicly and unequivo-cally their fentiments, touching the grand fundamental and conftitutional rights of this kingdom.

Refolved, That notwithftanding the iron hand of power hath long oppreffed and degraded the inhabitants of this king-dom, they have neverthelefs been diftinguifhed, not more by their unexampled exertions for the peace and defence of their country, than for their unfhaken attachment and loyalty to his Majefty's facred perfon and government.

Refolved,

Refolved, That we highly approve of the fpirit and moderation of the refolutions of the Ulſter Delegates affembled at Dungannon on the 15th of February laſt; and that we ſhall at all times be ready, at the hazard of our lives and fortunes, to co-operate with them and our other fellow-ſubjects, in every conſtitutional meaſure for carrying the purpoſes of the ſaid refolutions into full effect.

Refolved, That theſe refolutions be ſigned by our Chairman, and publiſhed three times in the Dublin Evening Poſt and Belfaſt News-Letter, and a copy tranſmitted to James Dawſon, Eſq; Secretary of the Ulſter Delegates.

JOHN M'CAMON.

Mr. John M'Camon having left the chair, and Captain John Ingram having taken it,

Refolved, That the thanks of this meeting be given to our worthy Chairman, for his proper conduct in the chair,

Refolved, That the thanks of this meeting be given to John Blackall, Eſq; for his very ſpirited exertions in convening this meeting, and in digeſting and drawing up the above refolutions.

---

# CARRICK MEETING.

*At a Meeting of Delegates from the following Corps,* Clanwilliam Union, Munſter Corps, Fethard Independents, Iverk Volunteers, Third Company of Waterford Infantry, *and* Waterford Union, *convened at* Carrick *by a requiſition of the* Waterford Union, *to re-conſider the Appointment of a Reviewing General, made on the 1ſt of February laſt.*

Captain HANNIBAL WILLIAM DOBBYN in the Chair.

The following refolutions were unanimouſly agreed to:

IT having been ſuggeſted that the corps, whoſe Delegates met here on the 1ſt day of February laſt, are bound in honour to abide by the refolutions of that day;

Refolved, That men of honour cannot be bound to what is diſhonourable.

Refolved, That we have ſeen ſince our laſt meeting the moſt improper influence exerted, to prevent the county of

Waterford

Waterford from inftructing their reprefentatives in parliament, (although convened for that purpofe by the Sheriff) and thereby from uniting in the general meafures for the redemption of our country.

Refolved, That the appointment of any perfon to be a reviewing general is the moft public approbation of his principles and conduct, and holds him forth as a character entitled to national efteem.

Refolved, That it would be dangerous to our country and difhonourable to ourfelves, to give weight and confequence to one of the moft active oppofers of out patriotic exertions, by putting him at the head of a confiderable body of Volunteers even in the ceremony of a review.

Refolved, That we refcind our refolution of the 1ft of February, appointing the Earl of Tyrone, our reviewing General.

Refolved, That the review be deferred, and alfo the appointment of a reviewing General, to a future day.

Refolved, That fuch corps as choofe to accede to our refolutions, are requefted to fend their names to our Chairman, in order to have them inferted in our refolutions.

HANNIBAL WILLIAM DOBBYN, Chairman.
Delegate from 3d Comp. of Waterford Infantry.

Thomas Ryan, Delegate from the Clanwilliam Union.
James Hackett, Delegate from the Munfter Corps.
John Congreve, Delegate from the Waterford Union.
J. Jacob, Delegate from the Fethard Independents.
Henry Brifcoe, Delegate from the Iverk Volunteers.

Major Hackett having taken the chair,

Refolved, That the thanks of this meeting be given to the Waterford Union, for its proper fpirit in convening us on this occafion.

Refolved, That the thanks of this meeting be given to Capt. Dobbyn, for his conduct as Chairman.

Refolved, That our Chairman be requefted to have thefe refolutions publifhed in the Dublin Evening Poft, and the Waterford and Clonmel Papers.

*Carrick,*                                        JAMES HACKETT.
*April 27, 1782.*

DUBLIN

DUBLIN VOLUNTEERS, commanded by his Grace the Duke of Leinfter.

*At a general Meeting of the Corps, purfuant to a fpecial Summons for that Purpofe, held at the* Eagle, Euftace-ftreet, *the 28th Day of April, 1782.*

## HENRY MONK, Efq; Major, in the Chair.

This corps having confidered, with the higheft gratitude, and moft heartfelt fatisfaction, the paternal regard and attention which his Majefty has been gracioufly pleafed to manifeft to this nation, in his meffage to our parliament, directing them to take our grievances into their moft ferious confideration, have

RESOLVED unanimoufly, That a conduct fo truly royal in our moft gracious Sovereign, muft make an indelible impreffion on the hearts of Irifhmen, whofe ftrongeft characteriftics are, affectionate loyalty to their prince, and the moft determined and perfevering exertions in the caufe of their country and her conftitutional rights.

Refolved unanimoufly, That we fhould hold ourfelves unworthy fuch royal favour, did we not feel the weight of the obligation, and determine moft fteadily to coincide with his Majefty's gracious intention, of delivering this his loyal kingdom from every grievance.

Refolved unanimoufly, That as citizens and foldiers, we feel ourfelves deeply impreffed with gratitude and efteem, for thofe refpectable and illuftrious characters in both Houfes of Parliament, who have fupported the honour and confequence of the Volunteers of Ireland, from a conviction that their manly determinations to enjoy the bleffings of a free conftitution, are the beft proofs of their unfhaken loyalty and attention to the true interefts of this country.

Refolved, That we receive the utmoft fatisfaction in finding, that the following refolution of this corps, publifhed the 9th day of June, 1780, has been fupported by the unanimous voice of the nation, viz.

" That the King, Lords, and Commons of Ireland only, are competent to make laws binding the fubjects of this realm, and that we will not obey, or give operation to any laws, fave only thofe enacted by the King, Lords, and Commons of Ireland,

Ireland, whose rights and privileges, jointly and severally, we are determined to support with our lives and fortunes."

Resolved unanimously, That Henry Grattan, Esq; in a peculiar manner, merits the thanks and confidence of every Irishman, for the distinguished exertion of his abilities, displayed on his proposition for a parliamentary declaration of rights, which we have now the happiness to see sanctified by both Houses of Parliament, with that unanimity its national importance demanded.

Resolved accordingly, That the thanks of this corps be presented to Mr. Grattan, and that a respectable deputation do wait on him with a copy of these resolutions.

The corps take the opportunity of thus publicly returning thanks to Major Monk for his conduct in the chair this day; and for his constant attention to the corps upon all occasions.

Ordered, That the above resolutions be published six times in the Dublin Journal, and Dublin Evening Post.

Signed by order,
**JOHN WILLIAMS, Sec.**

*The Committee appointed having waited on Mr.* Grattan *with said resolutions, he was pleased to return the following answer:*

To *the* Dublin Volunteers.

*Gentlemen,*

I RETURN you my most sincere thanks. We are embarked in the same cause, with one interest and one opinion; the same determination to be free, and the same desire to exhort those who endeavour to serve the public: your resolution is particularly agreeable to me: I enter into the generous spirit which inspired it, and shall be ambitious to retain that esteem which I am proud to meet with in this most flattering testimony of your liberality and your patriotism.

I am, Gentlemen,

With the greatest respect,

Your most humble, obedient

**HENRY GRATTAN.**

*At a Meeting of the* Youghal Union, *held the* 28th *Day of April,* 1782.

THOMAS GREEN, Major Commandant, in the Chair.

Resolved unanimously, That we highly applaud the patriotic and spirited resolutions of the Ulster Volunteers, represented at Dungannon, on the 15th of February last, and that we will heartily co-operate with our brethren Volunteers, in such constitutional measures as may appear expedient, for redress of grievances.

Resolved, That a copy of the above be transmitted by our Chairman, to the Secretary of the Ulster Delegates, and be published in the Dublin and Cork Evening Posts.

WILLIAM ROCH, Secretary.

## COUNTY of LEITRIM.

*At a Meeting of the Independent Freeholders of the County of* Leitrim, *who do not possess more than Fifty Acres of Land each in his own Right, assembled at* Castlecargin, *on Wednesday, May* 1, 1782.

ROBERT SADLER in the Chair.

The following resolutions were unanimously agreed to:

1. Resolved, That Honesty is the best Policy.
2. Resolved, That none but honest men can be truly great or good men.
3. Resolved, That it is for want of having *honest* men in power for the time past, that this country is poor and the inhabitants of it miserable, and that flaxseed, tobacco, sugar, cotton, &c. &c. bear such high prices as they do at present, to the ruin of the nation.
4. Resolved, That it is neither honest or wise, to buy or sell votes for an election of members to serve in parliament, because the man who buys us will sell us again to our own destruction.
5. Resolved, That we must be honest ourselves before we can reasonably expect our representatives should be so, who are only our trustees.

6. Resolved,

Refolved, That nothing under God, can make this country rich, and the people of all ranks happy, but an honeft
parliament, and that we deferve to live and die in flavery
and wretchednefs, if ever we vote for any who is or has been
the enemy of Ireland.

Signed,
ROBERT SADLER, Chairman.
and fixty others.

✦✦✦✦✦✦✦✦✦✦✦✦✦✦✦✦✦✦✦

## MUNSTER VOLUNTEERS.

*At a Meeting of Delegates from Eighty-fix of the Volunteer
Corps of the Province of Munfter, at Mallow, the 2d of
May, 1782.*

Colonel STAWELL in the Chair.

A committee being chofen for the purpofe of forming Refolutions, the following were reported and unanimoufly
agreed to.

Lord KINGSBOROUGH, Chairman of the Committee.

RESOLVED unanimoufly, That the refolutions of the
Volunteer Delegates affembled at Dungannon, exprefs with
fpirit and truth the rights and grievances of this kingdom ;
we therefore moft cordially accede to them.

Refolved unanimoufly, That we are determined, with our
lives and fortunes, to fupport our Houfes of Parliament, in
their late virtuous efforts to eftablifh the rights and privileges
of this realm.

Refolved unanimoufly, That it is the earneft wifh, and it
muft ever be the glory of Irifhmen, to be connected with Great
Britain, by friendfhip never to be broken; by affections never
to be changed; by interefts never to be feparated ; but we
conceive a mutual enjoyment of equal privileges (being united
under the fame foveieign, yet governed by diftinct and independent legiflatures) ean alone eftablifh fuch friendfhip, fuch
affections, fuch interefts.

Refolved

Refolved unanimoufly, That we have the moft ardent hope, that the adminiftration of Ireland will adopt that plan of retrenchment, which minifters have declared their intention of forming in England ; and we rejoice at the idea of " weeding corruption from the land," a fyftem much to be wifhed for in this kingdom, where we have feen the moft proftitute characters hold the moft honourable and lucrative employments.

Refolved unanimoufly, That when the rights of this realm fhall be univerfally acknowledged, it will be the indifpenfable duty of every Irifhman, to guard the conftitution againft future violation ; and as the infamous doctrine of *Power conferring right* hath been afferted, we therefore pledge ourfelves, and conjure our brethren Volunteers, not to relinquifh or flacken in the ufe of arms, as the beft means to repel any attempt of lawlefs power, to guard againft invafion, affift our fifter kingdom, and enforce the juft execution of the laws.

Refolved unanimoufly, That a committee of correfpondence, confifting of thirty-fix members, be elected (Seven to be a quorum) to meet and confult with the other Delegates of the kingdom.

Refolved unanimoufly, That no member of either Houfe of Parliament, who hath in or out of parliament, or by any other means, oppofed a declaration of rights for this kingdom, fhall be eligible as a committee man.

The Committee was formed of the following perfons :

*County of Cork.*
James Bernard, Efq.
Colonel Francis Bernard,
Lord Vifcount Kingfborough,
Sir John Conway Clothurft, Bart

*County of the City of Cork.*
Colonel Bagwell,
Colonel Boufield,
Richard Moore, Efq.
Richard Fitton, Efq.

*County of Limerick.*
Colonel Maffey,
Colonel Croker,
Colonel Ryves,
Colonel Maunfell.

*County of Waterford.*
John Congreve, Efq.
Colonel Keane,
Captain Mufgrave,
Captain Shee,

*County of the City of Waterford.*
Robert Shapland Carew, Efq.
Cornelius Bolton, Efq.
Henry Alcock, Efq.
Hannibal William Dobbyn, Efq.

*County of Kerry.*
Colonel Sir Barry Denny, Bart.
Colonel Arthur Blennerhaffett,
Major Godfrey,
Colonel Gun.

*County*

| *County of the City of Limerick.* | *County of Tipperary.* |
|---|---|
| Colonel Smyth, | Colonel Prittie, |
| Colonel Prendergaſt, | Edward Moore, Eſq. |
| Colonel Harte, | Samuel Jacob, Eſq. |
| Major Powell. | Samuel Allen, Eſq. |

*County of Clare.* Not yet returned.

Reſolved unanimouſly, That as we wiſh to ſee all the ſpirit, the virtue, and the ſtrength of the nation united, in the ſupport and defence of the juſt rights and conſtitution of Ireland, reſpectable men of every religious denomination, be admiſſible, by ballot (as uſual) into the Volunteer corps of this province.

Reſolved unanimouſly, That we ſhall ever acknowledge our obligations to thoſe members of parliament, who uniformly ſupported the rights, and preſſed for a redreſs of the grievances of this kingdom; and that ſuch men alone are worthy of our ſupport on every future election.

Reſolved unanimouſly, That the thanks of this meeting be preſented to colonel Henry Grattan, for his unwearied attention to the intereſt of Ireland ; and from whoſe exertions, aſſiſted by the Volunteers, and people in general, this kingdom is likely to derive great and laſting advantages.

Reſolved unanimouſly, That the following addreſs be preſented to colonel Henry Grattan ;

SIR,

" *A nation, for ages deſpoiled of her Liberty, conſiders* YOU *as the aſſertor of that bleſſing, without the enjoyment of which, riches ceaſe to be wealth, and peace to be tranquility. Look into yourſelf; revolve in your mind that you have made your country* FREE : *your own ſenſations muſt be ſuperior to all the thanks we can expreſs.*

Reſolved unanimouſly, That the Volunteer corps and inhabitants of Mallow merit the thanks of this meeting, for their attention, and for their polite and hoſpitable behaviour.

Reſolved unanimouſly, That the commanders of the ſeveral Volunteer corps of this province do return (upon honour) to the chairman, the date of their firſt aſſociation in arms.

Reſolved unanimouſly, That the proceedings of this meeting be publiſhed in the Dublin, Belfaſt, Cork, Clare, Limerick, Kerry, and Waterford News-papers.

Reſolved unanimouſly, That the thanks of this meeting be given to Henry Newſom, Eſq; for his proper conduct as ſecretary.

Reſolved,

Refolved unanimoufly, That this meeting be adjourned until fuch time as the anfwers to the addreffes of our parliament be received, as we are at this time uncertain, what meafure may be proper for Irifhmen to adopt: and that then, and on every other great national occafion, our committee of correfpondence be impowered, and are requefted to call a meeting of the Delegates of this province.

SAMPSON STAWELL, Chairman.

The Chairman having quitted the chair;
Refolved unanimoufly, That the thanks of this meeting be prefented to colonel Stawell, for the propriety of his conduct in the chair.

In committee, the chairman having quitted the chair;
Refolved unanimoufly, That the thanks of this committee be given to Lord Vifcount Kingfborough, for the propriety of his conduct in the chair; and we reflect with pleafure, on his patriotic conduct in parliament.

HENRY NEWSOM,
Secretary to the Munfter Delegates.

*To the Provincial Meeting of* Delegates *for* Eighty-fix Volunteer Corps *of Munfter, bolden at Mallow, May* 2, 1782.

*Gentlemen,*

IT is impoffible to convey in fewer words more decided fentiments, or more flattering approbation, than you have done in thofe very pregnant lines, for which I am now to return my fincere acknowledgments.

On the part of my country, and of myfelf, I am to thank eighty-fix corps; I am to thank them for conferring honour on the individual, for giving fupport to the caufe, and for combining both.

The grievances, for the removal of all and each of which we are committed life and fortune—foreign legiflature, appellant judicature and writ of error to England, unconftitutional power of the councils, a perpetual mutiny bill, will, I hope, fpeedily vanifh, and a free conftitution eftablifh itfelf on their ruins.

I thank you moft fincerely. I thank you for your fupport and your commendation, your efteem and your affiftance.

I am, Gentlemen,
With the greateft refpect and regard,
Your moft humble fervant,
HENRY GRATTAN.

P. S. Mr. Francis Bernard has done me the honour to prefent your addrefs; to the fame refpectable and independent
member I give the anfwer.

✦ ·❍·✦ ·❍·✦·❍·✦·❍·✦·❍·✦·❍·✦ ✦ ❍·✦✦ ❍·✦·❍·✦·❍·✦·❍·✦·✦·❍·✦·❍·✦ ✦

*At a Meeting of the* Loughinfhillin Battalion, *held at* Caftle-
Dawfon, *the 3d of May,* 1782.

Major DOWNING in the Chair.

RESOLVED, That at this awful and important hour,
when the fate of Ireland, as a nation, is depending, it would
be a dereliction of our rights longer to delay a publication of
our fentiments. We are now in full poffeffion of the feveral
opinions and demands of our countrymen armed, and unarmed, of the Volunteers, and of the people of Ireland.
We therefore, with hearts beating high for the honour of our
king, and the good of our country, do accede to the refolutions
of the Delegates affembled at Dungannon, on the 15th day of
February laft, as breathing the true fpirit of loyalty, liberty,
and toleration, and will ufe every conftitutional effort in fupport of fuch meafures, as may tend to promote the undoubted
liberties and commerce of this kingdom.
Refolved, That the interefts of Great Britain and Ireland
are infeparable, and that any attempts to difunite them deferve the execrations and refentment of every friend to both.
Refolved, That as we are willing to fhare her fate, fo it is
our decided determination to be *free.*
Refolved, That the thanks of this corps be given to thofe
worthy and independent members of parliament, who ftrenuoufly fupported the rights and liberties of Ireland, and that
we are happy in having this opportunity of expreffing our
moft grateful acknowledgments to the right hon. Thomas Conolly, our General, Col. Staples, and Lieut. Col. Dawfon,
for their generous donations, fteady fupport, and particular
attention to this battalion from its firft formation.
Refolved, That with heart-felt pleafure we reflect, that the
ftricteft harmony has ever fubfifted in this battalion, and that
our fentiments have on this, and every other occafion, entirely
coincided with thofe of our worthy commanders, whofe abfence at this time is owing to their indifpenfable duty in parliament.

Refolved,

Refolved, That our Chairman do immediately inclofe thefe our refolutions to James Dawfon, Efq; Secretary to the Dungannon meeting.

Refolved, That Col. Staples and Lieut. Col. Dawfon, be requefted to confer with the other Delegates of the Ulfter Volunteers, on all conftitutional meafures and queftions that may tend to the redrefs of grievances and injured rights of Ireland.

Refolved, That our Chairman fhall have thefe our refolutions publifhed in the Dublin Evening Poft, and Belfaft News-Letter.

JOHN DOWNING, Major.

Major Downing being requefted to leave the Chair, and Capt. Ellis to take it,

Refolved unanimoufly, That the thanks of this meeting be given to our worthy Chairman, for his polite and genteel behaviour on this and every other occafion.

HENRY ELLIS.

## AUGHINLOE MEETING.

*At a numerous and refpectable Meeting of the Freeholders and principal Inhabitants of the Parifh of* Aughinloe, *in the County of* Londonderry, *held at the Church of faid Parifh, on Friday the 3d of May,* 1782, *purfuant to public Notice.*

### PAUL CHURCH, Efq; in the Chair.

RESOLVED, That at this critical and important crifis, when the fate of this kingdom depends upon the wife and fpirited exertions of its virtuous inhabitants, we confider it an indifpenfible duty we owe to ourfelves, to our country, and to pofterity, to join with our fellow-citizens, in demanding thofe conftitutional privileges which are our unalienable birth-right as a free people.

Refolved, That as freemen we will be governed by our own laws only, that the King, Lords, and Commons of Ireland, are the only reprefentatives of this crown and people.

Refolved, That as the members of the Houfe of Commons are the reprefentatives of the people, and derive their power folely from them, every member of that houfe, who contemptuoufly tuously neglects the instructions of his constituents, betrays his trust, and is unworthy of confidence.

Resolved, That we will not support any man at the ensuing election, but such as are known to be men of real integrity, and friends to the King and constitution of Ireland.

Resolved, That our Chairman, with Messrs. Alexander Scott, Matthew Patten, David Rankin, John Forsyth, William Forsyth, Jacob Forsyth, William Hazlet, and Thomas Maxwell be appointed a committee, any five to be a quorum, to call future meetings of said parish, and act in concert with the committees of other parishes.

Resolved, That our warmest thanks are due to that saviour and deliverer of his country, Henry Grattan, Esq; and the rest of those worthy and patriotic Senators, who have so long, and till now so unsuccessfully laboured for the emancipation of Ireland.

PAUL CHURCH, Chairman.

Resolved, That the thanks of this meeting are due to our worthy Chairman, for his proper and polite conduct in the chair.

JACOB FORSYTH, jun. Sec.

O◄←•)►•►►•)►•)►◄←•)►◄←◄←◄←◄←◄←◄←•)►◄←•)►◄←←◄←◄←◄←C

## ARMAGH VOLUNTEERS.

*At a Meeting of the* Second Company *of Armagh Volunteers,
convened the 4th of May,* 1782.

RESOLVED, That our disapprobation of the Dungannon meeting was directed against the mode of convening that assembly, not the salutary measures resulting from it; these we do in the amplest manner accede to, having ever held them in the highest esteem, as conducing to the happiness and prosperity of our kingdom. And we declare, that we will always join with our brethren, in giving every constitutional support to obtain a redress of the grievances therein mentioned.

Signed by order,

JAMES CRAWFORD, Sec.

MAGHER-

# MAGHERAFELT MEETING.

*At a Meeting of the Inhabitants of the Parish of* Magherafelt, *held at* Magherafelt, *on Monday the 6th Day of* May, 1782, *pursuant to public Notice.*

## Mr. HENRY PATTERSON, Chairman.

The following resolutions were unanimously agreed to :

1. RESOLVED, That the welfare of the people ought to be the great design of every government.

2. That when the servants of the crown, by their corrupt influence, attempt to undermine the rights of the people, it becomes the indispensable duty of each individual to use every constitutional effort in their defence.

3. That we most cordially approve of, and accede to the resolutions entered into at Dungannon, by the Delegates of the Volunteers assembled on the 15th of February last, and the solemn declaration of the high Sheriffs, Grand Jurors, Freeholders, and Inhabitants of the city and county of Londonderry, convened at the last assizes, both which resolutions and solemn declarations merit, and shall receive our most determined support.

4. That we have with admiration beheld the efforts of those distinguished and illustrious citizens, who formerly composed the minority of the Irish parliament, in asserting, with such uncommon ability and unwearied zeal, the rights of Ireland, rejoicing that their able reasonings, seconded by the voice of the people, have forced conviction on every mind, and brought both Houses of Parliament unanimously to speak the sentiments of the people, in stating and claiming the ancient rights of this kingdom ; rights which ought to be asserted at every risk, and to be torn from us only with our lives.

5. We rejoice that those obstructions, which so lately diverted the rays of royal benificence, have been removed, by placing around the throne men of the most approved worth, and who possess the intire confidence of the people ; and we trust, a similar change of men and measures will take place in this kingdom, which we are persuaded would produce the most happy effects.

6. That such members as act contrary to the inclinations and interests of their constituents, or endeavour, by absence,

when

when important conflitutional queftions are depending in the houfe, to avoid both minifterial vengeance and popular odium, are unworthy of future confidence; and that, therefore, on every fubfequent election, we will fupport, with our votes and intereft, fuch candidates as are moft diftinguifhed for integrity and patriotic conduct.

7. That the interefts of Great Britain and Ireland are indiffolubly united, and by our being admitted into an equal fhare of the benefits of the Britifh conftitution, the bonds of mutual intereft and cordial affection will be rendered firm and permanent.

8. That the thanks of this meeting be prefented to our worthy chairman for his very proper conduct in the chair.

9. That the following gentlemen, major Patterfon, Rev. Mr. Downing, Rev. Mr. Chambers, Rev. Mr. Henry, Rev. Mr. Wilfon, Mr. Henry Patterfon, Doctor Caldwell, Captain Tracy, Mr. Robert Crawford, Mr. Samuel Crawford, Mr. Andrew Torrens, Mr. Theodore Williams, Mr. Hugh Crawford, Mr. Thomas Pollock, Mr. Abraham Mathews, Mr. Richard Dawfon, Mr. Samuel Strean, Mr. Quintin Dick, Mr. John Glenhorn, and Mr. Samuel Brown (five to be a quorum) be appointed a committee, to convene the inhabitants of this parifh, when they fhall think it neceffary, and to correfpond with the committees of the other parifhes, who may affociate for fimilar purpofes.

**HENRY PATTERSON, Chairman.**

❧✦❧✦❧✦❧✦❧✦❧✦❧✦◍✦❧✦❧✦❧✦❧✦❧✦❧

*At a numerous Meeting of the Inhabitants of the parifh of* Ballywalter, *convened by public notice the 6th May*, 1782.

The following Refolutions were unanimoufly agreed to:

1. RESOLVED, That at this important crifis, when refolutions are entered into by all ranks of our countrymen in every part of the kingdom, to obtain and fecure our conftitutional rights, we think it our duty to declare our fentiments, left our filence fhould be deemed an oppofition to our worthy patriotic brethren, or at leaft a want of regard to the interefts of our country.

2. Refolved, That the refolutions of the Volunteer Delegates, who met at Dungannon the 15th of February laft, and the addrefs of their committee, merit our warmeft approbation and fupport.

3. Refolved,

3. Refolved, That we will do all in our power to obtain an upright houfe of Commons, and a fair reprefentation of the people in parliament, by giving our votes, on the enfuing election, to fuch men only as we have reafon to believe will confult the good of Ireland, and fairly reprefent us; that as in the election of reprefentatives we are refolved to be free, fo this unalienable right of our brethren freeholders we will endeavour to fupport, by giving every affiftance in our power to fuch as may fuffer on account of their fteady attachment to the rights of citizens—the freedom of election.

4. Refolved, That Meffrs. Robert Allen, Robert Goudy, Francis Bailie, James Spence, John Mc. Kee, Robt. Park, Andrew Davifon, Daniel Kirkpatrick, Robert Mc. Kee, Wm. Mc. Kee, James Laughlin, Hugh Wallace, Andrew Mc. Cormick, and Archibald Scott, be a committee to collect our voluntary contributions for the relief of fuch virtuous fufferers, to call us together on any emergency, to convene us at leaft once in every year for the purpofe of reviving in our minds thefe our refolutions, and to correfpond with the committees of neighbouring parifhes.

Refolved, That thefe refolutions, be publifhed in the Belfaft News-Letter, figned in the name of 300 inhabitants, who were all prefent, by

JAS. COCHRAN, P. D. M.

✠✦✪✦✪✦✪✦✪✦✪✦✪✦✪✦✪✦✪✦✪✦✪✠

*At a numerous Meeting of the* Boyne Volunteer Corps, *held on 12th of May,* 1782.

Major BASS in the Chair.

The refolution of the Delegates of the Munfter Volunteers, " That refpectable men of every religious denomination, be admiffible into the Volunteer corps of this province," being read :

RESOLVED unanimoufly, That we do highly approve of, and accede to faid refolution, and that we will confider this corps as honoured by every refpectable man, of what religious denomination foever, who fhall propofe to be admitted a member of it.

JOHN BASS, Major.

MONAGHAN

## MONAGHAN RANGERS.

*At a Meeting of the* Monaghan Rangers, *on Saturday the* 13th *of May,* 1782.

### WILLIAM FORSTER, Efq; in the Chair.

RESOLVED, That it is the duty of freemen, publicly to exprefs their gratitude to the affertors and fupporters of liberty.

Refolved, That our fincere thanks, be prefented to Henry Grattan, Efq; and the other true reprefentatives of the people, who declared the authority and independence of the King, Lords, and Commons of Ireland.

Refolved, That our fincere thanks, be prefented to Barry Yelverton, Efq; and the other friends of the Irifh parliament, who endeavoured to refcue it from an ufurped unconftitutional interference.

Refolved, That our thanks be prefented to the Rev. Jofeph Warren, for his excellent fermon preached before this company, on Sunday the 7th inft.

Refolved, That our moft grateful thanks, be paid to the ladies of Monaghan, who prefented a fuit of colours to this company ; a compliment which could not be encreafed, but by the very genteel method they took of paying it.

By order,

WILLIAM LOWRY, Sec.

*At a Quarterly Meeting of the* Culloden Volunteers, *held on the* 13th *of May,* 1782.........

### Captain NEWSOM in the Chair.

RESOLVED unanimoufly, That we fubfcribe with pleafure to what the Munfter Delegates refolved on the fecond inftant, and we pledge ourfelves to them to be perfectly obedient to their directions.

Refolved unanimoufly, That we, as a corps of perfectly tolerating principles, wifh to be firmly united with all our countrymen, and for that purpofe we invite refpectable perfons of every religious denomination to become members of our corps.

HENRY NEWSOM.

## UNION R'ANGERS.

*At a Meeting of the* Union Rangers, *held at* Caftle-Dawfon, *May* 19, 1782.

### Rev. Mr. A. STEWART, Chaplain, in the Chair.

RESOLVED, That as the late formation of this troop has unavoidably delayed the publication of our fentiments upon matters of importance to this kingdom, we do now embrace the earlieft opportunity of difcharging this our indifpenfable duty.

Refolved, That we take a zealous and liberal part in the military affociation, as well in parliament as in the field, and in every effort, how inconfiderable foever, that may be conducive to the honour of that inftitution.

Refolved, That a body of men, voluntarily affociated in the manner and on the principles of our Volunteers of Ireland, may be confidered equally as the foldiers of the conftitution and kingdom, bound to affift in refcuing the one from abufe, and defending the other from foreign enemies.

Refolved, That the Volunteers of this country are to be confidered as an army grown out of national fpirit, public virtue, and preffing neceffity, who by regular behaviour, under conftitutional controul, with firmnefs and moderation affert their rights, and with equal refolution expect to convert the poffeffion of them to folid advantages.

Refolved, That upon the moft mature deliberation, we think that the refolutions of the Ulfter meeting at Dungannon, on the 15th day of February laft, are worthy the approbation of every honeft, unbiaffed mind, and therefore we moft heartily accede to them.

Refolved, That thoroughly fenfible of the bleffings we have already enjoyed under the beft of governments, and in full expectation of a confirmation of our civil and commercial liberties, we will ftrain every nerve in fupport of that government, as the great fource of Irifh happinefs.

Refolved, That the ftrength and exiftence of this and every other corps, depend upon their unanimity; keeping therefore conftantly in view the great caufe we have efpoufed, we will be unanimous and adhere moft ftrictly to the firft principles of our affociation, the defence of our King and conftitution, and the fupport of the juft rights of Ireland.

Refolved,

Refolved, That our fincere acknowledgments are due to our worthy Captain, Arthur Dawfon, Efq; (now abfent ferving his country in parliament) for his polite attention to this corps on every occafion.

Refolved, That a copy of thefe refolutions be tranfmitted to James Dawfon, Efq; fecretary to the Dungannon meeting.

Refolved, That our thanks are due to our worthy chairman, for the propriety of his conduct in the chair, and conftant attention to this corps.

Signed by order,

JOHN CRAWFORD. Sec.

## INDEPENDENT DUBLIN VOLUNTEERS.

*At a meeting of the Corps, Dublin, May 28, 1782.*

Rev. OLIVER MILLER, Chaplain, in the Chair.

IN order to teftify our attachment and affection to Great Britain, and our determination to *ftand and fall with her*, *fharing her liberties to fhare her fate*,

Refolved unanimoufly, That as foon as our reftrictions fhall be *unequivocally* done away, and our liberties *permanently* eftablifhed, that a delegate from this corps be appointed, to demand a meeting of the delegates of the province of Leinfter, to take into confideration the *juftice* and *neceffity* of making an offer to the parliament of Ireland of our fervices and exertions, under the command of the civil magiftrates, for the internal defence of the kingdom, and the protection of the public peace at our own expence, whereby a principal part of the army on this eftablifhment may be fpared to his Majefty againft his *European* enemies, having every conviction and proof, from the loyalty and public fpirit of our countrymen, that this, our idea, will be univerfally and cheerfully adopted.

Refolved, That the above refolutions be publifhed in Saunders's News-Letter, the Hibernian Journal, and the Dublin Evening poft.

Signed by order,

C. B. KIPPAX, Secretary.

*The Addreſs of the Committees of* Ulſter *and* Connaught *to the* Volunteers *of thoſe Provinces.*

*Friends, Freemen,* and *Fellow-Soldiers,*

WE have ſuſpended all obſervations on public affairs, until we ſhould receive that authentic information from our legiſlature on which we ſhould ground our proceedings. Appointed by the Volunteers of our reſpective provinces to ſuperintend the great cauſe in which we were engaged, we have been watchful ſpectators of its progreſs, and have waited, in ſilent expectation, for the fate of thoſe demands of juſtice, which our parliament, echoing the voice of the nation, had carried to the foot of the throne. We can now congratulate with our fellow-ſoldiers on the full completion of their wiſhes. The all-bountiful Providence, whoſe omnipotent hand guides the fate of nations, has led this country on to Glory; the people of Ireland, with the ſteady dignified moderation of conſcious rectitude, have boldly vindicated their Rights; and the magnanimity of Britain, forgetting all antient prejudices, has obliterated every ſource of jealouſy, by an act of ample and unequivocal juſtice. Let us bow down with gratitude to that Providence, whoſe divine protection has led us through the paths of peace to the ſummit of ſucceſs; let us cheriſh that ſpirit in ourſelves which has been the inſtrument of our deliverance; let us embrace our ſiſter kingdom with renovated affection, and evince that freedom is the ſtrongeſt cement of union and liberality, the firmeſt baſis of power.

The diſtinction between Engliſhman and Iriſhman is no more; we are now one people; we have but one intereſt, one cauſe, one enemy, one friend, and we truſt that the conduct of the Iriſh nation will demonſtrate to all mankind, that the ſame ſpirit which graſps at liberty and ſpurns at uſurpation, is equally alive to the impreſſions of friendſhip, of kindneſs, and of generoſity. Let this auſpicious æra, which at once reſtores us to the poſſeſſion of our conſtitution, and to the arms of our magnanimous ſiſter, be ever recorded in the annals of this country; and let the glory which ſurrounds it diffuſe its light to illuminate ſucceeding ages; let ſtructures ariſe to commemorate the tranſactions of this eventful period, and to hold up an example to ſtimulate poſterity to an emulation of the virtues of their anceſtors, and religiouſly to preſerve the ſacred truſt tranſmitted to them inviolate and uncontaminated; let the whole nation pour in the voluntary tribute of its feelings,

that

that every man who affifted in the attainment of the object may have the gratification of contributing to the meafure which is to record it, and that as the caufe is national, fo fhould the monument.

Amidft thefe effufions of public exultation; amidft thefe records of the glorious events of this memorable æra; while we pay every teftimony of heart-felt gratitude to thofe ever-to-be-honoured Senators, who, fuperior to all temptation, have boldly ftood forth in vindicating the rights of their country; while we offer every tribute of particular veneration to the illuftrious leader of the Volunteers of Ireland, the *Earl of Charlemont*, we fhould be wanting to our own feelings, to our fenfe of juftice, and to what we are convinced is the unanimous fenfe of the nation, did we not hold up that great and exalted character, *Henry Grattan*, as the object of peculiar commemoration and diftinguifhed national reward. It was the capacious genius of that honour to his country and mankind, which firft conceived the practicability of refcuing his native land from oppreffion; it was the power of his fplendid abilities which rouzed the public mind, and called forth all the talents and all the virtue in the nation to his aid; it was his perfeverance which, with fuch an aid, irrefiftibly bore down all oppofition to the parliamentary declaration, and the Britifh recognition of our conftitution. Services like thefe are fo blended with, and form fo leading a feature in the hiftory of the times, that one cannot be commemorated without the other, nor can any monument record the effect without diftinguifhing the caufe. But we fhould not ftop here; the Duke of Marlborough received Blenheim from the Britifh nation, as a tribute of gratitude for his military fuccefs; but as much as liberty is more valuable than conqueft, fo are the fervices of a *Grattan* fuperior to thofe of a *Marlborough*; and we truft the characteriftic generofity of the Irifh will not be inferior to that of Britain, in proportion to her ability. The reward to the individual is united to the political encouragement held out to public virtue, and if a nation fhould err in its retribution for diftinguifhed fervices, its error fhould ever be on the fide of liberality.

Impreffed with thefe opinions, we did intend to recommend it to your confideration, to apply in your capacity as freeholders to the Sheriffs of your refpective counties, to convene public meetings, for the purpofe of inftructing your reprefentatives in parliament, to confer an adequate, national reward on that truly deferving character; but finding the

fubject

fubject was laft night mentioned in the houfe of commons by a very refpectable member, and is foon to be taken under parliamentary confideration, we have only to exprefs our wifh, that every county in the kingdom may be convened to fanctify, by their approbation, the conduct of their reprefentatives on this occafion, and evince, that it is equally the defire of the people and the legiflature.

While we falicitate you on the glorious profpects which now begin to open in this country; while we view with wonder and exultation the tide of good fortune which poured in at once upon the Irifh nation and the empire at large, we cannot but particularly intreat you not to relax your military defcipline; we have now a coftitution as well as property to defend againft the common enemy; let us remember too, that there is a public fpirit and a high fenfe of honour annexed to the Volunteer inftitution, which, we have found the great fupport and incentive to national virtue; and which, having already made corruption fink before it, can alone prevent its rifing again into exiftence.

The late happy change in his Majefty's meafures and Minifters in Ireland, as well as Great Britain, feems the harbinger of profperity and indiffoluble union to both kingdoms; and we truft, that gratified in all thofe particulars mentioned in the late addreffes of our parliament, the people of this country will (as well as the legiflature) affure his Majefty, that while England adheres to the principle manifefted in her prefent conduct, no conftitutional queftion between the two nations will any longer exift, which can interrupt their harmony; and that we will fhew our fifter-kingdom and the world, that a government founded on the broad bafis of liberty, of purity, and public opinion, will ftand unftaken upon the fupport of the nation, and rife fuperior to all the arts of corruption. *Dublin, May 28,* 1782.

*For Ulfter.*

MERVYN ARCHDALL
FRANCIS DOBBS
JOSEPH POLLOCK.

*For Connaught.*

JOHN GEOGHEGAN
LEWIS FR. IRVINE
NEAL O'DONEL.

## ULSTER VOLUNTEERS, IRELAND.

*Dungannon, June* 12, 1782.

Colonel WILLIAM IRVINE in the Chair.

" At a Meeting of THREE HUNDRED and SIX COM-PANIES of this Province, purfuant to public Notice, the following Addrefs was unanimoufly agreed upon, and ordered to be prefented to his Majefty by the Chairman, Major Francis Dobbs, Captain James Dawfon, Captain Francis Evans, and Colonel Thomas Morris Jones.

To the KING's moft Excellent Majefty, the humble Addrefs of the Volunteers of Ulfter.

" *Moft gracious Sovereign,*

" WITH the moft unfeigned attachment to your Majefty's perfon and family, we approach your throne. You are our true and lawful Sovereign ; and we truft that every act of ours will evince, that we are your faithful and loyal fubjects.

" The addreffes of the Irifh parliament having difclaimed any power or authority, of any fort whatfoever, in the parliament of Great Britain over this realm, we fhall confider an unqualified and unconditional repeal of the ftatute of the fixth of George the firft, by the Britifh parliament, made in purfuance of the faid addreffes, a compleat renunciation of a principle hoftile to the rights of Ireland, and of all the claims contained in the faid ftatute ; and as fuch we will accept it and deem it fatisfactory. Thus united by the facred bond of freedom, we requeft our gracious Sovereign to affure our fifter kingdom, that we will be fharers in her fate, ftanding or falling with the Britifh empire.

" We humbly beg leave to exprefs our gratitude for the appointment of his Grace the Duke of Portland to the government of Ireland. Prevented by fituation from enjoying the prefence of our benevolent Sovereign, we rejoice in a viceroy, whofe character affures us that he will faithfully difcharge the duties of his ftation.

" The œconomy and retrenchment which your Majefty has been gracioufly pleafed both to recommend and practife, will, we humbly hope, be extended to Ireland. Should a more equal reprefentation of the people be alfo adopted, our profperity would be for ever fecured, and your Majefty's reign moft honourably diftinguifhed in the annals of mankind.

" We rejoice in the great and fignal fuccefs of your Majefty's arms : every enemy muft yield to the efforts of a great, a brave, a free, and an united people. Your Majefty's choice of thofe whom you have entrufted with the adminiftration of public affairs gives us the moft heart-felt fatisfaction ; public confidence is revived ; and we doubt not but your Majefty's crown and empire will fpeedily be raifed to the higheft pinnacle of human glory.

" We

" We have ever beheld with admiration your Majefty's domeftic virtues. May your Majefty, and the truly great and amiable partner of your throne, long, long live to blefs each other : may the offspring of your happy union reward your parental fondnefs, by a difplay of every grace and every virtue : and when, at length, the immutable law of nature fhall demand that tribute, which even Kings muft pay, may your mourning fubjects with one voice lament, that the great, the benevolent father of his people is no more.

WILLIAM IRVINE, Chairman.
JAMES DAWSON, Secretary.

## VOLUNTEER NATIONAL COMMITTEE.

*At a Meeting of the* Volunteer National Committee, *at* Dublin, *on Tuefday the* 18th *of June,* 1782.

The Rt. Hon. Lord KINGSBOROUGH in the Chair.

RESOLVED unanimoufly, That the addreffes of the Irifh parliament having difclaimed any power or authority of any fort whatfoever, in the parliament of Great Britain over this realm, we fhall confider a repeal of the 6th of George the firft by the Britifh parliament, made in purfuance of the faid addreffes, a complete renunciation of all the claims contained in the faid ftatute, and, as fuch, we will accept it, and deem it fatisfactory.

| Kingfborough, R. Sh. Carew, W. T. Monfel, Samuel Jacob, A. Blennerhaf. Wm Godfrey, Geo. Stacpoole | For Munfter. | Richard Talbot, William Burton, John Parnell, R. Nevill. Lewis Francis Irvine, Charles O'Hara, John Geoghegan. | For Lein. | Mer.Arch. F. Dobbs, J. Pollock. | Ulfter. |
| --- | --- | --- | --- | --- | --- |
| | | | | Connaught. | |

## BELFAST FIRST VOLUNTEER COMPANY.

*At a Meeting of the* Firft Volunteer Company, *in the* Market-houfe, *of* Belfaft, *on Thurfday the* 27th *of June,* 1782.

Capt. CUNNINGHAM in the Chair,

The following was ordered to be publifhed ;

RESOLVED unanimoufly, That as an advertifement from the national committee was publifhed on the 18th inft. we fhould think ourfelves culpable, were we (from perfonal attachment to any of the three Ulſter members who ſubſcribed it) not freely to declare our diſapprobation.

The advertiſement runs thus.—" Reſolved unanimouſly, that the addreſſes of the Iriſh parliament having diſclaimed any power or authority of any ſort whatever in the parliament of Great Britain over this realm, We ſhall conſider a repeal of the 6th of Geo. the firſt by the Britiſh parliament, made in purſuance of the ſaid addreſſes, a complete renunciation of all the claims contained in ſaid ſtatute, and as ſuch, *we will accept it and deem it ſatisfactory*."

Signed by four Delegates from Leinſter, ſeven from Munſter, three from Cannaught, and three from Ulſter.

The objections to that advertiſement, as far as the province of Ulſter is concerned, are ſo glaring as ſcarcely to require a comment.:—Three Delegates of the province, without any authority from the people they repreſent, decide on a great national queſtion, with which the liberty of a kingdom, gloriouſly ſtruggling for a free conſtitution, is intimately connected. The very men who ſummoned a general meeting of the province, to be held only three days after their publication appeared, attempted in this extraordinary manner to influence the proceedings of a great and reſpectable body, which had appointed them for purpoſes of a very different and much more limited nature. Beſide, the impropriety of their giving any public opinion whatever on the ſubject, the language they conveyed it in is, to every corps which claims the privilege of thinking for themſelves, juſt cauſe of complaint.

WADDELL CUNNINGHAM.

From the multiplicity of papers which the Editor was obliged to have recourſe to in collecting theſe different Reſolutions, miſtakes conſequently were unavoidable. Such, however, as were omitted in chronological order, are here inſerted, and the collection cloſed with others of a later date.

*The Delegates of the different Corps who attended the meeting held in the town of* Clonmel, *on* Thurſday *the* 14th inſt. *came to the following reſolutions :*

Colonel HENRY PRITTIE, in the Chair.

RESOLVED unanimouſly, that we highly approve of the ſpirited and liberal reſolutions and addreſs, of the Ulſter Volunteers, repreſented at Dungannon, the 15th of February laſt, and alſo the reſolutions entered into by the Grand Jury of this county, now aſſembled.

Refolved unanimoufly, that as Citizens and Volunteers, we will co-operate with the feveral corps whofe Delegates met at Dungannon, in every conftitutional mode of obtaining a redrefs of the grievances mentioned in their refolutions.

Refolved unanimoufly, that a Delegate be appointed from each corps, to attend the meeting of the Volunteer delegates in Dublin.

HENRY PRITTIE, Chairman.

Upon the above refolutions being agreed to, Col Prittie was requefted to leave the chair, and Col. Bagwell to take it, when the following addrefs was unanimoufly agreed to:

To HENRY PRITTIE, Efq.

SIR,

YOUR conduct as *one* of the reprefentatives in parliament for *this* county, having been highly meritorious, demands from us, our warmeft thanks and approbation; though critical the fituation of this country, and though her interefts are *deferted* in parliament by many of her reprefentatives, yet, judging of the future by the paft, we think it unnecef-fary to recommend any particular line for *you* to follow.

*To the Delegates of the different Volunteer Corps of the County of Tipperary, who met at* Clonmel, *on the* 14*th of March,* 1782.

*Gentlemen,*

YOUR approbation of my parliamentary conduct, raifes fentiments in my breaft, which words cannot exprefs; a fteady perfeverance in which, fhall ever be the invariable rule, of

Gentlemen,<br>Your much obliged,<br>And ever faithful,

*March*
16, 1782.
Humble fervant,<br>HENRY PRITTIE.

COUNTY of DOWN.

WE, the High Sheriff, Grand Jury, Freeholders, and In-habitants of the county of Down, affembled in Downpatrick, at an Affizes held for faid county, the 15th day of March, 1782, thinking it now peculiarly neceffary to declare our fen-timents refpecting the fundamental and undoubted rights of this nation, and defirous, by a feafonable explanation, to ter-minate

minate an anxious jealousy, and to prevent the possibility of any future contest, do declare, That we will, in every situation of life, and with all the means in our power, assert and maintain the constitutional right of this kingdom, to be governed by such laws only, as are enacted by the King, Lords, and Commons of Ireland, and that we will, in every instance, uniformly and strenuously oppose the execution of any statutes, except such as derive authority from said parliament, pledging ourselves to our country, and to each other, to support, with our lives and fortunes, this our solemn declaration; and farther, we bind ourselves, that we will yearly renew this necessary vindication of our rights, till such time as they shall be explicitly acknowledged, and firmly established by the authority of parliament.

Tho. Douglas, Sheriff.

Grand Jurors.

1 Richard Annesly, Foreman, by order of the majority of the Grand Jury.
2 Robert Ward
6 Matthew Ford
7 Nicholas Price
8 Gawin Hamilton
9 Simon Isaac
John Blackwood
Roger Hall
Pat. Savage
Edward Ward
Francis Price
John Echlin
Robert Lambert
James Ham. Clewlow
John Crawford
James Clewlow
Eldred Pottinger

11 Richard Magenis
12 Arthur Johnston
13 Alexander Stuart
14 James Waddell
15 Nicholas Harrison
16 Matthew Forde, jun.
17 Francis Savage
18 John Kennedy
20 Samuel Gibbons
21 Charles Innes
22 Robert Montgomery
23 James Crawford
Henry West
William Waring
Steele Hawthorne
John Aughinleck
William Hamilton
James Hamilton
Francis Turnley,
And five thousand eight hundred and sixty-two others.

*>*>*>*>*>*>*>*>*>*>*>*>CO*<*<*<*<*<*<*<*<*<*<*<*<*<

*At a full Meeting of the* Monaghan Rangers, *March* 17, 1780.

JOHN MONTGOMERY, Esq; Colonel, in the Chair.

The following Resolutions were unanimously agreed to:

RESOLVED, That in a time of great and anxious concern, we think it our duty to declare explicitly our sentiments on public Affairs. That

That, connected as we are to England only by a common sovereign, and fully entitled to the bleffings of an equal and independent legiflation, we cannot admit a right or power in the parliament of that kingdom, to bind Ireland in any cafe whatever; on which account it is highly expedient to have a total renunciation, and exprefs difavowal of that controuling power, claimed and ufurped by a foreign legiflature.

That, we cannot without indignant jealoufy, fuffer the Privy Council of this kingdom to be a legiflative body, or any part of our conftitution, which is compofed only of King, Lords and Commons; therefore it is equally expedient and neceffary, to have either a repeal or a modification of the law, called Poyning's, which vefts an unconftitutional power in the Privy Council, as our parliament in their virtue and wifdom .fhall adopt.

That effentially conjoined with the independence of our houfe of lords, is a reftoration of its conftitutional privileges and dignity, and that it be fupreme in all judicial appeals from the fubordinate courts of juftice in Ireland.

And further, That we are ready, at every hazard of life and fortune, to co-operate with the other Volunteers of this kingdom, in the attainment of thefe juft and national requifitions, in fecuring that equal freedom and jurifdiction which belong to all the parts of the Britifh empire; and for obtaining fuch a firm and indefeafible eftablifhment of our rights, that an excefs of prerogative, or the borrowed power of reprefentation, cannot hereafter deftroy them.

Signed by Order,
WILLIAM LOWRY, Sec.

＊✢✚✪✚✪✚✪✚✪✚✪✚✪✚✪✚✪✚✪✚✪✚✪✚✪✚✪✚✪✚＊

## KERRY LEGION.

*At a meeting of the* Kerry Legion, *held on the* 27*th of March,* 1782.

### MAJOR GODFREY in the Chair.

HAVING with the utmoft pleafure read the fpirited refolutions entered into by the Delegates of the Ulfter Volunteer corps, affembled at Dungannon, on the 15th of February laft;

Refolved, That we will be ready at all times to affift and co-operate with them, in obtaining a redrefs of thofe grievances they fo juftly complain of, and which we have fo long laboured under.

Refolved,

Refolved, That the above refolution be printed in the Dublin Evening poft, and Kerry Journal.

Refolved, That thefe refolutions be inclofed to Arthur Blennerhaffet, Efq; our Colonel, to be by him forwarded to the Chairman of the Dungannon meeting.

Refolved, That the thanks of this meeting be returned to our Chairman, for his polite and proper conduct in the chair.

JOHN HURLY, Sec.

## LISMORE VOLUNTEERS.

*At a full meeting of the* Independent Blues *of Lifmore, in the County of* Waterford, *on the 1ft of April,* 1782.

### ROBERT COOKE, Efq; in the Chair.

The following Refolutions paffed unanimoufly:

RESOLVED, That the King, Lords, and Commons of Ireland only, are competent to make laws to bind this kingdom, and that an ufurpation of this power by any other body of men, is unconftitutional, illegal and a grievance.

Refolved, That a Mutiny Bill in this kingdom, not limited in point of duration, as in England, is an invidious diftinction, unconftitutional, and a grievance.

Refolved, That the independence of Judges is equally effential in Ireland as in England, to the impartial adminiftration of juftice, and that a refufal or delay of this right to Ireland, is equally infulting to the abilities and integrity of the Judges of this realm, as oppreffive to the liberties of its people, and is unconftitutional and a grievance.

Refolved, That the numerous abfentees of this kingdom, from the immenfe fums annually remitted to them, are very detrimental, and very much contribute to the impoverifhing this nation; that a tax upon abfentees would be highly conducive to the profperity, honour, and happinefs of this kingdom; and that the revenue arifing from fuch tax fhould be paid into the Treafurer of the county, where the eftates of fuch abfentees lie, and be appropriated by the Grand Jury to fuch ufes in the county, as they may think fit.

Refolved, That the doctrine, that *power makes right*, is of a moft alarming nature to a free people, manifeftly tending to erect arbitrary power on the ruins of our happy conftitution; and that any claim or attempt to govern this kingdom, by fuch

an abfurd and wicked maxim, is unconftitutional and a grievance; and that we do confider any man who is capable of
making fuch a declaration, or entertaining fuch a fentiment,
as an enemy to his country, and deferving our utmoft contempt.

Refolved, That no other perfons but the blood royal, as
children of the public, and fuch, who from their fervices have
deferved the regards of their country, or thofe whofe fituation and birth entitle them to the confideration of the public,
ought to enjoy any penfion or finecure employment; and that
the alarming increafe of unneceffary places and heavy penfions
in this kingdom, beftowed on unworthy perfons, is equally
difgraceful to the meritorious, as oppreffive and injurious to
the nation.

Mr. Cooke having quitted the Chair, and Mr Wigmore
having taken it,

Refolved, That the thanks of this meeting be given to Mr.
Cooke, for his upright and proper conduct in the chair.

Signed by order,

JOHN CRANITCH, Sec. and Treaf.

●◇◇◇◇◇●◇◇◇◇◇◇◇◇◇◇◇◇◇◇◇◇◇◇◇◇◇◇◇◇◇◇◇◇◇◇

## COUNTY of DOWN.

*At two feveral very numerous meetings of the Freeholders of the
Barony of Dufferin, on the 3d and 8th of April, 1782, occafioned by the prefent alarming ftate of public affairs.*

GAWIN HAMILTON, Efq; at each meeting in the Chair.

RESOLVED unanimoufly, That the civil and religious
principles expreffed in the refolutions of the Ulfter Delegates
met at Dungannon, highly merit approbation and meet our
warmeft fupport ; and we pledge ourfelves to each other, and
to the public, that we will at all times endeavour, by every
conftitutional meafure in our power, at the rifque of life and
fortune, to maintain a conftitution, the effence of which is liberty, and its fubjection to any foreign controul, a virtual annihilation. And further, that we will be watchful over the conduct of our reprefentatives in parliament, and that we will
not, at any future election, give our fuffrages to any perfon
who fhall have deferted his duty in the houfe, reprobated the
inftructions of his conftitutents, or voted in parliament contrary to the fpirit of thefe refolutions ; and that we will fupport without any expence on our account, at all future elections, fuch, and fuch only, as fhall give us the moft folemn
affurances of his or their full approbation of thofe fentiments,

and

and determinations to conform thereto, during the term of the great truft to be repofed in them.

Refolved, That the warmeft thanks of thefe meetings be given to our worthy Chairman, for his very proper and polite conduct in the chair, and that he be requefted to publifh thefe refolutions in the Dublin Evening Poft and the Belfaft paper.

Refolved, That Sir John Blackwood. Bart. Gawin Hamilton, Efq; Dr. Little, Meffrs. James Baillie, William Willie, Francis Heron, Robert M'Dowal, James M'Connell, Robert Johnfton, James Richardfon, Thomas Lindfay, Thomas Taylor, the Rev. Hamilton Trail, the Rev. Jofeph Kinkead, Meffrs. William Moore, Thomas Potter, jun. John Stewart, Gawin Frew, Thomas Ofborn, Thomas Hewett, John Heron, Robert Morrow, James Lemon, and Robert Logan, be a committee to call future meetings of the Freeholders of this barony, as often as may be found expedient fo to do, and to correfpond with other Affociations; nine of the above fhall be a quorum.

✦✧✦✧✦✧✦✧✦✧✦✧✦✧✦✧✦✧✦✧✦✧✦✧

## COUNTY of KILDARE.

## NAAS RANGERS.

*At a full meeting of the* Naas Rangers, *on the 7th of April, 1782.*

### Captain NEVILL in the Chair.

RESOLVED, That we do approve, and highly applaud the patriotic refolutions and addrefs of the Delegates from the feveral corps of Volunteers affembled at Dungannon, the 15th day of February laft.

Refolved, That we will co-operate with our Volunteer brethren, in every conftitutional mode of obtaining a redrefs of the grievances mentioned in faid refolutions.

Refolved, That the thanks of this meeting be prefented Captain Richard Nevill, for his particular propriety of conduct in the Chair, and his attention, upon all occafions, to the corps.

Refolved, That the above refolutions be publifhed three times in the Dublin Evening Poft.

Signed by order,

ROB. FRA. MORGAN, Sec.

## GORTIN VOLUNTEERS.

*At a meeting of the* Gortin Volunteer Company, *the* 10th *of April,* 1782.

### Lieutenant LENNON in the Chair.

The following refolutions were unanimoufly agreed to:

1. THAT we adopt, in the fulleft extent, the feveral refolutions and addrefs of the Delegates affembled at Dungannon, on the 15th of February laft.

2. That we will, as Volunteers, Freeholders, and Proteftants, in our feveral capacities and relations, as men firmly and zealoufly attached to the unalienable rights, civil and commercial, of Ireland, co-operate with our brethren Volunteers, and fellow-citizens, in every conftitutional meafure, to confirm, eftablifh, and afcertain the freedom of this kingdom, and to unite us by indiffoluble ties of mutual intereft, attachment, and affection, to our fifter kingdom.

3. That the honourable Arthur Cole Hamilton, our commander, be requefted, and is hereby appointed a Delegate from this company, to confer with the other Delegates of the Ulfter Volunteers in Dublin, on all conftitutional meafures and queftions that may tend to the redrefs of grievances, and invaded rights of Ireland.

4. That we will attend the review to be held at Strabane, on the 18th of July next.

5. That the thanks of this company be given to Lieutenant Lennon, for his very proper conduct on the prefent occafion.

6. That thefe our refolutions be publifhed in the Dublin Evening Poft.    Signed by order,

JA. TAYLOR, jun. Sec.

## ARDS BATTALION.

*At a Meeting of the* Ards Battalion, *in the County of* Down, *on the* 22d *of April,* 1782.

### Colonel SAVAGE in the Chair.

RESOLVED unanimoufly, That the manly, laudable and moderate refolutions of the Ulfter Volunteers, met at Dungannon, have our warmeft approbation, and that we moft heartily accede to them; with pleafure we accept of their invitation, and think ourfelves honoured, by being admitted members of fo truly refpectable a body.

PAT. SAVAGE.

## COUNTY of DOWN,

*At a meeting of the* Diſſenting Congregation of Clough, *convened by public Notice on Sunday the 28th Day of April,* 1782.

### Mr. AUGHTRY LAW in the Chair,

The following Declaration was unanimouſly agreed to, and ordered to be publiſhed.

SENSIBLE of the rights of men from what we feel in our-ſelves, and animated by the pureſt ſentiments of liberty and benevolence, we cannot help expreſſing our ſatisfaction at the recent progreſs of religious toleration in the chriſtian world. The arm of authority is learning to unbend the chains which bigotry hath long rivetted; the mind is beginning to reſume a ſenſe of its native excellence, and the beſt conſequences may be expected.

We heartily partake with the friends of civil liberty, alſo, in the great ſelf-complacence which they muſt at preſent enjoy, from the flattering proſpects of ſucceſs in their virtuous ſtrug-gles. And we ſincerely congratulate our fellow-citizens in this kingdom, in particular, upon the extenſive unanimity, the firmneſs, and the moderate and generous ſpirit of their late reſolves. We ſee baneful counſellors ſkulking from the merited vengance of an injured people, and corruption totter-ing to its fall; we ſee the hand of juſtice ready to diſtribute equal privileges to all his Majeſty's ſubjects, and true policy anxious to unite the Britiſh empire in mutual confidence, proſperity, and peace; we ſee our *ancient* enemies trembling at the force which œconomy, patriotiſm, and union, are likely to bring againſt them; and we *rejoice.*

And we further declare, That the man who attempts to *ſuppreſs* the peoples voice in public affairs, or who barters the more general welfare to private emolument, ſhall, *hereafter,* meet our warmeſt oppoſition; as we look upon a *fair* repreſen-tation of the people as the beſt ſecurity of our conſtitutional rights; and are determined to co-operate with our fellow-citizens in every meaſure which may tend to promote the independence of parliament.

A. LAW, Chairman.

## SLIEVARDAGH LIGHT DRAGOONS.

*At a Meeting of the* Slievardagh Light Dragoons, *held at* Killenaule, *the* 10*th February,* 1780.

### JACOB SANKEY, Efq; in the Chair.

The following refolutions were unanimoufly agreed to :

RESOLVED, That we will not, on any future election, give our fuffrages or fupport to any Candidate, who will not give us the moft folemn affurance of protecting and fupporting the real conftitutional intereft and rights of this Kingdom.

Refolved, That we expect that our reprefentatives, as well for this county as for the burroughs, will ufe their moft ftrenuous efforts to have that act, called *Poyning's law,* repealed, as we apprehend it vefts a dangerous power in perfons who are no part of the real legiflative body of this kingdom.

Refolved, That we fincerely abhor and abjure an act made in the 6th of George I. known by the name of the *Declaratory Act,* and that we will oppofe its operation and tendency to the utmoft of our powers.

Refolved, That the power affumed by the Britifh legiflature of making laws to bind us, is ufurped and unconftitutional ; and that we will obey no laws but thofe made by our King, our own Lords and Commons.

Refolved, That though we cannot anfwer to our confciences or pofterity, to fuffer any infringement on our *liberties,* or unjuft *reftrictions* on our *commerce ;* yet, we look upon ourfelves bound, by the ftrongeft ties, to affift our brethren of Great Britain to the extent of our abilities ; and as we are governed by the fame Sovereign, breathe the fame fpirit of liberty, and in general have adopted the fame laws, we will always confider their enemies as ours, and behave in all refpects as the people of an effectionate, but at the fame time, an *independent fifter kingdom.*

Refolved, That as we have taken up arms for the defence of our rights and privileges, fo fhall we continue our affociation for the defence of the fame.

Signed by order

### THOMAS LANPHIER JOHN, Secretary.

*At a Meeting of the Officers of the* Volunteer Corps, *which attended the Review at* Monaghan, *August* 21, 1781.

Colonel LUCAS in the Chair.

The following Addrefs to the Reviewing General was unanimoufly agreed to :

## To ALEX. MONTGOMERY, Efq.

WHILE we acknowledge the very high pleafure which the noble appearance of Volunteers this day afforded us, we muft do equal juftice to our feelings, in expreffing great fatisfaction at the very public approbation you have avowed to our caufe.

We take the fame occafion to declare our refolutions of acquiring further knowledge in the ufe of arms, in fo far as the neceffary calls of civil life permit. A fecurity from foreign enemies, as well as from internal violence, and ftill more the prefervation of our conftitution in its pureft form, plead ftrongly for that continued exertion, and fhall have our moft active fupport.

We lament the policy of the prefent age, which has reduced corruption into a fyftem, and feparated the interefts of the people from that of their governors. But it is yet of fuperior concern that our conftitution, originally a glorious attempt at human perfection, fhould not have fufficient powers to check that deftructive evil, and that while a corrupt borough influence, and a confequent imperfect reprefentation continue, the people at large, however incorruptible, can afford but a partial relief.

Sir, holding an equality of civil and commercial freedom as conftitutional rights, we have been much hurt at the illiberal reftrictions, which have hitherto governed the liberties and trade of this kingdom. We hold it as a fettled principle, that the King, Lords and Commons of Ireland, are alone competent to make laws, and that the legiflative interference of the Privy Council is highly repugnant to fuch our conftitution. Making the regulation of the army perpetual is an act the more alarming and unneceffary, under the exiftence of a conftitutional army, which is equally determined to preferve the peace and liberties of the kingdom. And laftly, it is our wifh, and in this, Sir, you will witnefs our moderation, to have a liberal fyftem of government, which, detefting all monopolies of freedom as of trade, confults the common profperity of the Empire.

To you, Sir, who, with fuch confiftent rectitude, appear in the field and in the fenate the friend of Ireland, we thus make our folemn appeal, as in fupport of it we wifh to imitate your firmnefs and integrity.

FRANCIS LUCAS, Chairman.

···◄ ◆➤◆➤◄◄◆◄◄◆◆➤◆➤◆➤◆➤►····

*To the Officers of the* Volunteer Corps *which attended the Review at* Monaghan, *the 20th and 21st of August,* 1781.

*Gentlemen,*

I HAVE received the honour of your addrefs, and beg you will be affured, that I fhall, at all times, take a particular pleafure in expreffing my entire approbation of the Volunteers of Ireland, and that I fincerely hope they will continue to exert that noble fpirit, which has hitherto enabled them to do fuch offential fervice to their country.

I equally with you lament the prevalence of corruption, but I truft a remedy may be found in the virtue of the nation.

Perfectly agreeing with you, gentlemen, in your fentiments on thofe great public points that you have mentioned, you may reft affured of my beft exertions being employed (as they have hitherto been) to redrefs all evils affecting either our trade or conftitution. To have been appointed to fo confpicuous a fituation as you were pleafed to place me in, merits my warmeft gratitude, but when I reflect on the perfons from whom the appointment came, a body of men affociated upon the nobleft principles for the protection, peace and honour of their country, it excites emotions that leave me nothing to regret but my own unworthinefs.

I am, with the greateft efteem,

And fincerity, gentlemen,

Your moft obliged,

And faithful humble fervant,

ALEX. MONTGOMERY.

Refolved alfo unanimoufly, That the thanks of this meeting be prefented to Captain Young, exercifing Officer, for his conduct and attention to the different corps, before and during the review.

*The*

*The Addreſs of the Corps of* Independent Dublin Volunteers
*To the Right Hon.* Henry Flood.

S I R,

IN an age of diſſipation, when venality ſtands in the place of
virtue, and tainted ambition is ſapping the conſtitution, a
corps of Independent Iriſh Volunteers ſtand forth with their
warmeſt acknowledgments, and thank you for unfolding your
manly elocution in defence of the rights and liberties of the
kingdom.

Animated with the ſame glorious fire which governs all
liberal minds, we freely acknowledge your name will add
honour wherever it may be enrolled; we have therefore unanimoufly elected you an honorary member of our corps; a
ſmall, but grateful return for that noble eloquence, that language of conviction, ſo lately exerted for the advantage of
our trade, and limitation of an hateful law.

A ſteady perſeverance, we boldly affirm, may, on a future day, ſatisfy the wiſhes of the people, by reſtoring the
conſtitution to its priſtine form. It is through you, ſir, in
particular, and the virtuous part of the legiſlature in general,
that Ireland muſt become reſpectable; or loſe that rank in the
eſtimation of nations, which ſhe lately gained by the ſpirit of
her people.

*Royal Exchange,*     Signed by Order,
*Nov.* 27, 1781.     JAMES ROBINSON, Chairman.

To which the following Anſwer was returned:

*Gentlemen,*

I RECEIVE this mark of your generous approbation with
the moſt heart-felt ſatisfaction.

It gives me pleaſure to concur with you in thinking, that a
manly conſtitutional perſeverance will reſtore your rights.

I accept your honourable invitation, and am proud to enrol
myſelf in a corps which deſerves ſo diſtinguiſhed a place in
virtue and in arms. I have ever admired the Volunteers of
Ireland; and, having adopted, ſhall not be among the firſt
to relinquiſh the character.

I have the honour to be,
Gentlemen,
With the moſt perfect reſpect,
Your moſt obliged and obedient ſervant,
HENRY FLOOD.

# INDEX

## TO THE

# RESOLUTIONS.

# INDEX.

## ADVERTISEMENT.

*The continuation of this work is now in the preſs, which will contain the characters of our preſent Senators, impartially drawn. Such reſolutions as have eſcaped, or any other papers relative to this undertaking, will be thankfully received (poſt paid) by* Joſeph Hill, *at his houſe in* Park-place, *near* Townſhend-ſtreet, *(formerly called* Lazor's-hill) *or* C. H. Wilſon, No. 15, Mountrath-ſtreet, Dublin. *Mr.* Ogle, *of* Wexford, *having promiſed the particulars of the riſe of Volunteering in that county (which is generally thought to be the birth-place of it) they ſhall alſo be inſerted in the next volume. It is certain, this was compiled in a hurry, and—But I ſhall not attempt to apologize.* I am enough ſucceſsful as my theme ſucceeds.